American Risorgimento

American Risorgimento

*Herman Melville
and the
Cultural Politics of Italy*

DENNIS BERTHOLD

THE OHIO STATE UNIVERSITY PRESS
Columbus

Copyright © 2009 by The Ohio State University.
All rights reserved.
Library of Congress Cataloging-in-Publication Data
Berthold, Dennis.
  American Risorgimento : Herman Melville and the cultural politics of Italy / Dennis Berthold.
    p. cm.
  Includes bibliographical references and index.
  ISBN-13: 978-0-8142-1106-9 (cloth : alk. paper)
  ISBN-10: 0-8142-1106-2 (cloth : alk. paper)
  ISBN-13: 978-0-8142-9203-7 (cd-rom)
  1. Melville, Herman, 1819–1891—Criticism and interpretation. 2. Italy—History—1815–1870. 3. United States—Civilization—Italian influences. I. Title.
  PS2388.I8B47 2009
  813'.3—dc22
                                                    2009015560
This book is available in the following editions:

Cloth (ISBN 978-0-8142-1106-9)
CD-ROM (ISBN 978-0-8142-9203-7)
Paper (ISBN: 978-0-8142-5706-7)
Cover design by Laurence Nozik
Text and typesetting by Jennifer Shoffey Forsythe

for Pam

Contents

List of Figures / ix

Preface and Acknowledgments / xi

Introduction
1

Chapter 1
Italy in the American Imagination: A Divided Vision / 29

Chapter 2
Mardi's Dantean Intertext / 60

Chapter 3
Fleeing Revolution: The Rise and Fall of the Roman Republic / 95

Chapter 4
Machiavellian Aesthetics:
From *Pierre* to *The Confidence-Man* / 132

Chapter 5
The Triumph of Nationalism: Early Poems and *Battle-Pieces* / 175

Chapter 6
"The Italian Turn of Thought": *Clarel* and Late Writings / 227

Works Cited
265

Index
281

List of Figures

1. Map of Italy in 1815 — 28
2. Thomas Cole, *Dream of Arcadia* — 32
3. François Pascal Simon Gérard, *Portrait of Joachim Murat* — 37
4. Thomas Cole, *The Course of Empire: Desolation* — 58
5. "Dante Alighieri" — 65
6. William Blake, "Dante in the Empyrean, Drinking at the River of Light" — 69
7. *The Dying Gladiator* — 109
8. Broadside reprinted in Horace Greeley, *Hints Toward Reforms* — 119
9. The Iron Crown of Lombardy — 123
10. Benvenuto Cellini, *Perseus with the Head of Medusa* — 125
11. *Medusa Rondanini* — 126
12. John Flaxman, "Paolo and Francesca" — 138
13. Agasias of Ephesus, *The Borghese Gladiator* — 146
14. Map of Italy, 1859–70 — 177
15. Alexander Jackson Davis, "Winyah" — 179
16. Giuseppe Garibaldi, 1851 — 186
17. Giuseppe Garibaldi, 1852 — 187
18. Lajos Kossuth, 1851 — 187
19. Giuseppe Mazzini, 1852 — 188
20. Tin of Virginia tobacco with Garibaldi's image — 193
21. "General Giuseppe Garibaldi" — 194
22. John Tenniel, "Garibaldi the Liberator; or, The Modern Perseus" — 198

23. Guido Reni, *Perseus and Andromeda* — 199
24. William Hogarth, *Perseus Rescuing Andromeda* — 200
25. "Giuseppe Garibaldi: Died at Caprera, June 2" — 203
26. Medal, Society of the Cincinnati — 209
27. *Head of Medusa* — 214
28. Antoninus Pius — 254
29. Garibaldi statue, Washington Square, New York City — 263

Preface and Acknowledgments

All I wanted to do was understand why Herman Melville, more than any American writer of the antebellum period, alluded so frequently and knowledgeably to Italy. When I started this project in the early 1990s I had never heard the word "transnationalism" nor did I have much interest in literature and politics. My primary interest was visual art, and while it still drives much of this study, it was finally inadequate to explain the presence of Italy—which also means Rome, which also means Roman Catholicism—in Melville's work. Only when I began studying the Risorgimento, Italy's decades-long quest for independence, did I realize how profoundly Italy's experience paralleled America's, and how their mutual quest for a national art, history, and politics enacted Benedict Anderson's theories of nations as "imagined communities." While this insight complicated my task immensely, it has, I hope, resulted in a more analytic and significant book than I originally planned, and one that applies current theories of transnational American studies to a particularly appropriate nineteenth-century writer. If I have learned anything from my research it is how deeply antebellum Americans engaged Europe and how few scholars have pursued that topic in depth. While this remains a book about Melville, I hope readers will view it as exemplary, not definitive. Its aggressive historicism combined with transnationalism can be applied to other authors, times, and places, and can map new borders that reveal cross-cultural patterns of appropriation, reinvention, appreciation, and misunderstanding. Ideologies shift and alter under the pressure of experience and exchange, and the "cultural imperialism" Americanists have often lamented may be only one of the possible outcomes of transnational interactions.

It is less important to me that readers agree with my reading of Melville than that they appreciate my methodology and perhaps, someday, practice it in new and better ways themselves. Scholars better versed than I in European literatures could help Americanists understand why all of Emerson's "representative men" were Europeans, or why Charles Brockden Brown gave so many of his characters an Irish past, or whether aspiring globalists should pay more attention to James Russell Lowell, Henry Wadsworth Longfellow, or even Henry Theodore Tuckerman, some of the antebellum period's most cosmopolitan writers. The emergence of comparative American literary studies is one of the most exciting developments of the last fifty years, and I hope my book illustrates the richness of this approach even when applied to a much-studied author like Melville.

As my study grew from a narrow focus to encompass politics, religion, and history as well as art and literature, it required the help of more people than I ever expected. Among the hearty souls who read and commented on early drafts of this work no one deserves greater credit than Larry J. Reynolds, my colleague and friend for over thirty years. His pioneering study *European Revolutions and the American Literary Renaissance* (1988) is a landmark of transnational American studies and I proudly cite it often. He encouraged my early work on Melville and Garibaldi and twice helped me publish it in important venues, and as the study slowly grew into its present form he read the entire manuscript with a discriminating eye for the essentials, slashing dozens of extraneous pages from it to the benefit of its present readers. It is impossible to thank him enough. Lea Bertani Vozar Newman, the first scholar to study Melville's annotations of Dante, generously provided me with a photocopy of Melville's markings in his edition of *The Divine Comedy*. This saved me enormous amounts of time and travel and revealed a path that connected the political, the literary, the American, and the Italian. Even more generously, Lea read my Dante chapter before anyone else, and saved me from several linguistic blunders, yet still enthusiastically endorsed my general conclusions. She would not have had access to Melville's copy, of course, without the generosity of its owner, William Reese, who has repeatedly opened his collection to eager scholars. John Bryant reviewed a penultimate draft of the entire book and offered perceptive advice in addressing the concerns in my readers' reports. Sandy Crooms, editor of The Ohio State University Press, found outside readers who combined sharp critique with solid encouragement that helped me see more clearly how to organize and prune a previously unwieldy manuscript. Her own reading of the penultimate draft convinced her to pursue it through a major revision, and to shepherd it efficiently through the press. To all of these tireless and helpful readers, I offer sincere thanks.

I also benefited from the criticisms and observations of colleagues who heard me present an early draft of my introduction at a colloquium sponsored by the Melbern G. Glasscock Center for Humanities Research at Texas A&M University, including Jimmie Killingsworth, Marco Portales, Pamela Matthews, David McWhirter, Larry Reynolds, Marian Eide, and Jim Rosenheim, the director of the Glasscock Center. For providing the funding and space for such activities, I thank Melbern G. and Susanne M. Glasscock, two farsighted supporters of the humanities at Texas A&M. Other colleagues helped in surprising ways, as when J. Lawrence Mitchell loaned me an early edition of Dante that I needed to confirm some differences in translations, or when Mary Ann O'Farrell led me to Bruce Robbins' work, or when Craig Kallendorf put me in touch with Machiavelli expert Wayne Rebhorn at the University of Texas, who has the distinction of writing on Melville as well as Machiavelli and who patiently answered repeated questions about this tantalizing relationship.

Several people helped me with Italian, which I had studied just enough to realize I was no linguistic autodidact. Special mention must go to Paola Gemme of Arkansas Tech University, whose scholarly accomplishments are evident in my many references to her outstanding book *Domesticating Foreign Struggles: The Italian Risorgimento and Antebellum American Identity* (2005). Her scholarship is surpassed only by her willingness to assist others, as when she summarized several Italian essays for me and explained the nuances of many key terms, not the least of them "Risorgimento." My former colleague Howard Marchitello, now at Rutgers University-Camden, had the misfortune of being a close friend as well as an Italian speaker, which meant he was available to answer more questions about the language than anyone. Even though his field is the English Renaissance, he re-read *Moby-Dick* and co-taught it with me in a Shakespeare-Melville course, acts that went beyond friendship to Melvillean geniality. My colleague Giovanna del Negro also helped with translation, sometimes at the spur of the moment, and my history colleague Cindy Bouton recommended a French source for my *Clarel* chapter and confirmed my vague understanding of it over a welcome lunch.

Stanton Garner, a formidable Melville scholar whose passion for historical detail has inspired me and kept me honest, loaned me a half-dozen reels of microfilm of the *Pittsfield Sun* and the *Berkshire County Eagle,* and has let me use them for over a decade. Reading these newspapers convinced me that I was on the right track and spurred my investigation of other serial publications of the era. Merrill and Diane Whitburn, friends and colleagues from years past, opened their home to me in upstate New York and let me spend a week studying Melville's annotations in Vasari's *Lives of the Artists,* a work they purchased by accident in a big box of books. Although these annotations figure less conspicuously here than I had originally planned, they are rich with insights into Melville's aesthetics, and I hope to return to them in another context. Peter Norberg of St. Joseph's University in Philadelphia sent me photocopies of the table of contents of an edition of Shelley he determined identical to Melville's so I could be reasonably certain that Melville had seen Shelley's Italian poems. Thanasis Christodoulou sent me a digitally improved copy of the "Head of Medusa" that proved valuable for studying its details; Sam Otter provided invigorating insights about Melville's poetry, particularly "The Conflict of Convictions" in *Battle-Pieces* and the Piranesi allusion in *Clarel;* Walter Bezanson lent his prestige to my inductions about *Clarel*'s historical setting; and Hershel Parker replied promptly and precisely to a relentless barrage of e-mails requesting information about Melville's reading, particularly in poetry and such recondite works as *Modern British Essayists.* I also received useful comments from contributors to the online discussion group ISHMAIL, notably Kris Lackey, Robert Kilgore, and Tim Fretheim. Although it has been many years since I visited the Garibaldi-Meucci Museum on Staten Island, I still recall the warm welcome from Pat Whitehouse, a volunteer who guided me around the museum and showed me one of Garibaldi's red shirts, and the helpful answers about Garibaldi engravings from Anne Alarcon, the curator. Lindsey Borst and Ellen McCallister Clark of the Society of The Cincinnati answered numerous inquiries promptly and thoroughly, and undertook independent research to make sure they were providing the most appropriate images of the Cincinnati Medial for this volume. Finally, I want to pay homage to my preceptor, Merton M. Sealts, Jr., for his lifetime of impeccable Melville scholarship and his joyful help, even when he was fighting his last battle with cancer, with my questions about Melville's reading and annotations.

Melville knew that writing requires cash and time as well as patience, and Texas A&M University has helped me with all three. The Association of Former Students funded two faculty development leaves through the Office of the Dean of Faculties under Dean Karan Watson, one in 1999 and another in 2005, that allowed me to complete my writing. A grant from the Program to Enhance Scholarly and Creative Activities administered by the Office of the Vice-President for Research supported my work on *Clarel* in the summer of 2003, and I am grateful to Robert A. Kennedy, now president of the University of Maine, for beginning this program during his tenure at Texas A&M. A Glasscock Stipendiary Fellowship from the Center for Humanities Research supported book purchases and travel, and the English Department at Texas A&M provided able research assistance from several graduate students, among them Roger Reeves, Seunggu Lew, Kohei Furuya, and Young-Hyeon Ryu. Molly Johnson and Sook Hyun, my first two research assistants, deserve special mention for patiently and precisely photocopying and annotating relevant passages from the *Berkshire County Eagle* and the *Pittsfield Sun,* and Ji Nang Kim and Yonggi Kim deserve thanks for retrieving and printing periodical articles from the invaluable Making of America Web sites. The Office of the Dean, College of Liberal Arts, particularly Executive Associate Dean Ben M. Crouch, helped cover publication costs and supplemented English Department travel funds so I could present my work at two international conferences, one on Elizabeth Barrett Browning and another on Garibaldi. Jimmie Killingsworth, my department head, supplemented a grant from the Glasscock Center for indexing.

My enduring thanks and gratefulness go to Pamela Matthews, an extraordinary woman, spouse, teacher, scholar, and administrator who has, in all the ways that truly count, made this project possible through her support, understanding, patience, and concern. If these don't add up to love, I don't know what does. For those reasons and many others, I have dedicated this book to her.

My discussion of Persean iconography in *Moby-Dick* in chapter 3 and of Garibaldi in chapter 5 is modified from its first appearance in "Melville, Garibaldi, and the Medusa of Revolution," *American Literary History* 9 (Fall 1997): 425–59 (rpt. in *National Imaginaries, American Identities: The Cultural Work of American Iconography,* ed. Larry J. Reynolds and Gordon Hutner [Princeton, NJ: Princeton University Press, 2000], 104–38). Most of chapter 6 appeared in "The Italian turn of thought": Risorgimento Politics in *Clarel," Nineteenth-Century Literature* 59 (December 2004): 352–77.

Introduction

> Dante and Columbus were Italians, in their time:
> they would be Russians or Americans to-day.
> —Ralph Waldo Emerson, *The Conduct of Life* (1860)

> History and experience prove that foreign influence is one of the most baneful foes of Republican Government.
> —George Washington, "The Farewell Address" (1796)

> For the whole world is the patrimony of the whole world; there is no telling who does not own a stone in the Great Wall of China.
> —Herman Melville, *Redburn* (1849)

ONE MORNING in February 1857, on his first and only visit to Italy, Herman Melville left the Hotel de Genève in Naples to take a solitary stroll. He later jotted the following telegraphic impression in his journal: "Sallied out for a walk by myself. Strada di Toledo. Noble street. Broadway." (15:101).[1] Not "like" Broadway. Not "reminds me of" Broadway. Just "Broadway," an elliptical identification so congruent that it required no copula. Despite the vast religious and political differences between Italy and the United States, Melville, like many other Americans of his generation, sensed affinities between the two cultures that, from 1848–1871, linked their fates more closely than at any other time. Coincident with the years of Melville's ascent and decline as a successful novelist and his fertile turn to poetry, this period of cultural mutuality bore with special weight on the aspiring young writer whose neophyte literary persona Wellingborough Redburn believed "the whole world is the patrimony of the whole world; there is no telling who does not own

---

1. Parenthetical references to Melville's works by volume and page number are from *The Writings of Herman Melville*, 14 vols., ed. Harrison Hayford et al. (Chicago: Northwestern University Press and Newberry Library, 1968–).

a stone in the Great Wall of China" (4:292). So while he was a stranger in a strange place, ignorant of the language, suspicious of its religion, and critical of its government, for Melville the Strada di Toledo, Naples's busy, colorful main thoroughfare, constituted a familiar locale that bridged cultural differences and offered a glimpse of home.

Only four years later, America was engaged in civil war. In 1859 Giuseppe Garibaldi, the brilliant Italian military tactician and guerilla general, overthrew Francis II, the Bourbon king of the Two Sicilies, and brought Naples and Sicily into the new Kingdom of Italy under the constitutional monarch Victor Emmanuel II of Piedmont-Sardinia. The Risorgimento, Italy's long quest for national unity and freedom from foreign domination, was almost complete. So compelling was Garibaldi's triumph, so analogous his battle to unite Italy's northern and southern halves to the war besetting the United States, that in late July 1861, shortly after the disastrous Union defeat at Bull Run, Abraham Lincoln offered Garibaldi the post of major-general in the Union army, a two-star rank equivalent to that of George B. McClellan, commander of the Army of the Potomac.[2] American newspapers greeted the offer with enthusiasm, and Garibaldi considered the proposition seriously. He mistakenly believed he was an American citizen because, during his nine-month exile in New York from 1850–51, he had received a United States passport from the mayor of New York but never completed the naturalization process.[3] Garibaldi considered America his adopted country, and might have accepted the post except for one stipulation: he demanded that the United States immediately abolish slavery. Such a request, impossible to grant at the time, positioned Garibaldi as a more dedicated republican and advocate of universal freedom than Lincoln. Symbolically preempting America's role as the "Redeemer Nation," Italy, not the United States,

2. Howard Marraro, "Lincoln's Offer of a Command to Garibaldi: Further Light on a Disputed Point of History," *Journal of the Illinois State Historical Society* 36 (1943): 237–70, and Herbert Mitgang, "Garibaldi and Lincoln," *American Heritage* 26 (October 1975): 34–39, 98–101. Rumors that Garibaldi might join the Union forces were rife during the summer and fall of 1861, and numerous *Garibaldini* in fact joined the Union army. The Thirty-Ninth New York regiment of French, Italian, Hungarian, German, Swiss, and Spanish volunteers took the name "Garibaldi Guard" in honor of the general and fought with distinction throughout the war. See Frank Moore, ed., *The Rebellion Record: A Diary of American Events with Documents, Narratives, Illustrative Incidents, Poetry, Etc.*, 11 vols. (New York: G. P. Putnam and Van Nostrand, 1861–68), 1:306, and Andrea Viotti, *Garibaldi: The Revolutionary and His Men* (Poole, UK: Blandford Press Ltd., 1979), 136. Melville consulted *The Rebellion Record* for *Battle-Pieces* (1866).

3. For a thorough discussion of Garibaldi's interest in acquiring United States citizenship, see H. Nelson Gay, "Garibaldi's American Contacts and His Claims to American Citizenship," *American Historical Review* 38 (October 1932): 1–19.

momentarily provided the world a vision of national unity and emancipatory politics in Garibaldi, the charismatic "Hero of Two Worlds" who had fought wars of liberation in both South America and Europe. For a few months in the dark hours of 1861, a transnational Italian guerilla fighter emblematized liberal America's highest principles more boldly than America itself.

Melville in Italy, Garibaldi in America: these two instances, one intensely private, the other sensationally public, dramatize the intersection of American and Italian values at a crucial moment in their modern histories. During the mid-nineteenth century, both countries made the painful transition from a congeries of affiliated states to unified nations, simultaneously exposing deficiencies in federalist republican theory (the lack of strong central governments) and achieving long-desired ideals (abolishing slavery in the United States, eliminating foreign oppressors in Italy). Herman Melville, the most politically and culturally sensitive imaginative writer of the period, recognized these parallels and developed them more fully than any major nineteenth-century American novelist or poet. The telling document, what I call Melville's Neapolitan diptych, is his two-part unpublished poem "At the Hostelry" and "Naples in the Time of Bomba," probably begun around 1860 and clearly revised and amplified intermittently until the early 1880s.[4] The diptych praises both Giuseppe Garibaldi and Count Camillo Benso di Cavour, the military and diplomatic heroes of Italy's liberation, stages a dialogue among painters on the merits of the picturesque, and brings forth the genial innocent Major Jack Gentian to recount his visit to Naples, a trip much like Melville's in 1857. The poem begins with Garibaldi's 1859 invasion of southern Italy and ends with his death in 1882, while alluding variously to Italian art, Roman history, European revolutions, Dutch painting, and contemporary notions of progress. Long ignored in the Melville canon, it is the tip of an iceberg of Italian themes, references, and motifs in Melville's works that reveals the Risorgimento's impact on American culture and demonstrates Melville's standing as the exemplary nineteenth-century author in American transnationalist studies.

Extending from the Congress of Vienna in 1815 that dismembered post-Napoleonic Italy to the establishment of Rome as Italy's secular capital in 1871, the Risorgimento's dates bracketed the most creative years of every major writer of the American Renaissance. It was the one

---

4. For a full discussion of this poem's complicated and uncertain textual history, see chapter 5.

inescapable international event of their lifetimes, as significant as the Napoleonic Wars had been for William Godwin, Samuel Taylor Coleridge, and William Wordsworth, the Great War for F. Scott Fitzgerald, Ernest Hemingway, and William Faulkner, World War II for James Jones and Norman Mailer, and Vietnam for Tim O'Brien and Francis Ford Coppola. Melville's well-known openness to other cultures combines with his voraciously acquisitive imagination to make him a supremely important register of the Risorgimento's significance to Americans. Beginning with his third novel, *Mardi* (1849), Melville mined Italian art, history, and politics as a fictional and poetic resource. Every one of his subsequent works overflows with allusions and metaphors drawn from his developing knowledge of Italy, from its current political struggles back to the Renaissance and beyond to the dim legends of ancient Rome. Whether in Naples or New York, Italy was always with Melville, not just the Italy of tour guides and travel narratives, art museums and history books, but an imagined Italy constructed from his omnivorous reading and vitally cosmopolitan cultural surround. If Naples was Broadway, Broadway was Naples, both parts of a cultural exchange that made Italy (among other cultures) available to Americans, particularly New Yorkers such as Melville. Thus, when Melville finally visited Italy he had, in a sense, already been there.

The "Italy" of this study is therefore a cultural construction, one produced in America for Americans, satisfying American needs and desires in the turbulent and uncertain decades surrounding the Civil War. Just as we see in paintings what we have been trained to see, so we experience in travel what we have been conditioned to experience, whether we're following a Michelin guide or, as did Melville, a Murray *Handbook for Travellers*. Even before our visit, the actual place is already an imagined locale stamped on our inner vision which we corroborate by following the prescriptive tourism of histories, art catalogs, and guidebooks. We never see anything for the first time. Melville's Italy, then, is not so much a place as it is a state of mind, or, better, a constellation of texts, artifacts, and ideologies gathered and mediated by an aggressively acquisitive intellectual culture, the aspiring American Renaissance that agglomerates, like Whitman in "Song of Myself," all it sees and touches into an ostensibly new, inchoate, dynamic, national identity. Although some scholars have discountenanced parallels between Giuseppe Mazzini's "Young Italy" ("Giovine Italia") and Northern Democrats' "Young America" wing under which Melville temporarily nestled, the two movements both sought a democratic cultural nationalism reciprocally figured in metaphors drawn from either country.[5] Italians, suffering under a century of foreign oppression, drew hope from America's successful emergence from colonial status. Americans, devoid of the legendary Roman past which Italian nationalists constantly invoked, borrowed from the rich fund of Italian history to ground their own arguments for republican expansionism. In *America's Rome,* a massive interdisciplinary study of American appropriations and representations of the Holy City over two centuries, William L. Vance observes that American "representations of Rome thus serve as a kind of running commentary on the changes that America itself was undergoing. Once more, in representing Rome the Americans represented—and sometimes discovered—themselves."[6] Melville invested again and again in this widely practiced economy of Italianate reference, betraying both in his casual allusions and developed responses the unspoken depth of the Italian-American analogy and extending it beyond mere motif into an aesthetic and ideological resource.

TOWARD AN INTERCULTURAL AMERICAN EXCEPTIONALISM

At the end of the 1980s, American literary criticism began a paradigm shift from focusing on America's difference from Europe to stressing its affinities. The idea of "American exceptionalism," that America has unique origins along with a special, God-given destiny distinct from any previous country's, was questioned by William C. Spengemann in *A Mirror for Americanists* (1989) and Amy Kaplan and Donald Pease's influential anthology *Cultures of United States Imperialism* (1993), and has continued to be interrogated in numerous works analyzing the political, literary,

---

5. Two standard works on the topic, for example, John Stafford, *The Literary Criticism of "Young America": A Study in the Relationship of Politics and Literature, 1837–1850* (Berkeley: University of California Press, 1952) and Perry Miller, *The Raven and the Whale: The War of Words and Wits in the Era of Poe and Melville* (New York: Harcourt, Brace and Company, 1956), credit Cornelius Mathews with the term and systematically ignore foreign influences, even though Merle Curti's pathbreaking "Young America," *American Historical Review* 32 (October 1926): 34–55, mentions antecedent European movements such as "Young Ireland" and "Young Germany." The most recent study, Edward L. Widmer, *Young America: The Flowering of Democracy in New York City* (New York: Oxford University Press, 1999), argues consistently for the imbrications of the European and American movements and specifically cites Giuseppe Mazzini's Young Italy as an inspiration (5).

6. William L. Vance, *America's Rome,* 2 vols. (New Haven, CT: Yale University Press, 1989), 2:xxiv.

and theoretical relations between America and other cultures. The binary opposition of foreign and domestic, Kaplan argues, replicates the same gender, ethnic, and racial oppositions that impede American multiculturalism, and all of these must be explored "in relation to one another and to ideologies of nationhood through the crucible of international power relations."[7] As important as Kaplan's concerns are, they tend to foreground American literature after the Civil War, where issues of multiculturalism, imperialism, immigration, and international imbroglios are so evident. This emphasis is not only true of Kaplan and Pease's justly influential collection, but of much scholarship that has followed. What I hope to do is follow the path carved out by Leon Chai in *The Romantic Foundations of the American Renaissance* and Larry J. Reynolds in *European Revolutions and the American Literary Renaissance* who place classic American writers in European contexts in order to demonstrate their indebtedness to transatlantic literature and events.[8] In 1992 Lawrence Buell quite appropriately chose Melville as a springboard to call for studying American exceptionalism "as a myth that American authors broached and American critics formalized in a much more complicated transnational historical matrix that included contrary evidence and competing possibilities."[9] In the subsequent decade, while theorists debated the methodologies, labels, and boundaries of this emerging field, books and essays and conferences heeding Buell's call proliferated.[10] The American Studies Association chose transnationalism as the

---

7. Spengemann, *A Mirror for Americanists: Reflections on the Idea of American Literature* (Hanover, NH: University Press of New England, 1989); Kaplan and Pease, eds., *Cultures of United States Imperialism* (Durham, NC: Duke University Press, 1993), 16.

8. Chai, *The Romantic Foundations of the American Renaissance* (Ithaca, NY: Cornell University Press, 1987); Reynolds, *European Revolutions and the American Literary Renaissance* (New Haven, CT: Yale University Press, 1988). Some scholars hail Robert Weisbuch's *Atlantic Double-Cross: American Literature and British Influence in the Age of Emerson* (Chicago: University of Chicago Press, 1986) as a foundational text in American transnationalism, but to my mind it still rests on assumptions of American literary exceptionalism. Weisbuch argues that American literature could not establish its own identity until it liberated itself from English models, a process he traces using familiar nationalist texts and Harold Bloom's theory that writers must overcome their strong precursors before they can create something new. In contrast, Chai and Reynolds show how a variety of foreign forms and ideologies work their way into American writing in a productive cross-fertilization that reveals, in Chai's words, "some deeper sense of historical development, of the rise and transmission of different forms of thought and of the tendencies that underlie and produce these forms" (xii).

9. "Melville and the Question of American Decolonization," *American Literature* 64 (June 1992): 233.

10. Some of the notable theoretical discussions occur in special issues of leading journals: "America, the Idea, the Literature," ed. Djelal Kadir, *PMLA* 118 (Spring 2003); "American Literary Globalism," ed. Wai Chee Dimock and Lawrence Buell, *ESQ: A Journal of the American Renaissance* 50 (2004); and "Hemispheric American Literary History," ed. Caroline S. Levander and Robert S. Levine, *American Literary History* 18 (Summer 2006).

theme of its 2006 conference, and two new journals emerged, *Comparative American Literary Studies* (2003) and the online *Journal of Transnational and Transcultural American Studies* (2008). In 2007 Wai Chee Dimock's *Through Other Continents,* an ambitious attempt to theorize American literature's debt to other cultures and times, won Honorable Mention for the Modern Language Association's annual James Russell Lowell Prize, and her collection of original essays by various scholars coedited with Lawrence Buell, *Shades of the Planet,* brings a new breadth of vision to the field.[11] Still, transnational studies of antebellum writers remain rare, even though, as the example of Melville shows, they interacted long and productively with other national cultures.

An intercultural approach, as Kaplan notes of Buell, risks colonizing other literatures while ignoring its own imperialistic aims.[12] As transnational studies mature, however, "cultural imperialism" and "exceptionalism" are less the bogeymen of leftist literary studies and more the conduits for exchange among distinct nations, which I take to be a defining characteristic of contemporary transnational studies. Because every nation has a tradition of exceptionalism, the more it insists on its uniqueness the more unexceptional it becomes: "As an agent of national identity and as an incentive to the writing of national history," Hans R. Guggisberg points out, "American exceptionalism is problematic in many ways, but it is in itself not exceptional."[13] David W. Noble seconds this point, albeit more pessimistically, in *Death of a Nation,* which roots exceptionalism in fantasies of nature: "Paradoxically the middle classes in each modern nation saw their individual and rational relationship with nature as exceptional."[14] As these scholars realize, the very idea of exceptionalism necessitates a comparatist context to demonstrate how one nation differs from another, a process that uncovers both positive and negative instances of exceptional national behaviors and registers their change over time. Slavery certainly made America exceptional during the antebellum period, but so did the rapid extension of the franchise. Much later, the United States was

---

11. *Through Other Continents: American Literature Across Deep Time* (Princeton, NJ: Princeton University Press. 2006); *Shades of the Planet: American Literature as World Literature* (Princeton, NJ: Princeton University Press, 2007).

12. Kaplan and Pease, *Cultures of United States Imperialism,* 21.

13. "American Exceptionalism as National History?" in *Bridging the Atlantic: The Question of American Exceptionalism in Perspective,* ed. Elisabeth Glaser and Hermann Wellenreuther (Cambridge: Cambridge University Press, 2002), 276. For a conspectus of recent defenses of exceptionalism, see Ari Hoogenboom, "American Exceptionalism: Republicanism as Ideology" in the same volume, 43–65.

14. *Death of a Nation: American Culture and the End of Exceptionalism* (Minneapolis: University of Minnesota Press, 2002), xxvi.

equally exceptional for the civil rights movement and its economic inequities. Like any other feature of nation-building, exceptionalism should be questioned and criticized, but neither ignored nor valorized. If we are to understand the historical underpinnings of American transnationalism we must accept that something like "literary colonization" may accurately describe the attitudes of American Renaissance writers toward foreign cultures, however unpalatable that idea seems today. When Emerson chose examples for *Representative Men* (1850), all six—Plato, Swedenborg, Montaigne, Shakespeare, Napoleon, and Goethe—were Europeans; and, practical Yankee that he was, Emerson exhibited them for their "use or service" to his readers, effectively Americanizing them for moral purposes.[15] Employing a transatlantic intercultural typology, Emerson could even claim in "Fate" that "Dante and Columbus were Italians, in their time: they would be Russians or Americans to-day."[16] To Emerson, Dante's *Divine Comedy* and Columbus's founding of New Spain were avatars of America's national and increasingly imperial quest, aesthetic and political consolidations of nationhood that America might well emulate. America needed a Dante to consolidate its regional cultures into a vernacular whole, and it needed Columbian explorers like Lewis and Clark or Charles Wilkes to expand the nation's commercial power. Even more, to paraphrase Thoreau's injunction at the end of *Walden,* Americans needed Columbuses who would simultaneously explore their inner and outer worlds, undertaking the dual exploration of self and society that absorbed so much of Melville's career. Although such cultural appropriations might elide an individual's distinctive traits, they also give him or her contemporary relevance and open Thoreauvian opportunities for cross-cultural engagements and interchanges that might otherwise go unnoticed. To be American, then, is to be global, as Randolph Bourne envisioned in his 1916 essay "Trans-national America," perhaps the first published use of the phrase. While today's theorists would readily discern the nationalism and cultural ethnocentrism behind Bourne's essay, his call for ethnic diversity, dual citizenship, and cultural cosmopolitanism were designed "to weave a wholly novel international nation out of our chaotic America," an aim that necessarily targets foreign cultures for local ends.[17] Why incorporate a foreign practice if it has no value for you? What Bourne did not appreciate sufficiently was how those incorporations would hybridize the local culture and extend its artistic, linguistic, political, and social range

15. *Essays & Lectures,* ed. Joel Porte (New York: Library of America, 1983), 617.
16. *Essays & Lectures,* 962.
17. *Atlantic Monthly* 118 (July 1916): 97.

in ways often unpredictable and, to some, undesirable, as Homi Bhabha has theorized so powerfully in his classic statement on "cultural hybridity," "DissemiNation: Time, Narrative, and the Margins of the Modern Nation."[18] The exceptional American, then, is one who can read writers from Plato through Goethe and profit from each one, who recognizes what other nations can teach the United States, who finds herself, like Margaret Fuller reporting from the ramparts of Rome during the 1849 revolution, utterly changed by travel abroad, or who, like Melville, delves into the "Deep Time" of Roman history to critique the American present.[19]

While Italy has long been acknowledged as a presence in American writing, the specific political and cultural impact of the Risorgimento has been largely ignored. Van Wyck Brooks, Paul R. Baker, Nathalia Wright, James Woodress, James Tuttleton, and many others have written excellent accounts of writers' visits to Italy along with summaries of their works that depended on Italian themes.[20] But almost as if adhering to George Washington's admonition "that foreign influence is one of the most baneful foes of Republican Government," these critics ground their observations on writers' actual experiences in Italy, effectively partitioning Italian from American culture and emphasizing the artistic product over cultural and ideological exchange. If Italian settings, characters, or history figure in a particular work—say, James Fenimore Cooper's tale of Venetian intrigue, *The Bravo* (1831), or Washington Irving's romantic story "The Italian Banditti" in *Tales of a Traveller* (1824), or Nathaniel Hawthorne's allegory of Italian art and painting *The Marble Faun* (1860), or Henry James's Künstlerroman *Roderick Hudson* (1876)—scholars pursued Italian sources and influences. Barring such literal appropriations, the matter of

---

18. *Nation and Narration,* ed. Homi K. Bhabha (New York: Routledge, 1990), 291–322.

19. For the notion of "Deep Time" as an element in American transnationalism, see Dimock, *Through Other Continents,* esp. 1–6 and the chapter on Margaret Fuller, 52–72.

20. See Brooks, *The Dream of Arcadia: American Writers and Artists in Italy, 1760–1915* (New York: Dutton, 1958); Baker, *The Fortunate Pilgrims: Americans in Italy, 1800–1860* (Cambridge, MA: Harvard University Press, 1964); Wright, *American Novelists in Italy: The Discoverers: Allston to James* (Philadelphia: University of Pennsylvania Press, 1965); Woodress, *Howells & Italy* (Durham, NC: Duke University Press, 1952); Tuttleton, *The Sweetest Impression of Life: The James Family and Italy* (New York: New York University Press, 1990). The OCLC lists over twenty works on American writers and Italy, including specific studies of Thomas Jefferson, Benjamin Franklin, Emerson, Ernest Hemingway, and Ezra Pound. Additionally, there exist many studies of American sculptors and painters in Italy, notably James Thomas Flexner's classic, *The Light of Distant Skies, 1760–1835* (New York: Harcourt, Brace, 1954), and Theodore E. Stebbins Jr., *The Lure of Italy: American Artists and the Italian Experience, 1760–1914* (Boston: Museum of Fine Arts, 1992).

Italy was deemed insignificant. Nathalia Wright, whose *American Novelists in Italy* remains the most comprehensive guide to the subject, forthrightly limits her study to the effects of travel and "largely disregards [writers'] knowledge and conception of Italian culture acquired through books, reproductions of works of art, and other means available outside Italy."[21] While this orientation is understandable in traditional historicist criticism, and is perhaps a necessary limitation given the breadth of Wright's book, it remains evident even in Leonardo Buonomo's admirable study *Backward Glances: Exploring Italy, Reinterpreting America (1831–1866)*, which still focuses on writers who visited Italy and survived to write about it: Margaret Fuller and Julia Ward Howe, Cooper and William Dean Howells, Henry T. Tuckerman and Henry P. Leland, and, of course, Hawthorne.[22]

Such self-imposed critical constraints privilege personal experience over cultural context and, ironically, exacerbate an unquestioningly positive exceptionalist view of American culture. The unexamined assumption is that the Old World only affected those few authors who actually experienced it, while provincials who stayed at home remained insulated from European sophistication, free to develop a native literature uncontaminated by transatlantic practices. Emerson's famous dismissal of traveling as a "fool's paradise" targets precisely such literalist notions. However, as one of the earliest American readers of Dante in English, Emerson knew that Italian culture (among others) was a developing presence in American life, not only through accounts in newspapers, magazines, and travel narratives, but through poetry, novels, dramas, as well as architecture and painting, all materials available in the United States. In many ways, Canto IV of *Childe Harold's Pilgrimage* (1818) did more to shape American views of Italy than all the Murrays combined, and Madame de Staël's durable classic *Corinne; or Italy* (1807) influenced two successive generations of American women writers long before Daisy Miller visited the Coliseum at midnight.[23] Poe,

---

21. *American Novelists in Italy*, 7.
22. Madison, NJ: Fairleigh Dickinson University Press, 1996.
23. *Corinne* was immediately translated into English (often as "Corinna") and was widely available in the United States from 1808 on. Harper's alone published three different editions before 1860. Margaret Fuller, Lydia Maria Child, and Harriet Beecher Stowe all acknowledged its influence (Avriel H. Goldberger, "Introduction," *Corinne, or Italy* [New Brunswick, NJ: Rutgers University Press, 1987], xlix–1). The novel was immediately translated from French into English and was published widely in the United States from 1808 on. A long retrospective review in the *Southern Literary Messenger* for July 1849 demonstrates the novel's durable popularity as both a romance and a commentary upon Italian politics, society, and character (15:377–84). For a conspectus of its broad Euro-American influence, see Ellen Moers's chapter "Performing Heroinism: The Myth of Corinne," in *Literary Women* (New York: Oxford University Press, 1976), 173–210. See also Paul R. Baker, who acknowledges the importance of Samuel Rogers as well as de Staël and Byron (*Fortunate Pilgrims*, 27–28), and who suggests that, during "the first six decades of the

normally the most skeptical of critics, was so taken with the detail and vividness in Edward Bulwer-Lytton's novel *Rienzi, the Last of the Roman Tribunes* (1835) that he considered it truer than either Simonde de Sismondi's *History of the Italian Republics in the Middle Ages* (1807–1808) or Edward Gibbon's *Decline and Fall of the Roman Empire* (1776–88): "It is History. We hesitate not to say that it is History in its truest—in its only true, proper, and philosophical garb. Sismondi's works—were not."[24] By elevating fiction over history, Poe looks forward to Hayden White's theories of history as fiction, in which historical narratives employ the same literary techniques as novels, and from there it is a short jump to Benedict Anderson's notion of nations as imagined communities, essentially social fictions constructed out of political necessity.[25] During the heady antebellum days of mutual Italo-American cultural resurgence, nationalists in both countries were especially susceptible to such romantic interfusions of genre, and constantly recreated their histories to serve contemporary needs and ideals. George Dekker's analysis of Sir Walter Scott's influence on American historical romances is among the most convincing expositions of the multiple avenues of transcultural exchange taken by Americans eager to construct a fictional national history based on European models.[26]

Novels and poetry, although crucially important for American writers, were only the most obvious vehicles for intercultural borrowing and appropriation. Larry J. Reynolds convincingly demonstrates that the French Revolution of 1848 impacted Emerson, Fuller, Hawthorne, Melville, Whitman, and Thoreau through the multiple refractions of contemporary illustrations, literary iconography, newspaper accounts, magazines, and the letters and diaries of acquaintances. William L. Vance contextualizes American opinion not only in travel accounts, poetry, and fiction, but also in painting, statuary, monuments, tourist sites, landscapes, and the perdurable specter of Roman Catholicism. Jenny Franchot's *Roads to Rome* explores the mixed allure and repulsion Catholicism held for Americans, and shows how it seeped into the national consciousness despite recur-

---

nineteenth century, the American was probably better prepared for a visit to Italy than to any other foreign country except England" (200).

24. *Essays and Reviews,* 145, in Poe's 1836 review of the American edition of *Rienzi.*

25. White, *Metahistory: The Historical Imagination in Nineteenth-Century Europe* (Baltimore: Johns Hopkins University Press, 1973); Anderson, *Imagined Communities: Reflections on the Origins and Spread of Nationalism* (1983; rev. ed., New York: Verso, 1991).

26. *The American Historical Romance* (New York: Cambridge University Press, 1987). Buell, "American Literary Emergence as a Postcolonial Phenomenon," *American Literary History* 4 (Autumn 1992): 414, briefly analyzes a number of other pathbreaking studies of intercultural influence on American literature.

rent periods of anti-Catholic hysteria. Robert Levine, in *Conspiracy and Romance,* deploys Bakhtin's theories of heteroglossia and intertextuality to decipher the European subtext for American fears of Jacobinism, Masonry, Popery, and other ostensibly antirepublican ideologies. And Paola Gemme, directly addressing American appropriations of the Risorgimento, shows how exceptionalism and economic imperialism motivated American interest in Italy.[27] The cultural configurations that these and other studies trace provide, to my mind, the most fruitful methodology for understanding the peculiar place "Italy" assumed in the mid-nineteenth-century American imagination. They implicate American literature in transatlantic dialogue across multiple modes of transmission and reveal the cultural exchanges and hybridizations that occurred on many levels: aesthetic and ideological, elite and vernacular, cosmopolitan and local, figurative and literal, religious and secular, political and social.[28]

The cultural turn has also reinvigorated Risorgimento studies, as a recent collection of essays, *Making and Remaking Italy: The Cultivation of National Identity Around the Risorgimento,* reveals. While, like America's Civil War, the Risorgimento's political and military history has been exhaustively analyzed, less has been said about its role as a flexible framework for inventing and revisioning the idea of Italian nationhood itself. By taking a multidisciplinary approach to the effects of the Risorgimento and examining painting, poetry, music, film, monuments, celebrations, women's writing, private correspondence, philosophy, historiography, and journalism as contested sites of Italian identity, the essays in *Making and Remaking Italy* reveal "elements of unpredictability and fluidity in the making of nationalist narratives that many nationalists themselves prefer to ignore."[29] Traditional histories that link Mussolini with Garibaldi or Fascism with monarchism have their place, but ignore the larger process of cultural appropriation and reconfiguration that makes the Risorgimento a significant resource for constructing contradictory national myths. Depending

---

27. Franchot, *Roads to Rome: The Antebellum Protestant Encounter with Catholicism* (Berkeley: University of California Press, 1994); Levine, *Conspiracy and Romance: Studies in Brockden Brown, Cooper, Hawthorne, and Melville* (Cambridge: Cambridge University Press, 1989); Gemme, *Domesticating Foreign Struggles: The Italian Risorgimento and Antebellum American Identity* (Athens: University of Georgia Press, 2005).

28. For a recent collection that excerpts some of the essays I have cited here and places them in a broad, comparative scholarly context, see *Transatlantic Literary Studies: A Reader,* ed. Susan Manning and Andrew Taylor (Baltimore: Johns Hopkins University Press, 2007).

29. "Introduction," *Making and Remaking Italy: The Cultivation of National Identity Around the Risorgimento,* ed. Albert Russell Ascoli and Krystyna von Henneberg (New York: Berg, 2001), 3.

on current political needs, for example, one can choose among four distinct Risorgimento heroes to best represent the Italian character: the aristocrat Cavour, the monarch Victor Emmanuel II, the intellectual Mazzini, or the general Garibaldi, much as Americans, depending on their politics, variously honor Abraham Lincoln, Robert E. Lee, Stonewall Jackson, or Ulysses S. Grant. What is remarkable is how often the materials these essays find essential to Italian nationalism—the Roman Republic, Dante, the Florentine wars, the Sicilian Vespers, classical statuary, Renaissance painting, and many others—appear in antebellum American texts, particularly Melville's. These shared cultural artifacts and historical concerns form a virtual lingua franca of national identity and cultural formation that both exploits and critiques the transatlantic connection between Italy and the United States.

Such densely woven strands of cross-cultural influence suggest an even more complex vision of transnational American criticism than that envisaged by Buell or Dimock. America early and powerfully absorbed ideas about Italy and processed them to fit the contours of its own political landscape, merging them ineluctably with its own desire for literary nationalism in a web of global transcultural refigurations. One need not dismiss writers' well-documented quest for a native literature in order to promote the transatlantic agenda, for both Italian and American nationalists insisted on their own "exceptional" place in history.[30] Nor should cultural appropriation automatically earn the pejorative label "imperialistic," as though any borrowing necessarily subordinates the lender. One of the most exceptional qualities of American literary practice was its eager embrace of other cultures, from Washington Irving's *Sketch-Book* (1819–20) to Henry James's refinement of the international novel. American writers have interacted productively with English, German, Spanish, Dutch, and French literatures and, in other manifestations, African, Native American, Caribbean, and Pacific cultures. What became evident to some American writers was that the defining element of this acquisitive American culture would be its eclectic, sometimes avaricious appropriation of foreign models as it erratically progressed toward an identity constructed from a mosaic of other cultures, past and present.

30. For literary nativism, see such classic expositions as Benjamin Townley Spencer, *The Quest for Nationality: An American Literary Campaign* (Syracuse, NY: Syracuse University Press, 1957); J. Meredith Neil, *Toward a National Taste: America's Quest for Aesthetic Independence* (Honolulu: University Press of Hawaii, 1975); and Richard Ruland's anthology of primary documents, *The Native Muse: Theories of American Literature,* vol. 1 (New York: E. P. Dutton & Co., 1976). Von Henneberg and Ascoli notice the similarity between American and Italian Exceptionalism ("Introduction," 4–5).

Because of the perceived political homologies, real or not, between the United States and Italy, the Risorgimento presents a leading example of American interculturalism. The actual facts of Risorgimento history matter less than the "use or service" to which Americans put those facts, facts that were really just impressions filtered through newspapers, magazines, novels, travel books, and often obtuse personal experiences and recalcitrant nationalist and racist ideologies. The similarities of the terms, Renaissance and Risorgimento, entice. Literally "rebirth" and "resurgence," respectively, each carries overtones of the other, and connotes as well renewal, progress, redemption, and—more ominously—revolution, as Whitman understood when he titled his paean to 1848 "Resurgemus" (1850).[31] Both countries sought to create a national literature, a common impulse that drew Americans to such Italian literary nationalists as Vittorio Alfieri, Giacomo Leopardi, and Alessandro Manzoni and prompted the sweeping Dante revival in England and the United States. The overt rebellions that periodically erupted in Italy paralleled the conflicts over sectionalism, slavery, and class that characterized antebellum America and eventuated in the Civil War and Lincoln's astonishing appeal to Garibaldi. Both countries suffered through economic and cultural divisions along a North-South axis, a similarity that prompted the Southern historian Don H. Doyle to analogize Italy's quest for national unity to the Union struggle for hegemony during the Civil War: "Instead of understanding the United States as a sui generis nation, we may see it as part of a larger transatlantic enterprise that spawned a variety of national types."[32] When the full pangs of sectional revolt struck the United States in 1861, American violence outstripped anything Europe had ever seen and demonstrated America's own fragile national cohesiveness and even more urgent need for a unifying national culture.

From an intercultural perspective, such conflicts merge in figures like Washington and Garibaldi, or Lincoln and Victor Emmanuel II, men dedicated to many of the same republican and nationalist principles yet, conditioned by experience and necessity, willing to assert a tyrannical authority in the name of liberty and national union. Routinely praised in the American press as "the Washington of Italy," Garibaldi proudly

---

31. First published on June 21, 1850, Whitman included this homage to the revolutionaries of 1848 in every edition of *Leaves of Grass*, retitling it "Europe" in 1860. See *Leaves of Grass: Comprehensive Reader's Edition*, ed. Harold W. Blodgett and Sculley Bradley (New York: W. W. Norton & Company, 1965), 266.

32. *Nations Divided: America, Italy, and the Southern Question* (Athens: University of Georgia Press, 2002), 17.

assumed the title "Dictator" when he entered Naples in 1860 and reigned for two months as a triumphant figure of populist revolt. When Victor Emmanuel II arrived, Garibaldi readily offered his sword to the king in the name of a cause even greater than one man's conquests—a unified Italian nation. Revolution, independence, secularism, national unity, even freedom itself merged with monarchism in ways so historically particular and nuanced that they seem incomprehensible to twenty-first-century Americans. M. Wynn Thomas, borrowing a term from Eric Hobsbawm, terms this "Risorgimento nationalism" and finds it key to Whitman's vision of the United States: "Whitman's poetry (and prose) reproduces, in an arresting way, the great central ambivalence of the Risorgimento concept of nationhood; simultaneously libertarian and authoritarian."[33] It would be hard to encapsulate the dilemma better. Thomas's formula captures the appeal of Risorgimento ideology for many Americans, especially Melville. During these turbulent years surrounding the Civil War, Italy became for Americans a transnational cultural metonym for attitudes toward art, politics, history, and religion of urgent local importance, and merged at times almost invisibly with America's outward pretensions to literary nationalism. More than any writer of the period Melville offers a productive site for elaborating this affiliation. The international themes, motifs, and allusions that saturate his novels and poems create a consciously globalized and historicized context that simultaneously advances and critiques American exceptionalism. America can be "exceptional" without being provincial or isolated from the international community; in fact, when analogized to Italy, America's distinctive qualities, for good and ill, take on the international colorations Melville praised when Wellingborough Redburn argued, "You can not spill a drop of American blood without spilling the blood of the whole world" (4:169). Melville, plucking stones from the Great Wall of China to annihilate geographical boundaries in an eclectic quest for a poetics sufficient to his country, demonstrates this reciprocal process throughout his career.

33. "Walt Whitman and Risorgimento Nationalism," *Literature of Region and Nation*, ed. Winnifred M. Bogaards (Saint John, New Brunswick, Canada: Social Sciences and Humanities Research Council of Canada and University of New Brunswick in Saint John, 1998), 359.

HERMAN MELVILLE, COSMOPOLITA

Melville came of literary age in the late 1840s, during the sweeping European revolutions of 1848 and the electrifying months of the short-lived second Roman Republic, proclaimed in 1849. He tried to visit Italy that year, finally succeeded in 1857, and angled repeatedly to obtain a consular post in the country. He followed Garibaldi's campaigns of 1859 and 1860 in the Pittsfield newspapers, and when he returned to New York City in late 1863 found himself in a hotbed of American Italophilia. Living until 1891, he could assess both the triumphs and the failures of the Risorgimento and measure them against America's own nationalist consolidation and turn toward corporate capitalism and mass industrialism.[34] Nevertheless, as William Shurr notes in *A Companion to Melville Studies*, Melville's "affection for Italian Culture" remains "a subject so far untouched by scholarly inquiry."[35] Because most critics privilege Melville's fiction over his poetry, some of his most Italianate works remain unstudied except in specialized contexts; and because he set only one story in Italy, the sympathetic Melvillean Nathalia Wright felt duty-bound to omit him from *American Novelists in Italy*, even though he visited Italy and, as Wright acknowledged in a later article, wrote over a dozen poems with Italian settings.[36] Of all American Renaissance writers, Melville was the most sensitive to intercultural influences, from his attacks on Western political and religious imperialism in *Typee* (1846) to his multiethnic crew aboard the *Pequod* in *Moby-Dick* to the "intersympathy of creeds" in his international religious epic *Clarel* (1876).[37] He was equally multinational in his reading, exhibiting a transhistorical and global literary appetite that feasted equally on Livy, Shakespeare, Balzac, and Hawthorne, and Plutarch, Gibbon, Byron, and *Harper's Weekly*. He read eagerly and eclectically throughout his life, and we know from studies of his personal library, newspaper and magazine reading, and his abundant annotations and marginalia, much of what he read, when he read it, and what he thought about it.[38] He read history, politics, biography, memoir,

---

34. For a comprehensive statement of these movements, see Alan Trachtenberg, *The Incorporation of America: Culture and Society in the Gilded Age* (New York: Hill & Wang, 1982).

35. "Melville's Poems: The Late Agenda," *A Companion to Melville Studies*, ed. John Bryant (New York: Greenwood Press, 1986), 369.

36. "Herman Melville and the Muse of Italy," *Italian Americana* 1 (1975): 169–84.

37. The quoted phrase is William Potter's. See his study *Melville's Clarel and the Intersympathy of Creeds* (Kent, OH: Kent State University Press, 2004).

38. See Merton M. Sealts Jr., *Melville's Reading: Revised and Enlarged Edition* (Columbia: University of South Carolina Press, 1988); Mary K. Bercaw, *Melville's Sources* (Evanston, IL: Northwestern University Press, 1987); and Walker Cowen, *Melville's Marginalia*, 2 vols. Harvard Dis-

and reference works, along with many Italian writers whose contributions to his thought have gone unstudied.[39] He was intensely interested in Renaissance art, and began collecting engravings and prints around 1849, a practice he continued his entire life.[40] His lecture on "Statues in Rome" drew moral and aesthetic significance from Roman and Italian statuary, and offered a template for his classical allusions in *Billy Budd*, as Gail Coffler has shown.[41] So keen was his interest in Italian art that he signed his Galápagos sketches "Salvator R. Tarnmoor," a playfully constructed nom de plume that simultaneously parodied shopworn conventions of landscape description and paid homage to Salvator Rosa, an archetype of the outlaw artist. And when Melville idealized the perfect state, he saluted "The Age of the Antonines" of second-century Imperial Rome, a time when reason and order reigned in classic repose.

If at times Melville seems the most nationalistic of America's canonized authors—"Let us away with this Bostonian leaven of literary flunkeyism towards England," he exclaimed in "Hawthorne and His Mosses" (1850; 9:248)—he is also among its most cosmopolitan: "The origins of this cosmopolitanism," Lawrence Buell observes, "lay in his postcolonial anxiety to think transcontinentally, but it fully matured only after, and partially as a result of, going through a comparatively 'American' phase at midcareer, during which Melville more directly confronted the parochialism of national narratives and of national styles of expression."[42] As

---

sertations in American and English Literature, ed. Stephen Orgel (New York: Garland Publishing, 1987). Hershel Parker's massive biography, *Herman Melville: A Biography*, 2 vols. (Baltimore: Johns Hopkins University Press, 1996, 2002), provides numerous commentaries on Melville's use of his sources. Additional books that Melville annotated turn up periodically, as do speculations about his sources and reading.

39. In addition to the writers mentioned above, Sealts, using a rigorous standard of attested possession, includes Machiavelli's *Florentine Histories*, Goethe's *Letters from Italy*, the Harper Classical Library, Chambers's *Cyclopedia*, Lanzi and Vasari on Renaissance painting, and many other potential sources. Bercaw adds numerous readings based on internal evidence, such as *The Life of Benvenuto Cellini*, Barthold Niebuhr's *History of Rome*, Machiavelli's *The Prince*, *The Penny Cyclopedia*, and dozens of newspapers and journals.

40. Robert K. Wallace has inventoried and studied nearly every print available in Melville's extensive collection, work that began with "Melville's Prints and Engravings at the Berkshire Athenaeum," *Essays in Arts and Sciences* 15 (1986): 59–90, and continues in an impressive series of handsomely illustrated articles in the *Harvard Library Bulletin* and *Leviathan*. Christopher Sten edited *Savage Eye: Melville and Visual Arts* (Kent, OH: Kent State University Press, 1991), and Douglas Robillard analyzed Melville's use of *ekphrasis* in *Melville and the Visual Arts: Ionian Form, Venetian Tint* (Kent, OH: Kent State University Press, 1997).

41. Gail Coffler, "Classical Iconography in the Aesthetics of *Billy Budd, Sailor*," in *Savage Eye: Melville and the Visual Arts*, ed. Christopher Sten (Kent, OH: Kent State University Press, 1991), 257–76. For a complete record of Melville's references to Roman art, see Coffler's *Melville's Classical Allusions: A Comprehensive Index and Glossary* (Westport, CT: Greenwood Press, 1985).

42. Lawrence Buell, "Melville and American Decolonization," 232.

contemporary theorizing on cosmopolitanism suggests, even "national narratives" rooted in local prejudices and customs can enforce cosmopolitan principles, as in the 1850s when New York City's refusal to fund parochial education led to the creation of its first public schools.[43] Bruce Robbins, in his introduction to *Cosmopolitics: Thinking and Feeling Beyond the Nation,* broaches the notion of multiple cosmopolitanisms emerging from particularized, local contexts and colliding with each other in divergent notions of universal human value. Rather than exalting the cosmopolitan ideal for its transcendent detachment and enlightened humanity, Robbins suggests that we reconceive it based on a double assumption: "first, that any cosmopolitanism's normative or idealizing power must acknowledge the actual historical and geographic contexts from which it emerges, and, second, that such an acknowledgment need not prove fatal."[44] In a global economy, principles assumed to be universal (say, workers' rights or free speech) must be adapted to local conditions or risk cultural imperialism. What is cosmopolitan in one culture seems parochial in another (think of France banning headscarves in public schools, or the US Congress impeaching a president for an isolated sexual contretemps). In a transnational context, cosmopolitanism and multiculturalism, two ideologies associated with Melville, necessarily conflict, even as Risorgimento and Union nationalisms risked eradicating the cultural identities of the Italian and American Souths. As Robbins adds pithily, "Clearly, there is no inherent virtue in transnationality."[45] Nor is there any real homology between nations. Similarities are selected to fulfill particular local needs, as when Lincoln asked Garibaldi to accept a Union command, oblivious to the Italian's abhorrence of slavery. Americans took what they needed from Risorgimento nationalism, especially its mantle of Roman Republicanism and Imperialism, a respected aesthetics, and a liberatory politics, whether or not these concepts fit local American conditions. When Horatio Greenough created his famous statue of George Washington wearing nothing but a Roman toga below his waist, the public outcry indicated there were limits to such appropriations; yet Italo-American interculturalism continued, notably when architects modeled the new Capitol dome after Rome's Pantheon and hired Constantino Brumidi, a refugee from the second Roman Republic, to decorate its interior with

43. Edwin G. Burrows and Mike Wallace, *Gotham: A History of New York City to 1898* (New York: Oxford University Press, 1999), 631.

44. "Introduction Part I: Actually Existing Cosmopolitanism," in *Cosmopolitics: Thinking and Feeling Beyond the Nation,* ed. Pheng Cheah and Bruce Robbins (Minneapolis: University of Minnesota Press, 1998), 2.

45. *Cosmopolitics,* 11.

frescoes, Italianizing the heart of American power during the peak years of the Civil War.[46] Paradoxically, claiming affinities with the Risorgimento fed American nationalism and exceptionalism, even as Italians were constructing an exceptionalist identity of their own. One could, it seems, be intercultural, transnational, cosmopolitan, and nationalistic all at the same time.

The cosmopolitan culture and political liberalism of New York City, as Wyn Kelley has shown, played a crucial role in Melville's literary development and gave him, like Walt Whitman, abundant exposure to Italian music, art, literature, and the Risorgimento exiles who promoted them.[47] He began attending operas in February 1847 at Palmo's Opera House, the first New York theater with reserved seats, and after his move to Manhattan that September he saw at least two more operas at the new, elite Astor Place Opera House.[48] He attended the American Art-Union exhibition in the company of Evert Duyckinck, an Art-Union member, and saw idealized Italian landscapes hanging alongside American genre paintings (*Log*, 262). The following June he began building his personal library with one of his earliest purchases, a copy of Dante (*Log*, 278), and his literary circles widened to include some of the city's leading Italophiles, men and women who cared deeply about the current Italian situation and followed it closely. In 1849 he attended a Valentine's Day party at the house of Anne Lynch, where at least four of the guests—Nathaniel Parker Willis, Rev. Orville Dewey (who baptized Melville's children), William Cullen Bryant, and Henry Theodore Tuckerman—had published books on Italy, and two more—Caroline Kirkland and Catherine Sedgwick—would do so within two years.[49] Columbia University Italian Professor E. Felice Foresti, New York's leading Italian émigré, attended Lynch's soirées, as did Margaret Fuller, and since Lynch typically invited a lively mix of revolutionists, liberals, and conservatives, it's tantalizingly possible (although entirely undocumented) that Garibaldi himself dropped in during his

---

46. Barbara A. Wolanin, "Constantino Brumidi's Frescoes in the United States Capitol," in *The Italian Presence in American Art 1760–1860*, ed. Irma B. Jaffe (New York: Fordham University Press, 1989), 150–64. See also Donald R. Kennon and Thomas P. Somma, *American Pantheon: Sculptural and Artistic Decoration of the United States Capitol, Perspectives on the Art and Architectural History of the United States Capitol* (Athens: Published for the U.S. Capitol Historical Society by Ohio University Press, 2004).

47. See Wyn Kelley, *Melville's City: Literary and Urban Form in Nineteenth-Century New York* (Cambridge: Cambridge University Press, 1996).

48. Jay Leyda, *The Melville Log: A Documentary Life of Herman Melville, 1819–1891*, 2 vols. (New York: Gordian, 1969), 234, 267, 271. Future references are incorporated parenthetically.

49. Parker, *Herman Melville*, 1:606, 584; *Log*, 270. Parker considers Anne Lynch and Augusta Melville, Herman's sister, as "friends" (649). Lynch knew Melville and his work well enough to mention him familiarly in an 1849 review in the *Literary World* (*Log*, 323).

New York exile of 1850–51.[50] In 1855 Lynch married Vincenzo Botta, an Italian who served in the Piedmontese Parliament in 1849; he later wrote a book on Dante and another on Cavour, the architect of Italian unification.[51] Whenever Italy's nationalists achieved a victory, as when Mazzini ousted the pope from Rome in 1849, Garibaldi conquered Naples in 1860, or Victor Emmanuel II proclaimed Rome his capital in 1871, New Yorkers celebrated with huge public meetings. Speeches and public letters from Henry Bellows, Henry Tuckerman, Charles Sumner, William Cullen Bryant, and Horace Greeley identified Italy's sympathizers as highly placed, influential political and literary figures whose lives and works repeatedly intersected with Melville's. Italophiles were common in New York literary circles, and Melville frequently found himself among them.

While Melville learned much about Italy from his New York companions, he applied his knowledge rather differently than most writers, a primary reason his Italian interests have not been isolated as a force in his work. He set only one story, "The Bell-Tower" (1855), in Italy, and created only two developed Italian characters, Carlo in *Redburn* (1849) and Celio in *Clarel* (1876). Although he addressed the Risorgimento directly in his Neapolitan diptych, Melville more typically used allusion, iconography, metaphor, allegory, and oblique reference to confront Italy's turmoil and limn its implications for the United States. His very offhandedness reveals the pervasiveness of Italian culture in antebellum New York, for Melville expected discerning readers such as the guests at Anne Lynch's parties to supply the ideological ballast for his allusions. Given his literary instinct for metonymy, Melville didn't need and probably didn't want to make literal references to Italy; rather, he wove Italian materials seamlessly into a web of allusions and tropes that track the intersections of American and Italian culture with his own political and aesthetic obsessions, particularly his family's heritage of aristocratic pretension and political hubris.

Larry J. Reynolds and Michael Paul Rogin provide a valuable orientation toward Melville's appropriation of Italy, even though neither addresses it directly. Both scholars recognize not only the ideological conflict behind Melville's politics, but how those conflicts took shape in metaphors and iconography that blend the personal and political. Reynolds has amply demonstrated how the iconography of *Moby-Dick* registers and critiques the European Revolutions of 1848 and their aftermath, which reconstituted monarchies in France, Italy, and Austria. Melville recognized

50. Lynch's guests also included Melville's acquaintances Emerson, Rev. H. W. Bellows, and Bayard Taylor. See Lynch, *Memoirs of Anne C. L. Botta* (New York: J. S. Tait & Sons, 1894), 16.
51. Lynch, *Memoirs,* 89, 226.

the rebellions' origins in the French Revolution of 1789, a bloodbath that he, like many Americans, viewed with disgust: "Like Hawthorne," writes Reynolds, "he maintained a lifelong skepticism toward violent popular uprisings, and the developments in Europe, especially the French revolution, affected him deeply and endowed his work, in a lasting manner, with the dark hues of the conservative side of his thought."[52] Rogin analogizes the revolutions of 1848 to Melville's psychic battle with his aristocratic pedigree, and charts his ideological recoil from popular rebellions in the years before the Civil War. The revolutionary excesses of 1848, Rogin argues, led both French and American governments to seek stability: "Just as Bonaparte's [Napoleon III's] coup destroyed French liberty in order to preserve the social order, so the Fugitive Slave Law betrayed the principles of the Declaration of Independence to avert a civil conflagration."[53] Both writers realize that, although Melville was uncomfortable with any betrayal of democracy, and although he frequently dramatized the tension between revolt and authority (notably in "Benito Cereno," *Israel Potter,* and *Billy Budd*), his revolutionary heroes are ultimately failures, doomed to suffer under the "iron dome" of filial, religious, and political authority, the Roman-inspired iron dome of the new Capitol Melville watched rising in Washington, DC. Walter Bezanson identifies a similar skepticism in *Clarel* (1876) in the figures of Mortmain and Ungar, former rebels who disavow their revolutionary principles and typify Melville's mixed admiration and disdain for revolutionaries in general.[54] Conservative readings of *Billy Budd* build on these views to identify Melville's ultimate political philosophy with Captain Vere's, a continually contentious position that exposes the heart of the Melville problem. Melville's transnational sympathies reinforce these ideological interpretations, yet modify their reactionary tendencies with a cosmopolitanism that retains, on a more abstract metaphorical and historical level, the equally persistent progressive elements of his thought and art. This constitutes the paradox of liberty and authority at the heart of Risorgimento nationalism and the republican experiment in the United States as well. The whole matter of Italy, in other words, complicates Melville's attitudes toward revolution, authority, religion, and art, and qualifies as one of those "central historical and public issues" that Michael Rogin deems so influential in Melville's career.[55]

---

52. *European Revolutions*, 101; see also 99–100, 124.
53. *Subversive Genealogy: The Politics and Art of Herman Melville* (Berkeley: University of California Press, 1985), 103; see also 283.
54. See Bezanson's notes to *Clarel*, 12:626–28, 633–34.
55. *Subversive Genealogy*, 41.

I would not want, however, to imply that the Risorgimento offers a magic key that unlocks the secret to Melville's politics or establishes a unifying myth that gives coherence to his career. Quite the opposite. The shifting, pragmatic politics of the Risorgimento mirror the alternations, oppositions, and yoked incongruities that constitute both the ideological dynamics of the nineteenth century and Melville's profoundest meditations on freedom, art, and authority. Many of these ruminations come in his later writings, which are too often omitted from comprehensive studies of his career. Read against the matter of Italy, all of Melville's works take on richer contextual colorings, and place both his early and late literary practice and ideas more firmly within his own era. The result is a more ideologically complex Melville, one whose literary nationalism draws sustenance and critique from Risorgimento nationalism, effectively blending the local and the universal in a historically grounded, culturally specific transnational context. The Melville that results is very much a product of his age, not just the American 1840s and 1850s, where most studies of Melville stop, but of a global nineteenth-century culture that included Italy (as well as other countries) in its struggle for self-definition.

For these reasons my study moves chronologically through Melville's career, embedding each work in its immediate historical moment—and sometimes they are moments, mere weeks or months—and examining its Italianate allusions in the context of shifting American attitudes toward the Risorgimento. Chapter 1 assesses Italy's place in American culture from the Congress of Vienna in 1815 to the eruption of European revolutions in 1848, and identifies those in Melville's circle who followed events in Italy most closely. Young Americans such as Henry T. Tuckerman and Joel Tyler Headley debated whether Italians had the political maturity to accept republican institutions, particularly when they lived under the yoke of the Roman Catholic hierarchy. As a paradoxical object of desire and disdain within the American imaginary, Italy evolved from a "Land of the Dead" to a cauldron of "Red Republicanism" almost overnight, making it an ethnographic object as impervious to American understanding as the Typees had been to young Melville. Chapter 2 accounts for the tide of Dante studies that swept over Melville as he wrote *Mardi,* a novel simultaneously influenced by *The Divine Comedy* and the rapidly unfolding events of 1848. As Melville's first encounter with a major European author, Dante not only shaped the structure and politics of his third novel but, in the scholarly edition of Henry Cary, provided a template of intertextual borrowings, cross-references, allusions, and scholarly discussion. Dante offered Melville a *via media* between the extremes of tyranny and anarchy that are evident in King Media's scroll, and as a Catholic writer who sent popes to hell, provided cover for *Mardi's* antipapalism. Chapter 3 examines *Redburn* and *White-Jacket* against the rise and fall of the second Roman Republic, a period when New Yorkers were reading Margaret Fuller's dispatches from Rome that urged American support for the Risorgimento. Instead of addressing this issue directly, Melville immersed his narratives even deeper in Roman art and history to complicate Fuller's ardent radicalism with the somber lessons of the past. Carlo, the young Sicilian immigrant in *Redburn,* and Ushant, the rebellious old foretopman in *White-Jacket,* image a mediatory politics drawn from Italian iconography that balances liberty with authority and foreshadows the Risorgimento metaphors Melville uses to characterize Ahab's revolutionary excesses in *Moby-Dick.* Chapter 4 uncovers Melville's indebtedness to Machiavelli, whose history of Florence he consulted as he wrote *Pierre.* Although Italy had drawn away from revolution, the United States seemed to totter on its brink, and the anarchic career of young Pierre Glendenning, several short stories, *Israel Potter,* and *The Confidence-Man* all betray the increasing appeal of Machiavelli's insight that successful republics require order, diplomacy, and decisive leaders. Satire and irony become Melville's dominant narrative modes as he engages in a literary diplomacy of his own to question facile American notions of populist virtue and the hasty exaltation of European revolutionaries such as Louis Kossuth. Chapter 5 builds on the insights about art and history that Melville gained from his trip to Italy in 1857 and codified in his lecture "Statues in Rome." When Garibaldi liberated Naples in 1860, Melville, by now a confirmed poet, began his Neapolitan diptych and fused art and politics as never before, creating a complex poem that reveals his intimate knowledge of Risorgimento nationalism and finds in its successes and failures lessons for the United States. *Battle-Pieces* incorporates some of these ideas, notably in its "Supplement," which invokes Roman and Italian history as premonitory guides for the postbellum United States. Chapter 6 focuses on *Clarel,* especially Celio, the most developed Italian character in Melville's oeuvre and a sad but realistic figure of Risorgimento secularism. *Clarel* is as political as it is theological, and by articulating a cyclical view of history it vitiates American progressivism and optimism as well as naïve expectations of supernatural salvation. The austere imperialism of ancient Rome has devolved into the transnational ambitions of a politicized Roman Catholicism, an ideology Melville dismantles through his satirical portrait of the Dominican priest, and while Rome may lie in ruins its example still holds for modern civilization. The chapter and book conclude by examining the theme of revolution in *Billy Budd* through the optics of Risorgimento meliorism, an ideology that honors republican freedoms but, through Captain Vere, maintains a strong grip on the throne.

I hope this book is, finally, not just about Melville the writer but about Melville as a cultural metonym, a figure who embodies the paradoxes and contradictions of his times and challenges any easy assumptions about nineteenth-century ideologies. I think most of recent critics such as David S. Reynolds, Joel Porte, Nancy Fredricks, and John Carlos Rowe, who assume Melville's "ruthless democracy" and chart his career as a philosophical struggle for individual agency, but forget that "democracy" in 1850, when over two-thirds of the adult population could not vote, meant something very different than "democracy" at the end of the twentieth century.[56] Despite critics' best efforts, lapses into presentism seem endemic to Melville studies, partly because Melville does remain astonishingly relevant to our own times but also because too few critics embed him sufficiently in his era or adequately consider his entire career. Local events and contemporary history drove Melville's thought more than the abstractions of Kant and Hegel, and these events often surface in his works through a topical iconography unnoticed by modern readers. I subscribe to Rowe's call to revaluate American literature "in terms of both its critique of ideology—the traditional function of *aesthetic dissent*—and the discursive communities such literature helps constitute," but would contextualize that dissent in the broader matrices of transnational interculturalism and Melville's entire corpus. The paradox of authority and individualism that most critics correctly locate at the center of Melville's ideological anxieties often finds expression in non-American terms,

---

56. In *Beneath the American Renaissance: The Subversive Imagination in the Age of Emerson and Melville* (Cambridge, MA: Harvard University Press, 1989), David S. Reynolds, in a chapter entitled "Melville's Ruthless Democracy," argues that "*Moby-Dick* is the literary culmination of the radical egalitarianism that had its roots in Jacksonian democracy and that Melville used "paradoxical emblems of his newfound radical democracy" to subvert conventional norms (289–90). Joel Porte, *In Respect to Egotism: Studies in American Romantic Writing* (Cambridge: Cambridge University Press, 1991), believes Melville was a phallic democrat who grudgingly admired the Astor Place rioters (189–212), a position I contest in "Class Acts: The Astor Place Riots and Melville's 'The Two Temples,'" *American Literature* 71 (September 1999): 429–61. Nancy Fredricks, *Melville's Art of Democracy* (Athens: University of Georgia Press, 1995), believes critics have ignored Melville's class consciousness and his "attempt to create an art that embodies egalitarian and multicultural democratic values" (4). In a more nuanced argument, John Carlos Rowe, *At Emerson's Tomb: The Politics of Classic American Literature* (New York: Columbia University Press, 1997), reads *Pierre* against Hegel and Marx to demonstrate Melville's deconstruction of "the democratic pretensions of American capitalism" (94).

and offers possibilities of resolution invisible to strictly nationalist eyes. Wai Chee Dimock's notion of Melville's "Imperial Self" negotiates this paradox in nationalist political, ethical, rhetorical, and economic discourse, and through her fundamental oxymoronic metaphor captures tensions inherent in Risorgimento nationalism as well:

> Freedom not only entails an obverse; it is itself constituted by that obverse.... What animates this polarity, what gives it its characteristic structure, is not merely a logic of the literary text, but equally a logic of the self and, beyond the self, a logic of the nation—all three of them being double formations, all three bodying forth, separately and together, a kindred logic of freedom and dominion, sovereignty and subjection.[57]

Mutually constitutive opposites coexist within text, self, and nation, and escape the bounds of logical expression and conscious observation, emerging (if at all) in moments of narrative irruption and fissure. Italian art and history provided Melville with a cultural symbolic both to create such productive disjunctions and offer alternative resolutions literally and metaphorically "foreign" to American readers. The conflict between democracy and imperialism need not be figured only in Starbuck and Ahab; it can also be personified in the unitary image of Garibaldi, simultaneously a liberator and dictator, a squire and a knight, a rustic sailor and a cosmopolitan rebel. As an aesthetic resource drawn from the transnational imaginary, Garibaldi offered Americans a cosmopolitan refraction of their own conflicted identity and modeled a selfhood that negotiated the dilemmas of individualism and authority that Dimock and others see as central to Melville's nation-making vision.

For Melville, the "possibilities of democracy" were not, as they were for F. O. Matthiessen, couched in terms of the New Deal, or in terms of subaltern liberation, as they are for many postmodern critics, but in his actual experiences with nascent capitalism, aristocratic nostalgia, literary elitism, constitutional monarchies, populist economics, workers' rights, mob violence, and socialist revolutions. These were messy, unkempt ideas and events that provided little stable ground for constructing a coherent politics, and Melville, always evolving, never forged a conscious ideology consistent with modern notions of democracy (even something as simple

---

57. Dimock, *Empire for Liberty: Melville and the Poetics of Individualism* (Princeton, NJ: Princeton University Press, 1989), 111.

as "one man, one vote"—a catchphrase with its own obvious shortcomings). Scholars who study Melville within this complicated context find him, in Carolyn Karcher's formulation, both "a refractory conformist and a reluctant rebel."[58] Just how reluctant Karcher refines in a searching essay on *Battle-Pieces,* where she finds the erstwhile multicultural Melville retreating after the Civil War from his earlier ideals of interracial brotherhood and working-class solidarity.[59] John P. McWilliams traces a similar pattern in Melville's works, and concludes that after the Burgundy Club Sketches of the 1880s Melville was left with the paradoxical pain "of understanding his forever-disillusioning commitment to vile liberty," while other critics, such as James Duban, ironize Melville's most democratic effusions and find him essentially Whiggish all along.[60] These scholars, along with Rogin and Reynolds, embrace the contradictions of Melville's ideology along with the contradictions of American society. None of them, however, recognizes the analogies Melville intuited between Italy and America and how he exploited them to construct a borderless national identity that spanned ages and continents. What seems paradoxical to us—Dimock's "Imperial Self"—were normative terms of Risorgimento discourse, if not all nineteenth-century political discourse. By reading Melville through the Risorgimento, we can better understand him within the cultural politics of his own age and place, a time of ethical contradictions as apparent as ours. As twenty-first-century Americans have discovered anew, wars of liberation can quickly morph into wars of occupation and eventually wars of repression. When Byron asked in *Childe Harold's Pilgrimage* "Can tyrants but by tyrants conquered be?" he posed a question as relevant to Melville as to us.[61]

58. Karcher, *Shadow Over the Promised Land: Slavery, Race, and Violence in Melville's America* (Baton Rouge: Louisiana State University Press, 1980), 3.

59. Karcher, "The Moderate and the Radical: Melville and Child on the Civil War and Reconstruction," *ESQ: A Journal of the American Renaissance* 45 (3rd and 4th Quarters 1999): 187–257.

60. McWilliams, *Hawthorne, Melville, and the American Character: A Looking-Glass Business* (Cambridge: Cambridge University Press, 1984), 228. Duban, *Melville's Major Fiction: Politics, Theology, and Imagination* (DeKalb: Northern Illinois University Press, 1983).

61. *Selected Poetry of Lord Byron,* ed. Leslie A. Marchand (New York: Modern Library, 1951), 134; Canto IV, stanza 96. Melville parodied stanza 179 of Canto IV in "The Mast-head," chap. 35 of *Moby-Dick* (6:158), the famous apostrophe to Ocean ("Roll on, . . . ").

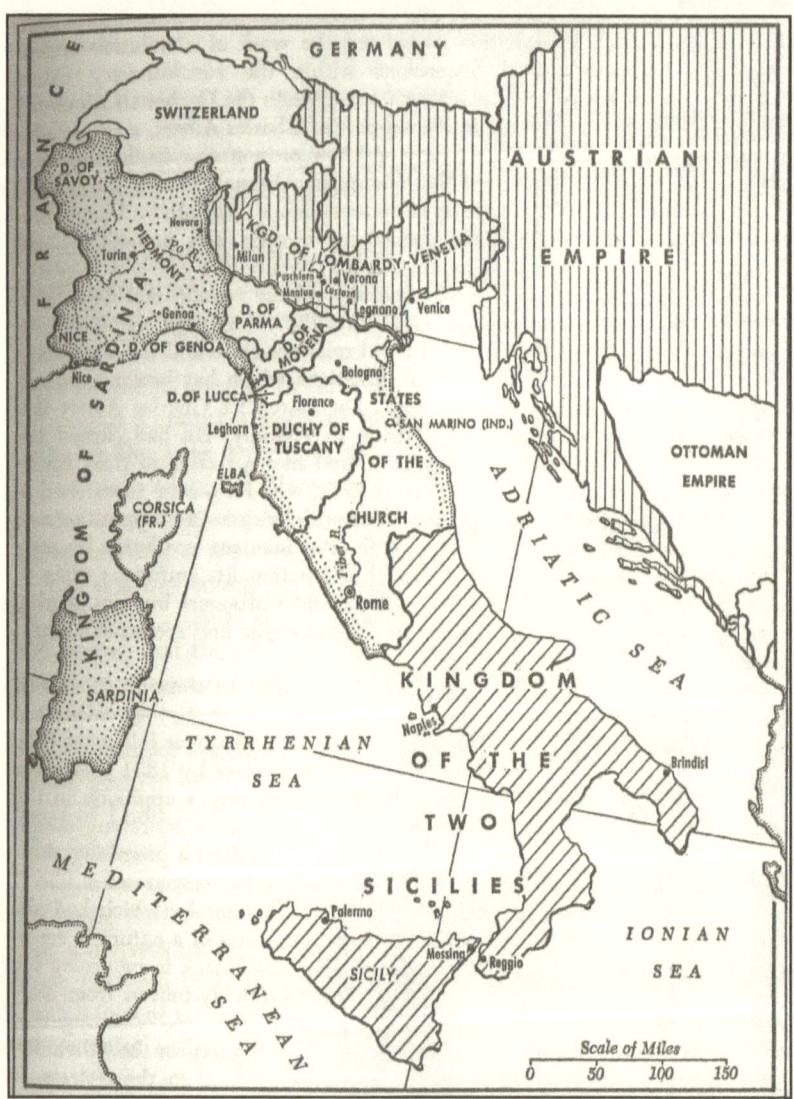

Figure 1. Map of Italy in 1815. Napoleon Bonaparte had consolidated Italy into a few large states, but the Congress of Vienna restored the peninsula to its fragmented condition and reinstated Austrian, Bourbon, and Papal rule. From Clough and Saladino, *A History of Modern Italy,* 29.

1

Italy in the American Imagination
A Divided Vision

> Italy is a geographical expression.
> —Prince Metternich (1849)

> Italy! Italy! Thou who'rt doomed to wear
> The fatal gift of beauty . . .
> Ah! Would that thou wert stronger, or less fair,
> That they might fear thee more, or love thee less.
> —Longfellow, "To Italy (From Filicaja)" (1869)

ACTUALLY, MELVILLE never visited Italy. Rather, he visited the Kingdom of the Two Sicilies, the Papal States, Tuscany, Lombardy-Venetia, and the Kingdom of Sardinia, the five states that, along with Modena, Parma, and Lucca, shared the Italian peninsula in 1857 (fig. 1).

"The great calamity of Italy, as of Germany," wrote a reviewer in the *North American Review* in 1825, "has been the severance of the members of that beautiful country, into rival and hostile states," a conventional lamentation that pervades antebellum discourse.[1] Except for a brief period of unity under Napoleonic rule, Italy before 1859 remained largely as it had since the Middle Ages, a congeries of city-states, kingdoms, and petty duchies with varying dialects, social conditions, cultural values, and political aspirations. For example, even though much of the case for Italian nationhood relied on the myth of a common peninsular language, at the time of reunification in 1860 only two-and-a-half percent of the population regularly spoke the ostensible "national" language, and for both the new king and his prime minister Cavour Italian remained a

---

1. "European Politics," 21 (July 1825), 149, rev. of J. C. L. De Sismondi, *A Review of the Efforts and Progress of Nations, during the last Twentyfive* [sic] *Years* (Philadelphia, 1825).

poorly spoken third language, after their regional dialects and French.[2] Austria occupied Lombardy-Venetia, the Hapsburg Leopold II ruled Tuscany, and the Two Sicilies remained under the oppressive Bourbon rule of Ferdinand II. Despite these problems, Italy remained the most popular continental destination for American tourists, a place where they could sate their burgeoning taste for picturesque travel and romantic history while indulging their sense of moral, religious, and political superiority.[3] Americans viewed Italy through a contradictory optics of repulsion and desire, condescension and admiration, despair and hope, in an irreconcilable binary that opposed politics and aesthetics. If states are necessary to create nations, as Ernest Gellner argues in *Nations and Nationalism*, Italy, even more than the United States, existed primarily as an imagined community, in Metternich's words a mere "geographical expression" seeking a state to make it whole.[4]

(EVADING) POLITICS IN THE LAND OF THE PICTURESQUE

Although Italy's fragmentation was evident in the irritating border crossings, customs inspections, and repeated visa applications experienced by all travelers to Italy, few Americans before the 1840s commented directly on the peninsula's political problems. Taking brief trips, almost always ignorant of the language, seldom interacting with the politically active Italian upper and middle classes, often confining their travel to a few select regions—Sicily, for example, made few itineraries—Americans instead elided political comment and viewed Italy only as "*the* land of the picturesque," as Leonardo Buonomo has argued, seeing it as a colorful

2. E. J. Hobsbawm, *Nations and Nationalism Since 1780: Programme, Myth, and Reality*, 2nd ed. (Cambridge: Cambridge University Press, 1990), 38–39, quoting Tullio de Mauro, *Storia Linguistica dell'Italia Unita* (Bari, 1963), 41; Doyle, *Nations Divided*, 33. Some Italian historians discount de Mauro's figure because many Italians spoke both their regional dialect and either spoke or understood the broader Italian vernacular. See the discussion in Derek Beales and Eugenio F. Biagini, *The Risorgimento and the Unification of Italy* (London: Pearson Education Limited, 2002), 74–80.

3. For the rise of picturesque taste in the United States, see Beth L. Lueck, *American Writers and the Picturesque Tour: The Search for National Identity, 1790–1860* (New York: Garland Publishing, 1997).

4. (Ithaca, NY: Cornell University Press, 1983). In his definitions of "state" and "nation," Gellner writes, "the state has certainly emerged without the help of the nation. Some nations have certainly emerged without the blessings of their own state. It is more debatable whether the normative idea of the nation, in its modern sense, did not presuppose the prior existence of the state" (6). Metternich is quoted in Stuart Woolf, *A History of Italy 1700–1860: The Social Constraints of Political Change* (London: Methuen & Co. Ltd., 1979), 227.

intermixture of past and present, nostalgia and gaiety, ruin and beauty, but no place for a republic.⁵ Americans consistently "idealized" Italy, Nathalia Wright observes, constructing it as a "fairy-land" free from the anxieties of revolutionary politics: "It is notable, too," Wright adds, "that though most of these writers were sympathetic with the contemporaneous movement for Italian independence, none treated it directly in fiction."⁶ Even the most notable American novels on Italy, such as Cooper's *The Bravo* (1831) and Hawthorne's *The Marble Faun* (1860), avoid politics, as do the most popular travel books, such as Caroline Kirkland's *Holidays Abroad* (1849) and George Stillman Hillard's *Six Months in Italy* (1853).⁷ Not surprisingly, such evasions also characterize American scholarship on Italy. When Van Wyck Brooks borrowed the title of Thomas Cole's 1838 painting *Dream of Arcadia* (fig. 2) for his influential survey of American

---

5. *Backward Glances*, 92, 12. The "variety of cultural individualities of cities and regions was not a prominent theme in most nineteenth-century American books on Italy," Buonomo adds, attributing this omission to a combination of cultural ignorance, willful idealization, and politically useful overgeneralization (17–18). Paul R. Baker states similar views in *The Fortunate Pilgrims*, 188–89.

6. Wright, *American Novelists in Italy*, 263.

7. Leonardo Buonomo compares *The Bravo* to Manzoni's *The Betrothed* (1827) as historical romances with oblique political meanings, but finally makes only a modest case for *The Bravo's* political currency: "Notwithstanding its unrealistic aspects and its eighteenth-century setting, *The Bravo* might be read as a commentary (however indirect) on the political situation in nineteenth-century Italy" (66–67). Robert S. Levine, "'Antebellum Rome' in *The Marble Faun*," *American Literary History* 2 (Spring 1990): 18–38, finds numerous allusions to the politics of 1848, particularly the notion that Italy might unify under papal leadership, but he admits that by 1860, when the romance was published, this idea had been relegated to the realm of fantasy. Mark A. R. Kemp, "*The Marble Faun* and American Postcolonial Ambivalence," *Modern Fiction Studies* 43, no. 1 (1997), finds Hawthorne effacing Italian nationalism with broad moral concerns that deflect attention from political reality (226, 230). Kirkland is more direct than the novelists, telling her readers, "I had always cared far more about Italian pictures than Italian politics," and "as for the 'affairs of Italy,' I had sedulously averted my eyes whenever I saw anything under that head in the newspapers *(Holidays Abroad; or Europe from the West*, 2 vols. [New York: Baker and Scribner, 1849], 1:182). In an insightful article Brigitte Bailey, "Gender, Nation, and the Tourist Gaze in the European 'Year of Revolutions': Kirkland's *Holidays Abroad*," *American Literary History* 14 (March 2002): 60–82, places Kirkland among those promoting a more aestheticized appropriation of European and Catholic iconography that disengaged them from their historical and religious uses, empowered women observers, and constructed an artistically richer national imaginary (62 esp.). Hillard, a good friend of Hawthorne's, made an extended journey to Italy from September 1847 to April 1848, yet fails to mention the popular revolts that spread throughout the country between January and March and resulted in constitutional governments in Sicily, Piedmont, Tuscany, the Papal States, and even Parma. Kirkland and Hillard may have been following the example of Charles Dickens, who prefaced his immensely popular *Pictures from Italy* (1845) by promising to avoid "any grave examination into the government or misgovernment of any portion of the country," an avowal that implies "misgovernment" existed but was not a suitable topic for a travel book *(Pictures from Italy*, ed. David Paroissien [New York: Coward, McCann & Geoghegan, 1974], 36). Evert Duyckinck pirated this title for his "Library of Choice Reading," a series he edited for Wiley and Putnam between 1845 and 1848.

Figure 2. Thomas Cole, *Dream of Arcadia,* c. 1838. Denver Art Museum: Gift of Mrs. Lindsey Gentry, 1954.71. Photo courtesy of the Denver Art Museum.

writing on Italy, he enshrined a visual archetype that illuminated Italy's aesthetic significance while obscuring its contemporary ideology, a perspective evident in later works by Paul Baker, Erik Amfitheatrof, and even Buonomo.[8]

Such avoidance seems deliberate. The *North American Review,* the *New-England Magazine,* and the *Democratic Review* published reviews of political and historical works on Italy which typically lamented the country's divided condition and praised its nationalistic liberals, even comparing them to the patriots of the American Revolution.[9] More broadly, Americans who steeped themselves in English romantic poetry—and there were many, including Melville—knew of Italy's political problems. Byron and Shelley attacked the Hapsburg betrayal of nationalistic and republican impulses that flickered to life under Napoleon, and composed verses that captured Italy's suffering for two generations of readers. "The Niobe of Nations!" Byron apostrophizes in his 1818 addition to *Childe Harold's Pil-*

---

8. Baker, *The Fortunate Pilgrims;* Erik Amfitheatrof, *The Enchanted Ground: Americans in Italy, 1760–1980* (Boston: Little, Brown and Company, 1980). This perspective, of course, was rooted in earlier British attitudes toward Italy: see Lytton Sells, *The Paradise of Travellers: The Italian Influence on Englishmen in the Seventeenth Century* (Bloomington: Indiana University Press, 1964).

9. See, for example, "Italy," *North American Review* 12 (January 1821): 198–229; "Americans in Italy," *New-England Magazine* 1 (July 1831): 50–54; "Retrospective View of the State of European Politics," *Democratic Review* 1 (October 1837): 123–42; and "Italy," *North American Review* 40 (1835): 438–40. For the comparison to American patriots, see "European Politics," 150.

grimage, "there she stands, / Childless and crownless, in her voiceless woe; / An empty urn within her withered hands, / Whose holy dust was scattered long ago."[10] Shelley's moving plea for Italian independence, "Lines Written Among the Euganean Hills," condemns Austrian hegemony and urges freedom to "awake / In her omnipotence, and shake / From the Celtic Anarch's hold / All the keys of dungeons cold" (ll. 150–53).[11] Even the genteel poet Samuel Rogers worked revolutionary sentiments into his enormously popular and predominantly nostalgic *Italy, A Poem* (1822–28) by attacking "those who now enslave thee" and envisioning a day when a united Italy will once again shine "among the nations of the world."[12] Melville breakfasted with Rogers in 1849 and owned, quoted, and annotated works by Byron and Shelley, giving him early and frequent access to literature that integrated the political and the aesthetic in a more complex understanding of Italian culture than pre-1848 American writing.[13]

The blended vision of a picturesque *and* a political Italy is evident in one of the most influential nineteenth-century books on Italy, the Englishman Joseph Forsyth's *Remarks on Antiquities* (1813), a work Melville owned and annotated perhaps as early as 1830.[14] Forsyth's *Travels*, as it

10. *Selected Poetry,* 130; Canto IV, stanza 79. Byron added Canto IV in 1818, when the full impact of Italy's occupation by foreign powers was clear. Niobe bore the twelve children who taunted Latona because she had born only two children, Apollo and Diana. In revenge, Apollo and Diana slew Niobe's children. Niobe's grief turned her to stone, yet the statue continued to weep for the murdered children as though it were alive

11. *The Complete Poetical Works of Percy Bysshe Shelley,* ed. William Michael Rossetti (London: John Slark, 1885), 2:39. The combination of the picturesque and political is evident in Shelley's note to another poem sympathetic to the Italian cause, "Ode to Naples": "The author has connected many recollections of his visit to Pompeii and Baiae with the enthusiasm excited by the intelligence of the proclamation of a Constitutional Government at Naples. This has given a tinge of picturesque and descriptive imagery to the introductory Epodes which depicture these scenes, and some of the majestic feelings permanently connect with the scene of this animating event" (*Complete Poetical Works,* 1:86.

12. *The Poems of Samuel Rogers* (New York: Hurst & Co., [1853]), 39. In other editions see part 1, canto 9, ll.15, 17. According to Maura O'Connor, *The Romance of Italy and the English Political Imagination* (New York: St. Martin's Press, 1998), the 1830 edition of Rogers's poem with the J. M. W. Turner engravings sold almost as many copies as Murray's travel guide to Italy (201n103). Robert K. Wallace, *Melville & Turner: Spheres of Love and Fright* (Athens: University of Georgia Press, 1992), believes that descriptions in *Mardi* and *Moby-Dick* were influenced by Melville's encounter with Evert Duyckinck's copy of the illustrated 1830 edition (142–50, 428–30).

13. For Melville's holdings in Byron and Shelley, see Sealts, *Melville's Reading.* The transcriptions in Cowen, *Melville's Marginalia,* 1:376–403, reveal extensive markings and several significant annotations in Melville's ten-volume edition of Byron's *Poetical Works* (1853).

14. Joseph Forsyth, Esq., *Remarks on Antiquities, Arts, and Letters, During an Excursion in Italy, in the Years 1802 and 1803,* ed. Keith Crook (1816; Newark: University of Delaware Press, 2001). Parenthetical references are to this edition. Forsyth's *Italy* was originally published in 1813 but

was commonly known, moves beyond picturesque conventions to infuse traditional moral and aesthetic readings of the country with a politicized grammar of Italian travel. "Every city in Tuscany having been once a separate republic, still considers itself a nation distinct from the rest, and calls their inhabitants foreigners," he writes, a situation that fosters endless feuds and makes Italians "the hypocrites of liberty" (22, 23). National unity seems a distant hope at best: "The strongest bond of union among Italians is only a coincidence of hatred" (63), and ancient rivalries among city-states erupt at border crossings and leave the frontiers lawless (145). Forsyth's "enlarged edition" of 1816, the basis for all subsequent editions including Melville's, takes advantage of Napoleon's demise to add even more explicit commentary on Italy's political woes. Italians flourish best under enlightened despots like Leopold I (207–11), Forsyth argues, but under the papacy "the national character is the most ruined thing in Rome" (219); meanwhile, Naples lingers in a "barbarian twilight" that countenances every immorality, and is little more than "a paradise inhabited by devils" (223, 225).[15] Forsyth's Italy is a country in chaos, a land of stiletto-wielding assassins, corrupt priests, degenerate aristocrats, hot-blooded monarchist mobs, outdated industries, stagnant economies, and superstitious masses neither capable of nor deserving republican self-rule. Far from an Arcadian paradise, Italy is a land devastated by internal dissension, vitiated tradition, blind religion, and foreign occupation, a vision of Italy that Melville exploits in *Mardi*.

Forsyth's jaundiced views surfaced in Melville's New York literary circle as early as 1834, when William Cullen Bryant began publishing travel letters from Italy in the *New York Evening Post*. Although he agreed with the general opinion that Tuscany under Leopold II was among the most enlightened states, it was still "little better than an Austrian province, like the other countries of Italy."[16] At Volterra Bryant ascribed the nobles' indolence to their exclusion from politics, finding them "soft and effeminate," and at the nearby fortress he observed four political prisoners, young men "guilty of offences against the state."[17] Naples, already syn-

---

was quickly "enlarged" for the 1816 edition, which became the basis for the editions of 1824 and 1835. Melville owned the 1824 edition which he may have acquired in the 1820s (Cowen, *Melville's Marginalia*, 1:xlvii). Sealts, *Melville's Reading*, #219, gives no acquisition date. Paul R. Baker attests to Forsyth's popularity: "It was probably the volume most often referred to by the Americans visiting Italy in the first half of the nineteenth century" (*Fortunate Pilgrims*, 27).

15. Forsyth places this remark in quotation marks, suggesting it was a well-known epithet for Naples.

16. New York *Evening Post*, May 12, 1835; rpt. in *Letters of a Traveller; or, Notes of Things Seen in Europe and America* (New York: George P. Putnam, 1850), 39.

17. *Letters of a Traveller*, 436 and 441.

onymous with unchecked tyranny, generated the worst horror. When the king's brother Prince Charles discovered an old man gathering wood on the royal grounds, the prince tied him to a tree and summarily executed him. "The royal family of Naples," Bryant wrote bitterly, "kill people by way of amusement."[18] Despite Italy's storied beauty, Bryant was, according to his biographer, ready "to leave a land where so much of what he saw reminded him of a cruel and repressive antiquity," and when he returned to New York he published one of the earliest pro-Risorgimento American poems, "To the Apennines" (1836).[19]

Similarly, Melville's literary friend Henry Theodore Tuckerman dismissed Italy's political dilemma in a popular formulaic rationalization that derives from Forsyth's jaundiced perspective: "Italy is not yet virtuous enough to maintain the forms or evolve the moral glory of genuine national freedom," he wrote in 1835,"[20] a candid view that was widely accepted before 1848 and conditioned Melville's first appropriations of Italian culture. As in Germaine de Staël's *Corinne,* the image of Italy as a beautifully feminine but politically emasculated land vainly seeking to reclaim its lost glory appeared in almost every major American poem about the Risorgimento,[21] necessarily complicating any single vision of Italy. Italy was beautiful, alluring, tragic, and doomed, a dangerously appealing place with what the seventeenth-century Italian poet Vincenzo da Filicaja called "the fatal gift of beauty," a phrase echoed again and again by British and American poets including Longfellow's well-known 1869 translation of Filicaja's poem "To Italy." This and other stock romantic tropes encouraged American interest but blocked understanding. Italy remained a land of contradictions, torn between nationalist longings and local loyalties, republican dreams and monarchical realities, a quest for independence and a heritage of foreign domination, a rich artistic past and an impoverished present—a land longing for a coherent cultural identity as much as the United States itself.

18. *Letters of a Traveller,* 38.
19. Charles H. Brown, *William Cullen Bryant* (New York: Charles Scribner's Sons, 1971), 230, 244.
20. [Henry Theodore Tuckerman,] *The Italian Sketchbook. By an American* (Philadelphia: Key & Biddle, 1835), 204. For the Tuckerman-Melville friendship, see Parker, *Herman Melville,* 1:572–73.
21. Roy M. Peterson, "Echoes of the Italian Risorgimento in Contemporary American Writers," *PMLA* 47 (1932): 220–40, traces Risorgimento references in the poetry of Whittier, Lowell, Longfellow, and others, where the motifs of feminized emasculation are abundantly evident. I have uncovered instances in American poetry dating back to 1831, for example "The Italian Exile," *New-England Magazine* 1 (1831): 10, and Buonomo finds these motifs persisting in Julia Ward Howe's *Passion Flowers* (1854) which genders Rome as a "Queen," "mailed virgin," "mass-frequenting crone," and "Sibyl, Iris, Sappho" (*Backward Glances,* 35–46).

DREAMING OF REVOLUTION
Carbonarism in New York

By the time Melville moved to Manhattan in 1847, New York City's literati had been sufficiently exposed to Risorgimento nationalism to endow particular events, people, and aesthetic objects with revolutionary meaning, creating a coded political language and iconography that found its way into *Mardi* and much of Melville's later writings. The influx of exiles from the failed Italian revolutions of 1820 and 1831 made New York a hotbed of Risorgimento sympathies, and combined with literary expostulations on Italy's plight to create a distinctively American view of the Risorgimento. This view bears only tangential resemblance to the political and diplomatic realities of Risorgimento history because it developed from the often impressionistic and inaccurate resources available in English, particularly those in the popular press, and blended history, legend, fiction, prejudice, and national desire into an image of Italy that might be unfamiliar to Risorgimento historians. Such alterations are to be expected in transnational borrowings, where countries appropriate—or, in Paola Gemme's useful term, domesticate—foreign cultures for their own purposes.

The first inklings of modern Italian nationalism came during the late 1790s, when Napoleon ejected Italy's Spanish and Austrian rulers and consolidated Italy's various northern states into the inelegantly named Cisalpine Republic. The south proved harder to occupy, but for five months in 1799 Neapolitan liberals established the Parthenopean Republic, one of the most romantic experiments in Italian self-rule that brought the term "Parthenope" into the English vocabulary. Simply by giving itself this ancient Greek name for Naples, the short-lived republic reinforced Italy's mythic status and its common political lineage with the United States, for it suggested that both were enlightenment republics sharing an Athenian genealogy. The name also strengthened Italy's feminine image, for it literally means "virgin" and comes from the siren Parthenope who drowned herself out of love for Odysseus and was cast ashore on the Bay of Naples. In comparison to Napoleon's bureaucratic attempts at nation-naming (he tinkered with "Cispadane" and "Transpadane" as proper republican names as well), the Neapolitan republicans understood the power of metaphor and chose a name that resonated years later in Melville's Neapolitan diptych: "Neapolitans, ay, 'tis the soul of the shell / Intoning your Naples, Parthenope's bell" (125; 9:11–12.).[22] Only when Lord Horatio Nelson offered

---

22. Parenthetical references to Melville's Neapolitan diptych are from Robert Allen Sandberg, "Melville's Unfinished *Burgundy Club* Book" (PhD diss., Northwestern University, 1989).

Figure 3. François Pascal Simon Gérard, *Portrait of Joachim Murat* (1800–1810), Museo di San Marino, Italy.

his services to the Neapolitan counterrevolutionaries were the republicans defeated and Ferdinand I (ruled 1759–1825) reinstated, symbolically rendering Naples a woman overcome by masculine power and providing historical sanction to gendered stereotypes of Italian nationalism. In 1808 Napoleon once more conquered the Kingdom of Naples and gave the throne to his brother-in-law Joachim Murat, whose military victories and courageous cavalry charges made him one of the most romantic figures to emerge from Napoleon's armies (fig. 3).

A flamboyant and independent figure who rose from humble beginnings to lead a kingdom, a sort of Napoleonic Andrew Jackson, Murat instituted numerous reforms that suggested that the erstwhile "Land of the Dead"—the historian Barthold Niebuhr's phrase for Italy—had life after all. As king of Naples, Murat eliminated the last vestiges of feudalism, suppressed brigands, and achieved immense popularity with the Neapolitan masses. His career ended in a welter of political intrigue as he broke with Napoleon, allied briefly with Austria, and then, in an important move for his place in Risorgimento history, advocated uniting Italy from Sicily to the Po. When Metternich broke his treaty with Murat and threw his support back to Ferdinand I, Bourbon troops executed Murat at a spot near Naples, making him a martyr to Italian dreams of a united country under an enlightened monarch. Murat's showy dress and dashing behavior put a masculine, romantic face on Italian politics and made him one of the few revolutionary figures to frame Melville's career. In *Mardi,* Melville compares a squall to "a white charge of cavalry; mad Hotspur and plumed Murat at its head" (3:117), a favorite image he Americanized in his 1849 review of Parkman's *Oregon Trail* by comparing Quincy A. Shaw's Great Plains buffalo-hunting to "Murat charging at the head of cavalry—in wild and ornate attire" (9:233). Given the radical associations of young Billy Budd, whose first words are "And good-bye to you, too, old *Rights-of-Man*" (49), Melville's late-life comparison of the "Handsome Sailor" to "a nautical Murat" (44) carries the ambiguous political associations of Murat's ill-fated attempts at combining monarchy and republicanism, the desire for order in tension with the impulse for freedom that vexes all readings of *Billy Budd.*[23] During his visit to Naples, Melville visited the site of Murat's execution and noted it tersely in his journal (15:101).

While he ruled Naples, Murat countenanced the rise of Carbonarism, the secretive nationalistic movement that spread throughout Italy during the post-Napoleonic era and was for twenty years Italy's leading revolutionary organization.[24] Many of New York's first Italian exiles were Carbonarists whose liberal cosmopolitanism smoothed their entry into the literary circles Melville frequented. Carbonarism originated in Italy's Masonic lodges and took on broadly secular, enlightened, and internationalist values, and emphasized Italian independence and constitutional government. Its politics varied from monarchism to Rousseaustic socialism, and in the face of Murat's failure and continued Austrian hostility, most members forsook the ideal of national unity. After the Congress of Vienna, Carbonarist associations increased in number and influence, particularly among nobles, intellectuals, professionals, military leaders, and writers, making it mostly a movement among Italy's small middle and upper classes. Carbonarists instigated a military revolt in 1820 that led to a temporary constitutional government in Naples and inspired Byron to

23. Parenthetical references to *Billy Budd* are from Herman Melville, *Billy Budd, Sailor (An Inside Narrative),* ed. Harrison Hayford and Merton M. Sealts, Jr. (Chicago: University of Chicago Press, 1962).

24. The information on Carbonarism comes from Bolton King, *A History of Italian Unity: Being a Political History of Italy from 1814 to 1871,* 2 volumes (London: James Nisbet & Co., Limited, 1899), 1:13–40, 110–125; Shepard B. Clough & Salvatore Saladino, *A History of Modern Italy: Documents, Readings, & Commentary* (New York: Columbia University Press, 1968), 15–38; and relevant articles in *Dictionary of Modern Italian History,* ed. Frank J. Coppa (Westport, CT: Greenwood Press, 1985).

join their movement in Ravenna, where he led a group of revolutionists called the *Cacciatore Americani,* the "American Hunters," an incident Thomas Moore described in his *Life of Byron,* a book Melville owned.²⁵ Repression quickly followed as Ferdinand I brought Austrian troops into Naples and, along with the duke of Modena and other Austrian puppets, mercilessly persecuted the Carbonari and drove their leaders into exile or prison. A second Carbonarist revolution in 1831 also failed, and Carbonarists moved their Supreme Lodge to Paris where their practical influence dwindled. But their secrecy and liberal principles gave them a legendary aura in the United States. In 1849 one book reviewer declared that "the objects of the Italian patriots [specifically, the Carbonari] were the same as of the American Revolution—INDEPENDENCE and UNION," and as late as 1859 they remained popular fodder for Melville's local weekly the *Berkshire County Eagle,* which reprinted a long article describing their rituals and politics.²⁶ Poe's unfortunate Fortunato in "The Cask of Amontillado" (1849) is perhaps American literature's most famous Carbonarist, one whose Masonic gestures, like the Carbonarists' two abortive revolutions, precede his death.²⁷ Despite its failures, largely due to its isolation from the Italian masses, Carbonarism fostered the development of men with the literary skills and political convictions able to articulate Italy's case to the international community, including Ugo Foscolo, Vincenzo Monti, Alessandro Manzoni, Piero Maroncelli, and the two writers Americans knew best, Silvio Pellico and Eleutario Felice Foresti.

Silvio Pellico (1789–1854), a professor and dramatist from Milan, was retained by Counts Porro and Confalonieri to edit *Il Conciliatore,* a journal that endorsed the romantic movements in England and Germany. As its title suggests, it was a moderate publication that advocated literary nationalism and liberal reform, but after the first Carbonarist revolution such opinions were enough for the Austrians to arrest Pellico in 1820 and condemn him to death. His sentence was commuted and along with Maroncelli he served ten years in prison, including seven in the Spielberg, an infamous Austrian fortress in Moravia. After his release in 1830, he published *Le mie prigioni (My Prisons,* 1832), a moving account of his

---

25. Leslie A. Marchand, *Byron: A Biography* (New York: Knopf, 1957), 2:867.
26. "The Italian Revolutions in 1848," rev. of *A Year of Consolation* by Mrs. Butler, late Fanny Kemble, *New Englander* 7 (February 1849): 75; "The Carbonari," *Berkshire County Eagle,* January 28, 1859, np. Most of the *Eagle* article was reprinted from an undated essay in *Chambers' Journal,* and presents Carbonarism as a strong if fanatical force against political tyranny up to 1815.
27. When Montresor fails to comprehend Fortunato's "grotesque" gesticulation, Fortunato asks if he is "of the brotherhood, . . . the masons," and asks for a sign; Montresor, with grim irony, shows him a trowel. *Poetry and Tales,* ed. Patrick Quinn (New York: Library of America, 1984), 851.

sufferings that gained immediate popularity all over Europe. The book appeared in two American translations, one in 1836 and one in 1844, and Henry David Thoreau proudly compared his one night in jail to Pellico's ten years in the Spielberg: "This is the whole history of 'My Prisons'" he wrote in "Civil Disobedience" (1849), an allusion so casual that Thoreau surely assumed his readers could gloss it.[28] A circular reprinted in the *Literary World* in 1848 claimed that *My Prisons* was "for many years the first book put into the hands of the student of Italian," and in 1859 Henry Tuckerman considered Pellico's story "as well known as that of the Arctic explorer or the English factory-operative."[29] But because Italy remained under the Austrian thumb, Pellico symbolized defeat, not victory. His meekness and resignation rendered him a victim rather than a hero, for he survived by humbly accepting his imprisonment as God's will, thus reinforcing stereotypes of Italian incapacity for the vigorous, masculine republicanism practiced in the United States. After his release in 1830 Pellico returned to Turin where he published his tragedies and, late in life, wrote increasingly pious works until his unheralded death in 1854.

In the long quest for Italian independence, Silvio Pellico was a minor player, yet his story endured in the American imagination and led Melville to memorialize him in two poems, "Pausilippo (In the time of Bomba)" and *Clarel* (1876). Based as it is on Melville's Italian journey, "Pausilippo" may have been written as early as 1857 and included in Melville's unpublished 1860 volume of poetry, and parts of it were once embedded in the Neapolitan diptych, as Parker's study of the manuscript shows.[30] While we cannot know how closely the version published in *Timoleon* (1891) corresponds to Melville's earlier drafts, that version cuts through Pellico's sentimental appeal and raises fundamental questions about Risorgimento nationalism that ripple out into larger issues of revolution and authority. How could Pellico promote independence without active resistance?

---

28. "Civil Disobedience," in *Walden and Civil Disobedience,* ed. Owen Thomas (New York: W. W. Norton & Company, 1966), 239. The two American translations are *My Prisons, Memoirs of Silvio Pellico,* tr. Mrs. Andrews Norton (Cambridge [MA]: Printed by C. Folsom, 1836), and *Memoirs of Silvio Pellico; or My Prisons,* trans. Hubert P. Lebfevre and M. J. Smead (New York: J. H. G. Langley, 1844). I use the Norton translation.

29. *Literary World,* March 4, 1848, 86. The circular, signed by Foresti among others, asked New Yorkers to purchase raffle tickets for Piero Maroncelli's library, which his impoverished widow was selling. Tuckerman, "E. Felice Foresti," *Atlantic Monthly* 4 (November 1859): 534. Tuckerman included Pellico in a collection of thirty biographical essays on figures as diverse as George Washington, Benjamin Franklin, Roger Williams, and Jenny Lind (*Essays, Biographical and Critical: or, Studies of Character* [Boston: Phillips, Sampson and Company, 1857], 428–40).

30. See Parker's extensive discussion of the relationships among the 1860 manuscript *Poems,* "At the Hostelry," "Naples in the Time of Bomba," and "Pausilippo" in *Herman Melville,* 2:418–23.

How could he preach republicanism and still pledge fealty to the pope? "Pausilippo" constructs an imagined encounter near Naples between a tourist and "Silvio," an old beggar "bleached through strange immurement long," a man so spiritually depleted that he can no longer play his harp, that is, no longer create art: "Hillward the quelled enthusiast turned, / Unmanned, made meek through strenuous wrong, / Preluding, faltering: then began, / But only thrilled the wire—no more ... Himself too spiritless and spent" (11:297; 15, and 298; 39–42, 46).[31] "Pausilippo," the place where the tourist sees the harpist, in Greek means "easement unto pain"; but here there is no comfort for the blighted, aged Silvio, whose "Vain liberation late" (11:298; 48, 36) has led only to impotence and artistic sterility. Mute himself, he depends on a girl to voice his despondency and confirm that Pausilippo, "Named benignly if in vain," "unravels not the pain" (11:299; 73). Melville's tourist hands the old man a bit of silver, futile ore for one so ravaged. Melville offers a similar picture of Pellico in *Clarel* (1876), imagining him leaving his dungeon "crippled and bleached" and uttering the words, "Grateful, I thank the Emperor" (I.37.107–8, 12:118). No such words occur in *My Prisons,* nor was Pellico literally in a "dungeon," nor did he die a beggar.[32] Melville, writing these poems after America's own quest for national unity had extracted its awesome toll in the Civil War, refashions Pellico as a transnational icon who shows that personal suffering does not guarantee freedom and that art alone cannot create a nation, a perceptive critique of simplistic appropriations of Risorgimento idealism for American purposes.

More radical politics made their way into Melville's circle through E. Felice Foresti (1793–1858), the best-known Italian expatriate in New York. Arrested for Carbonarism in 1819, he was so brutally treated by the Austrians that he attempted suicide by swallowing broken glass.[33] After a mock public execution in Venice's Piazza San Marco, he was incarcerated in the Spielberg along with Pellico and other Carbonari. Released on the condition of exile to America in 1836, Foresti arrived in New York City

31. For more on Pellico, see Walter Bezanson's note in the Northwestern-Newberry *Clarel* (12:756) and Hans-Joachim Lang, "Silvio Pellico, Melville's 'Dungeoned Italian,'" *Melville Society Extracts* 58 (May 1984): 4–5, which plausibly identifies the "dungeoned Italian" in *The Confidence-Man* (10:111) with Pellico.

32. Upon hearing that he and Maroncelli were free, Pellico surprised his jailer by showing sorrow rather than joy, asking him "to inform the Emperor of our gratitude; but, until we shall have news from our families, it is impossible for us not to fear that we may have been deprived of some of those whom we most tenderly love. This uncertainty oppresses us, even at a moment which should be one of the greatest joy" (*My Prisons,* 336). At the conclusion of his autobiography Pellico expresses gratitude to Providence but not the emperor.

33. For biographical information about Foresti, see the *DAB*. The anecdote of the broken glass is from Henry Tuckerman's obituary, "E. Felice Foresti," 530.

with twenty other "Martyrs of the Spielberg" and assumed a professorship in Italian literature at Columbia College and New York University.[34] He became a US citizen in 1841 and began directing Mazzini's central congregation of "Young Italy" in America, forming a conduit between the most radical form of Risorgimento nationalism and American supporters.[35] At the height of the 1848 revolutions, Theodore Dwight praised Foresti as one of the few Carbonarists to persist in his aims: "Out of so many that left those dungeons mere wrecks of humanity, he alone came out unbroken. He may be seen even now walking erect, cheerful, about the streets of New York. mild [sic], affable, in his manners, looked up to by the whole community."[36] Franklin Pierce appointed him US consul to Genoa in 1853, but Piedmont-Sardinia, still smarting from the revolutions of 1848, refused to seat such an ardent Mazzinian. Foresti returned to Italy in 1856 and gradually accepted the necessity of a constitutional monarchy, an ideological withdrawal from Mazzinism that led Sardinia to accept him as Genoese consul shortly before his death in 1858.

Foresti's actual views, like Pellico's, mattered less than the symbolic role both men played in creating a moderate image of the Risorgimento in America that distinguished it from the regicidal French Revolution of 1789. As Pellico symbolized piety and resignation, so Foresti symbolized strength and pragmatism. In a lengthy obituary in the *Atlantic Monthly*, Tuckerman extolled Foresti's defiance of authority, as when he openly professed his liberalism before an Austrian magistrate or threw scalding soup in the face of a jailer. Yet as he matured he wisely moderated his views while maintaining his liberal principles: "a fervent republican in sentiment, he yet recognized the radical benefits of a constitutional monarchy, like those of England and Sardinia."[37] Glossing over Foresti's Mazzinism—Tuckerman never mentions it—the obituary paints Foresti and his fellow exiles as genteel moderates: "As scholars, citizens, gentlemen, and, in more than one instance, authors of real genius, these Liberals stand alone, and are not to be confounded with perverse Radicals of a subsequent epoch," an allusion that in 1859 could refer only to Mazzini.[38] When John Greenleaf Whittier paired Pellico and Foresti in "The Prisoners of Naples" (1851), he used them to counsel patience

34. Amfitheatrof, *Children of Columbus*, 90. Other exiles included Pellico's cellmate Piero Maroncelli, his employer Count Confalonieri, and two Sicilians who became Harvard professors, Pietro Bachi and Luigi Monti.

35. Joseph Rossi, *The Image of America in Mazzini's Writings* (Madison: University of Wisconsin Press, 1954), 19.

36. Dwight, *The Roman Republic of 1849* (New York, 1851), 233, quoting Alexandre Aryane.

37. "E. Felice Foresti," 537, 538.

38. "E. Felice Foresti," 537.

among King Bomba's newest crop of political prisoners, the thousands incarcerated after the 1848 revolutions: "let them share / Pellico's faith, / Foresti's strength to bear / Years of unutterable torment, stern and still, / As the chained Titan victor through his will."[39] By combining Christian resignation with Promethean endurance and progressive but realistic political views, Whittier constructed Pellico and Foresti as nonviolent intellectuals brutally incarcerated for exercising the most basic American freedoms of speech and association. More martyrs than rebels, these two men legitimated rebellion through moderation, unlike the guillotining French or the ideologically dogmatic Mazzini.

YOUNG ITALY IN YOUNG AMERICA
The Tuckerman-Headley Debate

The demise of Carbonarism paved the way for Mazzini's *Giovine Italia*. Mazzini joined the Carbonari in 1829, but after the failure of the 1831 revolutions and his own exile to France, Switzerland, and finally England, he organized Young Italy to seek international support for an active Italian resistance. In 1833 he enlisted seven hundred exiles to invade Piedmont and recruited a young sailor, Giuseppe Garibaldi, to revolutionize the navy, an ill-conceived plan that failed miserably and only created further repression and more exiles, including Garibaldi, who fled to Uruguay and became a full-time revolutionary. Mazzini's supporters, often without his knowledge, engaged in scattered revolts over the next decade that fed the image of Mazzini as Europe's chief conspirator and terrorist. What Mazzini lacked in practical revolutionary ability he compensated for in his extensive theoretical writings as he forged alliances to advocate progressive ideals. In London from 1837–45 he developed friendships with Thomas and Jane Carlyle, John Stuart Mill, Gabriele Rossetti, William C. Macready, Samuel Rogers, Douglas Jerrold, Walter Savage Landor, Robert Browning, Bulwer-Lytton, Dickens, and a host of others whom American intellectuals read, admired, and knew personally.[40] He published constantly, from inflammatory pamphlets smuggled into Italy to formal essays

---

39. *The Complete Poetical Works of Whittier*, ed. Horace E. Scudder (Boston: Houghton Mifflin Company, 1894), 372.
40. For a good review of Mazzini's early years, see Denis Mack Smith, *Mazzini* (New Haven, CT: Yale University Press, 1994), 1–48. For his literary activities, see Harry W. Rudman, *Italian Nationalism and English Letters: Figures of the Risorgimento and Victorian Men of Letters* (London: George Allen & Unwin Ltd., 1940), 40–79.

in British periodicals. His influential analysis of Dante as "the patriotic prophet of national unity" and his aggressive cultural politics helped spark a nationalist literary revival in Italy, particularly in the operas of Verdi, Bellini, and Rossini.[41] His mantra of "Duty, God, and Country" appealed to young republicans worldwide, and in America his unequivocal antagonism to royalism and the papacy, combined with a fervent commitment to democracy, made him by 1848 the most visible Risorgimento figure in America.

Mazzini's Young Italy is sometimes credited with inspiring Young America, the well known but inchoate nationalist literary movement led by Melville's friends Cornelius Mathews and Evert Duyckinck in the 1840s.[42] The group's key organ, John L. O'Sullivan's Jacksonian journal the *United States Magazine and Democratic Review*, was perhaps the first American publication to support Mazzinism unequivocally, praising Young Italy's commitment to democracy and the masses while avoiding revolutionary extremism: "We do not find in it the violent diatribes and imprecations of an excited and revengeful jacobinism, but the moderation and gravity of true patriots and philanthropists."[43] In fact, as Joseph Rossi and Paola Gemme have shown, Young America diverged crucially from Mazzinian ideals on such fundamental issues as slavery, federalism, and Manifest Destiny, all key planks in Young America's jerry-built platform.[44] Moreover, as Denis Mack Smith has argued, Mazzini was not a narrow nationalist, as were the Young Americans; rather, he was a patriot who advocated the universal brotherhood of man and a united Europe based on Christian socialism, principles hard to square with American values of individualism and capitalism.[45] In a private letter of 1838 Mazzini even

---

41. The quote is from Rudman, 57; see also 42–46, for a discussion of Mazzini's contributions to the *Westminster Review, Tait's Edinburgh Magazine,* and other British journals. For Mazzini's influence on Italian literature at large, see King, 1:144–45. For an extended analysis of Mazzinian ideas in Verdi's operas, see Mary Ann Smart, "Liberty On (and Off) the Barricades: Verdi's Risorgimento Fantasies," in *Making and Remaking Italy,* 103–18.

42. Stafford, *Literary Criticism of "Young America,"* 6–11. The standard account of Melville and Young America is Miller, *The Raven and the Whale,* and a more political analysis is Widmer, *Young America.* Widmer distinguishes between the early, more literary Young Americans led by Duyckinck and the later, more politicized cohort assembled by George N. Sanders, who purchased the *Democratic Review* in 1851. As consul to London for a few months in 1853–54, Sanders actively courted Mazzini, Louis Kossuth, and other European revolutionaries, yet nothing came of his efforts (Widmer, 198–99). Paola Gemme has thoroughly analyzed the Sanders-Mazzini relationship and concludes that ideological differences over slavery and laissez-faire social policies far outweighed any temporary political alliances (*Domesticating Foreign Struggles,* 76).

43. "The Revolutionary Secret Societies of Italy," *United States Magazine and Democratic Review* 9 (September 1841): 275. The unsigned article is presumably by O'Sullivan.

44. Rossi, *Image of America,* esp. 1–14; Gemme, *Domesticating Foreign Struggles,* 41, 101–11.

45. Mack Smith, *Mazzini,* 12.

asked a friend to avoid speaking of America because, he wrote, "I feel a cordial antipathy for the very name of that country."[46] Mazzini's appeal to the Young Americans in Melville's circle lay less in his particular policies than in his integration of literature and politics, the sort of literary call to arms Melville trumpeted in "Hawthorne and His Mosses" (1850). By recognizing that words affected ideas and could change governments, Mazzini offered Young Americans a progressive, politically conscious art that embraced an optimistic vision of global democracy, a vague goal easily applied to local needs while retaining cosmopolitan cachet. In ground tilled by Pellico, Foresti, and a generation of British writers sympathetic to Mazzinian aims, Risorgimento sympathies grew rapidly in New York's literary circles during Herman Melville's most formative years.

Henry Tuckerman and Joel Tyler Headley, the first a close friend of Melville's, the second an acquaintance with whom he was publicly linked, offered Young Americans differing but still supportive views of Italian revolutionaries. Both drew American faces on Risorgimento nationalism that varied in features while preserving a generally favorable outline. Tuckerman, as America's most knowledgeable and dedicated Italophile, missed few opportunities to argue the case for Italian freedom, even though he expressed doubt, as we have seen, whether Italians were ready to govern themselves. He read and spoke Italian, made extended visits to Italy in 1833–34 and 1837–38, met Samuel Rogers in England, and frequented Anne Lynch's salon in New York where he developed friendships with Foresti and other Italian exiles. His unusual familiarity with southern Italy exposed him to the most impoverished, oppressed, and politically unstable region of the peninsula, and gave him a keen sense of the country's need for reform. His first published work, the *Italian Sketchbook* (1835), adheres to the conventions of picturesque description and largely follows Cooper's example in *The Bravo* for avoiding politics. A notable exception to this convention occurs at the end, in a moving portrait of a censored poet who wishes that he enjoyed America's freedom of the press (195–97). Although Paola Gemme has amply discountenanced Italy's debt to the American Revolution, Tuckerman's anecdote promoted American notions of republican exceptionalism and messianic nationalism and positioned Italy as a supplicant for American favors.[47] Tuckerman's second book was also set in Italy, only this time he combined travelogue, fictional narrative, and political commentary in his only novel, *Isabel; or, Sicily*.[48] *Isabel* fol-

---

46. Quoted in Rossi, *Image of America*, 14.

47. For an excellent discussion and critique of this idea, see Gemme, *Domesticating Foreign Struggles*, esp. 20–45.

48. (Philadelphia: Lea and Blanchard, 1839. Parenthetical references are to this edition. The

lows the Sicilian journey of Isabel Otley, an eighteen-year-old American on her way to reunite with her father who moved a few years earlier to Italy to assuage his grief over his wife's death. Accompanied by her uncle Clifford Frazier and their Italian host Count Vittorio, Isabel learns to appreciate both the aesthetic riches and political problems of Italy. For example, Vittorio explains how the operas of Vincenzo Bellini exploit the comparative freedom allowed to Italian composers:

> Although the censors jealously guard the actual verbal expressions attached to operas; to a true imagination and just sensibility, the mere notes of masterpieces are perfectly distinguishable, as expressive of the thousand sentiments which sway the heart. Bellini, it is believed, was one of that secret society, which has for some time existed, under the title of "Young Italy," whose aim is the restoration of these regions to independence; and we can read, or rather feel, the depth and fervor of his liberal sentiments, breathing in the glowing strains of his last opera—the Puritani. (53–54)

In a repressive society, free expression is still possible through a subversive art, a lesson Melville learned as early as *Mardi* and perfected in his short stories, as Marvin Fisher has argued.[49] Great art derives from conflict rather than consensus, for as Count Vittorio says, "The history of genius in every department is almost always a record of conflicts—of struggles against what is dominant" (52–53).

Count Vittorio, an aristocrat with revolutionary sentiments, presents Mazzinism in its most appealing guise, a moderate, historically justified, and responsible movement based on constitutional principles and enlightened leadership. Tuckerman's account of Vittorio's political education strives to give Risorgimento nationalism a moderate face, one that distinguishes rampant democracy from temperate republicanism. As Vittorio tells Isabel and Frazier, his father was a Carbonarist instrumental in the Palermo uprising of 1820, Sicily's attempt to win independence from the Bourbons of Naples. Although completely justified, the revolt led to violent excesses reminiscent of the French Revolution: "For several days anarchy reigned in Palermo. The rabble intoxicated with their temporary triumphs, gave themselves up to indiscriminate rapine and butchery. The horrid scenes then enacted, the license and brutality which prevailed indicated the utter unfitness of the people for the dignity and blessings of political freedom" (137). Only the moderating influence of Vittorio's

---

novel was reissued in 1852 as *Sicily: A Pilgrimage*).

49. Fisher, *Going Under: Melville's Short Fiction and the American 1850s* (Baton Rouge: Louisiana State University Press, 1977).

father, the wise patrician, restored order. Nevertheless, internal rivalries kept Sicilians divided and the revolution failed, sending Vittorio's family to England, then Malta, where Vittorio presumably converts to Protestantism. He returns to Sicily nursing a hatred for soldiers and priests but bent on more gradual reforms, for he has learned that popular movements are doomed to fail if they encourage "premature action on the part of those least fitted to assume the responsibility" (136). Americans, Count Vittorio reminds Isabel and Frazier, enjoy different traditions, and must be patient with those ordinary Sicilians who labor under years of oppression: "The existing poverty of this beautiful island, which Cicero called the granary of Rome, is chiefly attributable to inherited evils of government, and habits of idleness and vice, a disproportionate nobility, a pampered priesthood, and an utterly unenlightened lower order" (152). No class escapes Vittorio's critique, effectively rendering him a good middle-class American, a surrogate Mazzini who recognizes equally the dangers of mob rule and aristocratic privilege and balances democratic desire with republican restraint. His perfect English, Protestantism, rationality, and restrained demeanor—Tuckerman often says he has a "northern" rather than "southern" temperament—further Anglicize him and suggest American affinities with Italy's predominantly northern reformers. Had the novel ended with Isabel marrying Count Vittorio, a possibility hinted at in several conversations and longing looks, Tuckerman might have melded American and Italian nationalism as James did with Christina Light. Christina, the illegitimate daughter of a married American woman and her Italian courier, eventually marries an Italian prince and becomes an aristocrat who supports anarchist revolutionaries in *The Princess Casamassima* (1886). Tuckerman's characters never go so far. For all his sympathies with the Italian cause, Tuckerman remains skeptical of Italians' political maturity and convinced of America's republican uniqueness.

Tuckerman had to confront his own ambivalence about Italian politics when, shortly after his move into New York's Young American circles, the *Democratic Review* asked him to review Joel Tyler Headley's *Letters from Italy* (1845), the third book in Evert Duyckinck's new series for Wiley and Putnam, the "Library of American Books."[50] Like Tuckerman, Headley traveled to Italy for his health and returned a writer, spending about

50. New York: Wiley and Putnam, 1845; further references in text as *Letters*. Little scholarship on Headley exists. A good overview is Paola Gemme, *Dictionary of Literary Biography*, vol. 183 (Chicago: Gale Group, 1997), 162–67, supplemented by Owen Connelly and Jesse Scott, *Dictionary of Literary Biography*, vol. 30 (1984), 107–11. See also Gemme's discussions of Headley in *Domesticating Foreign Struggles*, especially her analysis of his essay "The One Progressive Principle," 19–20 and 25–26. For a good analysis of the political role that the Library of American Books played in Melville's circle, see Widmer, *Young America*, 103–11.

six months there in 1842–43. Unlike Tuckerman, Headley freely criticizes Italian character, customs, and politics, and largely avoids matters of art and landscape. Writing as a contemporary historian rather than a traveler, Headley judges Italians against an idealized American norm and finds them lazy, changeable, childlike, effeminate, untrustworthy, and morally deficient. In an earlier version of his book he frankly states, "These Italians, as a mass, I do not like. They are exceedingly civil, but heartless—frank in manners, but capable of great duplicity in action—fiery-hearted, but not steadily brave, and selfish to any amount of meanness. In one word, you cannot trust them."[51] In *Letters from Italy* he expresses "no hope in the multitude of conspiracies and outbreaks with which Italy is filled," for Italians "do not care enough for liberty to fight for it" and their leaders fail to inspire confidence: "The love of pleasure and its pursuit takes from the manliness of the Italian character, so necessary to a republican form of government" (*Letters,* 223). In his review Tuckerman rightly condemns Headley for his sweeping generalizations, hasty judgments, factual errors, and political pessimism: "Mr. Headley but partially recognizes the Italian character, and fails altogether in solving its apparent inconsistencies."[52] Yet Tuckerman's counterargument rings hollow, and depends on some of the same infantilizing stereotypes that Headley deploys, such as vague appeals to Italian spirituality, what he calls "the instinctive and characteristic life of her children": "the energy, the tact, the sentiment, that once made her great . . . still exist in the very blood of her sons. Tyranny has warped and marred her organic life, but amid all its infernal and persevering wiles, vitality has survived" ("Word," 205). Betraying an Emersonian cosmic optimism, Tuckerman finds at work in Italy "a benign and universal law—that of compensation" ("Word," 212), which offsets political restrictions with "social and individual advantages, vivid sensations, noble memories, delicious local attachments, rare and available means of culture" that will eventually lift Italy from centuries of oppression to a new era of liberty and freedom.

For all of his noxious stereotyping, Headley deserves credit for continuing Bryant's unflinching depiction of Italian tyranny and recognizing that many traits Americans ascribed to Italians—indolence, poverty, begging, superstition, indifference—stem from particular circumstances,

---

51. *Italy and the Italians: In a Series of Letters* (New York: I. S. Platt, 1844), 24; further references in text as *Italians.* This book inaugurated the "Prose Series" of Duyckinck's "Home Library," an abortive project for publishing American writers that is briefly discussed in Miller, *Raven and the Whale* (114) and provided the first eighteen chapters of *Letters from Italy.*

52. "A Word for Italy," *United States Magazine and Democratic Review* 17 (September 1845), 210. Further references in text.

not some inherent matter of "blood." In Naples, Headley expects to be assaulted by beggars but finds that a recent law has driven them from the streets. Reflecting on this, he confesses his earlier "prejudices" and recognizes that beggars are victims not exploiters. He inquires among the "lower classes" to determine "the amount of real distress" they suffer and discovers an "economy of tyranny" that first impoverishes the masses and then, when they turn to beggary, creates a police state that denies them even this meager profession. If a man looks on Naples's *lazzaroni* as no more than "heaps of rags that lie along church-steps" he will feel nothing for them; but

> if, on the contrary, he regards them as so many martyrs (degraded though they be) to a selfish and oppressive political and social system, starving to load another man's table, and dying to enliven another man's feast, their rags, as they drop, will appeal to him with a power he cannot resist. In that fragment of a man that turns his face to the wall with a moan, and drops at its base to die, he will behold a *brother* slain to make a king's holiday. (*Italians*, 59)

Headley's imagery prefigures Melville's in "Poor Man's Pudding and Rich Man's Crumbs" as well as "Bartleby, the Scrivener," and his final phrase alludes to Byron's memorable lament for the "Dying Gladiator": "Butchered to make a Roman holiday" (*Childe Harold's Pilgrimage*, 4:cxli). For every thoughtless generalization about Italian character, Headley makes a dozen assaults on Italian government as he exposes supposedly liberal Piedmont's heavy-handed censorship of painters and musicians (*Italians*, 21), heaps invective on its king, Charles Albert ("this traitor, and Jesuit, and religious bigot, and tyrant" [*Letters*, 215]), and deplores Neapolitan economic inequities ("the King of Naples has five palaces, while thousands of his subjects have not one blanket" [*Italians*, 49]). As a self-styled "young republican," Headley even carried a letter of introduction to Silvio Pellico, and although he failed to see him he clearly hoped to link America's cause with Italy's persecuted writer (*Italians*, 17, 40).

The Tuckerman-Headley quarrel shows that by 1845 Americans were doffing their picturesque lenses, recognizing Italy's political dilemma, and accepting the possibility of an Italian revolution. By largely stripping his account of conventional idealism, Headley ironically drives the more hopeful Tuckerman to acknowledge Italy's plight: it is, Tuckerman says in his review, a land of "beauty and anguish" (204), oppressed by "tyrants," "divided into eight states, between which all the arts of despotism are ceaselessly fomenting dissensions, which varieties of dialect, climate, habits and interest habitually create" (206). While Tuckerman may think more highly of Italian character than Headley, both men see the need for reform and differ primarily on its method and probability. Tuckerman, aligning himself with Pellico, trusts in the patience and endurance of the Italian people and the wise leadership of aristocrats like Count Vittorio, while Headley, though he admires Italy's upper-class liberals, locates his hope for Italian resurgence in Mazzinian radicalism. Headley dramatizes his politics by citing a figure from the Neapolitan past, the legendary Amalfi fisherman "Masaniello," a nineteenth-century icon of populist revolt whom Melville would later portray in his Neapolitan diptych. In 1647 twenty-five-year-old Tommaso Anniello led a spontaneous revolt against unjust taxes and gained a brief victory when Neapolitan authorities temporarily revoked the levy. Although he was soon killed by a mob, his memory inspired one of the nineteenth century's most popular and influential grand operas, Daniel Auber's *Masaniello* or *La Muette de Portici* [The Mute of Portici] (1828), which sympathetically and romantically portrayed the young rebel. *Masaniello* played hundreds of times in New York throughout the 1830s and 1840s,[53] so Headley knew his audience would understand him when he quotes his Neapolitan guide who is complaining about excessive taxes: "'We want another Massaniello [sic] to lead us. But the time will come—let us wait—the time will come when we will do thus to Kings,' drawing, as he spoke, a piece of board he held in his hands across his throat with a gesture no one could mistake" (*Letters*, 105). Masaniello, Headley opines, "is the People's Washington" (*Letters*, 105), a picturesque, even theatrical figure of republican revolt like Murat, Garibaldi, or the Hungarian nationalist Louis Kossuth.

One can object, as does Paola Gemme, to Headley's insistent Americanizing of Italian nationalism: "Toledo is the Broadway of Naples" (*Italians*, 58), he exults, foreshadowing and perhaps inspiring Melville's own comparison a decade later. Yet in terms of cultural politics, such chauvinistic, even imperialistic impulses encourage the cosmopolitanism necessary to foster cultural affinities that, however reconfigured, promote transnational ideologies. *Letters from Italy* went through six editions and launched Headley on a career that made him America's most popular historian. His success kept

---

53. From 1829 to 1848, *Masaniello* played nearly every season at a New York theater, sometimes as many as thirty-six performances. See George C. Odell, *Annals of the New York Stage* (New York: Columbia University Press, 1927), vols. 3–5, *passim*. In an extract from Byron's journal of 26 January 1821, Thomas Moore includes one of the poet's angriest outbursts at Austrian oppression: "If the Neapolitans have but a single Massaniello amongst them, they will beat the bloody butchers of the crown and sabre." See *The Works of Lord Byron: With His Letters and Journals, and His Life* (London: John Murray, 1833), 5:88.

alive Duyckinck's Library of American Books, which went on to publish another travel narrative in 1846—Herman Melville's *Typee*. Melville aimed his provocative blend of political opinion and exotic description at the same audience as Headley and like him and Tuckerman attacked cultural imperialism even as he practiced it, creating a paradoxical discourse that negotiates America's simultaneous commitment to universal republicanism and Manifest Destiny.[54] Although Melville never refers to Headley, they probably met at Duyckinck's Manhattan home in 1847, may have chatted at one of Anne Lynch's soirees, and unquestionably hiked and dined together during the Duyckinck circle's famous visit to the Berkshires in August of 1850.[55] Melville and Headley could even have discussed Charles S. Briggs's review in *Holden's Dollar Magazine* the previous February which considered them "the two most popular authors among us, just now," primarily due to "the perfect fearlessness with which they thrust themselves before their country men" (*Log*, 1:364).[56] Both young writers combined internationalist revolutionary sympathies with visions of a hegemonic *Pax Americana*, making them ideal candidates for Young America's sparse literary pantheon. One way or another, Melville was discovering a local version of Young Italy within Young America, and transmuting its vocabulary and values into his own emergent cosmopolitan art.

TAKING THE ROMAN OUT OF ROMAN CATHOLICISM

For Americans the single most resonant word in the Risorgimento lexicon was "Rome." The eagle, national emblem of both Imperial Rome and the fledgling United States, typologically linked the two nations in a powerful transhistorical icon of difference, identity, and destiny, as in

---

54. A study valuable for its international perspective is Jincai Yang, *Herman Melville and Imperialism: A Cultural Critique of Melville's Polynesian Trilogy* (Nanjing: Nanjing University Press, 2001). Yang finds Melville "both critical of colonial ideology and subordinate to it" (103), a position that identifies "Melville" with his narrators more than I think justified, yet one that offers a valuable corrective to liberal readings of the novels. See also the half-dozen essays debating *Typee*'s cultural imperialism in *"Whole Oceans Away": Melville and the Pacific*, ed. Jill Barnum, Wyn Kelley, and Christopher Sten (Kent, OH: Kent State University Press, 2007).

55. A letter from Evert Duyckinck to his brother George describes "Melville as a frequent visiter [sic] at No. 20[.] Headley too gets out at the same moment his 'Washington the Generals.' He comes of Sunday nights to fight his battles over again in the parlor." Letter of May 14, 1847, Evert Duyckinck Collection, New York Public Library (notes courtesy of Larry J. Reynolds). Parker, *Herman Melville*, 1:747–49, describes Headley leading Melville, Hawthorne, and Duyckinck through the "Icy Glen" and taking dinner at the Melville house. Headley's *The Adirondack; or, Life in the Woods*, was reviewed alongside *Mardi* in the *New York Tribune*, May 10, 1849, 1.

56. Miller, *The Raven and the Whale*, identifies the writer as Briggs (253).

Headley's observation of Rome's ravaged Campagna: "The mighty empire has become a desolate province, while [in America] the wilderness has become greater than an empire; Rome, the mistress of the world, rules now a territory less than the state of New York. The eagle that soared over the imperial city, has left it and her battling armies, and now sails with our commerce. Men flock to her to see *fading* glory—to our shores to behold *rising* glory" (*Letters,* 138). Less chauvinistically, Margaret Fuller invoked the same typology as she questioned where the new year, 1846, would lead her country: "At present she has scarce achieved a Roman nobleness, a Roman liberty, and whether her Eagle is less like the Vulture and more like the Phoenix than was the fierce Roman bird, we dare not say. May the New Year give hopes of the latter, even if the bird need first to be purified by fire."[57]

On the one hand, "Rome" evoked America's mythic identification with the first Roman Republic, evident not only in the eagle but in the writings of the founders, the architecture of the Capitol, the paintings of Benjamin West, the sculptures of Hiram Powers, the oratory of Daniel Webster, and most concretely and durably in the Latin inscriptions on the Great Seal of the United States.[58] On the other hand, "Rome" also connoted Roman Catholicism, a fusion of church and state long anathema to New England Puritans and now widely viewed as a grave and growing threat to American society at large. In a country already riven by ideological conflicts between isolationism and expansionism, slavery and abolition, states rights and federal authority, these antagonistic meanings of "Rome" created new fissures that further complicated American sympathies for the Risorgimento. A matrix of religious, political, sectional, racial, and cultural ideologies affected liberals and conservatives alike and made strange bedfellows as Whig Italophiles supported democratic revolutions abroad but opposed them at home, Northern Democrats courted Catholic voters but condemned papal rule, Southerners justified slavery by citing both the Bible and the Roman Republic, expansionists modeled Manifest Destiny on Imperial Rome, and evangelical Protestants seized

---

57. "1st January, 1846," rpt. in Judith Mattson Bean and Joel Myerson, eds., *Margaret Fuller, Critic: Writings from the* New-York Tribune, *1844–1846* (New York: Columbia University Press, 2000), 332.

58. For a brilliant essay summarizing and assessing these well-known analogies, see Robert A. Ferguson, *Reading the Early Republic* (Cambridge, MA: Harvard University Press, 2004). See also Vance, *America's Rome,* particularly 1:1–42. John C. Shields, *The American Aeneas: Classical Origins of the American Self* (Knoxville: University of Tennessee Press, 2001), poses Aeneas as an alternative to the myth of the American Adam, and Meyer Reinhold, *Classica Americana: The Greek and Roman Heritage in the United States* (Detroit: Wayne State University Press, 1984), traces classical learning in America through the nineteenth century.

on Italy's troubles as an opportunity to convert the country and topple the papal Antichrist.[59] Before Melville could employ Italian culture for literary ends, it had to be stripped of its Roman Catholic associations and redeployed as a Protestantized yet still cosmopolitan and politically liberal artistic resource.

Abetting this aim was what Ray Allen Billington has dubbed "the Protestant Crusade," a period from 1834–54 of church burnings, religious riots, lurid convent tales, and rising hysteria over "Popery," "priestcraft," and Jesuitism. In some places, mobs tore crosses off buildings, objecting even to this simple display of Christian iconography.[60] In his thirty-eight-page list of anti-Catholic narratives Billington includes Headley's *Letters from Italy*, an intersection of political liberalism and religious intolerance common among Risorgimento sympathizers that also surfaced, as Susan M. Griffin has shown, in nativist novels of the 1850s and persisted in the fiction of Howells, James, and a wide swath of Anglo-American writers.[61] Cloaking parochial aims in cosmopolitan ideals, Americans seized on Carbonarist and Mazzinian anti-papalism to attack Roman Catholic beliefs and practices, failing utterly to distinguish between Italian liberals' desire to end the pope's temporal power and their continuing respect for the religion he represented. In one of the weirder manifestations of anti-Catholic hysteria, many propagandists claimed that a republican Italy would dethrone the pope and send him to America where he would establish a new Holy See in the trans-Mississippi west.[62] Such irrational fears gained ground as the rising tide of Catholic immigrants from Ireland and Germany during the 1840s linked anti-Catholics with nativism in a powerful xenophobia that fueled the rise of numerous "Native American" political parties, notably the "Know-Nothings" (the American Party) which rose from nowhere in the early 1850s to dominate American

---

59. In 1842 a group of New Yorkers founded the Christian Alliance with the aim of converting Italy to Protestantism, considered a necessary first step on the road to republicanism that the dogmatically Catholic and comparatively uncultured Irish could never take. While the group had little practical effect, it reinforced New York's position as the American center of Risorgimento activism and gave a veneer of Protestant respectability to Italian culture. Paola Gemme sees this as an attempt to infuse modern Italians with the Roman "republican self-reliance that Irish immigrants allegedly lacked" (*Domesticating Foreign Struggles*, 144), further valorizing Italians above other immigrant groups. Joseph Rossi devotes a whole chapter to the Christian Alliance, and traces Mazzini's shifting attitudes toward it (*Image of America*, 31–46).

60. *The Protestant Crusade 1800–1860: A Study of the Origins of American Nativism* (New York: Rinehart & Company, 1938). Despite the sixty-year frame in Billington's title, the book focuses on the years 1834–54, from the first convent burning to the decline of the Know-Nothing Party.

61. Billington, *Protestant Crusade*, 464. Griffin, *Anti-Catholicism and Nineteenth-Century Fiction* (Cambridge: Cambridge University Press, 2004), esp. 91–113 and 187–206.

62. Billington, *Protestant Crusade*, 118–41.

politics. In 1854 the party won nearly every seat in the Massachusetts legislature while New Yorkers elected as their new secretary of state none other than Joel T. Headley.[63]

Anti-Catholic politics added fault lines of religion, class, and ethnicity to New York's already complicated political landscape. New tastes for Dante, opera, classical sculpture, Renaissance painting, and classical landscapes such as Thomas Cole's famous *Course of Empire* series created an Italianate substrate to the emerging national aesthetic, and bathed the city's Italian exiles in an aura of cultural prestige unavailable to other groups.[64] The vastly more numerous Irish supported the unwavering papalism of Irish-born John Hughes, bishop and archbishop of New York 1842–1864, and consequently bore the brunt of anti-Catholic prejudice despite their rising political power.[65] Theoretically, Protestant republicans should have opposed the Risorgimento in order to keep the pope in Rome, but in practice anti-Catholic prejudice reinforced American sympathies for Risorgimento nationalism and carved a safe harbor for Italian culture in Protestant America. Etymologically separating "Roman" from "Catholic," American Italophiles reminded their audiences that papal Rome was but one corrupt phase of the larger flow of Italian history, beginning with the pre-Christian Roman Republic and continuing through Risorgimento patriots who struggled, as had Americans themselves, against foreign tyrants.

One acquaintance of Melville's who negotiated this conflict of aesthetics and ideology was the Rev. Orville C. Dewey, a Unitarian and lifelong friend of the Shaw family, Melville's in-laws. Dewey delivered Judge Lemuel Shaw's funeral oration in 1861, baptized Melville's two daughters in 1863, and preached occasionally at All Soul's in New York in the 1870s when Melville was a congregant. Melville may have attended his sermons at the Church of the Messiah in New York sometime before 1848, met him at Anne Lynch's Valentine's Day party in 1848, or attended his Lowell Institute Lectures in Boston in 1851.[66] While Hershel Parker is right to

---

63. The 1855 Massachusetts House of Representatives consisted of one Whig, one Free-Soiler, and 376 Know-Nothings (Billington, *Protestant Crusade,* 415); the party was widely expected to win the presidential election of 1856. For Headley, see Gemme, *Dictionary of Literary Biography,* 183:166.

64. For the appeal of Italian art, see Jaffe, *Italian Presence in American Art.*

65. Tammany Hall relied on Irish support, and Melville's older brother, Gansevoort, actively courted the New York Irish vote during the 1844 election. Parker provides a full account, and notes Uncle Thomas Melville's "resentment about this unseemly meddling with the Papists" (*Herman Melville,* 1:318).

66. See Parker, *Herman Melville,* 2:469–71, 549, 773, and 65–67; for Anne Lynch's, see *Log,* 270.

distinguish Dewey's positions on slavery and the poor from Melville's, on the matter of Catholic art Dewey formulated a rationale that empowered Protestant Democrats like Melville to exploit Italy as an artistic resource without endorsing its religion. In *The Old World and the New* (1836), an account of his Italian travels in 1833, Dewey blends Roman history and Renaissance art with liberal Protestantism and republican politics to present one of the more favorable views of Italy in the period.[67] His subjective and overwrought artistic judgments echo conventional sentiments, including ones that surface later in Melville's writings. Before the Apollo Belvedere he can scarcely resist "exclamations and tears" (2:108), he praises Guido's *Aurora* at the Rospigliosi (90), and he independently confirms that Raphael's *Transfiguration* and Domenichino's *Communion of St. Jerome* are the two greatest paintings in the world (2:94). Yet unlike Headley and Tuckerman, Dewey freely admits the aesthetic attractions of Catholic worship and attends several services whose forms and ambience "commend themselves, not merely to the imagination, but to the most unaffected sentiments of devotion" (2:150). Americans could learn from such outward manifestations of piety, he feels, and he wishes "religion were stamped, more than it is with us Protestants, upon the whole face of life" (2:109). Yet he distinguishes clearly between Catholic ritual and belief: "if it were not for the faith, I should like many of the forms very well" (2:150).

Dewey's travel book offers primary evidence of what Jenny Franchot calls "the Protestant gaze on Rome": "In the cautious turn toward the redemptive powers of the material dimension, issues of the body, of church architecture, of art, and of food converged to form a distinctive Protestant gaze on Rome, a gaze that acknowledged its spiritual desire, celebrated Catholicism as spectacle, and fantasied the consumption of this foreign substance rather than conversion to it."[68] Such confident cosmopolitanism thinly veils a self-righteous liberalism barely indistinguishable from Know-Nothing anti-Catholicism. Dewey proudly states that he has "none of the Protestant horror at a Catholic church; not a particle of it!" (2:111); finds a party at a cardinal's house much like "a great New-York or Boston jam" (2:127); and allows that many Italians are devout, educated, well-meaning, and spiritual. But he abhors "The Roman Catholic System," particularly its celibate priesthood, reliance on ritual, public piety that masks private immorality, intolerance for other forms of Christianity, and "the great evil . . . that imagination and sentiment are substituted for

67. Rev. Orville Dewey, *The Old World and the New; or, a Journal of Reflections and Observations Made on a Tour in Europe*, 2 vols. (New York: Harper & Brothers, 1836). Parenthetical references are to volume 2 of this edition. This was also published in London in 1836 and 1844.
68. *Roads to Rome*, 234.

real feeling and virtue" (2:170). Clearly addressing a Northern audience with metaphors that link Catholicism and slavery, Dewey contends that Catholicism provides a "safe bondage, in preference to dangerous freedom" that leads the ignorant into "mental slavery and superstition" (2:165, 166). Dewey tolerates Catholicism for the same reason many Northerners tolerate slavery: he is sure of its imminent decline (2:154–55). He understands innately that popular institutions require a masculinized Protestant belief in contrast to an infantilized and regressive Catholicism: "I will venture to say of the system, that it seems to be the childhood of Christianity, while Protestantism I consider to be its manhood. And although this manhood has its own peculiar exposures, yet for the same reason that I would advocate freedom in civil affairs, would I advocate freedom in religious affairs. The republicanism of Christianity is Protestantism" (2:166).

In Melville's Young America, Dewey's smug rationalizations allowed liberals to justify their anti-Catholic prejudices by cloaking Protestant religious superiority in aesthetic sophistication and supercilious ecumenism that played to their cosmopolitan self-image. Even Fuller, a sincere Mazzinian and religious liberal, found Roman Catholicism unsuitable for true republicans. Writing in Horace Greeley's *Tribune* for 1845, Fuller argued that "as the Irishman or any other foreigner becomes Americanized, he will demand a new form of religion to suit his new wants. The priest, too, will have to learn the duties of an American citizen; he will live less and less for the Church and more for the People, till, at last, if there be Catholicism still, it will be under Protestant influences, as begins to be the case in Germany."[69] Catholic forms and aesthetics exercised their charms, yet Catholic governance and politics remained suspect. Dewey was certain that priests used the confessional to betray Italian liberals to the Austrian authorities, maintaining the "twofold despotism under which Italy is suffering" (2:11–12), thus compounding religious with political errors that no good republican could countenance. For all its attractions, Catholicism remained to American observers a superstitious and hierarchical religion fundamentally inimical to republican progress.

Melville's first two novels address the Catholic issue with something of Dewey's liberal bonhomie. Tommo cites one commentator on the Marquesas who makes the islands seem "more severely priest-ridden than even the inhabitants of the papal states" (1:170), and while he questions his own observation, he nonetheless describes Kolory, one of the high

---

69. "The Irish Character," *New-York Daily Tribune*, July 15, 1845, 1; rpt. Bean and Myerson, 157.

priests, in distinctively Catholic terms: he wears a "mitre" on his head, leads the "priesthood," and seems both the "Lord Primate of Typee" and "a sort of Knight Templar—a soldier-priest" (1:174). Readers in tune with anti-Catholic stereotypes must have found humor in both the pun on "primate" (an archbishop and an ape) and the allusion to the sexually corrupt Knights Templars (made explicit in "The Paradise of Bachelors"). In *Omoo* (1847) Melville offered a more appealing Friar Tuck stereotype in his portrait of Father Murphy, a fat, jolly, and bibulous Irish priest whose company and liquor are so desirable that the imprisoned sailors begin attending mass every morning (2:142–44). Melville leaves the most overt anti-Catholicism to the Protestantized Tahitians who support banishing two French Roman Catholic missionaries—"emissaries of the Pope and the devil" (125)—and consider Masses as "evil spells" and priests as "diabolical sorcerers" (141). The narrator clearly deplores such intolerance but still wishes that Catholic missionaries had settled "upon some one of the thousand unconverted isles of the Pacific, rather than have forced themselves thus, upon a people already professedly Christians" (126), hardly a ringing endorsement of religious diversity. While Melville generally directs his displeasure at Protestant missionaries, Catholics come off little better, and their presence in his first two novels serves more to indicate Melville's culturally encoded anti-Catholicism than to illustrate his vaunted religious tolerance.[70]

THE MIRROR OF ITALY

Americans' contradictory vision of Italy not only conditioned Melville's literary appropriations of Roman art and history, Dante, Renaissance painting, and Catholicism, it affected his perceptions of what it meant to be an American. Many years ago Paul R. Baker observed that by interacting with the "alien culture" of Italy, which "offered much that [Americans] deeply admired and a great deal they wholeheartedly rejected, they revealed a great many facets of the ideological structure of their own culture."[71] As Melville and other thoughtful American writers began to understand more about the Risorgimento, they realized that it exposed nationalism as a theoretical construct and their own country as decidedly unexceptional. Neither the United States nor Italy nor any country

---

70. According to David S. Reynolds, *Beneath the American Renaissance,* this scene exemplifies Melville's subversive adaptations of popular reform literature. Reynolds finds its imputed anti-Catholicism "semipornographic" in its suggestions of the priests' "womanizing" (140).

71. Baker, *Fortunate Pilgrims,* 223.

Figure 4. Thomas Cole, *The Course of Empire: Desolation* (1836). New-York Historical Society. Oil on canvas.

for that matter was a homogeneous organic whole ordained by God or Nature, but a congeries of competing interests struggling to *become* a nation, an adminstrative invention, as Benedict Anderson has defined it so emotionally, that "people are ready to die for."[72] A reviewer of J. C. L. Sismondi's popular *History of the Italian Republics* recognized in medieval struggles between Guelph and Ghibelline, Bianchi and Neri, Milan and Florence and Rome, important lessons for America: "Those lessons are, the necessity of union, and of watchfulness over those entrusted with the interest of the state; the ruinous effects of party spirit; the dangers of unbounded prosperity, and of the accumulation of wealth and power, in the hands of the few."[73] Gazing into the mirror of Italy exposed the fallacies of progressive theories of history, a view that Melville voiced in such works as *The Confidence-Man* and *Clarel*. Italy was nearly a century behind the United States in achieving political unity, but measured on a grander historical scale she was millennia ahead, for her political roots reached to the Roman Republic. If Italy revived its republican institutions, the Roman toga would pass from America back to Italy and undermine the linear theory of history, the notion that civilization moved inexorably from East to West and culminated in the United States. Ital-

72. *Imagined Communities*, 141.
73. Anon., "Review of *History of the Italian Republics, by J. C. L. Simonde De Sismondi; in Lardner's Cabinet Cyclopaedia*," *Southern Quarterly Review* 1, no. 1 (1842), 172.

ian nationhood would prove that history is cyclical, that empires can regenerate themselves, that the last panel of Cole's *Course of Empire* (fig. 4) is hopeful, not despairing, and implies that the whole series will simply start over again. But if empires can revive they can also fall, even the currently nascent American empire, an idea too horrifying for the infant nation to entertain. On a psychological level, then, it was important for Americans to maintain Joseph Forsyth's view of Italians as "hypocrites of liberty" even as the Risorgimento gained momentum in the late 1840s. America was not really Italy, liberals insisted, even though both countries were bitterly divided by internal dissensions, wary of foreign domination, and harbored beneath their idealism the respective cankers of slavery and foreign oppression.

American writers who matured during the second quarter of the nineteenth century clung to their inherited a vision of Italy as simultaneously "priest-ridden" and beautiful, "malarial" and picturesque, "despotic" and sublime, undermining the three basic principles of aesthetic value with epithets that assuaged their own fragile sense of cultural superiority. Despite its great beauty and glorious past, Italy remained a fallen country whose architectural ruin imaged its repressive political institutions, medieval religious beliefs, and dissolute populace. As Protestant republicans with definite ideas about work, individual liberty, and sexual virtue, Americans felt aesthetically inferior but politically and morally superior to Italians, a point Hawthorne makes repeatedly in his Italian notebooks as well as *The Marble Faun*. A true interculturalism, however, as Melville exhibited in *Typee,* requires humility, tolerance, understanding, and good humor, as well as an appreciation for the historical and social circumstances that shape people's lives. Despite Tommo's refusal to submit to facial tattooing and so expatriate himself for life, and despite the novel's ultimate questioning of Polynesian virtue, *Typee* presents a powerful indictment of ethnocentrism and opens the way for readers to value the Other, whether Marquesan or Italian. "Civilization," Tommo realizes, "for every advantage she imparts, holds a hundred evils in reserve" (1:124), and it is premature for any nation to claim its superiority. When Melville moved into the intellectual and artistic crucible of New York to begin *Mardi,* his most ambitious novel to date, he found himself confronting the matter of Italy in all its ambiguity and complexity, and began discovering the remarkable literary resource it provided for his supple mind.

2

Mardi's Dantean Intertext

> Italy, for example, poor Italy lies dismembered, scattered asunder, not appearing in any protocol or treaty as a unity at all; yet the noble Italy is actually *one:* Italy produced its Dante; Italy can speak!
> —Thomas Carlyle, "The Hero as Poet. Dante; Shakespeare"
> (*Heroes and Hero-Worship*, 1841)

> Dante's praise is that he dared to write his autobiography in colossal cipher, or into universality.
> —Emerson, "The Poet" (1844)

FROM 1846 TO early 1849 American hopes for the Risorgimento fluctuated wildly from traditional despair to inflated optimism to an even darker cynicism after the failure of the 1848 revolutions. In the midst of this turmoil Melville moved to New York in October 1847 and joined the ardently pro-Italy circles of the city's literary elite, especially writers affiliated with Evert Duyckinck's new weekly paper the *Literary World,* where Melville published several book reviews. Only two months after Melville's arrival New York proved itself again the center for the American Risorgimento. On November 29 New Yorkers held a meeting supporting "the liberal measures of Pope Pius IX, and the efforts of the Italian People for National Independence and Constitutional Freedom,"[1] perhaps the first of the pro-Italy meetings that occurred in New York and other large American cities over the next twenty years. Speakers and attendees included Greeley, Tuckerman, Bryant, and David Dudley Field (whom Melville would meet three years later at the Monument Mountain picnic), and the meeting concluded with a speech in Italian by

---

1. Quoted from a pamphlet on the proceeding in Howard Marraro, *American Opinion on the Unification of Italy, 1846–1861* (New York: Columbia University Press, 1932), 5.

E. Felice Foresti. Letters of support came from numerous notable politicians, including former president Van Buren, Secretary of State James Buchanan, and Senator Thomas Hart Benton of Missouri, all Jacksonian Democrats.[2] This pattern of combining politics and literature was a constant feature of New York's pro-Italy meetings and they garnered widespread publicity that Melville could not have missed. The *Literary World,* not especially noted for its political articles, closely followed events in Italy and registered Young America's alternating pessimism and hope for Italian republicanism, making it a major conduit into Melville's imagination while he was working on his third novel, *Mardi,* a novel that itself went through various phases from travel adventure, philosophical romance, to political allegory.[3] At the same time, new English editions of Dante's *Commedia* became widely available and gained the Tuscan poet a far wider American readership than he had enjoyed in the two preceding decades. Linked with the Risorgimento through the efforts of Mazzini, Foresti, and other Italian patriots, Dante offered new literary resources for imagining the Risorgimento in American terms by expanding the range of politically charged allusions and iconography. In the midst of *Mardi's* final, most politicized phase, Melville purchased a copy of the *Commedia* and appropriated it as a key intertext for his most ambitious novel to date, initiating his lifelong interest in Italy and illustrating how a boundlessly ambitious novelist could infuse an American novel with a transnational poetics and ideology.

THE RISE AND FALL OF A "LIBERAL POPE"

For many progressive Americans, the major obstacle confronting Italian republicans had been Pope Gregory XVI (served 1831–46), an aged and reactionary pontiff who opposed industrialization, banned railroads and other improvements in the Papal States, and perpetuated the feudal economic system that Forsyth and others had denounced. Upon his death in June 1846 he was succeeded by Pius IX (served 1846–78), a younger man of humble origins who many hoped would embrace the Risorgimento. Pius initiated a series of reforms that promised a more liberal, democratic

---

2. Details here and in the preceding sentence are from Marraro, *American Opinion,* 5–10.
3. *Mardi's* exact genealogy is complicated and problematic, but critics generally agree on the stages I list here. See Elizabeth S. Foster, "Historical Note" (3:657–81); Watson Branch, "The Quest for *Mardi,*" in *A Companion to Melville Studies,* 124–30; and Branch, "The Etiology of Melville's *Mardi,*" *Philological Quarterly* 64 (Summer 1985): 317–36.

future for Italy, such as a general amnesty to political prisoners and exiles, a commission on railways, proposals for free trade among all Italian states, and advisory councils that gave voice to Young Italy's nationalist yearnings. The US Congress upgraded its representation in Rome from consul to chargé d'affaires, opening diplomatic relations with the Vatican for the first time and looking forward to establishing commercial and trade relations with the Papal States.[4] Throughout 1847 the *Literary World* ran articles praising the new pope for his humanity, common touch, and liberal sympathies, and in one book review Henry Tuckerman sharply contrasted the "system of intolerance and brute force" under Gregory XVI with the "singular firmness and wisdom" of Pius IX: "From the darkest cloud of the Italian heavens breaks forth the light; from the fountain of corruption gush the healing waters; from the very temple of civic despotism is heard the cry of freedom."[5] Sure that liberalism was ascendant Tuckerman even wrote a sonnet, "To Pius IX," praising the pope as a "Benign Reformer!" who made the Vatican "Freedom's home": "Vain is the Jesuit wile, the Austrian steel; / That sceptre which so long betrayed the earth / In thy pure hands is swayed for human weal."[6] From her perch in Rome Margaret Fuller too hoped that Catholics had finally elected a liberal pope who would lead Italy into a democratic future, and despite reservations about his ability to accomplish all he intended she considered him one of the "genuine kings of men."[7] Even *Yankee Doodle,* Cornelius Mathews's humor magazine that published Melville's "Anecdotes of Old Zack" (9:212–29), expressed support by punning on the Italian word for ninth: "if the Italians think so much of their new Pope Pius the IX, instead of shouting on every ocoasion [sic] *Viva! Pio No no!* they ought to shout *'Viva Pio! Yes, yes!'*"[8] Tuckerman revised his *Italian Sketch Book* in

---

4. For a full account of Pius IX's initial popularity in the United States, see Marraro, *American Opinion,* 5–27. For an analysis of the economic motives behind American recognition of the Papal States, see Gemme, *Domesticating Foreign Struggles,* 57–88.

5. Favorable views of Pius IX can be found in the *Literary World* for May 1, 300; September 25, 179; October 2, 203. Tuckerman's comments come in his review of Gabriele Rossetti's attack on papal despotism, *Rome in the Nineteenth Century* (1846), in the *Literary World,* October 20, 301. While sympathetic to Rossetti's argument, Tuckerman believes the new pope has so altered Catholic policy that a "peaceful revolution" is now possible.

6. *Literary World,* November 27, 1847, 405.

7. Margaret Fuller, *"These Sad but Glorious Days": Dispatches from Europe, 1846–1850,* ed. Larry J. Reynolds and Susan Belasco Smith (New Haven, CT: Yale University Press, 1991), 172–73. This dispatch was written on December 17, 1847, and appeared as "Things and Thoughts in Europe. No. XIX" in the *New-York Daily Tribune* on January 29, 1848.

8. *Yankee Doodle,* "Long Life to His Holiness," October 2, 1847, 248. Mathews expressed hope in Pius IX's reforms as early as December 19, 1846, in an article on "The Pope Turned Politician." An Italian informant assures me that no Italian would have associated the negative "no" with Pius's Italian title, but as his politics grew reactionary, English speakers increasingly

1848, almost reversing his gloomy assessment of Italy in the editions of 1835 and 1837, and in its favorable review of May 20 the *Literary World* quoted Tuckerman's placement of Pius IX "among the honored reformers of our day."[9] In July J. T. Headley hastily reissued *Letters from Italy* with a new preface correcting his low opinion of Italian character and terming Pius IX "a more liberal and a better man than his predecessor," although he still warned that "extravagant hopes" for constitutional liberty "were altogether too premature.[10]

Within months Headley's skepticism proved correct. Encouraged by papal reformism, Sicilians shouting "viva Pio Nono" rebelled against Ferdinand II on January 12, 1848, and began the Revolutions of 1848 that swept across France, Germany, and Austria-Hungary in a matter of months. Many rulers, including Pius IX, immediately granted constitutions to pacify angry republicans; but when King Charles Albert of Piedmont-Sardinia (ruled 1831–49) declared war against Austria, the pope abandoned his liberalism. On April 29 he issued his infamous allocution that refused to support the Piedmontese, repudiated the idea of national unity, and advised Italians "to abide in close attachment to their respective sovereigns, of whose good will they have already had experience."[11] Fuller was shocked: "A momentary stupefaction received this astounding performance, succeeded by a passion of indignation, in which the words *traitor* and *imbecile* were associated with the name that had been so dear to his people."[12] As the pope distanced himself ever further from reform the Roman populace grew restive, and after an unidentified assassin killed his prime minister Pellegrino Rossi on November 15, Pius IX left Rome in disguise for his Neapolitan fortress at Gaeta. Gleefully, the *Literary World* published a comic poem, "The Carnival in Europe," that celebrated the European Revolutions in general and mocked the pope's hasty escape in particular:

---

did so.

    9. Vance, *America's Rome*, 2:109, 120–22, points out the changes in Tuckerman's *Italian Sketch Book;* the review was published May 20, 1848, 304–5.

    10. *Letters from Italy,* new and rev. ed. (New York: Baker & Scribner, 1848), xii, vii–viii.

    11. Reprinted in D. Mack Smith, ed., *The Making of Italy 1796–1870* (London: Macmillan, 1988), 150–52. For details on the early risings, see Beales and Biagini, *Risorgimento,* 87–91.

    12. Fuller, *"These Sad but Glorious Days,"* 228. Published as "Things and Thoughts in Europe. No. XXIV" in the *New-York Daily Tribune,* June 15, 1848. This dispatch, titled by Reynolds and Smith "Noble Sentiment and the Loss of the Pope," offers a good summary of Pius IX's reversals and how they shattered liberal hopes in both Europe and the United States.

> O when his turn was come, who joins the Carnival quicker
> Than the Pontifex Supremus, and universal vicar?
> Not long it takes his Holiness to practise the deceiver,
> He doffs the saintly cassock, and he dons the modern beaver,
> And whirls in footman's livery, and a frightful false moustache,
> Through the *Porta San Giovanni,* and across the Pontine Marsh.
> Now surely to good Protestants right pleasant must it be,
> In such a state of things as this, to see the Holy See,
> The Head of all the Church, they think, a tonsured old buffoon,
> St. Peter's chair, a rocking-chair, the Keys all out of tune;
> The Vatican at last for good by the man of sin vacated,
> And that great toe that bothers them so, for ever dislocated.[13]

Fuller lost any lingering compassion for Pio Nono when he threatened his opponents with excommunication, a move she condemned for "its silliness, its bigotry, its ungenerous tone," while Tuckerman recanted his praise of the "liberal Pope" in an angry second sonnet "To the Same: in 1849," calling Pius IX a cruel bigot, an "apostate," and a tyrant: "Thou art the skeleton at Freedom's feast, / To which thy voice so blandly called the world. / How soon the man was vanquished by the priest, / And in the dust the faith of nations hurled!"[14] The ever-opinionated Headley, who despised Charles Albert and had never been confident of Pius IX's commitment to republican values, now identifed the pope with every other European monarch, calling him "a conscientious despot" as bent on achieving supreme political power as the emperor of Austria.[15] As Melville reoriented *Mardi* toward ever more contemporary and political themes, he drew upon Young American disenchantment with the "liberal pope" in his satirical portrait of "Hivohitee MDCCCXLVIII," a thinly veiled and entirely negative portrait that initiated his long involvement with Risorgimento imagery and ideology.

---

13. "The Colonel's Club: Meeting CXLVIII," February 3, 1849, 109.

14. Fuller, *"These Sad but Glorious Days,"* 253, in a dispatch dated February 20, 1849, and published in the *Tribune* on March 31, 1849. Tuckerman's sonnet appears in the *Literary World,* September 1, 1849, 201, alongside his earlier sonnet which he retitled "To Pius IX: in 1848" to emphasize the pontiff's rapid political turnaround.

15. Quoted from Headley's essay "Pope Pius IX and Italy" (1849) in Gemme, *Domesticating Foreign Struggles,* 143.

Figure 5. "Dante Alighieri." Frontispiece to *The Vision*, ed. Henry Cary (1847). Cary's editions used several different frontispieces over the years. This one is in the edition Melville owned and annotated. Author photograph.

THE AMERICAN DISCOVERY OF CARY'S DANTE

On June 22, 1848, in the midst of writing *Mardi,* Melville purchased the British edition of Henry Cary's translation of Dante, *The Vision; or Hell, Purgatory, and Paradise* (*Log*, 278; fig. 5), the book that began his lifelong interest in Italy.[16]

Benedict Anderson plausibly contends that a distinctive requirement of nineteenth-century nationalism was "national print-languages," vernacular works of literature that could articulate and codify the aspirations of a culturally disparate populace.[17] Mazzini, a Dante scholar himself, instinctively understood this demand, and recruited Dante to the banner

---

16. Long considered lost, Melville's copy surfaced at auction in 1985 and was purchased by William Reese of New Haven, Connecticut, in 1989. Reese has made the volume accessible to scholars, and one of these, Lea Newman, generously provided me with a photocopy of the annotated pages for my own use.

17. Anderson, *Imagined Communities,* 67.

of the Risorgimento early on;[18] in Cary's English translation Dante could perform the same work for Americans, modeling a national poet for a people as hungry as the Italians for a literary culture. Dante could satisfy Melville's cosmopolitan aspirations, his desire to create a transnational literature not only out of his maritime experience but from his increasingly wide reading. *The Divine Comedy*—a poem that blends aesthetics, ethics, philosophy, and politics—establishes a vernacular literary tradition that feeds nationalist ambitions and promotes cultural unity, and offers, in the words of Andrea Ciccarelli, a "dynamic concept of literature" in which "the instability of experience includes the possibility of change from a negative to a positive mode of existence."[19] Living in an America as riven by internecine divisions as Dante's Florence, Melville found in *The Divine Comedy* a politically charged and aesthetically complex work that offered new insights into Italy, the Risorgimento, and America itself.

Cary's *Vision,* completed in 1814 and slightly revised in 1844, quickly surpassed Henry Boyd's 1802 translation to assume the preeminent position as the best and most popular English version of *The Divine Comedy.* It was, as Kathleen Verduin shows, absolutely crucial in creating the Dante revival that swept England and America in the early nineteenth century and elevated the hitherto obscure Florentine to the ranks of Homer and Shakespeare.[20] After Samuel Rogers praised Cary's edition in an 1818 article in the *Edinburgh Review* and Samuel Taylor Coleridge commended it in a lecture before the Royal Institution, it quickly became the most celebrated and accessible vehicle for the American study of Dante.[21] In an 1819 article in the *North American Review* John Chipman Gray compared the Boyd and Cary translations and distinctly preferred Cary's blank verse literalism to Boyd's rhymed sestets: "As a mere assistant to the English

---

18. Mack Smith, *Mazzini,* 3. Mazzini actually completed Ugo Foscolo's unfinished four-volume commentary on the *Divine Comedy* so Italians could understand their cultural heroes (26).

19. "Dante and the Culture of the Risorgimento: Literary, Political or Ideological Icon?" in *Making and Remaking Italy,* 80, 79–80. Ciccarelli challenges the notion that Risorgimento writers such as Alfieri, Foscolo, Leopardi, and Manzoni truly followed the Dantean poetic model, and claims they were too pessimistic, in the Petrarchan tradition, to accept Dante's cosmic optimism. Nevertheless, her essay traces Dante's influence on Risorgimento literature effectively and concisely.

20. Kathleen Verduin, "Dante in America: The First Hundred Years," in *Reading Books: Essays on the Material Text and Literature in America,* ed. Michele Moylan and Lane Stiles (Amherst: University of Massachusetts Press, 1996), 16–51. American editions of Cary's *Inferno* were available as early as 1800; when the complete translation appeared in 1814, at least eight American publishers issued reprints. For a brief review of Dante's decline during the Renaissance and subsequent rise during the Romantic period, see the introduction to *Dante's Modern Afterlife: Reception and Response from Blake to Heaney,* ed. Nick Havely (New York: St. Martin's, 1998), 1–14.

21. Verduin, "Dante in America," 18–19.

reader, [Cary] deserves the greatest praise, and in doing justice to all the striking merits of the original, far excels Boyd."[22] In 1823 historian William Prescott asked George Ticknor to help him find Cary's translation, and in 1825 Ralph Waldo Emerson purchased a copy, the same year that the Italian exile Lorenzo Da Ponte was recommending it to New Yorkers.[23] By the 1840s Cary's Dante had assumed the status of "standard edition," a benchmark for subsequent translations like Henry Wadsworth Longfellow's, an early version of which Edgar Allan Poe attacked "as by no means equal to Cary."[24] As Dante's popularity increased, literary couples like Sophia Peabody and Nathaniel Hawthorne whiled away the hours in 1843 by "reading aloud Cary's Dante, with Flaxman open before us," as Sophia recorded in a letter.[25] British sculptor and engraver John Flaxman's 1793 portfolio of Dante prints proved such a fitting accompaniment to Dante that James Russell Lowell included the Flaxman engraving "Dante and Virgil Entering the Dark Wood" in his short-lived but distinguished periodical the *Pioneer* in 1843, and in 1845 Appleton's brought out a handsome edition illustrated with twelve Flaxman line engravings, a book Poe esteemed as "one of the most beautiful volumes ever issued from the press of Appleton" and "a very important service to the literature of the country."[26] By 1850 Poe considered Dante, along with Homer, Shakespeare, and Southey, as one of those rare writers who does not require "Mr." before his name.[27] Even as additional translations multiplied, Cary's maintained its popularity in numerous cheap reprints, especially when accompanied by the popular Gothic illustrations of Gustav Doré, a version that first appeared in 1866.[28] Still in print from Everyman, Cary's Dante opened the window on the *Commedia* to American eyes and gave readers the one line every English reader knows: "All hope abandon, ye who enter here" (Hell, III:9).

22. John Chipman Gray, [Review of *La Divina Commedia*], *North American Review* 8 (1819): 322–47; rpt. in *Dante in America: The First Two Centuries,* ed. A. Bartlett Giamatti (Binghamton: SUNY Binghamton, 1983), 6.
23. Verduin, "Dante in America," 20.
24. Poe, *Essays and Reviews,* 771. The original review appeared in the *Aristidean* for April 1845, and was part of Poe's well-known series of articles condemning Longfellow for plagiarism and other literary sins.
25. Quoted in Lea Bertani Vozar Newman, "Hawthorne's Summer in Florence: Reliving a Honeymoon, the Dante Connection. and the Nascent *Marble Faun,*" in *The Poetics of Place: Florence Imagined,* ed. Irene Marchegiani Jones and Thomas Haeussler ([Florence, Italy]: Leo S. Olschki Editore, 2001), 57. Newman points out the extended presence of Dante in Hawthorne's writing from "The Devil in Manuscript" (1833) through *The Marble Faun* (1860).
26. Quoted in Verduin, "Dante in America," 21–23. Poe's original review was in the *Broadway Journal,* 1845.
27. *Essays and Reviews,* 1042, from *Graham's Magazine,* January 1850.
28. Verduin, "Dante in America," 41–42.

To be sure, Melville eventually read or even owned other versions of the *Commedia*. In the top margin of Cary's version of Hell III:26 Melville quoted John Aitken Carlyle's 1849 prose translation of the same line: "And sounds of hands among them";[29] but he probably preferred Cary's more lyrical rendition, "With hands together smote that swell'd the sounds." Emerson, out of friendship with Thomas Carlyle, urged Harper's to publish Thomas's brother John's translation, and when it appeared he distributed the book widely among his Concord friends, making this version available to an influential audience.[30] Melville must also have known of Longfellow's heavily promoted, extensively reviewed translation of 1865–67, one of the few editions to challenge Cary's for preeminence. Melville also knew Dante's illustrators, even though his personal edition contained only a frontispiece, for specific allusions to "Flaxman's Dante" in *Pierre* (1852) indicate that he consulted or even owned the Flaxman prints. In 1870 he acquired Alexander Gilchrist's *Life of William Blake, "Pictor Ignotus"* (1863) which reproduced dozens of Blake illustrations, including one from the unpublished Dante series "The Circle of the Traitors," illustrating Hell: XXXII. Gilchrist's appendix describes Blake's drawing of Paradise XXX (fig. 6), Dante at the river of light, a passage in Cary that Melville sidelined and annotated "Blake" on the left and "Botticelli" on the right, bracketing the eleven lines that reminded him of their art. So in addition to knowing about Blake's illustration, he knew that Sandro Botticelli had also sketched this scene.[31] Given Melville's characteristic interest in literary pictorialism, particularly later in his career, it seems likely that he also knew Doré's illustrations that appeared in portfolio in 1863 and in Cary editions published in New York in 1866 and 1871.

Despite these multiple avenues of access to Dante, there is no question that Melville read Dante primarily through Cary, a volume he consulted throughout his life and marked even more thoroughly than his set of Shakespeare. Before acquiring volumes by Sir Thomas Browne, Milton, Shakespeare, or even Hawthorne, all major influences on Melville's prose, Melville possessed Cary's Dante. Dante mapped the course for

29. Hershel Parker speculates that Melville purchased the John Carlyle translation sometime during the 1850s (correspondence with the author).
30. Verduin, "Dante in America," 26–29.
31. Howard H. Schless, "Flaxman, Dante, and Melville's *Pierre*," *Bulletin of the New York Public Library* 64 (February 1960): 65–82, believes Melville bought a complete set of Flaxman prints in Paris in 1849, although there is no external evidence for this purchase. Pierre alludes to Flaxman's engraving of Paolo and Francesca, an illustration that was not included in Appleton's edition of Cary. Melville made his "Blake" and "Botticelli" annotations at Paradise XXX:60–70. In one of his last of many acts of kindness to me throughout my career, Merton M. Sealts, Jr., confirmed my reading of these two annotations.

Figure 6. William Blake, "Dante in the Empyrean, Drinking at the River of Light." Object 101 in the unpublished collection *Illustrations to Dante's "Divine Comedy,"* 1824–27. Pen and ink and water colors over pencil. Melville wrote "Blake" in the margin of *Paradise*, Canto 30, which describes this scene. ©Tate, London 2008.

Mardi, Moby-Dick, Pierre, and *Israel Potter,* all literal journeys projected into mythopoetic quests that transvalue space into powerful metaphors of spiritual and intellectual growth. Dante remained for Melville a rewarding companion on actual journeys, too. Twelve years after his initial purchase, he took Cary along on his voyage around Cape Horn with brother Tom in 1860, along with his Homer, Béranger, and new copy of *The Marble Faun.*[32] His copious markings, particularly in the heavily sidelined third book "Paradise," parallel his late interest in theology, and may have been made while he was writing *Clarel,* and the Blake annotation is coeval with Melville's deepening interest in art after 1870. My hunch is that Melville returned to Cary's Dante throughout his career, using it as a resource not only for his immediate writing projects, most obviously in *Mardi* and *Pierre,* but as inspiration for his turn to poetry in the late 1850s and beyond.

The Cary edition was important not only as the standard translation of Dante's verse, but for its scholarly apparatus, something other editions lacked. Cary offered Melville an example of serious, comparatist literary scholarship, perhaps the first he had observed in depth. Although he had a truncated classical education and borrowed scholarly editions from Evert Duyckinck, Cary's Dante was his first personal reference work for classical scholarship. Cary heavily annotated the text with cross-references to prior translators and their emendations and glosses. Some notes take up entire pages. Cary integrates the *Commedia* into a larger European literary tradition and presents Dante as a highly original author who describes local political conflicts in his native idiom while engaging the grand Western literary tradition of the Bible, Plato, Virgil, Ovid, Chaucer, and dozens of other classical writers. Here, in one volume, was a formula for literary greatness, for becoming a cosmopolitan writer whose influence extends across centuries and nationalities. Cary explains how Dante's terza rima prefigures the cadences of *Paradise Lost,* and the translation itself self- consciously displays a rugged, sometimes tortured literalism in order to infuse the poem with the vigor of Shakespeare and Homer. Such scholarship showed Melville that no literary work exists independently of its earlier versions: each participates in an unfolding continuum of texts, commentators, translations, and interpretations, a series of Talmudic glosses upon glosses, editions upon editions. Ishmael's well-known complaint that his book is but a "draught of a draught" (6:145) finds corroboration in Cary's Dante, where the editor revises prior translations and

---

32. Sealts, *Melville's Reading,* 132n.

imply alternate readings that imply the fluidity of texts.[33] Cary's extensive footnotes, introduction, historical information, linguistic glosses, lists of allusions, even his index, offered Melville a view of literature as a product of multiple sources and voices, a multireferential creation that outstripped its own time even as it immersed itself in its own localized present.

LIBERATING TOMMO

Melville's first two novels oscillated between fact and fiction, autobiography and romance, travelogue and novel, pleasing a literal-minded publisher and fulfilling authorial dreams of literary greatness. As Cary wrote in a section of the introduction Melville sidelined, the *Commedia* validated such generic indeterminacy:

> To this singular production, which has not only stood the test of ages, but given a tone and color to the poetry of modern Europe, and even animated the genius of Milton and of Michael Angelo, it would be difficult to assign its place according to the received rules of criticism. Some have termed it an epic poem; and others, a satire: but it matters little by what name it is called. It suffices that the poem seizes on the heart by its two great holds, terror and pity; detains the fancy by an accurate and lively delineation of the objects it represents; and displays throughout such an originality of conception, as leaves to Homer and Shakespeare alone the power of challenging the pre-eminence or equality. *The fiction,* it has been remarked, is admirable, and the work of an inventive talent truly great. (my emphasis)[34]

Like these three great authors, Dante created his own rules and demanded that readers accommodate him on his own terms. The *Commedia* validated Melville's emerging practice of composing mixed-genre narratives, an already popular form as Sheila Post-Lauria has pointed out,[35] but one that

---

33. Melville, of course, had already written what John Bryant calls a "fluid text." See *Melville Unfolding: Sexuality, Politics, and the Versions of Typee* (Ann Arbor: University of Michigan Press, 2008), esp. 277–97.

34. Henry Cary, "Life of Dante," introduction to *The Vision; or Hell, Purgatory, and Paradise of Dante Alighieri* (New York: D. Appleton and Company, 1858), 36–37. Except for pagination and the illustrations, this edition is identical with Melville's 1847 edition, and is cited parenthetically in the text.

35. *Correspondent Colorings: Melville in the Marketplace* (Amherst: University of Massachusetts Press, 1996), 101–22.

now, with the Dante revival, gained the imprimatur of classical scholarship. An author could write a blend of epic, satire, allegory, love story, political tract, theological treatise, encyclopedia, or whatever—wrap it up in that malleable category that Cary calls "the fiction"—and place it on the shelf next to the greatest writers in the Western tradition. Lea Newman, the first scholar to study Melville's annotations in Cary, finds in this passage strong evidence for the *Commedia's* influence:

> Here, in Cary's commentary, was evidence that, like [Melville's] work-in-progress, Dante's acknowledged world masterpiece encompassed more than a single genre and refused to be neatly categorized. Given the quest motif of his romance, a plot structure closely identified with epic poetry, and his penchant for satire, the mode that was to eventually dominate the last half of his book, Melville could well have seen in *The Divine Comedy* a model to emulate.[36]

Although Melville began *Mardi* in 1847, perhaps as much as a year before he acquired the Cary edition, he revised it heavily during the summer and fall of 1848, making numerous plot adjustments to develop the Taji-Hautia-Yillah romance and inserting new chapters and sections, including perhaps chapter 180 on Lombardo.[37] Some of the borrowings are so specific that the various hypotheses of composition should probably be altered to account for the Dantean influence. For example, many scholars believe that the Maramma section, chapters 105–117, was composed in 1847; yet, as Newman has shown, they so closely parallel Dante that either Melville was reading Dante before he purchased his own edition or he wrote these chapters later. Newman specifically identifies the Maramma chapters, chapter 119 on "Dreams," and chapters 184–188 on Serenia as the novel's most densely Dantean sections. She notes recurrent verbal echoes, shared theological and cosmological concepts (especially Neoplatonism), overlapping figures of speech, and shared patterns of light and circle imagery, and concludes by linking Taji with Dante's Ulysses as fellow spiritual explorers beset by pride. I would extend Newman's list by noting numerous broad, even obvious similarities: early on, Samoa guides Taji as Virgil guides Dante; Taji searches for Yillah as Dante searches for Beatrice; circular imagery gradually increases until chapter 188, "Babbalanja relates to them a Vision," a title that echoes Cary's title for the *Commedia, The Vision.* Read intertextually with the *Commedia, Mardi* seems

---

36. Lea Bertani Vozar Newman, "Melville's Copy of Dante: Evidence of New Connections Between the *Commedia* and *Mardi*," *Studies in the American Renaissance* (1993): 307–9.

37. Branch, "Quest for *Mardi*," 124–30, and "Etiology of *Mardi*," 317–36.

like Taji's description of Heaven, a place where "grim Dante [will] forget his Infernos, and shake sides with fat Rabelais" (3:13), a work that, unlike *Typee* and *Omoo,* consciously engages elite literary texts to extend its reach well beyond personal experience.

Cary's scholarly apparatus and principles of translation helped liberate Melville from the linguistic negotiations he confronted in *Typee* and *Omoo* where Polynesian dialects made the author an often uncomprehending mediator between his Marquesan subjects and his English readers. For example, in *Mardi* Melville borrows the Dantean phrase "l' ultima sera" (Purgatory I:58) as the title for chapter 185, a phrase Cary translates as "the farthest gloom."[38] Rendered literally, as in Philip H. Wicksteed's translation (1903), this means "the last hour." Cary justifies his figurative version by citing passages from Ariosto, Filicaja, and a "Mr. Mathias," each of whom uses the Italian phrase to connote death, not time. Since *Mardi*'s chapter 185 records the approach of a stormy night and a bowsman's sudden death in a dark sea, the phrase's double connotation of gloom and death precisely fits Melville's purpose, as Cary believed it did Dante's. To inventive geniuses like Melville and Dante, language is a function of imagination, a malleable tool forged for the writer's special aims. Cary's rare metaphorical translation better suits Dante's dark mood (and Melville's dark chapter) than would a more literal version. The choices authors make as they write, Melville was discovering, complexly combine past practice, personal desire, and contextual constraints. Meanings, like translations, multiply.

As Melville revised and extended his new novel in light of Dante, he recognized a metafictional analogy between the *Commedia* and *Mardi* and a biographical parallel between Dante's career and his own. *Mardi* develops these relationships in Babbalanja's inserted story of the Koztanza, the fictional epic by Lombardo, Mardi's national poet.[39] Lombardo, clearly an Italian name, conflates several proper names in the *Commedia*. In Purgatory XVI, the first canto Melville marked in that section, Marco Lombardo answers Dante's questions about free will and necessity (11:46–149) and reassures Dante, more than Melville himself was ever assured, that human beings have free will. The name also refers to Italians in general, for as Cary explains in a note to Purgatory XVI:127, "All the Italians

---

38. Newman, "Melville's Copy of Dante," 317.
39. Newman notes Maxine Moore's identification of the Koztanza with *Mardi* in *That Lonely Game,* but believes the books are too different for close comparison ("Melville's Copy of Dante," 334n). Augusta Melville's comment on the completion of *Mardi* is well known: "The last proof sheets are through. 'Mardi's a book!–'Ah my own Koztanza! child of many prayers. Oro's blessing on thee" (*Log,* 287).

were called Lombards by the French" (309). Of course, the name also recalls Lombardy, fusing person and place and implying the indebtedness of art and identity to region. And finally, it recalls Baldassare Lombardi, a Dante editor Cary frequently cites both as an authority to be respected and a source to be corrected. Lombardi, whose edition appeared in 1791, exemplifies the scholarly obscurantism that Melville at once values and ridicules, as does Cary,[40] a critical dilemma authors confront when they cite *any* authority. From William Ellis in *Typee* through William Scoresby Jr. in *Moby-Dick* to the hapless Amasa Delano in "Benito Cereno," Melville incurred debts to lesser authors which he repaid with sarcasm and scorn even while acknowledging their priority. Lombardi-Lombardo represents an archetype of great learning and experience combined with little understanding or imagination. Authors like Melville who use such writers as fodder must simultaneously acknowledge dependence and difference, a paradox that is a prime source of Melvillean irony. Cary's abundant notes revealed to Melville the literary ancestry behind genius and gave him a more sophisticated notion of originality, and by inserting notes and acknowledgments in his own works he placed himself in the same anxious relationship to authority as Dante and Cary, the poet and the scholar. More personally, Lombardi-Lombardo also represents unsung genius, a figure that assumed greater importance for Melville later in life and included Dante himself, an author undergoing rediscovery even as Melville lapsed into obscurity.

The name of Lombardo's epic, the Koztanza, also originated in Dante. King Manfredi of Naples and Sicily alludes to his grandmother Queen Costanza and his daughter Costanza in Purgatory III:110–12. Cary's notes identify all three historical figures. Lombardo's Koztanza is thus feminized, perhaps an emblem of its fecundity mixed with fragility, and likely Melville's wry attempt at parodying Cary's recondite annotations. Cary's relentless commentaries on the *Commedia* can be as picky as those of Verbi, the critic "who detected a superfluous comma" in the Koztanza (3:596–97), and *Mardi* itself goes forth to a world of reviewers who, like the waspish Zenzori, may ask the writer "where he picked up so much trash" (3:598). Lombardo is also an antitype of Dante, as is Melville, with

40. Just citing examples from pages Melville marked, we find Cary calling one Lombardi gloss "somewhat ludicrous" (Paradise, XXVI:97n), while another complains that Lombardi repeatedly "misrepresents the readings of other editions" (Hell, XXII:51n); on the other hand, Cary favorably quotes some of Lombardi's interpretations at length (see Paradise, I:77n). One gloss that Melville marked identifies Dante's allusion to "the rose" as a reference to the Virgin Mary, whom Roman Catholics call the "Rosa Mystica," according to Lombardi (Paradise, XXIII:71n). This interpretation would have interested the late Melville, author of the "Rose Poems."

all three writers struggling to create "the creative" (3:595) while remaining true to that "one autocrat within—his crowned and sceptered instinct" (3:597). They know, as Babbalanja says in another Dantean allusion, that "to scale great heights, we must come out of lowermost depths. The way to heaven is through hell" (3:594).

Cary's Dante made Melville a more self-conscious writer and showed him how multiple sources and competing authorities could be melded together into one mixed-genre narrative. While it is commonplace to see *Mardi* as a rehearsal for *Moby-Dick,* Cary's Dante has been insufficiently credited as an enabling document in Melville's growth, one he returned to again and again and found indispensable in his efforts to develop a transnational fiction of his own.

THE DANTEAN POLITICS OF *MARDI*

For all of *Mardi*'s verbal echoes of the *Commedia,* Newman concludes that Melville had limited use for Dante's thought:

> Ambivalent as ever, Melville recognizes in Dante a genius of a time long passed, another in some measure like himself—a writer committed to fulfilling his destiny as an artist, a man open to visions and their consequences. Melville was undoubtedly intrigued with Dante's imagination and poetic skill, but in spite of Babbalanja's conversion, he was clearly not persuaded by Dante's theological precepts. (330)

Yet Dante's thought was more than theological. It was also political, a running commentary on the partisan ideologies of his time, as Cary's edition constantly reminds readers. The timeline that follows Cary's introduction links specific historical events to sections of the *Commedia* and offers a perfect example of how poetry memorializes and comments upon contemporary events. It lists the various papal and monarchical successions during Dante's lifetime along with events in Dante's personal life keyed to corresponding lines in the *Vision.* It includes some events whether Dante alludes to them or not, for example Marco Polo's return from Venice in 1295, the death of Sadi in 1296, the execution of William Wallace in 1305, and the birth of Boccaccio in 1313 (47–49). Art, such a timeline implies, is embedded in history, even those events it fails to mention. And history, as Dante's poem illustrates, can be profitably accessed through art. Who would know of Paolo and Francesca without

Dante? Or Count Ugolino's grotesque death by starvation? Or the sins of popes, knights, friars, and other ostensibly moral leaders? A work like Dante's bridges the gap between history and fiction and suggests that all writing is, ultimately, mixed-genre, and that to separate the two, as readers of *Typee* and *Omoo* had struggled to do, is an exercise in futility. Through Babbalanja's response to a legend recounted by the poet Yoomy, Melville reveals his awareness of the intermingling of history and fiction: "what are vulgarly called fictions are as much realities as the gross mattock of Dididi, the digger of trenches" (3:283).

Dante's conspicuous choice of the Tuscan vernacular was also a political act, one with special significance for American writers. From Noah Webster's first efforts to distinguish an American lexicon through Whitman's praise of English as "the dialect of common sense" in his preface to *Leaves of Grass*, American writers sought to create a distinctive national idiom.[41] Italians, divided by linguistic barriers of region, class, and dialect, also desired a unifying national language commensurate with their political yearnings. Early on in the Dante revival, Longfellow noticed that the *Commedia* employed a variety of Italian dialects, simultaneously acknowledging the country's linguistic diversity even while constructing a national literary language:

> The facts which we can gather from the contending arguments, lead us to embrace the opinion that the classic Italian is based upon the Tuscan, but adorned and enriched by words and idioms from all the provinces of Italy. In other words, each of the Italian dialects has contributed something to its formation, but most of all the Tuscan; and the language thus formed belongs not to a single city, nor a single province, but is the common possession of the whole of 'Il bel paese là dove il sì suona' [literally, "the beautiful country where Yes sounds," that is, Italy]."[42]

Rather than ignoring regional differences, Dante subsumed them in a grand inclusive national vernacular designed to speak to the disparate cultures of early Renaissance Italy, making the *Commedia* a model for Ameri-

---

41. *Complete Poetry and Collected Prose*, ed. Justin Kaplan (New York: Library of America, 1982), 25. For Noah Webster's crucial role in the development of a literary language in the United States, see Michael P. Kramer, *Imagining Language in America: From the Revolution to the Civil War* (Princeton, NJ: Princeton University Press, 1992).

42. Review of *A History of the Italian Language and Dialects*, *North American Review* 35 (October 1832): 288–99. Rpt. in *Dante in America*, 43. Longfellow quotes from *Inferno* 33:78, which Cary translates as "In that fair region where the Italian voice / Is heard." Cary supports his version by citing Dante's *De Vulgare Eloquentia*, a Latin treatise on language and style. Dante distinguished Italian dialects by the way they pronounced *sì*, or "yes."

can writers striving to develop a national literature in a country riddled with sectionalism. Lowell, noting that Dante had originally intended to write his epic in Latin, praises his decision to turn to the vernacular:

> Instead of endeavoring to manufacture a great poem out of what was foreign and artificial, he let the poem make itself out of him. The epic which he wished to write in the universal language of scholars, and which might have had its ten lines in the history of literature, would sing itself in provincial Tuscan, and turn out to be written in the universal dialect of mankind. Thus all great poems have been in a certain sense provincial.[43]

A sophisticated cosmopolitan himself, Lowell prefigures Bruce Robbins's argument for the complementarity of the local and the universal, or what Jahan Ramazini has tentatively denominated the "translocal": "Neither localist nor universalist, neither nationalist nor vacantly globalist, a *translocal poetics* highlights the dialogic intersections—sometimes tense and resistant, sometimes openly assimilative—of specific discourses, genres, techniques, and forms of diverse origins."[44] Melville established such a dialogic relationship with Cary's Dante, as he did with many other authors, and thereby involved his works in a conversation at once global, historical, classical, and politically contemporary.

For American and English enthusiasts, reading Dante became synonymous with supporting the Risorgimento. "The Land of the Dead" came to life under Dante's influence and showed the promise of national unity facilitated by artistic vision. Thomas Carlyle, in his 1840 lecture on Dante and Shakespeare, argued that the political role of the "*Hero-Poet*," although subordinate to his philosophical or aesthetic role, was nevertheless central to his lasting historical significance and influence: "Italy, for example, poor Italy lies dismembered, scattered asunder, not appearing in any protocol or treaty as a unity at all; yet the noble Italy is actually *one:* Italy produced its Dante; Italy can speak!"[45] Melville's Dante was the heroic Dante of the Risorgimento, not the Middle Ages, a nineteenth-century Dante translatable to American aims and desires, one who represented an emerging nation much as did Melville. Whereas Dante sought to unify his culture by appealing to a deeply idealistic, Platonic vision of

---

43. "Dante," in *Among My Books,* 2nd ser. (Boston: Houghton Mifflin Company, 1876), 100. First published in the *North American Review,* 1872.

44. Robbins, *Cosmopolitics,* 2; Ramazani, "A Transnational Poetics," *American Literary History* 18 (Summer 2006): 350.

45. *On Heroes Hero-Worship and the Heroic in History* (1841; London: Oxford University Press, 1974), 150.

Christianity, with the questing self piously subordinated to divine law, Melville created an "Imperial Self," as Dimock has argued, an equally idealized but primarily secular figure representing the unrestrained energy of America's paradoxical impulses toward hegemony and individualism.

As twin imperial selves, Dante and Melville create truths that surpass the mere facts of history. A rather convoluted and transcendental defense of poetic truth in *Mardi* supports this view. Prior to relating Samoa's "incredible tale" of replacing part of a man's brain with a pig's brain, Taji asks the reader to exercise faith rather than knowledge because "a thing may be incredible and still be true; sometimes it is incredible because it is true" (3:296). Samoa's tale originates in his travels, and travelers are proverbially known as great liars. Yet Taji insists this proverb is false. After all, Dante excludes the well-traveled exaggerator Sir John Mandeville from the circle of Hell reserved for liars: "And though all liars go to Gehenna; yet, assuming that Mandeville died before Dante; still though Dante took the census of Hell, we find not Sir John, under the likeness of a roasted neat's tongue, in the infernalest of infernos, The Inferno" (3:298). Thus, we should follow Dante's example and *believe* travelers' tales, even Samoa's "incredible tale" of primitive brain surgery. Nor would it matter if Melville knew that *Mandeville's Travels* was published after Dante's death in 1321 and that Mandeville himself was the spurious creation of the book's true author, a French physician. Such facts only heighten the comic effect of Melville's defense of poetry, for Samoa's tale is manifestly false as were Mandeville's stories and Dante's account of a journey through hell to paradise. Yet our suspension of disbelief, in *Mardi* as in the *Commedia*, allows us to perceive the deeper allegorical truths that fiction and poetry reveal. By invoking the *Commedia* as the standard of poetic truth, Melville pays tribute to Dante's cultural authority and makes him a type of Emerson's "liberating gods," those poets who make us intellectually and politically free.[46]

Dante's aesthetic independence carried into his politics and made him a valuable intercessor in reconciling Americans' anti-Catholic prejudices with their Risorgimento sympathies. As the chief of the Priors, the supreme magistrates in Florence, he negotiated an agreement between the Papal party of the Guelphs and the Imperial party of the Ghibellines that

---

46. "The Poet," *Essays & Lectures,* 462. The whole passage is worth quoting: "The poets are thus liberating gods. The ancient British bards had for the title of their order, 'Those who are free throughout the world.' They are free, and they make free." In the first paragraph Emerson includes Dante in his list of "the highest minds of the world" who explore the "manifold meaning of every sensuous fact" (447).

satisfied neither faction.[47] He thus typifies the political independent, one who places principle before party and freely criticizes both opponents and allies. "So truly Catholic is he," wrote Lowell in 1872, "that both parties find their arsenal in him. The Romanist proves his soundness in doctrine, the anti-Romanist claims him as the first Protestant; the Mazzinist and the Imperialist can alike quote him for their purpose."[48]

When Melville assumed a mediatory role in his "Supplement" to *Battle-Pieces* (1866), a carefully measured argument for Northern mercy toward the South, he compared the two sides to Guelphs and Ghibellines and asked them to rise above the divisiveness "that animated a triumphant town-faction in the Middle Ages" (11:187). The ambiguous politics scholars have endlessly debated in Melville's works—*Billy Budd* is only the most notorious example—finds precedent in Dante, as Melville alternates between liberty and authority in an art so all-encompassing that it substitutes its own more comprehensive "vision" for the bipolar world of everyday politics. Michael Rogin, Larry Reynolds, and John McWilliams are among the scholars who have managed to take Melville's politics on its own terms, to accept his contradictory professions of Jacksonian democracy along with his fear of mob rule and evident need for authority.[49] But rather than seeing this as some sort of concession to his father-in-law, Judge Lemuel Shaw, or the increasing conservatism of Evert Duyckinck, or a reaction to the increasing radicalism of the "Young America" movement, or the excesses of the French Revolution, as do these scholars, I see Melville following a line traced by Dante, pursuing a pragmatic ideology that balances personal liberty with the rule of law, even at the risk of personal isolation. After all, Dante's judgments left him an exile from Florence under sentence of death by burning (Cary, 48), a fate not unlike Melville's after his move from New York to Pittsfield where his popularity gradually diminished. Courageously hewing out his own belief system, Melville criticizes Christian missionaries in *Typee* yet argues in "Hawthorne and His Mosses" that Americans should praise "those writers, who breathe that unshackled, democratic spirit of Chris-

---

47. Newman believes *Mardi*'s reference to "Petrarchs and Priors" (3:367) is one of many covert allusions to Dante, and derives from Melville's familiarity with Cary's introduction ("Melville's Copy of Dante," 311). Information later important to Melville in *Battle-Pieces* is Cary's distinction between Guelph and Ghibelline: "The factions were now known by the names of the Neri and the Bianchi, the former generally siding with the Guelphs, or adherents of the papal power, the latter with the Ghibellines, or those who supported the authority of the emperor" (14). Cary also discusses the origins of these names in a long footnote to Paradise VI:107.

48. "Dante," 100.

49. Rogin, *Subversive Genealogy;* Larry J. Reynolds, *European Revolutions;* McWilliams, *Hawthorne, Melville, and the American Character.*

tianity in all things" (9:248). Clearly, Melville attached his own meanings to words like "democracy" and "Christianity" and was discovering, like Dante, that it was much harder to combine politics, art, and religion in a unique brew of one's own creation than follow the party line of one faction over another. The risk was always, as Melville acknowledged to Hawthorne in 1851, the paradoxical temporal failure of timeless success: "Though I wrote the Gospels in this century, I should die in the gutter" (14:192). His religious metaphor bespeaks the Dantean intertext, and suggests how seriously Melville took his literary task.

MEDIA'S SCROLL
An Independent Voice

In *Mardi*'s long political allegory, chapters 145–69, and in the Maramma chapters, 105–117, Melville combines the *Commedia*'s narrative organization and thematic aims with contemporary politics and cultural prejudices to paint an acerbic portrait of democratic struggles at home and abroad. While readers from the novel's first reviewers to its most recent critics have placed these and other satirical passages in the tradition of Swift, Rabelais, Montaigne, Browne, and others, none of them have had at hand Melville's copy of Cary's Dante, a source that makes us rethink Melville's creative process as well as the genealogy of *Mardi*. Even though disagreements over the novel's dates of composition render precise parallels to current events problematic, too many references to European and specifically Italian political developments support the established view that Melville added long sections to *Mardi* through the tumultuous summer and fall of 1848, as Elizabeth Foster notes (3:662).[50] This makes *Mardi*, like Dante's *Inferno*, a thinly veiled topographical allegory of Melville's own time, a satire of national stereotypes and political personalities that exposes the hypocrisy of conservatives and progressives alike.

In chapters 145–69 Taji and his friends visit one island after another, moving through space like Dante and Virgil, albeit horizontally rather than vertically. Just as Dante placed Guelphs, Ghibellines, popes, and pagans in the Inferno, Melville pillories both sides of the political spectrum, recognizing that no one party or system has all the answers. Dominora (England) and Vivenza (the United States) share in Melville's scorn, the

---

50. Branch, "Etiology of *Mardi*," argues that the political allegory was completed by April 1848 (326), a position he modifies somewhat in his later piece "Quest for *Mardi*" (128–29).

first for its unbridled imperialism and rigid class system, the second for its hypocritical acceptance of slavery and emergent imperialism under the motto of Manifest Destiny. The American Congress, "the grand council of Vivenza," listens to the lunatic "Alanno," whose spread-eagle nationalism and Anglophobic bellicosity viciously parody Senator William Allen of Ohio. Daniel Webster, before his infamous accommodation of the Compromise of 1850, appears as the Roman "Saturnina" with a God-like brow as noble as "St. Peter's grand dome"(3:515). In sharp contrast is John C. Calhoun, portrayed as "Nulli: a cadaverous, ghost-like man, with a low ridge of forehead" (3:532). Although the phrenological contrast leaves little doubt as to Melville's sympathies, by including caricatures of Western, Northern, and Southern politicians, Melville cartoonishly limns a politics of his own making: "Whatever his intentions when he began writing current events into *Mardi,*" Hershel Parker observes, "Melville in these political chapters was freeing himself from the political factions and parties to which his acquaintances, friends, and relatives were vehemently allying themselves."[51] The strategy is much like Dante's in his City of Dis, where both Farinata degli Uberti, a Ghibelline, and Cavalcante Cavalcanti, a Guelph and the father of Dante's best friend, suffer together for their Epicureanism in a flaming open tomb (Canto 10). For committing simony, Dante condemns Popes Nicholas III, Boniface VIII, and Clement V to the eighth circle of Hell (Canto 19), and even Dante's beloved teacher, Brunetto Latini, suffers for sodomy in the seventh circle (Canto 15). It is precisely this evenhanded justice that undergirds Dante's poetic authority, says Latini, in words that apply equally to Melville: "For thee, / Thy fortune hath such honor in reserve, / That thou by either party shalt be craved / With hunger keen" (15:69–72). The truly independent writer must dramatize unpleasant realities, even to placing one's preceptor in Hell; but the victim can still speak truth, and his art—Latini's epic poem influenced Dante—can remain undiminished by his personal failings. Melville's critique of Vivenzan politics requires a similarly nuanced political morality that forces readers to confront the paradoxes and hypocrisies they have ignored. In the constructed worlds of *Mardi* and the *Commedia,* comfortable partisan dichotomies crumble before the searching vision of the independent, morally questing authorial self.

The mysterious scroll in chapter 161, "They hearken unto a Voice from the Gods," epitomizes Melville's Dantean politics not only because it critiques a popular cause, democracy, but also because it grounds its critique in Roman history, a two-thousand-year-old narrative dramatizing

---

51. *Herman Melville,* 1:605.

the competing claims of monarchy and popular rule. America's founders conventionally cited the first Roman Republic to exemplify the dangers republicanism faced from tyranny on the one hand and democratic excess on the other, Caesar versus the mob. Yet they believed, according to Robert Ferguson, that their history would be different: "they expected it to grow in a new and glorious fashion instead of repeating the past in endless cycles of rise and fall."[52] Intended to rectify Vivenzans' ignorance of past examples, the scroll draws on this tradition but questions its optimistic application to the American experiment. According to the scroll, the "sovereign-kings" of Vivenza, that is, the Jacksonian individuals of the United States, hold to one "grand error," a providential teleology based on "the conceit that Mardi is now in the last scene of the last act of her drama; and that all preceding events were ordained, to bring about the catastrophe you believe to be at hand,—a universal and permanent Republic" (3:525). To such nationalistic messianism the scroll opposes a cyclic view of history: "'Each age thinks its own is eternal. But though for five hundred twelve-moons, all Romara, by courtesy of history, was republican; yet, at last, her terrible king-tigers came, and spotted themselves with gore'" (3:526). This pattern, repeated throughout history, can occur again in Vivenza, warns the scroll:

> In nations, sovereign-kings! there is a transmigration of souls; in you, is a marvelous destiny. The eagle of Romara revives in your own mountain bird, and once more is plumed for her flight. Her screams are answered by the vauntful cries of a hawk; his red comb yet reeking with slaughter. And one East, one West, those bold birds may fly, till they lock pinions in the midmost beyond.
>
> But, soaring in the sky over the nations that shall gather their broods under their wings, that bloody hawk may hereafter be taken for the eagle.
>
> And though crimson republics may rise in constellations, like fiery Aldebarans, speeding to their culminations; yet, down must they sink at last, and leave the old sultan-sun in the sky; in time, again to be deposed." (3:527)

Echoing Margaret Fuller's 1846 imagery of Roman eagles transmuting into American vultures, the scroll portrays an America given over to the hawk of the Mexican War and the extension of slavery which are rapidly undermining its moral authority and rendering it little better than the

---

52. *Reading the Early Republic*, 175.

British monarchy it overthrew. In fact, because of the stain of slavery America may already be too corrupt to inherit Rome's republican mantle. Webster's Roman brow may prove unequal to the task of quelling the Vivenzan mob (as in fact it was), thus demonstrating the truth of the scroll's most controversial antiegalitarian statement: "Civilization has not ever [that is, "has not always"] been the brother of equality" (3:527). At first shockingly jacobinical, on reflection this opinion simply mirrors the historical realities of 1848, when America, the most progressive republic on earth, still countenanced slavery, and liberty-loving England clung to a dehumanizing class system that bred starvation in a land of plenty (3:478). Nations behave badly because they are all too human, subject to that "Calvinistic sense of Innate Depravity and Original Sin, from whose visitations, in some shape or other, no deeply thinking mind is always and wholly free," as Melville wrote in his "Mosses" review (9:243). Exhibiting as sharp a sense of human limitation as Dante and bespeaking a Calvinism deep-seated in Melville's personal past,[53] the scroll finally argues for political meliorism based on the human propensity to err:

> Now, though far and wide, to keep equal pace with the times, great reforms, of a verity, be needed; nowhere are bloody revolutions required. Though it be the most certain of remedies, no prudent invalid opens his veins, to let out his disease with his life. And though all evils may be assuaged; all evils can not be done away. For evil is the chronic malady of the universe; and checked in one place, breaks forth in another. (3:529)

The scroll is more a warning than a doctrine, a historically contingent fiction indexed to the political turmoil of 1848 and the violence it encouraged. As Larry Reynolds observes, "The scroll's interpretation of the past contains nothing antidemocratic. However, when it comments upon recent revolutionary events, it offers a pessimistic view of human nature and radical reform that would remain thereafter a salient feature of Melville's thought and art" (108). Written, like the *Commedia,* during a time of intense factionalism, the scroll seeks a wisdom that looks beyond politics for social harmony, a wisdom that drove Melville deeper into human nature even as it drove Dante deeper into theology. The scroll continues:

> Thus, freedom is more social than political. And its real felicity is not to

---

53. For a searching analysis of Calvinism's influence on Melville, see T. Walter Herbert, Jr., *Moby-Dick and Calvinism: A World Dismantled* (New Brunswick, NJ: Rutgers University Press, 1977).

be shared. *That* is of a man's own individual getting and holding. It is not, who rules the state, but who rules me. Better be secure under one king, than exposed to violence from twenty millions of monarchs, though oneself be of the number. (3:528–29)

The scroll directly addresses the problem of authority and rebellion at the core of Melville's politics. McWilliams believes Media's authorship of the scroll undermines its authority,[54] but in terms of Dantean and Risorgimento politics, it actually reinforces it. Media, as his name implies, is a mediatory figure, a king who believes in divine right but who also acknowledges the divinity of his companions. He continually defers to Taji, follows him on his quest, and listens patiently to the opinions of Babbalanja the philosopher, Mohi the historian, and Yoomy the poet. Just after Media's authorship of the scroll is decided, Media redefines his politics in social rather than traditional terms to reveal Melville's deep-seated skepticism of a classless society: "My children's children will be kings; though, haply, called by other titles. Mardi grows fastidious in names: we royalties will humor it" (3:541). Authority of some kind is inevitable, even in a democracy, whether it be what some have called in our time the "Imperial Presidency" or what others inveigh against as corporate power. This is confirmed by the experience of revolutionary Franko (France), which repeatedly fights revolutions only to fall back into monarchy:

"Franko!" cries Babbalanja, "thou wouldst be free; yet the free homage is to the buried ashes of a King; thy first choice, the exaltation of this race. In furious fires, thou burn'st Ludwig's throne; and over thy new-made chieftain's portal, in golden letters print'st—'The Palace of our Lord!'" (3:553)

Even France, which Larry Reynolds rightly cites as Melville's *bête noir* of revolution, refused to abandon its fealty to Napoleon Bonaparte and elected, on December 10, 1848, his grandson Louis as president. As Media's scroll predicts, Louis Napoleon grew as tyrannical as his grandfather, becoming the foe of revolution everywhere and the defender of the Papal State no matter how repressive it became. "Regicides but father slaves" (3:541) Media believes, in a cutting allusion to those self-styled Young Americans who preached freedom and democracy while supporting the Mexican War, the extension of slavery, and compromise with the South. Hypocrisy is as much the bane of liberals as conservatives, democrats as monarchists; neither Guelph nor Ghibelline, as Dante

---

54. *Hawthorne, Melville, and the American Character*, 151.

realized, has a monopoly on virtue, and the author's job is to point out such inconsistencies while striving to find "Truths" beyond the immediate moment. Media's position is not just a lingering paternalism, as Rogin believes,[55] but a principled attack on hypocrites, whom Dante, we recall, placed far beyond redemption deep in the eighth circle of Hell (Canto 23).

In its attempt to balance revolution and tyranny, Media's scroll reveals Melville's detailed knowledge of events in Italy, as a resonant metaphor makes clear: "For, mostly, monarchs are as gemmed bridles upon the world, checking the plungings of a steed from the Pampas" (3:525). During the 1830s and 1840s, Giuseppe Garibaldi was a political exile in South America fighting first to liberate the province of Rio Grande do Sul from Brazil and then to defend the Uruguayan Republic from Brazil and Argentina. In 1846 he won a decisive victory against Argentina and cemented his fame as a successful guerilla warrior, a "steed from the Pampas" whose daring exploits ignited revolutionary imaginations around the world. From this period stem his famous red tunic and gaucho outfit, habiliments that became the symbol of Italian nationalism and made Garibaldi an instantly recognizable, picturesque figure of revolution.[56] After the Palermo rising in January 1848, Garibaldi returned to Italy to join the fight for independence. He arrived in June and offered his sword to King Charles Albert of Piedmont, who he hoped would lead a united Italy against Austria. Garibaldi was ready to check his steed of revolution with the bridle of monarchy and so distinguish his revolutionary aims from the regicidal French, who had by this time toppled their "citizen-king" Louis-Philippe. But Charles Albert only wanted to drive the Austrians from Northern Italy. Fearing Garibaldi's reputation for radicalism, he refused the offer. Garibaldi moved on to Lombardy where he organized an independent guerilla army. When Piedmont lost to Austria at Custoza in August 1848, Garibaldi refused to disband his troops and, under Mazzini's leadership, joined the fight for an Italian republic. The revolution reached Rome in November 1848, the pope fled to Gaeta, and Garibaldi joined those who declared Rome a republic in February 1849. Had Charles accepted Garibaldi's services, Piedmont might have fared better on the battlefield, and monarchs rather than republicans might have led the struggle for Italian nationalism. By refusing to bridle the steed of revolution, Charles Albert abdicated in March 1849 and made it impossible to balance liberty with authority as Media's scroll advocates.[57]

55. *Subversive Genealogy*, 62.
56. Mack Smith, *Garibaldi: A Great Life in Brief* (New York: Alfred A. Knopf, 1956), 24.
57. Dates are from the timeline in Viotti, *Garibaldi,* 218. See also Mack Smith, *Garibaldi,*

UNMASKING THE POPE

American travel accounts of the period, as William Vance has shown, often viewed the papacy as the chief Catholic threat to political and religious liberty in both Italy and the United States, and grounded their position on the abuses, excesses, corruption, and totalitarianism associated with this unique institution.[58] *Mardi's* brief description of Italy in the list of European nations in chapter 145 stresses this association, along with the stereotype of a *dolce far niente* culture:

> the many chiefs of sunny Latianna; minstrel monarchs, full of song and sentiment; fiercer in love than war; glorious bards of freedom: but rendering tribute while they sang;—the priest-king of Vatikanna; his chest marked over with antique tatooings; his crown, a cowl; his rusted scepter swaying over falling towers, and crumbling mounds; full of the superstitious past; askance, eyeing the suspicious time to come. (3:467)

While this description sounds more like Pope Gregory XVI than Pius IX, in the Maramma chapters of *Mardi,* 105–117, Melville explicitly attacks Pius IX in one of the strongest denunciations of the papacy in canonical American fiction. Emboldened by Dante's example of pontifical damnation and American disgust with the pope that characterized the last half of 1848, Melville paints the Papal States in gothic hues and portrays Pio Nono as a cynical, indifferent scion of incest. He concludes by parodying the papal audience which some Americans, despite their Protestant beliefs, considered an obligatory ritual of Italian travel.[59]

Outspoken criticism of religion was not new to Melville, as both *Typee* and *Omoo* illustrated. In *Mardi,* however, Melville joined the chorus of papal critics by overtly satirizing a particular figure, Pope Pius IX, indulging an anti-Catholicism most students of Melville's religion avoid.[60]

32–35.

58. Vance, *America's Rome,* 1:24–40.

59. See, for example, Caroline Kirkland's account of her fifteen-minute visit with Pope Pius IX in June 1848 in *Holidays Abroad* (1849), 2:48–53. Even anti-Catholics like Joel T. Headley bolstered their traveling credentials by basking in the pontifical limelight. Headley was invited to see Pope Gregory XVI but declined because he didn't have the proper clothes: "It was a matter of very little consequence, however, as I had on several occasions been within a few feet of him an hour at a time, and heard him speak, and got, as I supposed, a very good idea of the *MAN*" (*Letters,* 151).

60. In the essay on Melville's religion in *A Companion to Melville Studies,* the word "Catholic" doesn't even occur, nor is it addressed in such books as Stan Goldman, *Melville's Protest Theism: The Hidden and Silent God in* Clarel (DeKalb: Northern Illinois University Press, 1993),

Melville's associations with N. P. Willis, Orville Dewey, and Joel Tyler Headley linked him with writers who by 1845 had all published derisive portraits of the pope, and when he visited Rome in 1856 he sought but did not find the American art collector James Jackson Jarves (15:106) whose *Italian Sights and Papal Principles* (1856) remains one of the period's most vitriolic anti-Catholic publications. While never as obviously anti-Catholic as these writers, Melville's work sometimes reflects their religious biases and reinforces perceptions of Roman Catholic despotism, corruption, sensuousness, and deception, as Jenny Franchot has shown in her analysis of "Benito Cereno" and "The Two Temples."[61]

The Maramma chapters open Book Two of *Mardi,* initiating the narrative's turn toward political allegory. Maramma, a large island in the Mardian archipelago and the residence of Mardi's religious leader, blends an actual Italian region with Dante's imagined Inferno to create a geographical horror that images American prejudice toward Italy and its medieval religious practices, something like Mark Twain's vision of England in *A Connecticut Yankee in King Arthur's Court* (1888). Maremma (as it is actually spelled) is an important agricultural site on the west coast of Tuscany, extending from Cecina in the north to Orbetello in the south, a distance of about seventy miles. Varying in width from ten to fifteen miles, the Maremma is a large irregular tract of low-lying land punctuated by hilltop towns. It enjoyed periods of reclamation under the early Roman emperors but then returned to swampland during the Middle Ages, leading Dante to characterize it as a snake-infested "marsh" (Hell XXV.18–20) and a stinking, "pestilent fen" (Hell XXIX.44–50), clearly a suitable locale for a husband to murder his wife (Purgatory V.128–33). In the nineteenth century travelers were routinely warned of its backward culture, lawlessness, and malarial climate. Knight's *Cyclopedia* (1855) warned that sleeping one night in the Maremma could prove fatal (3:699), and tourists—including Melville in 1857—routinely took steamers from Livorno (Leghorn) to Rome in order to avoid the area. Forsyth's *Travels* painted a grim landscape of the Maremma in 1802, a picture that influenced later descriptions and likely influenced Melville's as well:

> In some parts, the water is brackish and lies lower than the sea: in others, it oozes full of tartar from beds of travertine. At the bottom or on the sides of hills are a multitude of hot springs which form pools, called

---

which stresses Melville's affinities with Judaism. William Potter, *Melville's Clarel*, emphasizes the poem's ecumenism, but even he talks broadly about Christianity rather than Roman Catholicism in particular.

61. *Roads to Rome,* 172–91.

Lagoni. A few of these are said to produce borax: some which are called *fumache,* exhale sulphur; others, called *bulicami,* boil with a mephitic gas. The very air above is only a pool of vapours which sometimes undulate, but seldom flow off. It draws corruption from a rank, unshorn, rotting vegetation, from reptiles and fish both living and dead.

All nature conspires to drive man away from this fatal region; but man will ever return to his bane, if it be well baited. The Casentine peasants still migrate hither in winter to feed their cattle: and here they sow corn, make charcoal, saw wood, cut hoops, and peel cork. When summer returns they decamp, but often too late; for many leave their corpses on the road, or bring home the Maremmian disease. (68)[62]

Forsyth goes on to disparage what culture remains in the godforsaken region: "This country is full of little, local superstitions, and overgrown with monkish faëry. Every ruin is haunted, every spring has its saint, every district maintains its *strega,* or witch" (69). Forsyth's vivid description reinforced popular notions of a degenerate, medieval Italy locked in priestly superstitions and resistant to change, and assumed the status of encyclopedic fact when Longfellow cited Forsyth's passage to gloss Canto XIII of the *Inferno,* Dante and Virgil's journey through a dark forest.[63] In the 1830s Grand Duke Leopold II of Tuscany (mentioned sarcastically as "King Leo" in *Mardi,* 3:353) resumed the ancient Roman reclamation projects and successfully counteracted the region's malaria; yet this goes unmentioned in *Mardi,* either from ignorance or a willful desire to portray Maramma in the worst possible light, the hell on earth that papal misgovernment was creating even as Melville wrote. Melville's Maramma is a true transnational milieu, blending Dante, Forsyth, Italy, and Polynesia to construct an appropriate setting for building on Dante's critique of ecclesiastical abuses to authorize Melville's own depiction of papal corruption and venality. If even the devout Dante placed popes in hell, how much more readily would the Protestant Melville.

When Media, Babbalanja, Yoomy, Mohi, and Taji arrive at Maramma, the island, like war-torn Italy in 1848, is at an economic standstill, and even its agriculture suffers from religious superstition: "'It is not that the soil is unproductive,' said Mohi, 'that these things are so. It is extremely fer-

---

62. Geoffrey Stone, writing from a Roman Catholic point of view, noticed the similarity of Maramma to Maremma and the anti-Catholicism of this section of *Mardi,* but made no connection to Forsyth or Dante (*Melville* [New York: Sheed & Ward, 1949], 95).

63. *The Divine Comedy of Dante Alighieri,* trans. Henry Wadsworth Longfellow [1865]. In *The Writings of Henry Wadsworth Longfellow,* vol. 9 (Cambridge: Houghton Mifflin & Co., 1886), 249.

tile; but the inhabitants say that it would be wrong to make a Bread-fruit orchard of the holy island'" (3:324); hence, as Babbalanja says, Maramma "lies one fertile waste in the lagoon" (3:325), a symbol of great potential negated by the stultifying effects of the church. Entering Maramma is like entering Rome itself. The travelers first encounter a greedy beggar, Pani, who seeks to guide them to Yillah. Rejecting him, they next encounter a huge palm tree overgrown with banyan vines that reminds them of one of the Vatican's most famous statues: "Laocoon-like, sire and sons stood locked in the serpent folds of gnarled, distorted banians" (3:330). They continue through a landscape right out of Forsyth, a dark, slimy fen of "perpetual night" and "poisoned air" filled with emblems of death: "Owls hooted from dead boughs; or, one by one, sailed by on silent pinions; cranes stalked abroad, or brooded in the marshes; adders hissed; bats smote the darkness; ravens croaked; and vampires, fixed on slumbering lizards, fanned the sultry air" (3:331). This is Mardi's Inferno, a blend of Forsyth's Italy and Dante's Hell constructed as a religious-political allegory of papal corruption and presenting an Italy as "priest-ridden" and superstitious as anything conjured by ardent Protestants. "*Hell is in Rome nowadays,*" Joel T. Headley quoted an Italian acquaintance in Rome as saying (*Letters,* 127), a metaphor reified in Melville's ghoulish landscape.

Ensconced in the noxious isle of Maramma is "Hivohitee MDCCCXL-VIII," Melville's caricature of Pope Pius IX.[64] By the time Melville wrote these chapters in the summer of 1848, "Pio Nono" had issued his allocution of April 29 that ended all hopes for a republic and turned American liberals against him. It's difficult to have an audience with Hivohitee, the visitors are told, because he will be invisible for a few days (3:332), that is, as insubstantial as Pio Nono's promises of reform. Moody, haughty, unapproachable, Hivohitee has a reputation for great authority but in reality exercises little of it: "his assumptions of temporal supremacy were but seldom made good by express interference with the secular concerns of the neighboring monarchs; who, by force of arms, were too apt to argue against his claims to authority; however, in theory, they bowed to it" (3:333). Pius IX's refusal to support Charles Albert's war against Austria bent his policies toward those of Ferdinand II of Naples and Leopold II of Tuscany, not to mention the Austrian emperor, neighboring monarchs whose antirepublican sentiments were well known. But what could one expect from the product of 1,847 generations of incest: "The present

---

64. Maxine Moore, *That Lonely Game: Melville, Mardi, and the Almanac* (Columbia: University of Missouri Press, 1975), believes "Hivohitee MDCCCXLVIII" satirizes the Holy Office itself, not any particular pope (146). In the summer of 1848, however, Pius IX was being discussed everywhere, and Melville's caricature seems pointedly aimed at him.

Pontiff's descent was unquestionable; his dignity having been transmitted through none but heirs male; the whole procession of High Priests being the fruit of successive marriages between uterine brother and sister. A conjunction deemed incestuous in some lands; but, here, held the only fit channel for the pure transmission of elevated rank" (3:333). Dripping with sarcasm, these and other passages in *Mardi* render Pius IX a prime example of political cowardice, a hedging, mendacious, hair-splitting representative of Roman Catholic venality.

What Melville does with Pius IX is no worse than what Dante did with Pope Nicholas III, who hangs from his heels in Hell. But where Dante attacked papal excesses, Melville attacks the papacy itself, the whole system that gives one person spiritual authority over another and so denies the "democratic spirit of Christianity." Hivohitee MDCCCXLVIII dwells in an apocalyptic, post-revolutionary landscape of "polluted waters" and woods "haunted by the dismal cawings of crows" on a mountain "Strown over with cinders, [where] the vitreous marl seemed tumbled together, as if belched from a volcano's throat" (3:359). Conventionally a potent icon of revolution, the volcanoes of Maramma are dead, snuffed out by Pius IX's betrayal of republican ideals: surrounding the pontiff's dwelling are "five extinct craters. The air was sultry and still, as if full of spent thunderbolts" (3:359). When Yoomy interviews Hivohitee in his aerial hut, it is so dark the poet can barely see the pontiff:

> "What see you, mortal?" [asks Hivohitee]
> "Chiefly darkness," said Yoomy, wondering at the audacity of the question.
> "I dwell in it. But what else see you, mortal?"
> "The dim gleaming of thy gorget."
> "But that is not me. What else dost thou see?"
> "Nothing."
> "Then thou hast found me out, and seen all! Descend." (3:360–61)

Melville's parodic papal audience presents religion that depends upon pomp, ceremony, ritual, hierarchies, and mystery as no better than superstition. More skeptical than Fuller, Melville follows Headley and Dewey by recognizing the futility of expecting a pope to lead a revolution. The papacy, enshrined in superficial trappings for centuries—the incestuous closed-mindedness of 1,848 generations of popes—lacks the conviction or experience to advocate genuine reform. After he fled Rome in November 1848, Pius IX didn't return until 1850, over six months after the French drove the republicans from Rome. Although *Mardi* was completed before these events, Melville presciently recognized in Pius IX a repetition of the endless cycles of liberty and tyranny that characterized Italian history. The papacy is inherently corrupt, as the images of popes and monarchs inscribed on a rock at the Isle of Fossils reveal: "One's hand was on his stony heart; his other pledged a lord who held a hollow beaker. Another sat, with earnest face beneath a mitred brow. He seemed to whisper in the ear of one who listened trustingly. But on the chest of him who wore the miter, an adder lay, close-coiled in flint" (3:416). Perhaps betraying his Calvinist heritage, or his experiences with unjust authority at sea, or his growing skepticism of all reform, Melville registers the incompatibility of revolution and Roman Catholicism, a position even the enthusiast Fuller finally articulated. In her last dispatch from Italy on January 6, 1850, she wrote: "Not only Jesuitism must go, but the Roman Catholic religion must go. The Pope cannot retain even his spiritual power. The influence of the clergy is too perverting, too foreign to every hope of advancement and health" (321). After 1849, even the most sympathetic and hopeful American supporters of Italy had come round to an anti-Catholic viewpoint.

Mardi's references to Maramma multiply beyond the noxious realm of Hivohitee's island and become a leitmotif of anti-Catholicism. The novel mentions Maramma over a dozen times, at first neutrally, as the abode of religious tradition, but increasingly as a place of "gloom" (619), "persecutions" (623), and even slavery: "Maramma champions it!—I swear it!" cries Nulli, the Calhoun figure (533). Franchot explains that abolitionists characteristically viewed the American South as "Romish," notably in Harriet Beecher Stowe's depiction of Augustine St. Clare in *Uncle Tom's Cabin* (1853), and that Nativist Americans such as Ned Buntline asserted Catholicism was itself simply another form of slavery, a view Franchot finds pervasive in "Benito Cereno."[65] Indeed, "The chronicles of Maramma were full of horrors," says *Mardi*'s narrator (341), horrors as dehumanizing as anything on Simon Legree's plantation: a rebellious prophet, Foni, is defeated and driven into the woods where, years later, he is discovered and slain (341–42); at the temple of Oro (God), a boy avows his personal devotion to Oro but refuses to bow to his image, and is summarily executed (347); idols are manufactured and marketed like any other commodity, and the Pontiff shares in the profits (353), the crime of simony that landed the three popes in Dante's *Hell*. After Mohi offers a history of Alma, the Christ-figure who last appeared on Maramma and inspired its practices, Babbalanja notes the island's divergence from true

65. Franchot, *Roads to Rome*, 103–4, 174.

Christianity: "Nay: take from your chronicles, Mohi, the history of those horrors, one way or other, resulting from the doings of Alma's nominal followers, and your chronicles would not so frequently make mention of blood ... every thing in this isle strengthens my incredulity; I never was so thorough a disbeliever as now" (349). Encrusted with meaningless and inhumane rituals, bereft of respect for the individual believer, corrupted by idolatry and indulgences, and intolerant of all other beliefs (one of Orville Dewey's chief objections to Catholicism), Maramma epitomizes all the vices Americans identified with the Catholic church. "Ah!" says Babbalanja, in a long critique of religious narrowness, "how shall these self-assumed attorneys and vice-gerents be astounded, when they shall see all heaven peopled with heretics and heathens, and all hell nodding over with miters!" (3:428).

THE LESSON OF DANTE

Mardi's anti-Catholicism locates Melville's transnational politics in an American Protestant provincialism that resists the philosophical influence of Dante and blunts the novel's thrust toward universal appeal. *Mardi* attempts to forge a coherent geography of knowledge analogous to Dante's *Commedia,* but in the heated nationalism of 1840s America the task proved impossible. Systematic, cosmic thinking was for the Middle Ages, not the rapidly changing, pragmatic nineteenth century. While he would continue to study the great Tuscan poet all his life and acknowledge the appeal of Catholic ritual and tradition in *Clarel*,[66] Melville could not accompany Dante into Paradise. In *Mardi*'s strongly Dantean chapters on Serenia, where circle imagery derives explicitly from *Paradise,* only the Mardian travelers find refuge. Taji, Melville's alter ego, is too rebellious to accept religious authority yet too isolated from his fellow travelers to construct an alternative. He remains in the Inferno of endless creation and decreation, unable to accept the stasis that accompanies spiritual peace, as his last words suggest: "Hail! Realm of shades!" (3:654). If Taji, the novel, its whole cast of characters, and even the reader become subordinate to an increasingly dominant authorial voice, as Wai Chee Dimock argues,[67] so does Melville himself, whose fecund creativity overpowers

---

66. Vincent Kenny, *Herman Melville's Clarel: A Spiritual Autobiography* (New York: Archon Books, 1973), takes a fairly measured view of Melville's mixed admiration and skepticism toward the Roman Catholic Church in *Clarel* (132–45).

67. *Empire for Liberty,* 67–75. In support of her view, Dimock quotes Richard Brodhead's

his liberal, democratic values. By participating in the parochial politics of anti-Catholicism, he limits his understanding of a truly catholic, universalizing, Dantean art, and distorts Italian antipapalism with American religious prejudices. Such Americanizing of Risorgimento ideology might make the Italian revolution more acceptable in the United States, but it also created intercultural divisions within the United States itself that undermined the nationalist project both Italian and American liberals encouraged. A strong, secular, civic nationalism could never take hold by denying authority altogether, yet that is just where *Mardi* ends, with Taji's individualism thwarting Media's commands.

Nevertheless, Melville had moved far from the narrow, autobiographical rendering of *Typee* and *Omoo,* and was finding ways to meld politics and poetics along classical lines. Just as ideology untransmuted into art would have made Dante little more than a political hack, it would have kept Melville from being little more than a political satirist for *Yankee Doodle*. As Carlylean poet-heroes, however, each writer could make his own literary rules and create a language and form adequate to the complex political vision his times demanded. Writing in Dante's shadow, Melville was willing to risk reviewers' charges of disunity, allegory, political ambiguity, and irreligion in order to achieve the spiritual heights attributed to the *Commedia*. Given the comparable political turmoil of fourteenth-century Florence and antebellum America, cosmopolitan writers such as Dante and Melville would, like the patriots of the Risorgimento, find themselves unable to commit to any one faction and would courageously face the criticism their independence received. The confidence inspired by Dante saved Melville from succumbing to the adverse reviews of *Mardi,* as he indicated in a June 5, 1849 letter to Richard Bentley:

> Besides, the peculiar thoughts & fancies of a Yankee upon politics & other matters could hardly be presumed to delight that class of gentlemen who conduct your leading journals; while the metaphysical ingredients (for want of a better term) of this book, must of course repel some of those who read simply for amusement.—However, it will reach those for whom it is intended; and I have already received assurances that "Mardi," in its higher purposes, has not been written in vain. (14: 131–32)

---

judgment that "the real object of [*Mardi's*] quest is nothing [Melville's] characters seek but the mental world he himself discloses through the act of creating his book" (67). This is the tendency Dimock calls "Author as Monarch," a fusion of literature and politics broadly characteristic of the romantic period in Europe and America.

Caught between the disdain of conservative editors and the resentment of popular audiences, nineteenth-century literary equivalents to Italy's Guelphs and Ghibellines, Melville remained certain that he was on the path to literary immortality taken by Dante, who combined politics with metaphysics to achieve those "higher purposes" that forever elude superficial readers. In its highest purposes—the author's desire for literary freedom and immortality—*Mardi* was as much a quest for salvation as the *Commedia:* salvation from artistic commercialism, British sneers, American puffery, and the low expectations of popular audiences.

Although religion and revolution proved incompatible in Italy in 1848–49, Melville continued his quest for ethical reform balanced between revolutionary demands for individual rights and conservative demands for authority and order. Somewhere between these two lay the deliberate progress articulated in Media's scroll. The new element Melville had to deal with was violent reaction to revolution, a state violence as vicious as anything purveyed by the French mob in 1789. Repression and revolution would characterize the next decade of the Risorgimento, and the scholarly exposure to Italian history Melville gained from Cary's Dante prepared him for dealing with war, terrorism, assassination, foreign intervention, and the most severe political oppression Europe had faced in centuries.

3

Fleeing Revolution

The Rise and Fall of the Roman Republic

> Ah! after all, I find my Italy somewhere, wherever I go.
> —*Redburn* (1849)

> Let us leave the Past, then, to dictate laws to immovable China;
> let us abandon it to the Chinese Legitmists of Europe.
> —*White-Jacket* (1850)

> But in gazing at such scenes, it is all in all what mood you are in; if in the
> Dantean, the devils will occur to you; if in that of Isaiah, the archangels.
> —*Moby-Dick* (1851)

THE EUROPEAN Revolutions that fueled *Mardi*'s globalist political allegory reached their apex when Risorgimento nationalists proclaimed the second Roman Republic on February 9, 1849. The republic's meteoric rise destabilized the American image of Italy and complicated the ideological context of Melville's allusions to Italian and Roman history, making them an ambiguous compound of Margaret Fuller's enthusiasm and King Media's skepticism as the young novelist continued to grope for a politics sufficient to his aesthetics.

Fuller, who was in Rome during the revolution, wrote ten dispatches that appeared in Horace Greeley's liberal *New York Tribune* from January through October 1849, and that pressed Americans to make common cause with Risorgimento patriots and support them privately if not officially:

> How I wish my country would show some noble sympathy when an experience so like her own is going on. Politically she cannot interfere; but formerly when Greece and Poland were struggling, they were at least

aided by private contributions.... It would make me proud to have my country show a religious faith in the progress of ideas, and make some small sacrifice of its own great resources in aid of a sister cause, now.[1]

Recurring to classical iconography, she reported that "The Roman Eagle recommences her flight," a metaphor that meant America was no longer the only second Rome but Rome itself was a second Rome, enacting on European shores the millennial vision previously reserved to the United States.[2] Leonardo Buonomo has noticed how "the transition from the Italian to the American scene in [Fuller's] letters is always swift and effortless" and how intensively she argues that the Risorgimento is driven by "the same animating principle that was at the basis of America's own revolution,"[3] a view that many shared. The *New York Herald* claimed that 90 percent of all Americans supported the Roman Republic, and letters and editorials in New York newspapers generally advocated American recognition of Mazzini's new government.[4] For the first few months of 1849, it seemed as though Italians might prove worthy of political independence and forever dispel the stereotypes of ideological indifference and administrative incompetence that had made them "hypocrites of liberty" in Joseph Forsyth's eyes. Fuller forcefully articulated this hope in her dispatch of May 27, Americanizing and Protestantizing the Risorgimento as never before:

> When I first arrived in Italy, the vast majority of this people had no wish beyond limited monarchies, constitutional governments. They still respected the famous names of the nobility; they despised the priests, but were still fondly attached to the dogmas and ritual of the Roman Catholic Church. It required King Bomba, it required the triple treachery of Charles Albert, it required Pio IX, and the "illustrious Gioberti" [a discredited Roman moderate who advocated an Italian federation under the pope], it required the naturally kind-hearted, but, from the neces-

---

1. *These Sad but Glorious Days,* dispatch of February 20, 1849, 255, 259. Although Secretary of State James Buchanan appointed Lewis Cass chargé d'affaires to revolutionary Rome in January 1849, the Polk administration explicitly forbade official relations. Buchanan and Cass thought the pope would soon be restored, and no Democrat wanted to alienate the growing power of Catholic voters. See Marraro, *American Opinion,* 26, 69–71. Later analysts believed that, had the United States granted official recognition to the Roman Republic, the French would have stayed out and liberal democracy have taken root, but such is the stuff of speculation.

2. Fuller, *These Sad but Glorius Days,* 255.

3. *Backward Glances,* 32. Buonomo credits Italian scholar Rosella Mamoli Zorzi with noticing the intensified Americanness in Fuller's Roman dispatches.

4. Marraro, *American Opinion,* 69, 63–69.

sity of his position, cowardly and false Leopold of Tuscany, it required the vagabond "serene" meannesses of Parma and Modena, the "fatherly" Radetzky [the oppressive Austrian commander-in-chief in northern Italy], and finally the imbecile Louis Bonaparte, "would-be Emperor of France," to convince this people that no transition is possible between the old and the new. *The work is done;* the revolution in Italy is now radical, nor can it stop till Italy become independent and united as a republic. Protestant she already is.[5]

Fuller's version of events in Italy in the spring of 1849 countered Melville's gloomy picture of Maramma and intertwined the historical fates of America and Italy in a heady republican optimism that linked both countries' missions with ancient Rome. Rome was no longer a theoretic historical analogue, but a living lesson for modern, empire-building, republican Americans. The Old World, for a change, seemed to be leading the New.

At the same time, this "radical" shift in Italian politics fed reactionary opinion in the United States among both Irish Catholics and Protestant conservatives. Mazzini's antipapalism drew powerful opposition from Bishop John Hughes who castigated the Italian republicans for their "reign of terror," thus solidifying Irish Catholic opposition to the Risorgimento.[6] New York's Christian Alliance identified Mazzinism with "Red Republicanism," the anarchic, bomb-throwing, populist socialism previously associated with the worst excesses of the French.[7] Although Mazzini was no doctrinaire socialist, his attacks on laissez-faire economics and the unequal distribution of wealth were enough to link him with the "sanguinary schemes" and proletarian violence advocated by Europe's most radical revolutionaries and give American Italophiles pause.[8] While liberty was fine, anarchy was worse, and socialism unthinkable, particularly to the ideologues in Young America. To these Americans, the Italian republicans seemed to be going the way of the French, a view that marginalized Fuller politically and led her friend Hawthorne to consider her,

---

5. Fuller, *These Sad but Glorious Days,* dispatch of May 27, 1849, 278.

6. Marraro, *American Opinion,* 59, in his summary of an article on Hughes in the *New York Herald* of June 27, 1849.

7. Rossi, *Image of America,* 45.

8. For a nuanced assessment of Mazzini's views on socialism, see Mack Smith, *Mazzini,* 196–202. Rossi quotes from an angry letter of 1847 that Margaret Fuller wrote attacking the *London Times* for its reference to "the sanguinary schemes of Mazzini": "to couple the epithet, sanguinary, with the name of Mazzini," Fuller wrote in Mazzini's defense, "would be simply absurd, as to speak of the darkness of light" (*Image of America,* 56).

in Larry Reynolds's words, a "misguided subversive."⁹ When Duyckinck reprinted one of her *Tribune* dispatches in the *Literary World,* he omitted all political commentary, including her references to Mazzini as "a man of genius" and a latter-day Rienzi, the legendary Italian patriot, and published only her descriptions of American painters and sculptors.¹⁰ More indicative of Young American attitudes was a reviewer in the next issue of the *Literary World* who confessed that he "never felt quite at our ease since the Pope went to Gaeta" and found his politics wrestling with his aesthetics: "We are tempted to forget our sympathies with the Progress of Republicanism in Italy, in the weary sadness that comes over us in thinking of the havoc that is making of so much that is grand and venerable; in the desecration of so many shrines sacred to the choicest and most classic of associations; in the destruction of so many invaluable memorials of ancient and modern art and magnificence."¹¹ Once Rome was an actual republic, it no longer fit Arcadian stereotypes. It was Vesuvius in eruption, formerly dormant but now boiling with the potential to bury centuries of papal and foreign oppression in a flood of popular outrage, the kind of revolutionary outburst that would give Melville pause.

Despite the valiant efforts of Garibaldi's legions, the Roman Republic fell to French troops under General Oudinot on, ironically, July 4, 1849. Mazzini had failed to shake his image as a dangerous antipapalist in league with socialist radicals, and Louis Napoleon cannily seized the opportunity to placate conservative Catholic opinion and extend French authority in Italy by supporting the papal party. Italy was once again the tool of the great powers, this time a pawn in the geopolitical maneuvering between Austria and France. The United States delayed recognizing the republic until it was too late, and the rapid collapse of revolutionary movements in France, Austria, Germany, and Hungary made European support impossible. France, now the guarantor of papal power, joined Austria and the Bourbon monarch Ferdinand II of Naples in maintaining foreign domination over Italy and plunging her citizens once more into political servitude. While Mazzini returned to exile in London in 1850, New York City enthusiastically greeted Giuseppe Avezzana and, more quietly, Garibaldi, two other heroes of the Roman Republic.¹² In

9. *European Revolutions,* 76.

10. "American Artists in Italy, &c," *Literary World,* May 26, 1849, 458. For Fuller's original review, which appeared in the May 16, 1849 *Tribune,* see *"These Sad but Glorious Days,"* 260–74. The comparison to Rienzi is on 262 and the characterization of Mazzini is on 264.

11. Rev. L. Mariotti, *Italy, Past and Present,* and Rev. Robert Turnbull, *The Genius of Italy,* June 2, 1849, 474, 473.

12. Rudman, *Italian Nationalism,* 89; Marraro, *American Opinion,* 165–69. Because of the opposition of Archbishop John Hughes and many of New York's Irish Catholics, Garibaldi, an

Italy, however, thousands of republicans were executed or imprisoned. By the end of August 1849 Fuller's *Tribune* dispatches had grown grim, and in November she reported that Marshal Radetzky was indiscriminately flogging men and women in Milan and had applied the bastinado to over four hundred people in Parma, as reaction and repression swept across Italy.[13]

For Melville, more attuned to moral ambiguity than most of his contemporaries, Italy's political oscillations made it a fruitful literary resource. In the convoluted Italian mirror Melville found reflected issues Americans had evaded for their first seventy years: slavery, sectionalism, economic inequities, immigration, anti-Catholicism, ahistoricism, and an emerging class system, with many of these problems particularly visible in Young America's New York City.[14] *Redburn, White-Jacket,* and *Moby-Dick,* more topical novels than his previous three, register this new complexity by making Italy a site where the "Redeemer Nation" topos confronts political and historical reality in an anxious mix of warring ideologies, most famously in the Ahab-Ishmael dichotomy. Absorbed in contemporary events, rapidly written, deliberately realistic, and intensely autobiographical, these three novels reveal the increasing importance of Italy as a metaphorical, even typological resource for Melville's expanding exploration of a more conservative ideology, one that tethers the free-floating Jacksonian individual to the constraints of nation, art, and history. The rise and fall of the second Roman Republic validated the skepticism of Media's scroll; dramatized the fragility of *all* republics, including the United States; and undermined faith in global political progress. Melville was coming to see that no matter how noble the intentions or glorious the rhetoric, republics were not a foreordained final stage of civilization. They were only a stage in some larger, inchoate evolution of nations unforeseen by popular typologies; or worse, the typology might be accurate and America's fate would be similar to Rome's. Through Melville's increasing familiarity with Italian history, art, and current events, Risorgimento Italy emerged in his imagination as a bipolar metaphor for his

---

outspoken antipapalist, declined public recognition. He stayed in New York less than one year, living most of the time on Staten Island at the home of Antonio Meucci, a candlemaker and inventor. Meucci's house is now a museum. Avezzana remained in New York until 1860 when he returned to Italy. New York was beginning to rival London as a refuge for Italian exiles, who continued to arrive in small groups throughout the 1850s. See Amfitheatrof, *Children of Columbus,* 89–104, and Marraro, *American Opinion,* 169–85.

13. Fuller, *"These Sad but Glorious Days,"* 317–18; King, *A History of Italian Unity,* 1:361–66.

14. See, for example, Sean Wilentz, *Chants Democratic: New York City and the Rise of the American Working Class, 1788–1850* (New York: Oxford University Press, 1984), esp. 327–59.

politics: initially it represented the hope of creating an Old World republic to match and validate America's role in the New World; but when it collapsed it revealed the fragility of republican ideals. Like a mirror into the future, the rise and fall of the second Roman Republic exposed the contradictions in American society masked by the millennialist rhetoric of *Redburn, White-Jacket,* and *Moby-Dick* as doubts about the Risorgimento led to doubts about American political idealism as well.

SUBVERSIVE ART IN *REDBURN*

> For who was our father and our mother? Or can we point to any Romulus and Remus for our founders? Our ancestry is lost in the universal paternity; and Caesar and Alfred, St. Paul and Luther, and Homer and Shakspeare are as much ours as Washington, who is as much the world's as our own. We are the heirs of all time, and with all nations we divide our inheritance. On this Western Hemisphere all tribes and people are forming into one federated whole; and there is a future which shall see the estranged children of Adam restored as to the old hearth-stone in Eden. (4:169)

This is the heady millennialism of America as a "Redeemer Nation,"[15] an international refuge and universal savior for Western culture. Precisely because America, unlike Rome, has no fixed originating myth, its telos is equally unfixed, even infinite, allowing it to incorporate not only Roman but all European history, political, religious, and artistic. At the same time, Melville's allusions to Romulus, Remus, and Caesar—rhetorically if not logically the origins of America's genealogy—remind readers that America extends the ancient Roman ideal of a homogeneous world civilization into a timeless future when the world's diverse nationalities will merge into one culture on America's shores. These sentiments are too common in Melville's writing to dismiss as the naive reflections of a youthful narrator or Melville's ironic sallies at Young American chauvinism, as James Duban has argued.[16] They run throughout *White-Jacket* (particularly chap.

---

15. The classic study is Ernest Lee Tuveson, *Redeemer Nation; The Idea of America's Millennial Role* (Chicago: University of Chicago Press, 1968).

16. James Duban, *Melville's Major Fiction: Politics, Theology, and Imagination* (Dekalb: Northern Illinois University Press, 1983). Duban argues that Melville's satire of Vivenzan politics in *Mardi* establishes a norm that exposes the ardent democratic messianism of *Redburn, White-Jacket,* and *Moby-Dick* as deliberate satires. He cites critiques in the *American Whig Review* and numerous passages in Melville's later work, notably the attack on Young America in *Pierre* and the skepti-

36, "Flogging not Necessary"), "Hawthorne and His Mosses," the effusive letters to Hawthorne, and culminate in Ishmael's paean to the "great democratic God" in *Moby-Dick* (117). Yet Duban is right to point out the countercurrents to such liberal optimism that run deep throughout Melville's early works, as I have shown with the scroll in *Mardi;* and as these currents continue to flow in *Redburn,* they swirl and eddy around the fate of Italy.

Melville probably wrote most of *Redburn* in May and June 1849 (4:318–19), the glory days of the Roman Republic when the Mazzinian dream seemed possible and Fuller's most optimistic dispatches were appearing in the *Tribune.* Melville's more cautious view appears strikingly in Carlo, the fifteen-year-old organ-grinder who abruptly enters the narrative in the final chapters. An avatar of Young Italy thrust onto American soil, Carlo allows America to play its redemptive role by ushering him into its New World Eden. At the same time, Carlo remains a stereotype of Arcadian Italy, a handsome, carefree, and charming but impoverished young musician. To these conventional oppositions Melville adds a third, complicating element suggested by analogies between the Risorgimento and the French Revolutions of 1848: he makes Carlo a worker, a representative of what Fuller called the "LABORING CLASSES."[17] As a proletarian and hence a potential rebel, Carlo is an antitype of Masaniello and prefiguration of Billy Budd, an iconic figure who combines the appeal of the smiling, picturesque "beggar boy" with the newer, more frightening specter of the Mazzinian "red republican." At once a figure of desirable assimilation and dangerous otherness, Carlo metonymizes the mixture of hope and fear that characterized Young American perceptions of the Roman Republic.

Carlo is a wholly imagined character: no Italians sailed on the *St. Lawrence,* the merchant ship that took Melville on his first journey abroad in 1839 and inspired *Redburn.*[18] The reviewer in *Holden's Dollar Magazine,* possibly Charles F. Briggs (*Log,* 360), dismissed the entire Carlo episode as rhapsodic "rigmarole about the hand organ at sea,"[19] and to an extent he was right, for Melville fetishizes Carlo in digressively overwrought

---

cism of the *Confidence-Man,* for evidence. Duban performs valuable work in demonstrating the prevalence of antidemocratic opinion during this period, yet underestimates Melville's dialogic technique of expressing contradictory opinions through varied personas and his sensitivity to rapid shifts in national and international politics.

17. Fuller, *"These Sad but Glorious Days,"* dispatch of March 29, 1848, 211.
18. William H. Gilman, *Melville's Early Life and Redburn* (New York: New York University Press, 1951).
19. Hershel Parker and Brian Higgins, eds., *Herman Melville: The Contemporary Reviews* (New York: Cambridge University Press, 1995), 289.

aesthetic terms:

> The head was if any thing small; and heaped with thick clusters of tendril curls, half overhanging the brows and delicate ears, it somehow reminded you of a classic vase, piled up with Falernian foliage.
>
> From the knee downward, the naked leg was beautiful to behold as any lady's arm; so soft and rounded, with infantile ease and grace. His whole figure was free, fine, and indolent; he was such a boy as might have ripened into life in a Neapolitan vineyard; such a boy as gipsies steal in infancy; such a boy as Murillo often painted, when he went among the poor and outcast, for subjects wherewith to captivate the eyes of rank and wealth; such a boy, as only Andalusian beggars are, full of poetry, gushing from every rent. (4:247)

Monstrously introduced with an objectifying definite article "the" rather than the expected personal pronoun "his," Carlo anticipates Hawthorne's Donatello, the child-man who looks uncannily like the Faun of Praxiteles. Both characters are predominantly sensuous yet disturbingly infantilized, androgynous intermixtures of art and nature, myth and reality. Carlo similarly anticipates Billy Budd, an Apollonian "beauty" who is "feminine in purity of natural complexion" and reminds Captain Vere of "a statue of young Adam before the Fall" (48, 50, 94). Both young men are orphans—Billy is a "foundling" and Carlo has "no sire" (52; 4:248)—and both are musically gifted—Billy can sing and Carlo plays a hand organ. Carlo's ancient instrument reminds the impressionable young Wellingborough Redburn of the "old fiddles of Cremona" (4:249) as it produces a huge gamut of sounds ranging from "bubbling brooks," "ten thousand brazen trumpets," and the gush of the Alhambra's "Fountain of Lions," to "goblin sounds" that conjure "Medusa, Hecate, she of Endor, and all the Blocksberg's, demons dire" (4:250). Carlo vitalizes the romantic image of the carefree Italian or Spanish beggar, a figure so commonplace that Fuller casually refers to "Murillo boys in the sun just as usual" in one of her dispatches, trusting her audience to conjure the image.[20] Carlo's youth, beauty, and simple artistic talent, like Billy's, imply a harmless and charming prelapsarian innocence.

Yet beneath the rhapsody lies Melville's coded awareness of recent events in Italy that subvert the Arcadian dream with revolutionary anxiety.

---

20. Fuller, "*These Sad but Glorious Days,*" dispatch of February 20, 1849, 256; see also Vance's discussion of "The Politics of the Picturesque" in *America's Rome,* 2:139–60.

Just as Billy's farewell to the "*Rights-of-Man*" carries loaded political meaning for the *Bellipotent's* officers (49), Carlo's music connotes Mazzinian revolution to the *Highlander's* upper-class English passengers. Forming a rudimentary Catholic brotherhood of the poor, Carlo prefers to play for the steerage passengers, the poor Irish emigrants who compensate him by "furnishing him his meals" (4:261). But when he plays for the wealthy English, presumably all Protestants, they complain to the captain that the "organ was a most wretched affair, and made a horrible din," and show their disgust in the only fashion they know—with money—by rewarding Carlo with "three copper medals of Brittania and her shield—three English pennies" (4:261). While Redburn interprets the low tip as evidence of elitist niggardliness, which it certainly is, readers can discern a political iconography that represents England's failure to offer more than token aid to Sicilian revolutionaries during the early stages of the 1848 rising. After capitulating to demands for a constitution, Ferdinand II reversed course and decided to crush the Sicilian independence movement by brutally bombarding Messina from September 3–7, 1848. The British fleet, which had been supplying the Sicilian rebels under Palmerston's policy of destabilizing potential French allies, stood by and did nothing. This infamous event unleashed the reactionary forces that eventually crushed the Roman Republic and gave Ferdinand II his opprobrious nickname "Bomba," one that Melville remembered when he titled half of his Neapolitan diptych "Naples in the Time of Bomba." Messina capitulated on September 7, 1848, enduring four days of Neapolitan savagery before the English and French imposed an armistice, effectively replaying Nelson's suppression of the Parthenopean Republic in 1799.[21] Nelson's statue in Liverpool had earlier reminded Redburn of American slavery and the city's central role in the slave trade (4:155); the English passengers' condescension toward Carlo suggests similarly racialized prejudices.[22] Significantly, Carlo landed in Liverpool "from a Messina vessel" (4:248), effectively a refugee from King Bomba's counterrevolutionary attacks and British diffidence, the lat-

---

21. For the role of British policy in this event, see King, *A History of Italian Unity*, 1:316–18. Nelson's service on behalf of Ferdinand I, later the first king of the Two Sicilies, has long been considered a blot on his career, and was thoroughly presented as such in Robert Southey's *The Life of Nelson* (1813), a popular biography that Melville used as a source for *Billy Budd* (Sealts, *Melville's Reading*, #481). I discuss this further in chap. 6, 261.

22. Liverpool also had a proud antislavery past in the person of William Roscoe (1753–1831), a banker, historian, and poet whom *Redburn* presents as "the modern Guicciardini of the modern Florence" (148). Vigorously antislavery, Roscoe's *Wrongs of Africa* (1787–88) attacked Liverpool's complicity in the slave trade. By comparing him to Francesco Guicciardini, author of *Storia d'Italia* (1561; not translated until 1859), Melville draws a tenuous link between Italy's struggle for nationhood and the abolitionist movement. This association strengthened during the Civil War.

ter imaged here by the pathetic three-penny tip. As a picturesque beggar embellishing Melville's experience aboard the *St. Lawrence* in 1839, Carlo typifies romantic Italy; but as a symbolic character imagined in the spring of 1849 when Melville wrote the book, Carlo represents revolutionary movements that drove Louis-Philippe and Pius IX from power, the brutal reaction of Naples's despotic "King Bomba," and the refusal of ostensibly well-meaning European governments to support Italian liberation.

Carlo, like many Italian refugees before him, finally arrives in New York harbor and discovers a new transcultural identity. Gazing into the waters off the Battery, like Ishmael in the opening chapter of *Moby-Dick*, Carlo finds mirrored his inner desires: "This America's skies must be down in the sea; for, looking down in this water, I behold what, in Italy, we also behold overhead. Ah! after all, I find my Italy somewhere, wherever I go. I even found it in rainy Liverpool" (4:298–99). He goes ashore playing "Hail Columbia!" to pay for his passage from ship to dock (4:301), immediately exhibiting the cultural adaptability America encourages and suggesting a successful future for this remnant of Italy, whether viewed as artistic wonder, economic entrepreneur, or political exile. A nascent cosmopolitan, Carlo seemingly validates America's redemptive role and links its fate with the "Young Italy" of Fuller and Mazzini, a happy ending for all.

In such comforting confirmation of messianic progressivism, however, Melville rests uneasy, for Carlo images a heightened class consciousness and renewed Anglophobia that disturbs Italian stereotypes and American national identity. On the surface an ideal immigrant, a resourceful and engaging young man ready to accommodate himself to American ideals of self-reliance, he is nevertheless a far cry from Foresti, the educated exile from northern Italy who became a professor at Columbia. He is, rather, a poor Sicilian refugee who, along with the debilitated and impoverished Irish emigrants aboard the *Highlander*, portends the demise of Anglo-Dutch Protestant hegemony in New York and New England. Hawthorne recognized this when he translated Carlo into the disruptive organ-grinder who plays outside the decaying Pyncheon mansion in *The House of the Seven Gables* (1851). Clifford Pyncheon's initial delight in the organ-grinder and his monkey turns to tears when he realizes what the pair represents: a tawdry and invasive commercialism in a society rapidly shifting from a homogeneous Yankee aristocracy to an ethnically heterogeneous plebeianism (chap. 11). The picturesque, viewed up close, quickly becomes the "povertiresque" as Melville realized in *Pierre* where he coined the word in 1852 (7:276). The povertiresque's social and political ramifications render figures like Carlo a wedge for religious and social change in America. As one of the "LABORING CLASSES," Carlo embodies the revolutionary potential William L. Vance and Theodore E. Stebbins, Jr., have deciphered in Martin Johnson Heade's painting *Roman Newsboys* (1848) in which two seemingly innocent boys stand before a wall and distribute papers. Only close inspection reveals that the wall is covered with revolutionary graffiti and the papers are incendiary pamphlets supporting revolution, iconography that gives a new and disturbing meaning to the contented "Murillo boys" of genre painting.[23] When Redburn was in Liverpool, he compared dockside con-men to "Italian assassins" (194). Might Carlo revert to such behavior in the mean streets of New York? Revolutions, even failed ones, have consequences, here the creation of displaced persons with the potential to reshape America in their own foreign image. As a deeply problematic figure for Americans, Carlo—a surrogate for the Roman Republic, Catholicism, working-class revolution, and changing ethnic identities—suggests that politics, religion, class, and nationality, all contentious issues in Melville's New York, challenge America's idealized role as a "Redeemer Nation."

FLOGGING ROMAN HISTORY TO DEATH

The allegorized political tensions of *Mardi* and *Redburn* assume reality in *White-Jacket,* animated by Melville's impassioned attack on flogging in the US Navy, an issue that resonated with Risorgimento democrats as well as American sailors. John Lockwood's articles in the 1849 *Democratic Review,* one of which Melville may have read while writing *White-Jacket* (5:421), reignited this longstanding debate, and it appeared the same month that Marshal Radetzky began flogging in Milan and Charles Louis, duke of Parma, initiated the "reign of the lash" and even whipped a servant to death for jesting about his infant son.[24] Against this tide of cruelty, Melville opposed the combined authority of the Bible and Roman law, linking Christianity and paganism in a virtuous alliance against present vice. Wellingborough Redburn initiates this connection when, observing the well-trained horses that pull trucks along the Liverpool docks, he admires their size, power, and dignity: "Thou shalt not lay stripes upon these Roman citizens; for their docility is such, they are guided without rein or

---

23. Vance, *America's Rome,* 2:126, fig. 1; Stebbins, *The Life and Work of Martin Johnson Heade: A Critical Analysis and Catalogue Raisonné* (New Haven, CT: Yale University Press, 2000), 10–11.

24. King, *History of Italian Unity,* 1:375, 378. Fuller reported on these atrocities in her dispatch of November 15, 1849, but it was not published in the *Tribune* until January 9, 1850 (*"These Sad but Glorious Days,"* 316–18).

lash; they go or come, halt or march on, at a whisper" (4:197). Melville's specific source is Acts 22:25 where Paul claims Roman citizenship to avoid a beating. As horses, the working-class identity of the "Roman citizens" is clear, and their docility links them, albeit unceremoniously, with the typical loyal sailor. In *White-Jacket,* Melville repeats Paul's injunction as a question in his powerful chapter on "The Evils of Flogging": "Is it lawful for you to scourge a man that is a Roman? asks the intrepid Apostle, well knowing, as a Roman citizen, that it was not. And now, eighteen hundred years after, is it lawful for you, my countrymen, to scourge a man that is an American? to scourge him round the world in your frigates?" (5:142). By insistently applying naval vernacular to the *Neversink*'s crew, repeatedly calling them "the people," Melville universalizes flogging as a symbol of tyranny and raises the larger question common to all frustrated republicans after 1849: "How shall the people prevail?"

Melville's answer lay not in the revolutionary idealism and violence of the second Roman Republic, but in his moderate revolutionary figure Jack Chase, a literate political cosmopolite who has "sailed with lords and marquises for captains" (5:16) yet is deeply committed to republican ideals, having once deserted in order to join a revolution in Peru: "Though bowing to naval discipline afloat; yet, ashore, he was a stickler for the Rights of Man, and the liberties of the world" (5:17). When Captain Claret considers reneging on his promise of shore leave at Rio, Jack takes up the cause of the crew by assuming the role of Cola di Rienzi (1313–1354), the charismatic Roman revolutionary who led a bloodless coup in 1344 against the city's nobles: "I'm your tribune, boys; I'm your Rienzi" (5:225), he cries, as he counsels patience. The next day liberty is granted, a modest concession that reinforces Jack's leadership yet keeps him within the bounds of "naval discipline," unlike the historical Rienzi who ultimately overreached and was destroyed.[25] Maligned by Gibbon in *The Decline and Fall of the Roman Empire* and by Mary Mitford in her play, *The Tragedy of Rienzi* (1828), Rienzi was sympathetically portrayed in Bulwer-Lytton's popular historical romance of 1835, the version of Rienzi's life that Jack, a great reader of Bulwer (5:14), seems to follow. "Every person who reads at all will read Rienzi," wrote Poe in an uncharacteristically laudatory review, "and indeed the book is already in the hands of

---

25. Rienzi began as a moderate, allying himself with Pope Clement VI and claiming he would reestablish Rome's former glory. After the nobles left in disarray, Rienzi became dictator, a true tribune of the people, yet his arrogance and extravagance quickly alienated him from the pope and he left Rome only a few months after his coup. With a new pope's blessing, he reentered Rome ten years later in 1354, but his cruelty and imposition of high taxes soon antagonized the people and a mob murdered him within two months.

many millions of people."²⁶ Deliberately setting out to rehabilitate Rienzi, Bulwer explicitly admitted that he was "vain, ostentatious, and imprudent—always an enthusiast—often a fanatic; but his very faults had greatness of soul, and his very fanaticism at once supported his enthusiastic daring, and proved his earnest honesty."²⁷ It is precisely such "greatness of soul" in Jack that led Melville to dedicate *Billy Budd* to "that great heart" in 1891 (42). And it was just such sympathy that Fuller found missing in an American friend when they heard the second Roman Republic proclaimed: "I longed to see in some answering glance a spark of Rienzi, a little of that soul which made my country what she is"—but her companion remains "impassive."²⁸ As a latter-day Rienzi, Chase exhibits that "spark of Rienzi" without bursting into revolutionary flame, and always stops short of overturning the greater rule of "naval discipline."

Chase's moderation plays a key role in the novel's central flogging scene, "The Great Massacre of the Beards" (chaps. 85–87). During the long voyage "the people" have allowed their beards to grow to outrageous lengths, and Captain Claret, hewing to naval regulations, demands they all be trimmed. With more than a hint of sarcasm that distinguishes him from the ordinary seaman, White-Jacket makes fatuous comparisons to the St. Bartholomew's Day Massacre, the Sicilian Vespers (355), and the "mutiny of the Nore" (357), exaggerating the issue to the point of humorous absurdity: "Train your guns inboard, let the marines fix their bayonets, let the officers draw their swords; we *will not* let our beards be reaped—the last insult inflicted upon a vanquished foe in the East!" (5:357). The men refuse and actually instigate an "incipient mutiny" that is only quelled when Mad Jack, the one officer the men admire, leaps into the "mob" and cajoles them out of their anger (5:358). Mad Jack's ability to "wink at transgression" reminds White-Jacket of Caesar and Germanicus, Roman leaders confident of their men's essential loyalty and their own established authority (5:359). The next day, the beards are dutifully shorn, including Jack Chase's, for "in his cooler moments, Jack was a wise man; he at last deemed it but wisdom to succumb" (5:360). Just as Lieutenant Jack embodies wise Roman authority, even though he is "a bit of a tyrant," so Sailor Jack displays pragmatic Roman loyalty even though he is (like Rienzi) "a little bit of a dictator" (5:34, 15). The two

26. Poe, *Essays and Reviews*, 144; review of *Rienzi, The Last of the Tribunes, Southern Literary Messenger*, February 1836.
27. Bulwer, *Rienzi*, ed. E. H. Blakeney (New York: E. P. Dutton & Co., 1911), 440. One nineteenth-century reviewer evidently had Bulwer in mind when he offered Rienzi as an exemplary forebear of republicanism: see "Review of *History of the Italian Republics*," 160.
28. *These Sad but Glorious Days*, 257.

Jacks share more than their first names: they both recognize that social order is more important than either inflexible laws or individual desires, and have the "wisdom" to bend rules in order to preserve the nautical commonwealth. They model the strength of ancient Rome, a less ideologically driven and more pragmatic acceptance of gradualism, political difference, and social conservatism, compromises the Roman Republic of 1849 refused to make.[29]

True radicalism has a place in *White-Jacket,* however, in the person of John Ushant, the grizzled old Captain of the Forecastle. Along with a few of the oldest tars, Ushant refuses to shave his beard, a principled stand that should have shamed Captain Claret to concede. Instead, Claret's non-Roman inflexibility reveals him as a "Scythian," a barbarian, for "as the Roman student well knows, the august Senators themselves, seated in the Senate-house, on the majestic hill of the Capitol, had their holy beards tweaked by the insolent chief of the Goths" (5:363). The bearded sailors assume senatorial stature while Claret lapses into a Gothic chieftain tweaking sanctified beards. After all the tars but Ushant submit to shaving, Claret throws the old man in the brig and the next day administers twelve lashes, symbolically violating Roman law, the code of Justinian (5:145). Claret's recourse to flogging identifies him topically with Austrian tyrants like Radetzky, and undermines both his natural merit and his legal authority. Jack Chase almost intervenes but thinks better of it and watches while Ushant submits. The lashes have no effect on Ushant's indomitable spirit, and after the punishment is complete he "only bowed over his head, and stood as the Dying Gladiator lies" (5:366).

Ushant's passive resistance conflates art, history, and politics in one powerful aesthetic metaphor of personal rebellion. One of the most famous statues in the world, *The Dying Gladiator* (fig. 7) had a political history that made it an apt symbol of Italian nationalism. Originally placed in the Capitoline Museum in the 1730s, it was removed to Paris by Napoleon's armies in 1798 and then restored to Rome in 1816 and displayed in its own room.

In *Childe Harold's Pilgrimage* Byron captured the *Gladiator*'s essential meaning for the nineteenth century, rendering the statue a symbol of the common man's noble suffering under tyranny:

---

29. The counterrevolution in Naples succeeded because the lowest class, the *lazzaroni,* supported Ferdinand II and were willing to march on Rome to restore the pope. Elsewhere, class conflict, regional jealousies, and religious disputes fractured Italian unity and drove frightened peasants into the arms of their traditional monarchs (Beales and Biagini, *Risorgimento,* 96–99).

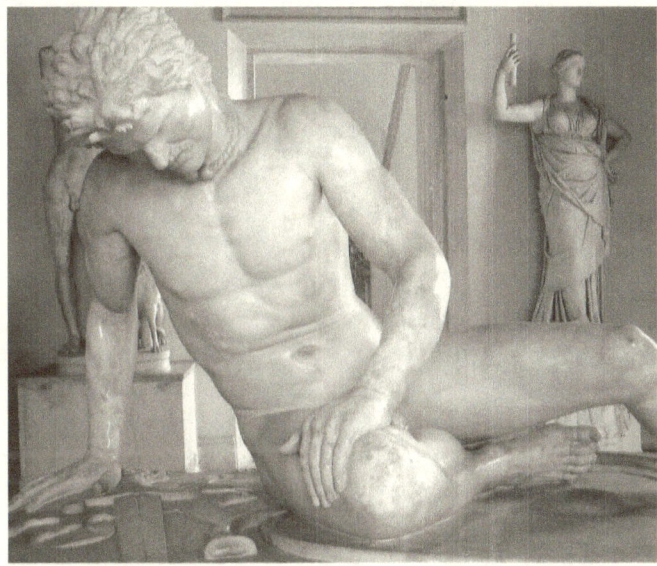

Figure 7. The Dying Gladiator. Capitoline Museum, Rome. Third century BCE. Marble.

I see before me the Gladiator lie:
He leans upon his hand—his manly brow
Consents to death, but conquers agony,
And his drooped head sinks gradually low—
And through his side the last drops, ebbing slow
From the red gash, fall heavy, one by one,
Like the first of a thunder-shower; and now
The arena swims around him—he is gone,
Ere ceased the inhuman shout which hailed the wretch who won.

He heard it, but he heeded not—his eyes
Were with his heart—and that was far away;
He recked not of the life he lost nor prize,
But where his rude hut by the Danube lay—
There were his young barbarians all at play,
There was their Dacian mother—he, their sire,
Butchered to make a Roman holiday—
All this rushed with his blood—Shall he expire
And unavenged?—Arise! ye Goths, and glut your ire![30]

30. *Selected Poetry,* Canto IV, stanzas 140 and 141, 147.

Inspired by a moonlit visit to the Colosseum where such gladiators died, Byron's lines merge domesticity with revolutionary vengeance in a powerful appeal to republican virtue that molded American reaction to the statue. Such popular travel writers as Joel Tyler Headley and George Stillman Hillard referenced these stanzas, as did the Murray guidebook Melville used in 1857.[31] Headley and Hillard elided Byron's final call to revolt, a moral too anarchic for their American audiences, especially when the exact nature of the *Gladiator*'s foe was uncertain; instead, they stressed the statue's noble image of suffering humanity. Orville Dewey too became "a convert entirely to the common opinion about the Dying Gladiator," namely that it shows "the triumph of mind over the sinkings of nature in its last hour" and invited respect rather than pity, admiration rather than sympathy.[32] And even Childe Harold backs away from proletarian anger when the moon rises over the Colosseum and creates a "magic circle" that hallows the mighty ruin: "Heroes have trod this spot—'tis on their dust ye tread" (4.CXLIV.8–9).

Melville followed this convention in his 1857 lecture on "Statues in Rome" when he expresses his compassion for the Dying Gladiator and then quotes Byron's most often-cited lines, "where his rude hut by the Danube lay / *There* were his young barbarians all at play" (9:405), bringing the ancient spectacle into the sentimental and religious economy of his audience: "Some hearts were there that felt the horror as keenly as any of us would have felt it," Melville continues. "None but a gentle heart could have conceived the idea of the Dying Gladiator, and he was Christian in all but the name" (9:405). Like the *Dying Gladiator,* Christian endurance not revolutionary ideology ennobles John Ushant, a nonviolent passivity that legitimates resistance to unjust authority much as Thoreau argues in "Civil Disobedience." Ushant's name is not only a pun on "you shan't," but also the name of a famous maritime landmark, the Isle d'Ouessant (pronounced and spelled "Ushant" by the English) off the western tip of Brittany that marks the entrance to the English Channel. Like the landmark and the Dying Gladiator's supposed final thoughts Ushant's passive rebellion leads home and makes him a domesticated, sentimental icon of universally suffering humanity beset by tyrannical authorities.

Yet as in the Risorgimento, such oppositions are not clear-cut. *The Dying Gladiator* had been a contested site of political, aesthetic, and ethi-

31. Headley, *Letters from Italy,* 149; Hillard, *Six Months in Italy,* 181–83; *A Handbook of Rome and Its Environs,* 5th ed. (London: John Murray, 1858), 232. Hillard bases his whole reaction to the statue on Byron's characterization of the gladiator as a "husband and father" (182), a purely subjective association.

32. Dewey, *The Old World and the New,* 99, 100.

cal interpretation since the seventeenth century, a popularly known fact reflected in the statue's alternate title, *The Dying Gaul*. Headley's remarks reveal this uncertainty along with the American preference for a sentimental reading:

> I care not whether it be a fancy piece, or a slave, or a Gallic herald, or a dying gladiator. There he lies dying—dying from a wound a foe has given him—dying too, innocent. His whole expression tells of a man who fought from necessity, not will. There is no anger in it, but the reverse; none of the fierce passions that kindle in the human face when foe meets foe. The whole countenance is beyond expression mournful. (Letters, 149)[33]

More is at stake here for Melville than art historians' quibbles. If the statue portrays a gladiator, the dying figure is the plaything of empire. If he is a "Goth" with "barbarian" children, as Byron styled him, he is no Roman and *can* be flogged, just like Ushant. If he is a slave, he becomes a disturbing reminder of American chattel slavery, still subject to the lash. But if he is a Gaul serving in the Roman legions, he could be either an unwilling conscript or a heroic volunteer, either a victim or defender of empire. Edwin Forrest chose the former interpretation when he assumed the statue's pose in the death scene of *Spartacus*, a popular play valorizing servile rebellion.[34] Eschewing sentimentalism and Christian resignation, Forrest exploited the statue's revolutionary implications as he brought Roman iconography alive to working-class audiences and deployed classical allusions for democratic aims.

Melville's seemingly offhanded allusion to *The Dying Gladiator* vexes the scene's politics and empowers the contemporary reach of Roman allusions. Claret may be a crude and ruthless martinet, yet White-Jacket defends him from the charge of unusual cruelty. Most of the sailors, White-Jacket believes, consider him a "lenient officer" (5:367) and, while

---

33. Vance, *America's Rome*, comments at length on the conflict "between historical factuality and transcendent beauty" in American reactions to Roman statuary (1:189ff). For the statue's provenance and various meanings, see "Dying Gladiator" in *Taste and the Antique: The Lure of Classical Sculpture 1500–1900*, ed. Francis Haskell and Nicholas Penny (New Haven, CT: Yale University Press, 1981), 224–27. For a summary of the debate in sources closer to Melville's time, see Robert Ball, "On the Dying Gladiator," *Royal Irish Academy, Proceedings* 6 (1853/1857): 152–54, or Theodore Lyman, "The Statue Called the Dying Gladiator," *Old and New* 2 (December 1870): 718–28. In a letter of 1881 Richard Henry Dana mentioned yet another current interpretation, that the statue portrayed "only some stray Gaul who had committed suicide to prevent falling into slavery" (quoted in Brooks, *Dream of Arcadia*, 19n).

34. "The Drama," *Literary World*, April 10, 1847, 234.

they are indignant at Ushant's flogging, see no good reason to denounce it (5:369). Authority has its prerogatives, and crews must obey their captains. Moreover, risking mutiny over something as trivial as a beard seems a foolish way to defend "manhood," for beards signify war while clean-shaven chins signify peace (5:368), and Melville can hardly be called an apostle of war.[35] Ushant's beard flows with "a Gothic venerableness" (5:363), making him as non-Roman as Claret, and White-Jacket's earlier contrast between neat and unkempt beards makes them symbolize everything from royalty to savagery (5:354). As political icons, they carry uncertain, even opposite meanings. After his flogging Ushant persists in muttering against Captain Claret, who immediately breaks him from Captain of the Forecastle to common seaman, effectively ending Ushant's military career and political effectiveness as a principled model to young sailors. Chase, with his combination of nautical skill, intellect, judgment, learning, and Rienzi-like charisma, follows a pragmatic course that leaves him both a heroic figure to the sailors and Captain of the Maintop, an important office that positions him to effect gradual political change from within. The *Neversink* may sail under the American Articles of War, but true leadership comes from flexible, quick-thinking pragmatists like Mad Jack and Jack Chase, men who adapt their decisions to the circumstances. Stubborn idealists like Claret and Ushant, two "barbarians" at the antipodes of authority and rebellion, are doomed to constant conflict.

Class, then, is no sure marker of *civitas*. White-Jacket points us this way early on when he defends naval discipline by contrasting it to aristocratic anarchy: "Were it not for these regulations a man-of-war's crew would be nothing but a mob, more ungovernable stripping the canvass in a gale than Lord George Gordon's tearing down the lofty house of Lord Mansfield" (5:9). In 1780 Gordon led riots against new legislation moderating strictures against England's Roman Catholics, and during the riots, Lord Chief Justice Mansfield's house was burnt. Melville surely remembered that George Gordon was Byron's father, making Byron's call for revolution—"Arise, ye Goths!"—as inappropriate as his father's reactionary call for overturning the toleration acts. All classes are capable of lawless acts, whether in the name of personal desires or political principles, and can be manipulated into rebellion by demagogues from either the patrician or plebian ends of the social spectrum.

---

35. "Melville's passion against war was a great dynamic in his imagination and a main shaping force in his art" (Joyce Sparer Adler, *War in Melville's Imagination* [New York: New York University Press, 1981], 3).

Again Melville turns to Jack Chase and Roman example to bridge the gap between classes and find a third way of creating social order. Chase attends to Lemsford, the ship's sailor-poet, "like Mecænas listening to Virgil, with a book of the Æneid in his hand" (5:41), replicating a noble Roman collaboration between a wealthy politician and an epic poet. Lemsford teaches Jack to distinguish between "the public," "the addle-pated mob and rabble" that fails to appreciate true art, and "the people," the ordinary, independent-minded individuals who follow their hearts rather than the opinions of society. "The public and the people!" ponders Jack; "Ay, ay, my lads, let us hate the one and cleave to the other" (5:192). This is the distinction that drove Melville and Duyckinck to sign the Macready petition that defended the refined acting at the Astor Place Opera House against the working-class bombast of Edwin Forrest at the Bowery Theater and led to a riot that cost twenty-two lives.[36] However Whiggish it sounds today, this distinction grows increasingly important in Melville's political thinking and draws sustenance from the example of Italian history. Mobs represent the worst of the public, and republics that would prosper, as King Media argued and Mazzini failed to recognize, must deny them power. For all of Ushant's sentimental appeal, he is finally a dangerous and unstabilizing figure whose personal desires threaten legitimate authority. Whereas Ushant's republican principles end with his chin, Chase's extend to all oppressed humanity, and he acts upon them with restraint and judgment. *The Dying Gladiator* is no model for political action. An abject figure, he is as dead as Mazzini's and Fuller's dream of a second Roman Republic. The times demanded a more pragmatic approach to the vexing issues of liberty and authority, and in the coming months Melville would discover even more resources in Italian history and art to address them.

THE RISORGIMENTO CONTEXT OF *MOBY-DICK*

Melville wrote his greatest novel in the shadow of autocratic reaction abroad. The restoration of monarchs in Italy, particularly the reaccession of Pope Pius IX in April 1850, set before Americans concrete images of illegitimate authority, persistent reminders of both the failure of revolution and the need for continued struggle, and prodded cautious Young Ameri-

---

36. Dennis Berthold, "Class Acts: The Astor Place Riots and Melville's 'The Two Temples,'" *American Literature* 71 (September 1999): 429–32.

cans like Evert Duyckinck to take more sympathetic notice of Italy's woes. Ferdinand II's repression was so harsh that William H. Gladstone famously declared that at Naples "the negation of God was erected into a system of government," while republican sympathizers in England consolidated their support by forming the Society for the Friends of Italy, which included many literary figures familiar to Melville such as Leigh Hunt, Walter Savage Landor, playwright Douglass Jerrold, and actor William Charles Macready.[37] Melville visited England in late 1849 and hoped to continue on to Italy, but when he failed to obtain an advance for *White-Jacket* he reluctantly shortened his trip: "Bad news enough," he wrote in his journal on November 17, "I shall not see Rome—I'm floored" (15:20).[38] He did, however, breakfast twice with England's most famous friend of Italy, Samuel Rogers, and their conversation could have touched on the fall of the Roman Republic and the plight of Risorgimento exiles.[39] By the time Melville returned to America in February 1850, the mood had turned angry, as John Greenleaf Whittier, William Cullen Bryant, and other poets denounced Neapolitan repression and the *Literary World* opened its 1850 volume with a poem by John Reuben Thompson condemning France for its part in destroying the second Roman Republic:

> How shall we blush for the Republic, France,
> That she among the spoilers should appear!
> Who has not shed the sympathizing tear
> For Freedom stifled in Rienzi's home,
> That men who boast their liberty should rear

---

37. For the reaction, see King, *History of Italian Unity*, 1:361–84; for Gladstone, see W. E. Gladstone, *Two Letters to the Earl of Aberdeen on the State Prosecutions of the Neapolitan Government* (1851), as cited in Marraro, *American Opinion*, 102. Gladstone's letter was widely circulated and his charges were corroborated by such American visitors as Benjamin Silliman and John Van Schaick Lansing Pruyn, a Melville family acquaintance (and perhaps a distant relative) from Albany (Marraro, 103–5). For the English Friends of Italy, see Rudman, *Italian Nationalism*, 97.

38. Around September 12, 1849, Melville put Evert Duyckinck "all in a flutter" by proposing "a cheap adventurous flying tour of eight months, compassing Rome!" that would include Evert's brother George, who had been in Paris during the 1848 revolutions and loaned Melville *Murray's Guidebooks to Northern and Central Italy* for the trip (*Log*, 313 and Sealts, *Melville's Reading*, #s 375, 377; for George's Parisian visit, see Reynolds, *European Revolutions*, 7–10).

39. Rudman, *Italian Nationalism*, 189. Samuel Rogers supported the Dante scholarship of Dante Gabriel Rossetti's father, Gabriele Rossetti, a refugee from the 1820 revolutions who helped Henry Cary with his Dante translation. Mazzini himself attended some of Rogers's breakfasts and praised his grasp of the Italian situation (Maura O'Connor, *Romance of Italy*, 72). Thirteen years later Melville confirmed his appreciation for Rogers in a marginal note defending him from William Hazlitt's attack on his poetry: "Rogers, tho' no genius, was a painstaking man of talent who has written some good things. 'Italy' is an interesting book to every person of taste" (15:368n).

Their frowning guns to shatter arch and dome
Upon the sacred hills of everlasting Rome?[40]

The next issue reprinted "Nightfall in Hungary," a moving poem by Anne C. Lynch condemning Austrian oppression, and a report on conditions in Naples made the connection between art and politics explicit: "The government, not content with putting down literature, is persecuting authors." In April appeared "Lines on the Late Carnival at Rome" by Christopher P. Cranch, a satiric verse predicting more revolutionary strife for Italy and using imagery Melville had employed in *Mardi:* "Under the thrones a volcano / Moans, not in vain—and the hour must come when the forces electric, / Justice, and Truth, and Freedom, no longer can slumber inactive."[41] This image of southern Italy endured until 1859 when Melville alluded familiarly to "the miseries of government" at Naples in his lecture "Traveling" (9:422).

English and American sympathies for the Risorgimento fused in June and July 1851 when the *Literary World* lived up to its name and reprinted generous excerpts from Elizabeth Barrett Browning's moving political eulogy "Casa Guidi Windows," a long poem that recounts in two parts the inspiring events of 1848 and the dismal reaction that followed in 1849. The Brownings moved to Florence in 1847 and observed firsthand the euphoria when the Grand Duke granted the people civic freedoms and the despair when he withdrew them, a betrayal that the *Literary World* illustrated with two paired quotations from "Casa Guidi Windows." The first, which the reviewer titled "Freedom's Hopeful Day," describes the people's joyful procession to the Pitti Palace to thank the duke for instituting the National Guard on September 4, 1847, the first step toward granting a constitution; the second, titled "The Return of the Grand Duke," bitterly recounts Leopold II's entry into Florence on July 28, 1849, accompanied by thousands of occupying Austrian troops. These passages show, writes the reviewer with a shade of optimism, "the fair and active morning of 1848 sinking into the heavy lethargic noon of 1851; but it is not evening or night yet." Nevertheless, the reviewer finds "Dantesque foot-prints throughout the poem," a moral darkness that leads him to compare Margaret Fuller's untimely death in 1850 to Anna Garibaldi's

---

40. "A Retrospect of 1849," *Literary World,* January 5, 1850, 14. Thompson was the editor of the *Southern Literary Messenger.* For Bryant and Whittier, see Peterson, "Echoes of the Italian Risorgimento," passim.

41. "Nightfall in Hungary," January 12, 1850, 37; report on Naples, January 12, 1850, 40; "Lines on the Late Carnival at Rome," April 13, 1850, 376.

death in the retreat from Rome.⁴² In a "second notice" a few weeks later the reviewer—perhaps Tuckerman—published additional excerpts praising Italian art and nature and concluded that "We all love Italy. That northern love of Italy—it is America's too."⁴³ Years later, when Melville marked his personal copy of "Casa Guidi Windows," he triple-checked an authorial footnote that underscored, like the two-part structure of the poem itself, the dizzying changes in Italy between 1849 and 1851: "The event breaks in upon the meditation, and is too fast for prophecy in these strange times—E.B.B."⁴⁴

Despite reprinting such long excerpts from Browning's aggressively political poem, Duyckinck's journal remained moderate. The reviews omit passages condemning the pope, linking Dante with the revolutionaries, and reproaching Italians for not following the example of Brutus by assassinating tyrants. More telling, they avoid lines that compare American slavery and Italian oppression. Browning wrote that "the slave's despair / Has dulled his helpless miserable brain / And left him blank beneath the freeman's whip / To sing and laugh out idiocies of pain" (Part II:393–96), and asked "No mercy for the slave, America?" (II:646),⁴⁵ yet the genteel Young Americans at the *Literary World* omitted these challenging comparisons, tilting its politics toward the status quo. After the fall of the Roman Republic, compromise was the order of the day in both the United States and Italy, as the Compromise of 1850 accommodated the slavocracy while canny diplomats like Camillo Benso di Cavour of Piedmont-Sardinia advocated parliamentary monarchy and federalism as the best hope for Italian independence. With their revolutionary leaders in exile or in prison, many Italians began to give national unity priority over republican governance, and even Foresti began to see a constitutional monarchy as the most realistic way to unify his homeland.⁴⁶ Repressing his anger with King Bomba, the Quaker Whittier counseled patience and nonviolence by advising incarcerated rebels to "share / Pellico's faith, Foresti's strength to bear / Years of unutterable torment, stern and still, /

---

42. "Casa Guidi Windows," *Literary World,* June 21, 1851, 491, 492; July 5, 1851, 7.

43. "Mrs. Browning's Italian Poem," *Literary World,* July 5, 1851, 7.

44. Cowen, *Melville's Marginalia,* 1:366. Melville acquired Barrett Browning's *Poems* (1860) in 1864 (Sealts #93), a complete edition that included "Casa Guidi Windows." He knew of her work at least since August 1850 when Cornelius Mathews gave Elizabeth Melville a signed manuscript copy of Browning's "The Cry of the Human" (1842), a universal appeal for sympathy toward impoverished humanity (Sealts, *Melville's Reading,* #92).

45. *The Complete Poetical Works of Elizabeth Barrett Browning,* ed. Harriet Waters Preston (Boston: Houghton Mifflin Company, 1900), 248, 251.

46. Marraro, *American Opinion,* 206n.

As the chained Titan victor through his will!"[47]

The Dante revival continued unabated, but the rapid alternation of events in Italy gave it more urgent and obvious political meanings. The *OED* records the first use of the word "Dantesque" in 1833 and "Dantean" in 1850, words that quickly became part of the popular idiom and fused the horrors of Hell with the evils of social injustice. On June 22, 1850, the *Literary World* titled a laudatory review of Dickens's grim descriptions of workhouses "Dantesque and Hogarthian Sketches of London," extending Dante's moral judgments to contemporary economic inequities.[48] Melville Americanized Dante in his 1850 review "Hawthorne and His Mosses" when he determined that Hawthorne's "great power of blackness" emerges best in "Young Goodman Brown," a story "deep as Dante" (9:243, 251), a simile that identified Puritan with Italian probings into the roots of human evil. And he appropriated "Dantean" for *Moby-Dick* (6:378) and "The Tartarus of Maids" (9:324) to exploit the word's fusion of damnation and politics. In "Tartarus," the "Dantean gateway" that ushers the narrator into the hellish world of sexually exploitative capitalism inverts Dante's quest for Beatrice by placing the virginal maids symbolically in Hell, not Paradise.

Both Young America and Young Italy were reassessing their programs by taking into account conservative strength, popular inertia, and the vague, contradictory ideology of their own platforms, complications that enriched the figurative complexity of Italian references. How could American imperialists cling to a progressive view of history when they had just seen cyclical history repeated in the precipitous decline and fall of a second Roman republic? How could Protestants link their secular destiny with Italian Catholics once a reactionary, hypocritical pope reassumed power? And how could New Yorkers, especially, after having suppressed the Astor Place riots, continue to idealize violent revolutionaries such as Mazzini and Garibaldi? As Melville developed a more supple and nuanced language in *Moby-Dick,* Italian tropes no longer connoted only freedom and nationalism, but intermixed hope and despair, freedom and authority, art and ideology in a semiotic web of increasing moral and political complexity.

---

47. "The Prisoners of Naples" (1851), *Complete Poetical Works,* 372.
48. *Literary World,* June 22, 1850, 615–16. Continuing textual interest in Dante led Duyckinck to publish, without editorial comment, contrasting translations of the *Inferno's* opening lines on February 23 (169) and March 9 (224).

THE VESUVIAN INKSTAND
Moby-Dick's Semiotics of Italy

Trying to describe the vastness of Leviathan in chapter 104, "The Fossil Whale," Ishmael cries out for tools adequate to the task: "Give me a condor's quill! Give me Vesuvius' crater for an inkstand! Friends, hold my arms!" (6:456). Pens dipped in Vesuvian ink, as Melville well knew, dripped with the blood of revolution. Nominally a metaphor of size, Melville's enormous inkstand implies political turmoil and trepidation, for volcanic eruptions are sudden, unpredictable, and destructive. Constructing a book with such immense and dangerous tools might help Ishmael capture cetacean grandeur, but they also carry the risk of explosive insights that shatter faith, trust, orthodoxy, and confidence into meaningless shards—the great theme of Melville's fiction after *White-Jacket*. Yet volcanoes also go dormant, and while Vesuvius remained smoking literally and figuratively during Melville's most productive years, the failures of 1848 and 1849 tempered his enthusiasm for sun-striking revolt and steered him toward the political gradualism increasingly embodied in the Risorgimento. On his voyage to England, Melville quizzed the captain with a standard debate question from his youth: "which was the best, a monarchy or a republic?"[49] *Moby-Dick* addresses this issue by confronting, among many questions, the central political issue "Who shall rule?"—a key theme in Shakespeare's histories and tragedies, the present dilemma in Risorgimento Italy, and the constitutional conundrum between the states and the federal government in the United States.

Melville began *Moby-Dick* shortly after his return from England. On his voyage over he had read Caroline Kirkland's *Holidays Abroad* and heard passengers discussing Germaine de Staël's immensely popular novel *Corinne, or Italy* (15:9). He must have mentioned *Corinne* to Bentley, for his publisher presented him with a copy before he left London, and he may have read it on his return trip along with Goethe's *Letters from Italy*.[50] The new book that contained the most significant reminder of Risorgimento politics was Horace Greeley's *Hints Toward Reforms*, a collection of lectures and editorials on progressive causes. Inside, among Greeley's old essays, was a bold broadside praising "The Martyrs to Human Liberty, who fell during the siege, May and June, 1849, as Defenders of Rome" (fig. 8).[51]

---

49. Parker, *Herman Melville*, 1:665.

50. See Sealts, *Melville's Reading*, for detailed information on all these titles. They are also included on Melville's list of the books he acquired in London (15:144).

51. *Hints Toward Reforms, in Lectures, Addresses, and Other Writings* (New York: Harper &

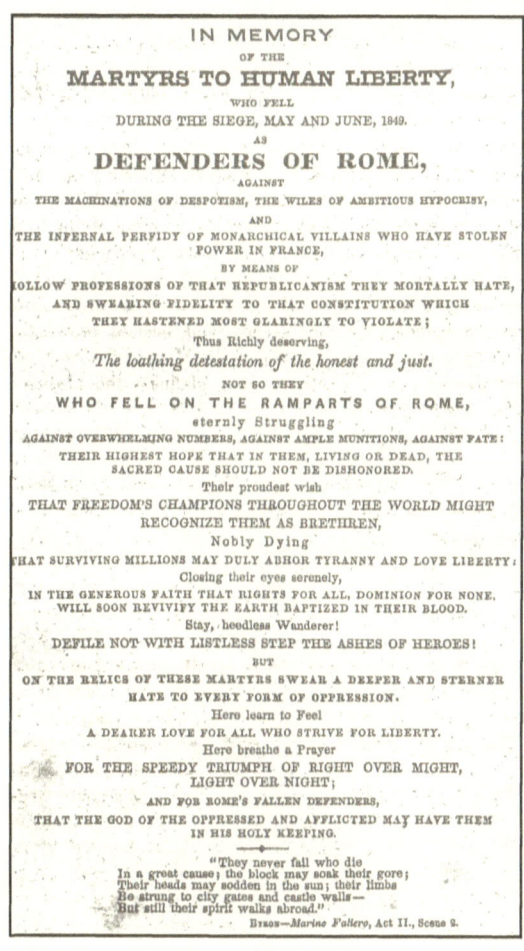

Figure 8. Broadside reprinted in Horace Greeley, *Hints Toward Reforms* (1850), which Melville acquired in May 1850. Author photograph.

Apparently added at the last minute, since none of Greeley's essays address the Italian cause, the graphic broadside set before Melville one of the strongest denunciations of European anti-republican reaction available in the United States. It attacks the "infernal perfidy of monarchical villains who have stolen power in France" and ennobles the Roman Republic's

---

Brothers, 1850). Greeley's book advocated for labor unions, public education, "practical Christianity," Emersonian idealism, and other progressive causes, including one dear to Melville, abolishing flogging in the US Navy. Melville purchased this book on May 21, 1850 (Sealts, *Melville's Reading,* #234).

martyrs as "Freedom's Champions," people who died "that surviving millions may duly abhor tyranny and love liberty," like Byron's Marino Faliero. Reprinting this sheet in a book advocating labor reform identifies the democratic aspirations of the Risorgimento with those of working-class Americans, a linkage that surfaces repeatedly in *Moby-Dick*. In this context the novel's dozens of allusions to Rome, Renaissance painting, Catholicism, the pope, and similar Italian topics take on international political significance even though they are embedded in the narrative of a Nantucket whaleship.

Alan Heimert's classic article "*Moby-Dick* and American Political Symbolism" identifies Ahab with John C. Calhoun and other senatorial histrios of the 1840s and 1850s.[52] In the transnational context of Risorgimento politics, more distant figures emerge in the novel's debate between authority and freedom and wrap it in a web of art, history, and religion that goes far beyond American boundaries. When Ahab assumes total authority over the officers and crew, he creates a ritual replete with Shakespearean drama and Roman Catholic liturgy:

> And now, ye mates, I do appoint ye three cup-bearers to my three pagan kinsmen there—you three most honorable gentlemen and noblemen, my valiant harpooneers. Disdain the task? What, when the great Pope washes the feet of beggars, using his tiara for ewer? Oh, my sweet cardinals! your own condescension, *that* shall bend ye to it; I do not order ye; ye will it. (6:166)

If the mates are his cardinals, Ahab is pope. The Catholic hierarchy and rituals—those elements Mazzinism sought to purge from Italian political life—provide Ahab useful scripts to support his rule. His factitious appeal to papal humility is clearly ironic, for Ahab never stoops to anyone; yet as theater it's enormously persuasive, an essential element in his daring prelatical performance. Americans who visited the papal court were invariably impressed with its ceremonious pomp, and even the waspish and apolitical Kirkland moved from seeing Pio Nono as a comical "Grand Lama" to "feeling a warm personal interest in him" and supporting his moderate course toward reform, including his refusal to support Charles Albert's war against Austria.[53] By the spring of 1850 few American lib-

---

52. *American Quarterly* 15 (1963): 498–534. John Staud, "'What's in a Name?' The *Pequod* and Melville's Heretical Politics," *ESQ: A Journal of the American Renaissance* 38 (4th quarter 1992): 339–59, extends Heimert's approach by unpacking the antitypological symbolism of the *Pequod*'s name and Melville's allusions to Dante and Tarquin.

53. *Holidays Abroad*, 2:8, 50–53. When Kirkland hears a revolutionary soldier condemn Pio

erals retained such regard for the pope, particularly in New York where Bishop Hughes had just praised the return of Pope Pius IX to Rome on May 12, sparking new outbreaks of anti-Catholicism.[54] Starbuck's reaction to Ahab's Romish rites mirrors such sentiments: "Who's over him, he cries;—aye, he would be a democrat to all above; look, how he lords it over all below!" (6:169). Starbuck echoes the critique American newspapers launched against Hughes when he defended the Irish rebellion against the English but denounced the Italian overthrow of Pio Nono. It was, said the *New York Herald,* "narrow and inconsistent in Bishop Hughes to take up the cause of liberty and lay it down again as he would his cassock."[55] "What a candidate for an archbishoprick, what a lad for a Pope were this mincer!" (6:420) cries Ishmael in "The Cassock" (chap. 95), wrapping Archbishop Hughes in the pelt of a whale's penis, attacking his hypocritical word-mincing, and making a "prick" of a leader whose authority depends on the empty vestments of ritual.

Ishmael, even though he enthusiastically joins the hunt for Moby Dick, understands Ahab's performative gestures as clever theatrical politics, not just Romish tricks. In "The Specksynder" (chap. 33), one of the novel's most perceptive analyses of leadership, Ishmael explains how Ahab manipulates appearances to maintain his authority. Ahab avoids the "elated grandeur" practiced by some whaling captains, opting instead to address his crew "in unusual terms, whether of condescension or *in terrorem,* or otherwise" while still adhering to the "forms and usages of the sea" (6:147). Consequently, "That certain sultanism of his brain, which had otherwise in a good degree remained unmanifested; through those forms that same sultanism became incarnate in an irrestible dictatorship" (147). Ishmael, unlike the pious Starbuck, recognizes these "forms" as trumpery, "external arts and entrenchments, always, in themselves, more or less paltry and base" (148); yet, like Starbuck, he feels the power of such "small things," particularly when combined with "extreme political superstitions" (148), the kind with which the crew invests Ahab or Catholics invest the pope. No "tragic dramatist," neither Ishmael, Ahab, Melville, nor Shakespeare, dare ignore this artistic and rhetorical truth, and will use precisely such "arts and entrenchments" to portray "moral indomitableness," to make a "poor old whale-hunter" look like an emperor or

Nono as a poltroon, she disregards his opinion and reluctantly sides with the pope (2:130–31), and in a footnote evidently inserted into the book version of her previously serialized travel articles, she continues to support Pius IX even after he asked foreign armies to help him regain his temporal power, probably a reference to Napoleon III's attack on the Roman republicans in April 1849.

54. Marraro, *American Opinion,* 97.
55. Quoted in Marraro, *American Opinion,* 54.

king (148). Just like "Hivohitee MDCCCXLVIII" in *Mardi,* Ahab masks his "Nantucket grimness and shagginess" with the discredited trappings of popery. In *White-Jacket,* the true leader Jack Chase used a democratic drama to express rebellion (5:89–95); in *Moby-Dick,* the false leader Ahab uses Vatican rituals to enforce authority. Both performances demonstrate, as Melville learned from the Astor Place riots, that theater was a powerful site for contested ideologies.[56] By employing it on opposite ends of the political spectrum—as a vehicle for rebellion and authority—Melville claimed it as a paradoxical metaphor for his own dialogic narratives.

Larry Reynolds has forcefully argued that Ahab's theatrics implicate him in the post-1848 restoration of illegitimate authority all over Europe. A latter-day Napoleon, initially democratic and Promethean, a seemingly desirable leader, Ahab succumbs to his "fatal egotism" and merges with failed leaders such as Louis Philippe, Metternich, and Charles Albert even while ominously foreshadowing the rise of Napoleon III.[57] This devolution of authority gains extra force, I believe, from its Roman and Italian associations, investing Ahab with a timelessness that awes his crew. Capable of taking many parts, Ahab plays Charlemagne, Caesar, and Tarquin as well as Napoleon, figures of universal despotism who abash their "kingly commons" (Ishmael's phrase, not Ahab's, 6:117) with the rhetoric and ritual of oppression. Ahab's tragic monologue right after the quarterdeck scene reinscribes the Shakespearean cliché "Uneasy lies the head that wears a crown" (*King Henry IV, Part II,* iii.i.30) in an artfully contrived Italian trope:

> Is, then, the crown too heavy that I wear? this Iron Crown of Lombardy. Yet is it bright with many a gem; I, the wearer, see not its far flashings; but darkly feel that I wear that, that dazzlingly confounds. 'Tis iron—that I know—not gold. 'Tis split, too—that I feel; the jagged edge galls me so, my brain seems to beat against the solid metal; aye, steel skull, mine; the sort that needs no helmet in the most brain-battering fight! (6:167)

Ahab knows how the iron crown looks (fig. 9) and Melville understands its political symbolism. Supposedly fashioned from a nail of the true cross found by Constantine I, the crown was eventually encased in a gold band incrusted with precious stones.

Thus its exterior is "bright with many a gem" but its essence is iron, making it another piece of deceptive imperial stagecraft designed to daz-

---

56. Berthold, "Class Acts," 445–53.
57. *European Revolutions,* 117.

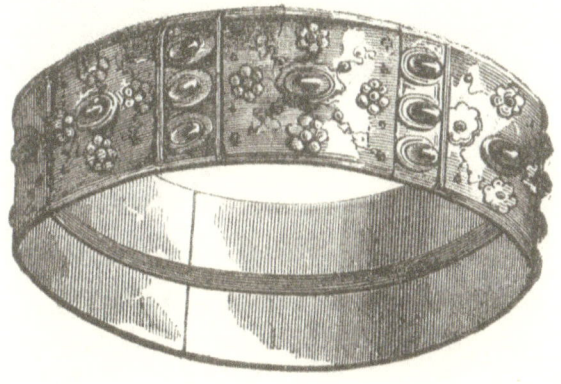

Figure 9. The Iron Crown of Lombardy. Sixth century CE. Its inner band was formed by a nail from the true cross, and gems and gold were added later. The Holy Roman Emperors, who were also nominal kings of Italy, wore this crown until the eighteenth century. It now reposes in the Cathedral of Monza near Milan, Italy.

zle and impress. Its "jagged edge" comes from the original iron nail, an icon of Christian humility and sacrifice, and while in Ahab's mind it seems to penetrate his brain, his own "steel skull" resists such religious ideals. Worn by Holy Roman Emperors from Charlemagne on, during the Risorgimento the iron crown symbolized foreign oppression. Because of its nationalist significance, Austria kept it under lock and key in the cathedral at Monza, near Milan, off the tourist track yet still famous enough to merit notice in Bayard Taylor's *Views A-Foot,* a popular book Melville purchased in 1846.[58] Rightfully belonging to Italian monarchs, the iron crown had been most famously worn by Spain's Charles V and France's Napoleon I, who exclaimed when he put it on, "Dieu me la donne, gare a qui la touche!" ("God gives it to me, beware who touches it!").[59]

By invoking the "Iron Crown," Ahab initiates a series of motifs that link him to oppressive, counterrevolutionary regimes. Moby Dick's white-

---

58. Sealts, *Melville's Reading,* #495. Taylor mentions the iron crown in a reverie at Charlemagne's tomb in Cologne Cathedral: "He lived in a stern age, but he was in mind and heart a man, and like Napoleon, who placed the iron crown which had lain with him centuries in the tomb, on his own brow, he had an Alpine grandeur of mind, which the world was forced to acknowledge" (*Views A-foot: or Europe Seen with Knapsack and Staff,* 2 vols. in one, 9th ed. [New York: George P. Putnam, 1850], 50). Melville owned a first edition, 1846. Taylor's cousin Frank accompanied Melville to England in 1849 and the two contemplated further travel together (Parker, *Herman Melville,* 1:664).

59. Quoted in the *Berkshire County Eagle,* June 10, 1859, 1. In order to keep the crown from falling into Italian hands, the Austrians moved it from the cathedral at Monza to their fortress at Mantua on April 22, 1859.

ness, the "colorless, all-color of atheism" that so enrages Ahab, is a blank slate for Ahab's totalizing dominance. Among the many significations of whiteness, Ishmael tells us, stand Austrian hegemony and Catholic ritual, the two forces most tyrannizing contemporary Italy. White is the royal color of "the great Austrian Empire, Caesarian heir to overlording Rome" (188) and in the "Romish faith" white is "specially employed in the celebration of the Passion of our Lord" (189). Insofar as Ahab mirrors the whale, he exhibits its imperial and papistical associations by arbitrarily enforcing his will and, like Pio Nono, squelching republican liberty. Later on, when Ahab needs a new leg and the earth-bound carpenter complies, Ahab laments his debt to the very proletarians he would dominate. He expresses his tragic plight in Roman metaphors, yearning for illegitimate, unearned dominion even while he knows he is only a "poor old whale-hunter": "I would be free as air; and I'm down in the whole world's books. I am so rich, I could have given bid for bid with the wealthiest Prætorians at the auction of the Roman empire (which was the world's); and yet I owe for the flesh in the tongue I brag with" (6:472). Instead of paying his debts, Ahab wants to eliminate ledgers in an economy of usurpation valorized by imperial Roman precedent. Finally, in "The Hat," Ishmael associates Ahab with Tarquin, the legendary fifth king of Rome, whose son's cruelty led citizens to establish the first Roman Republic. A Sicilian seaman notices a black hawk stealing Ahab's hat, which reveals to Ishmael the fragile authority of kinghood: "An eagle flew thrice round Tarquin's head, removing his cap to replace it, and thereupon Tanaquil, his wife, declared that Tarquin would be king of Rome. But only by the replacing of the cap was that omen accounted good. Ahab's hat was never restored" (6:539). Ishmael, who understands how "arts and entrenchments" reinforce authority and how history can be manipulated to justify despotism, reads Ahab's inability to fulfill Tarquinian prophecy as an omen of his eventual demise. Tyrants like Tarquin and Ahab necessitate revolution, the kind Romans took in 510 BCE, Americans began in 1775, and Italians attempted in 1849, the latter a connection Kirkland makes in *Holidays Abroad* and Melville continues in *Moby-Dick*.[60]

No wonder Ahab seeks revenge on the whale. It combines oppositional meanings unknown to iron-crowned, antirevolutionary Ahab, whose "fixed purpose is laid with iron rails, whereon my soul is grooved to run.... Naught's an obstacle, naught's an angle to the iron way!" (6:168).

---

60. While visiting Chiavenna, a town in Lombardy, Kirkland recalls "that two hundred and twenty citizens had left their homes to join the army of liberty. We remembered, too, the honor in which we had been taught to hold our revolutionary fathers, and that these men were earning in the same way the respect of future generations" (*Holidays Abroad*, 2:131).

Figure 10. Benvenuto Cellini, *Perseus with the Head of Medusa.* Loggia dei Lanzi, Florence, 1554. Bronze on marble base. © Marie-Lan Nguyen / Wikimedia Commons.

As coldly fixed as "Cellini's cast Perseus" (6:123), "standing like an iron statue at his accustomed place beside the mizen rigging" (6:483), rigid Ahab cannot see the "far flashings" on the exterior of his iron crown but keeps looking inward, penetrating into the dark heart of his own being rather than looking outward to art, history, community, politics. As Perseus (fig. 10) Ahab is the slayer of Medusa, one of the nineteenth century's most potent icons of revolutionary horror, as Neil Hertz has shown.[61]

61. "Medusa's Head: Male Hysteria under Political Pressure," from *Representations* 4 (Fall 1983), reprinted with a postscript in *The End of the Line: Essays on Psychoanalysis and the Sublime* (New York: Columbia University Press, 1985), 160–93. Hertz brilliantly combines Freud's reading of Medusa as a symbol of male horror of the vagina with nineteenth-century iconography

Figure 11. Medusa Rondanini. Possibly first century CE. Glyptothek Museum, Munich, Germany. Marble. Johann Goethe made this sculpture famous when he praised it in his letters from Italy (1786–88), recasting the previously horrifying Medusa head as a figure of beauty.

Melville would have read in *Letters from Italy* Goethe's description of the Medusa Rondanini as an alluring figure of mixed beauty and terror (fig. 11), and later on, if not in 1850, he knew Shelley's poem "On the Medusa of Leonardo Da Vinci in the Florentine Gallery" (1819), which further developed Goethe's paradoxical observations.[62] Cellini's cast *Perseus* is clearly the most brutal and sexualized depiction, a statue that, according to John Freccero, was conceived as a warning against revolution: Cosimo de Medici, Cellini's patron, "meant the statue to have a

---

of decapitated revolutionary women.

62. It was probably Goethe who ushered in the romantic phase of appreciation for Medusa's paradoxical qualities in 1788 when he expressed extravagant praise for the Rondanini mask in Rome: "the Medusa Rondanini—a marvelous, mysterious and fascinating work, which represents a state between death and life, pain and pleasure" (*Italian Journeys,* trans. W. H. Auden [New York: Pantheon, 1962], 489). See Jerome J. McGann, "The Beauty of the Medusa: A Study in Romantic Literary Iconology," *Studies in Romanticism* 11 (1972): 3–25. For Melville's later knowledge of Shelley, see chapter 5 below. See also my discussion of Medusan and Persean tropes in "Melville, Garibaldi, and the Medusa of Revolution," *American Literary History* 9 (Fall 1997): 425–59.

political significance: he imagined himself to be a Perseus, putting down the Medusa of republicanism."[63] Like Moby Dick, Medusa presents Ahab-Perseus with an intolerable image of ambiguity, whether sexual, aesthetic, political, or philosophical. As Perseus beheads women, so Ahab beheads whales (see chapters 74–76), both impossible attempts to decapitate and destroy ambiguity itself. Ahab, locked within the iron confines of his quest, refuses to heed the warnings of either history or prophesy and, like Alexander cutting the Gordian knot, resolves the endless debate on monarchies versus republics by imposing his own illegitimate authority on the cetacean world.

The whale's centrality to Melville's semiotics of Italy is well illustrated in chapter 86, "The Tail," where Roman and Renaissance allusions counterpoint conventional images of Dantean darkness to convey how opposed meanings reside within the same signifier, here a complex part of the whale's anatomy that challenges simple binaries and invites subjective interpretation:

> Out of the bottomless profundities the gigantic tail seems spasmodically snatching at the highest heaven. So in dreams, have I seen majestic Satan thrusting forth his tormented colossal claw from the flame Baltic of Hell. But in gazing at such scenes, it is all in all what mood you are in; if in the Dantean, the devils will occur to you; if in that of Isaiah, the archangels. (6:378)

Ishmael's mood is "Dantean," as his infernal dream indicates; yet Italian architecture and art, more widely considered, offer alternative metonyms that give aesthetic sanction to the intermixture of strength and beauty contained within the whale's flukes. Initially noting that the tail's strength derives from a tripartite internal structure like "old Roman walls" (6:375), Ishmael ropes together a wildly diverse herd of allusions that projects the tail into an article of Christian faith:

> Take away the tied tendons that all over seem bursting from the marble in the carved Hercules, and its charm would be gone. As devout Eckermann lifted the linen sheet from the naked corpse of Goethe, he was overwhelmed with the massive chest of the man, that seemed as a Roman triumphal arch. When Angelo paints even God the father in human form, mark what robustness is there. And whatever they may reveal of the divine

---

63. John Freccero, "Medusa and the Madonna of Forlì: Political Sexuality in Machiavelli," in *Machiavelli and the Discourse of Literature,* ed. Albert Russell Ascoli and Victoria Kahn (Ithaca, NY: Cornell University Press, 1993), 178.

love in the Son, the soft, curled, hermaphroditical Italian pictures, in which his idea has been most successfully embodied; these pictures, so destitute as they are of all brawniness, hint nothing of any power, but the mere negative, feminine one of submission and endurance, which on all hands it is conceded, form the peculiar practical virtues of his teachings. (6:376)

Perhaps thinking of the Farnese Hercules he later saw in Naples and praised in "Statues in Rome" or of Michaelangelo's humanized painting of God in the Sistine Chapel which he visited in 1857, Melville endows the whale's tail with the same religious paternity as Protestant America, originating in Roman republicanism and eventuating in the "practical virtues" of Horace Greeley's *Hints Toward Reforms.* Unlike Ahab, whose present rage drives him to challenge natural order, sperm whales live within history to combine strength with elasticity, masculinity with femininity, power with gentleness, as their "infantileness of ease undulates through a Titanism of power" (6:376).

The whale, with its many-layered Roman tail, moves through a universe of contraries as does *The Divine Comedy,* capable of smashing whaleboats and gently feeling a sailor's whisker, of raging in seas of bloody foam or paradisiacal circles of calm (as in "The Grand Armada"). Like Rome, the whale is both imperial and republican, contrary values rooted in its nature and experience as they are in system-challenging characters like Melville's noble mutineer Steelkilt. The sperm whale has a head shaped like "a Roman war-chariot" and Steelkilt has "a head like a Roman," paired allusions that authorize rebellious temperaments through history and nature (6:333, 246). With its ambergris like "old Roman tiles," the whale embodies and organically produces history, and when incarnated as the sea-monster that "for half a century stove the ships of a Roman Emperor" the whale, like the Roman-profiled Steelkilt, justifies revolt (6:407, 210). The whale is both king and subject, a law unto itself like the legendary Italian Robin Hood Rinaldo Rinaldini (6:204). When viewed in *all* moods and considered in *all* parts, such as its remarkable spout, the whale transcends Ahabian monomania to take its place among "all ponderous profound beings, such as Plato, Pyrrho, the Devil, Jupiter, Dante," from whom "there always goes up a certain semi-visible steam, while in the act of thinking deep thoughts" (6:374). As with its tail, its skin, "all over obliquely crossed and re-crossed with numberless straight marks in thick array, something like those in the finest Italian line engravings" (6:306), borrows from Italian art the potential to mirror multiple meanings and connect diverse historical periods in one grand semiosis of moral and aesthetic complexity.

Ishmael's recognition of the whale's multivalence leads him toward a more nuanced appropriation of Dante. "Dantean" normally connotes the torments of Hell, as though the *Divine Comedy* consisted of only one book, and Melville often used the neologism this way, as when he compared London in November to "a city of Dis (Dante's) cloud of smoke—the damned &c" (15:14). One of his primary sources for *Moby-Dick*, J. Ross Browne's *Etchings of a Whaling Cruise* (1846), compares the try-works to "Dante's pictures of the infernal regions,"[64] a hint that led Melville to the most Dantean chapter of the book, "The Try-Works" (chap. 96). Yet Melville knew Purgatory and Paradise as well as Hell, as *Mardi* demonstrates, and these books too are part of Ishmael's total try-works epiphany. Notable for its representation of the *Pequod* as a groaning "red hell" plunging blindly into "that blackness of darkness" and thus seeming "the material counterpart of her monomaniac commander's soul" (6:423), "The Try-Works" records one of Ishmael's earliest shipboard experiences, when the fires to render the blubber are first lighted (somewhere around chapter 61). Still a greenhorn, Ishmael takes the helm one night and finds himself transfixed by the "Tartarean shapes of the pagan harpooneers" stoking the flames (6:423). He nods off, and while sleeping turns to face the stern. Suddenly he awakes, utterly confused, and in a panic almost capsizes the ship before he realizes his mistake. Only recorded after Ishmael has developed an "equal eye" that balances the "wisdom that is woe" with the "woe that is madness" (6:425), "The Try-Works" goes beyond infernal uses of Dantean imagery to move like *The Commedia* from Hell to Paradise: "And there is a Catskill eagle in some souls that can alike dive down into the blackest gorges, and soar out of them again and become invisible in the sunny spaces" (6:425). After having wickedly parodied Bishop Hughes and Roman Catholic rituals in the immediately preceding chapter, "The Cassock," Melville employs Dante's orthodox Catholicism to serve the aims of Presbyterian Ishmael, reanimating Italian religion and literature as metaphors of secular redemption from the whaleship's fiery, capitalistic, industrially driven, madly questing enterprise. The lesson that Dante teaches Melville, and that Melville imagistically echoes in Ishmael's harrowing try-works nightmare, is to look not too long in the face of the fire, to persevere

---

64. Quoted in Howard P. Vincent, *The Trying-Out of Moby-Dick* (1949; rpt. Kent, OH: Kent State University Press, 1980), 330.

through the Inferno toward the Paradise beyond, even if for democratic Ishmael it be only the paradise of personal integrity. This was the lesson Young Goodman Brown failed to learn when he resisted the experience of universal depravity and denied himself the human community that Ishmael finds squeezing sperm or writing his book.

Still, in 1850–51 the matter of Italy was too fluid to provide Melville with a stable body of metaphors to gloss American politics. As firmly reinstated as European monarchs seemed to be, revolutionary plots swirled beneath the thrones. *Harper's* reported in December 1850 that "Red Republicans" were conspiring to assassinate the crowned heads of Europe, and Mazzini was busy raising funds for the liberation of Italy among his English "Friends of Italy."[65] In *Moby-Dick* Starbuck considers assassinating Ahab but rejects it, and to the end he and the crew persist in the hunt and pay with their lives. Melville suggests that personal desire is an inadequate basis for rebellion, and that only some larger, more providential force, something with the natural and historical sanction of the whale itself, can justify revolt. Who shall rule? *Moby-Dick* unequivocally replies, "not Ahab." Yet that negative answer leaves a void at the helm. Among the officers Starbuck lacks the fortitude, Stubb the seriousness, and Flask the strength. Steelkilt, the mutineer, is sometimes posited as an alternative, but his "Venetianly corrupt" origins along the Erie Canal and his murderous intentions toward Radney undermine his republican desires as much as the iron crown undermines Ahab's authority (6:249). Significantly, Steelkilt ends up on a ship "headed for France" (6:258), home of the "Red Republicans" that Americans loathed for their communism, socialism, and violence. In the hiatus between the defeat of the second Roman Republic and Garibaldi's liberation of Naples, between the Compromise of 1850 and the Civil War, citizens of both Italy and the United States were unsure who should lead. The conflict between illegitimate authority and revolutionary action that had burst out so gloriously in the Roman Republic of 1849 was now suspended, like the *Pequod*'s sailors who hear the cry of seals in the morning dark "and, for the space of some moments stood, or sat, or leaned all transfixedly listening, like the carved Roman slave, while that wild cry remained within hearing" (6:523).[66] John Ushant went down fighting, like the Dying Gladiator; Ahab's crew, under the

65. "Monthly Record of Current Events," 2 (December 1850): 127; for Mazzini, see Mack Smith, *Mazzini*, 95–96.
66. The rich conflation of metaphors is Melville's, not that of his source, Colnett, as Vincent points out (*Trying-Out*, 382–83).

spell of an illegitimate authority, succumbs to the paralysis imaged in an unidentified Roman statue that connotes abjection, weakness, and despair. A new, more powerful King Media was needed to resolve these polarities in the spirit of compromise that dominated the early 1850s.

4

Machiavellian Aesthetics

From Pierre *to* The Confidence-Man

> My Dear Augusta: I want you not to forget—if you please—to bring with you from Allan's when you return, Machiavelli's Florentine history which Allan borrowed from me. Dont forget."
> —Melville's letter of December [4?], 1851

> Damned be the hour I read in Dante!
> —*Pierre (1852)*

> *Seeking to conquer a larger liberty, man but extends the empire of necessity.*
> —Epigraph to "The Bell-Tower" (1855)

BY THE TIME Melville began *Pierre* in 1851, the papacy and the old Hapsburg and Bourbon monarchies of Italy seemed more entrenched than ever. The restorations of monarchies in Europe confirmed American exceptionalism and drove Melville to search more deeply within his own country's past to understand the meaning of democracy, nationalist art, and America's place in global culture. To be sure, Melville maintained his transnational perspective, placing the good Yankee sea captain Amasa Delano between African slavery and Spanish desuetude in "Benito Cereno," satirizing democracy and Manifest Destiny in his Galápagos sketches "The Encantadas," and composing his only prose work with an Italian setting in "The Bell-Tower." His three "diptychs," paired stories that explicitly compare social, economic, and gender inequalities in England and the United States, implicate America in global politics and culture as much as any literature of the period. When Roman and Italian references do arise, they purvey the old image of Italy as the "Land of the Dead," a tonal reaction that reflects American disappointment in the Risorgimento and flagging hopes for European republicanism in general. The lawyer in "Bartleby, the Scrivener" compares the scrivener to "Marius brooding among the ruins of Carthage,"[1] Delano almost falls into the sea when the *San Dominick*'s "Venetian-looking" decayed balustrade gives way, Galápagos tortoises look like "three Roman Coliseums in magnificent decay," an earthquake levels Bannadonna's bell tower and leaves it a "lichened ruin," while in *The Confidence-Man* a "crazy beggar," usually identified as the failed aesthetic idealist Edgar Poe, begs for alms "under the form of peddling a rhapsodical tract": "Nothing," writes Melville, "could exceed his look of picturesque Italian ruin and dethronement" (9:28, 73–75, 131, 174; 10:195).

As this chronology of allusions indicates, from 1853–57 Melville's image of Italy remained, like the country itself, fairly static. Cavour, ever the pragmatist, attempted to ingratiate Piedmont with France by joining her, England, and Austria in the Crimean War against Russia (1854–56), a game that backfired when the Congress of Paris confirmed the status quo, leaving Austria in control of northern Italy and the pope the ruler of Rome. Such unsatisfactory compromises left liberal nationalists like Mazzini "Marking Time," to quote Denis Mack Smith's chapter title for this period in Mazzini's life, further marginalizing him as a "Red Republican" reduced to hatching shady plots and failed insurrections.[2] After leaving New York in the summer of 1851, Garibaldi busied himself with trade and seldom ventured into the heady world of international revolutionaries. He agreed to serve King Victor Emmanuel, moved to the island of Caprera in 1855, and tended to his personal life.[3] Foresti, whom Sardinia rebuffed as US consul to Genoa in 1853, was accepted for the post in 1858 because he, like Garibaldi, now recognized the advantages of a constitutional monarchy.[4] "There never was a time when revolt was more hopeless," lamented an 1856 report on the Congress of Paris in *Littell's Living Age,* a New York weekly that kept Americans informed of European politics, and a reviewer of Hillard's apolitical *Six Months in Italy* wearily claimed that, politically speaking, "Italy, indeed, has exhausted her destiny.... The people have shown themselves as unworthy of freedom, as they are incapable of achieving it by their own efforts."[5] As Cavour's

1. Not all connotations of this image were negative, as William L. Vance has shown in *America's Rome,* 27–30. In the context of "Bartleby" and Italy in the 1850s, however, the more somber reading of it predominates.
2. *Mazzini,* 106–28.
3. Mack Smith, *Garibaldi,* 52–64.
4. Marraro, *American Opinion,* 206.
5. "The Italian Peninsula," *Littell's Living Age,* August 9, 1856, 383 (reprinted from the British publication the *Press* of June 21, 1856); rev. of *Six Months in Italy, North American Review*

moderate policies took effect foreign financial support for the Risorgimento diminished, Victor Emmanuel claimed increasing allegiance from liberals at home and abroad, and a republican Italy seemed farther away than ever.[6]

During this interregnum Melville discovered Machiavelli's *History of Florence,* most likely the edition that contained *The Prince,* and drew upon it in *Pierre* as well as his other writings through 1857. Machiavelli's political philosophy complicated the old debate question of which was better, a monarchy or a republic, and counterpointed Dante's cosmic idealism with an earthly pragmatism suitable to the increasingly polarized American of the 1850s. The rapid rise of the xenophobic, anti-Catholic Know-Nothings (officially, the American Party) destroyed the elite, temporizing Whig party and for a time gave political power to the partisans of a narrowly nativist ideology that exposed the conservative and reactionary face of American democracy. The Fugitive Slave Law of 1850, the Kansas-Nebraska act of 1854, the Anthony Burns riots in Boston that motivated Thoreau to write "Slavery in Massachusetts" (1854), the Dred Scott decision of 1857, John Brown's raid on Harpers Ferry in 1859, and the outbreak of the Civil War in 1861 justified the premise of Media's scroll: "evil is the chronic malady of the universe; and checked in one place, breaks forth in another" (3:529). Machiavelli's account of the rise and fall of Florentine republicanism corroborates the scroll's cyclical view of history, and his antipapalism, ardent republicanism, nationalism, measured appeals to Roman virtue, and antifactionalism made him a valuable guide through America's current political thickets. Cavour considered federalism as a realistic option for Italian unification; but its inability to stabilize the United States undermined the American model of republicanism and increased the appeal of strong central governments, a chief aim of Machiavellian politics and one that seemed increasingly desirable in a dividing Union. In *Pierre* and other late fiction, Melville employs Machiavellian principles to leaven Dante's cosmic optimism and weigh noble American ideals such as abolitionism, patriotism, democracy, religion, and charity in the cold scales of experience.

---

77 (October 1853): 522–23.

    6. See Marraro, *American Opinion,* 186–224 for an extensive survey of American newspapers and journals that convincingly demonstrates the steady shift away from Mazzinism and toward constitutional monarchy during the 1850s.

IRONIZING DANTE

Seemingly Melville's least political and most domestic novel, with its focus on the hermetic Oedipal struggle of its young protagonist, Pierre Glendinning of upstate New York, *Pierre* nevertheless counterpoints its protagonist's sentimental individualism with Machiavelli's moral pragmatism and adds to Melville's semiotics of Italy the devastating subversiveness of irony and satire, the literary modes that dominate his fiction after *Moby-Dick*. Unlike *Mardi*'s travelers to Serenia, the *Paradiso* of the South Seas, Pierre Glendinning fails the Dantean test of persevering through the Inferno to Paradise and dies clinging to mindless rebellion, epitomized in the futile heroism of the Titan Enceladus. Like Ahab, Pierre sacrifices himself and others for an unattainable and hypothetical ethical purity that is nothing more than his own erotic projections on Isabel, the beautiful young woman whom he embraces as sister, lover, and self-destructive Medusa. Michael Rogin rightly points out that Pierre flees the consequences of 1848, but he is wrong in attributing this same motive to Melville.[7] Through indirection and irony, Melville constructs in *Pierre* an ever more nuanced politics derived from a pragmatic reaction to republican excesses and failures combined with a more informed adherence to the Risorgimento's aim of national unity. Isabel, like Moby Dick a resonant and duplicitous symbol of the ambiguous Other, embodies multiplicity and paradox in an icon of male horror, lust, and desire combined with overtones of revolutionary chaos and violence. Isabel infuses gender into Melville's American Risorgimento and anticipates the sexual politics that dominate "The Tartarus of Maids," *Clarel,* and *Billy Budd*. As Melville's first full-scale representation of Medusa, Isabel is at once victim and victimizer, attractive and repulsive, paradisiacal and infernal, mythic and real, a chaotic representative of the alluring dangers of revolution itself.

Scholars have long noted that *Pierre* uses Dante ironically to undermine Pierre's shallow innocence and artistic pretensions. G. Giovannini believes that Pierre discovers the "universality of evil" only to reveal his incapacity to deal with it; Nathalia Wright finds Pierre guilty of numerous Dantean sins, yet too immature to comprehend Dante's larger vision, for he has apparently "not read the *Purgatorio* or the *Paradiso*"; and Howard Schless, citing John Flaxman's popular illustrations to Dante, believes that Pierre inverts Dante's quest for Beatrice, for Pierre is motivated by fear rather than love and consequently gets no further than the "City of Dis,"

---

7. *Subversive Genealogy*, 186.

the hellish New York of the novel's concluding chapters.[8] These studies, written without benefit of Melville's annotated copy of Cary's Dante, understandably focus on *Pierre* as an "Inferno dream" (7:318), Charlie Millthorpe's joshing name for the novel Pierre writes. The irony they all recognize testifies to Melville's skill in undercutting his antihero Pierre and implying a positive counterpoint beyond the frigid hell of Pierre's dystopic New York. In light of Melville's knowledge of Cary's Dante, including *Purgatory* and *Paradise,* Pierre's obsession with the *Commedia*'s first books is even more deeply ironic, for unlike Pierre Melville knew that there was more to Dante's vision than the Inferno.

Far less noticed is *Pierre's* debt to Machiavelli, an important figure in the Risorgimento's turn toward a more realistic political philosophy. Plotinus Plinlimmon and Glendinning Stanly, pragmatic cosmopolitans who confute Pierre's provincial idealism, represent ethical systems that rest on the premise of human evil and justify actions by its consequences, not its methods or intentions. Melville, as T. Walter Herbert has shown, knew about the universality of evil from Calvinism, a theology he later abandoned.[9] Yet a profound sense of human shortcomings remained with Melville and found support in Machiavelli, whose account of Florentine mendacity and selfishness is even more powerful than Calvin's theology because it rests on empirical evidence. Whereas the *Divine Comedy* takes the reader through evil, sin, and punishment to a vision of hope, mercy, love, and community, a journey more like Ishmael's than Pierre's, Machiavelli's secular narrative describes the cycles of tyranny and revolt that plague all societies and render impotent individual efforts at salvation. Melville's conscious appropriation of Machiavelli counterbalances his earlier regard for Dante and extends the dialectic between pragmatism and idealism with allusions to two key figures of Risorgimento nationalism.

Pierre's moral confusion begins when, some weeks before the novel opens, he notices the olive-cheeked face of a strange young black-haired woman while visiting a neighbor's sewing circle (7:46). When she hears his name she shrieks, so transfixing Pierre with her beauty and mysterious demeanor that he becomes obsessed. Although he doesn't learn her name until later this is, of course, the face of Isabel Banford. He shares

---

8. G. Giovannini, "Melville's *Pierre* and Dante's *Inferno,*" *PMLA* 64 (March 1949): 75; Nathalia Wright, "*Pierre:* Herman Melville's *Inferno,*" *American Literature* 32 (May 1960): 181; Howard H. Schless, "Flaxman, Dante, and Melville's *Pierre,*" *Bulletin of the New York Public Library* 64 (February 1960): 79. See also Rita Gollin, "*Pierre's* Metamorphosis of Dante's *Inferno,*" *American Literature* 39 (January 1968): 542–45.

9. This is Herbert's persuasive thesis in *Moby-Dick and Calvinism.*

the experience with Lucy Tartan, his blonde, blue-eyed fiancée who finds Pierre's revelation disturbing yet wants to hear more about it (7:37). As Pierre prepares to entertain Lucy on the first evening of the novel, he masks his fears of emotional betrayal by refusing to let her see "Flaxman's Dante," the popular portfolio of prints that Melville's friends the Hawthornes had enjoyed for years:[10]

> Then Flaxman's Dante;—Dante! Night's and Hell's poet he. No, we will not open Dante. Methinks now the face—the face—minds me a little of pensive, sweet Francesca's face—or, rather, as it had been Francesca's daughter's face—wafted on the sad dark wind, toward observant Virgil and the blistered Florentine. No, we will not open Flaxman's Dante. Francesca's mournful face is now ideal to me. Flaxman might evoke it wholly,—make it present in lines of misery—bewitching power. No! I will not open Flaxman's Dante! Damned be the hour I read in Dante! more damned than that wherein Paolo and Francesca read in fatal Launcelot! (7:42)

Hell, Canto 5, lines 69–138, tells the story of Paolo and Francesca, who fell in love while reading the story of Lancelot and Guinivere and were later executed by Francesca's enraged husband. Pierre's precise allusion makes it seem as though he knows his Dante well—but he doesn't. His problem isn't "the hour I read in Dante"; it's the many hours he avoided reading *all* of Dante. Cary's note on Lancelot refers the reader to *Paradiso* 16:13–15, where Dante compares Beatrice to the female servant whose cough emboldened Guinivere to encourage Lancelot's affections, implying sympathy if not sanction for impassioned lovers. Pierre ignores such subtleties and fabricates Francesca's daughter, who does not exist in Dante, in order to distance his passion for Isabel from Dante's Francesca. Dante may place Francesca in hell, but her (mythical) daughter can start life anew under Pierre's impassioned tutelage. Pierre also misreads Flaxman's illustration (fig. 12), for it reveals no "face," allowing him to project his obsessions on verbal and pictorial representations of sin and reinscribe them to suit his desires.

---

10. On Hawthorne's first visit to the Peabody home in 1838, Elizabeth Peabody entertained the author and his sisters by showing them Flaxman's illustrations. Sophia Peabody was an ardent admirer of Flaxman, and after her marriage to Hawthorne she decorated their homes with sketches from Flaxman and even earned money sketching Flaxman scenes on lampshades. See Edwin H. Miller, *Salem Is My Dwelling-Place: A Life of Nathaniel Hawthorne* (Iowa City: University of Iowa Press, 1991), 124, 210, 274–75.

Figure 12. John Flaxman, "Paolo and Francesca," line engraving for *The Divine Comedy*, Hell, Canto 5, lines 135–38. Melville's edition of *The Vision* had only a frontispiece of Dante, but in *Pierre,* Book II.7, Melville refers directly to this drawing (6:42), which he probably saw in a separately published portfolio of Flaxman's prints. Virgil watches over Dante's prostrate body while the two doomed lovers resume their punishment. Author's scan from a nineteenth-century edition of *The Divine Comedy*.

In failing to read beyond *Hell,* Pierre misses the redemptive love promised by Beatrice and remains transfixed by a "face" that seems a compound of "hell and heaven," "ever hovering between Tartarean misery and Paradisaic beauty" (7:43). The narrative comment on Pierre's outburst against Dante makes clear that he is as naïve as Young Goodman Brown, for "as yet [Pierre] had not seen so far and deep as Dante, and therefore was entirely incompetent to meet the grim bard fairly on his peculiar ground" (7:54). "Rash," "untutored," "ignorant," Pierre's view of Dante arises "from that half contemptuous dislike, and sometimes selfish loathing, with which, either naturally feeble or undeveloped minds, regard those dark ravings of the loftier poets, which are in eternal opposition to their own finespun, shallow dreams of rapturous or prudential Youth" (7:54). By satirizing Pierre's literary pretensions, Melville satirizes the Dante revival itself, which undoubtedly had its share of dilettantes, and widens even further the distance between himself and his callow protagonist.

Rather than following a guide, as does Dante, Pierre follows his feelings, and when Isabel claims to be his half-sister, he immediately believes her. Even though her relationship remains unverified, makes an adulterer of Pierre's father, divides Pierre from his mother, tortures Lucy, and eventuates in death for Isabel, Lucy, and Pierre, Pierre believes he intuits the truth of her claim when he notices a resemblance between Isabel and the "chair-portrait," an old painting of his father. At this epiphanic moment, Pierre quotes Dante's description of Agnello Brunelleschi transformed into a serpent: "Ah! how dost thou change, / Agnello! See! thou art not double now, / Nor only one!" (7:85; Hell, 25:60–62).[11] To Dante, this grotesque metamorphosis results in a horrifying "image miscreate" (25.69), a symbol of satanic punishment. In *Pierre,* this monster is Pierre himself. The fusion of his father's portrait with Isabel's face overturns his ethical system and makes him a "soul in anarchy" (7:87), driven like Ahab to create his own moral order irrespective of history or community. Facing Isabel, like facing Medusa, requires the knowledge and support of others. But where Perseus had Athena, and Dante had Virgil, Pierre has only himself, an isolation that compounds his subjectivity.

The dark and light heroines Isabel and Lucy may originate in Sir Walter Scott's conventionalized women, but they remained current in Staël's Italian Corinne and English Lucile, twinned dark and light lovers that divide Lord Nelvil's sexual and nationalist attentions.[12] Pierre imagines Isabel to be French, for that comports with his memory of Aunt Dorothea's story of his father and a group of emigrants who fled the French Revolution (7:75–76). Yet Isabel could as easily be an Italian like the dark improvisatrice Corinne, as her stereotypical olive cheek, black hair, and facility with the guitar suggest. Her childhood memories image scenes as reminiscent of Italy as France, particularly Savoy, that politically contested region between the two countries, a connection reinforced by her bilingual upbringing (7:114–116). Melville's readers would read Italian associations into her name from Tuckerman's *Isabel, or Italy* (1839; reissued in 1852 as *Sicily: A Pilgrimage*) and Willis's Florentine play *Tortesa, the Usurer* (1839), whose heroine is named Isabella. Furthermore, Isabel's nickname "Bell" not only echoes Jezebel and Baal, the Old Testament queen and god who attract and damn, but "bella," Italian for "beautiful." Dangerous and alluring, as in Filicaja's durable personification of Italy's "fatal beauty," these legendary women embody sexual and aesthetic power

---

11. Melville quotes accurately from Cary with the exception of "not" for "nor." Schless, "Melville's *Pierre,*" reproduces Flaxman's drawing (73) and rightly notes that this quotation "goes to the essential irony of the plot" (71). Parker, *Herman Melville,* finds psychological significance in the quotation (2:13).

12. Leon Howard, *Herman Melville: A Biography* (Berkeley: University of California Press, 1951), noticed this similarity between *Corinne* and *Pierre* (193–94). *Pierre* appeared three months before Hawthorne's tale of light and dark heroines, *The Blithedale Romance,* which Hawthorne sent Melville in July 1852 (14:229–31).

that combines with the nationalist imperatives of the Risorgimento to inspire political action. A republican Italy, gendered female, reifies Staël's Corinne in a new nation where history, art, and politics blend into a unified culture, achieving what Young Americans hoped for the United States. Pierre, however, lives outside of history and the moral complexity it teaches. He ignores the lesson of Dante and prematurely exalts Isabel into a false Beatice, totally misreading the *Commedia* and inverting its narrative into a journey from Paradise to Hell.

After his first interview with Isabel at Walter Ulver's farmhouse, Pierre becomes smitten with her beauty and mystery. On slim evidence, he quickly accepts her as a sister when he actually wants her as a lover, and to forestall incest and rationalize his pursuit he transforms her into an untouchable figure of spiritual desire: "Isabel wholly soared out of the realms of mortalness, and for him became transfigured in the highest heaven of uncorrupted Love" (7:142). Pierre imagines himself another Dante, willing to accept exile and enter the gates of Hell to pursue his self-generated ideal as shown when he reads almost verbatim from Cary the famous inscription over the gate of Hell:[13]

> Through me you pass into the city of Woe;
> Through me you pass into eternal pain;
> Through me, among the people lost for aye.
> ....
> All hope abandon, ye who enter here. (7:168)

Again, Pierre privileges Hell over the rest of Dante's *Vision*. And here the narrative seems to support him, creating a caricature of Dante's biography to justify Pierre's resolution to renounce Lucy, pretend he has married Isabel, and move to New York: "The man Dante Alighieri received unforgivable affronts and insults from the world; and the poet Dante Alighieri bequeathed his immortal curse to it, in the sublime malediction of the

---

13. The other English translations available to Melville vary considerably from Cary's rendition: Henry Boyd, *The Divina Commedia* (1802), has "Thro' me, the newly-damn'd for ever fleet, / In ceaseless shoals, to Pain's eternal seat; / Thro' me they march, and join the tortur'd crew.... Here bid at once your ling'ring hope farewell"; Ichabod Charles Wright, *The Inferno of Dante* (1833), has "Through me ye enter the abode of woe: / Through me to endless sorrow are ye brought: / Through me amid the souls accurst ye go, ... All hope abandon—ye who enter here"; and John Aitken Carlyle (1849) has "Through me is the way into the doleful city; through me the way into the eternal pain; through me the way among the people lost ... leave all hope, ye that enter." Cary's translation is "Through me you pass into the city of wo: / Through me you pass into eternal pain: / Through me among the people lost for aye.... All hope abandon, ye who enter here" (3:1–3, 9). These comparisons were made using Google Books.

Inferno. The fiery tongue whose political forkings lost him the solacements of this world, found its malicious counterpart in that muse of fire, which would forever bar the vast bulk of mankind from all solacement in the worlds to come" (7:168–69). This not only ignores Dante's second two books but Cary's introduction as well. Although Dante was exiled from Florence for the last nineteen years of his life he found many friends and benefactors among the Ghibellines, the emperor's party to which he turned after renouncing the papal Guelphs.[14] Pierre, "unprovided with that sovereign antidote of a sense of uncapitulatable security, which is only the possession of the furthest advanced and profoundest souls" (7:169), fails to read beyond his own desires. Reinvesting his text with irony, Melville's narrator reminds readers that "the thoughts we indite here as Pierre's are to be very carefully discriminated from those we indite concerning him" (7:167), so that when Pierre tears "into a hundred shreds the printed pages of Hell and Hamlet" (7:170), the two works that alternately anger and paralyze him, he reveals his infantile inability to profit from literature that exposes his self-delusions. "Eight-and-forty hours and more had passed" (7:170), as 1848 has passed, yet Pierre remains obsessively convinced of his revolutionary ideals and the chapter concludes with a Dantean apocalypse: "Now indeed did all the fiery floods in the Inferno, and all the rolling gloom in Hamlet suffocate him at once in flame and smoke" (7:171).

The "Young America in Literature" section consolidates Melville's break with the movement and exposes Pierre as a reverse Dante, a writer in exile but unable to compose a great original work of national significance or to engage in the political life of his country. His first night in the city reenacts Dante's entrance to the City of Dis, here a police station filled with a ragtag mob of thieves and prostitutes from the "infernoes of hell" (7:240). Fleeing such anarchy, Pierre isolates himself in a freezing New York apartment as cold as Dante's ninth circle of Hell where he "Immaturely Attempts a Mature Work" (7:282), a latter-day version of Dante's first book as his lighthearted friend Charlie Millthorpe realizes: "Ha, ha! well, my boy, how comes on the Inferno? That is it you are writing; one is apt to look black while writing Infernoes; you always loved Dante" (7:317). While Pierre has been "hammering away at that one poor plaguy Inferno!" (7:317), Charlie has published ten treatises, attended numerous meetings, edited a scientific work, and argued five legal cases. To be sure, Melville satirizes "silly Millthorpe" and his superficial productivity even as he satirizes Young America itself; yet Pierre's "Inferno dream" never sees

---

14. Cary, *The Vision*, 20.

daylight, a publisher condemns it as a blasphemous plagiarism, and even Isabel calls it "that vile book" (7:338, 318, 356, 348). Whatever Pierre has written, it is no *Divine Comedy*, nor has Pierre engaged national issues as did Dante's vernacular poem or Melville's earlier novels. In contrast, Pierre's literary efforts isolate him in a narcissistic dreamworld stimulated by early overpraise of his trivial adolescent poetry (7:244–56), a figure less like Dante and more like Poe's Thingum Bob.

"A COOL TUSCAN POLICY"
Machiavellian Cosmopolitanism

"My Dear Augusta: I want you not to forget—if you please—to bring with you from Allan's when you return, Machiavelli's Florentine history which Allan borrowed from me. Dont forget" (14:214). Written in December, 1851, as Melville was completing the final chapters of *Pierre*, this brief but insistent letter to his sister (who was visiting brother Allan in New York) indicates how important Machiavelli had become to the novel. Although scholars have not identified the exact "Florentine history" that Melville owned, only two editions are possible, C. Edwards Lester's American translation of the *Florentine Histories* or the English Bohn edition, *The History of Florence* which was titled "The Florentine History" on its first page of text.[15] Both were recent translations that indicate renewed Anglo-American interest in Machiavelli. The British historian J. G. A. Pocock argues that Machiavellian ideas permeated English political theory and filtered into American constitutionalism,[16] and Machiavelli's moving pleas for national liberation in the last chapter of *The Prince* positioned him as a leading political theorist of the Risorgimento, a far cry from his usual association with tyranny. By the late 1840s Machiavelli was a transnational figure of increasing importance, and Melville gained a favorable

---

15. Sealts suggests that Melville owned Niccolò Machiavelli, *The Florentine Histories*, trans. C. Edwards Lester, 2 vols. (New York: Paine and Burgess, 1845). See Sealts, *Melville's Reading*, #340a. Equally plausibly Hennig Cohen suggests that Melville owned *The History of Florence* (London: Henry G. Bohn, 1847), which includes *The Prince* and several additional documents by Machiavelli. See Cohen's richly annotated edition of *Israel Potter* (New York: Fordham University Press, 1991), 387n. Parenthetical references are to the Bohn edition.

16. J. G. A. Pocock, *The Machiavellian Moment: Florentine Political Thought and the Atlantic Republican Tradition; with a New Afterword by the Author.*, 2nd ed. (Princeton, NJ: Princeton University Press, 2003). Daniel S. Malachuk, "The Republican Philosophy of Emerson's Early Lectures," *New England Quarterly* 71, no. 3 (1998): 419, has discerned Machiavellian roots in Emerson's doctrine of self-reliance.

opinion of his ideas from Thomas Babington Macaulay whose famous *Edinburgh Review* essay of 1827 was included in *The Modern British Essayists,* a multivolume anthology that Melville acquired in 1849.[17] Macaulay acknowledged the infamy that attached to Machiavelli's name but traced it to the calculated slanders of his political enemies and defended him as "a zealous republican" who was exiled, imprisoned, tortured, and impoverished in "the cause of public liberty. It seems inconceivable that the martyr of freedom should have designedly acted as the apostle of tyranny" (260). Macaulay's corrective view runs through conservative and liberal American commentary of the times and exalts the Florentine diplomat as an authority on maintaining republican values in times of national stress and demonstrating that Italians are fully capable of self-rule.[18] Macaulay's defense percolates into the introductions of both Lester's American translation and the English Bohn edition, with the latter quoting extensively Macaulay's witty attack on Machiavelli's calumniators (xv). Americans may also have been drawn to Machiavelli because he opposed papal government. Almost as soon as Machiavelli's works were posthumously published the church placed them on the *Index Librorum Prohibitorum,* a decision that aligned Machiavelli with anti-Catholic opinion: "Machiavelli and other Italian statesmen have seen in the pretensions of the church, the greatest barrier to the independence and union of Italy," said an article in the *New Englander* in 1849, and further argued that Italians must learn from Machiavelli's critique of their political lassitude if they are to succeed in their revolution and be "fit for liberty."[19]

Macaulay's imprimatur validated Machiavelli's voice in American Risorgimento discourse and made his works an essential source for understanding how republics could survive the extremes of tyranny and

17. Melville purchased this seven-volume set in February 1849 (Sealts, *Melville's Reading* , #359). Because these volumes are so rare, I quote from the original publication "Machiavelli," rev. *Oeuvres Complètes de Machiavel,* traduites par J.V. Perier, *Edinburgh Review* 45 (March 1827): 259–95. It is identical to the version Melville owned.

18. This is the opinion of the exiled Italian patriot G. F. Secchi de Casali. "Italy in 1846," *American Whig Review* 5 (April 1847): 360. In 1835 the *North American Review,* "Machiavelli," 41, no. 88 (July 1835): 72–73, reviewed Italian and French editions of Machiavelli's works and studiously defended him from the groundless accusations of criminality leveled by the popular British historian William Roscoe (1753–1831). John Chapman, a Christian publishing house in London, anthologized the *North American's* essay in 1846 in order "to rescue that great man's name from the obloquy of ages." See John Chapman, ed., *Characteristics of Men of Genius: A Series of Biographical, Historical, and Critical Essays,* The Catholic Series (London: J. Chapman, 1846). In September 1845 the *Democratic Review's* "Notices of New Books" praised Lester's *Florentine Histories* by reprinting an extended passage from Macaulay's "great article" (17:237–38), and two years later published a laudatory article by Casali who called Machiavelli "the greatest political genius the world ever produced" ("Times and Life of Machiavelli," 20 [May 1847], 402).

19. "The Italian Revolutions in 1848," 89, 91, 93.

anarchy whether emanating from pope, king, or mob. Americans admired Machiavelli's ardent republicanism, his promotion of citizen militias, and his critiques of monarchy, papal rule, arrogant nobles, and factionalism, notably the divisive battles between Guelph and Ghibelline that hamstrung his native Florence for centuries. Lester explicitly intended his translation as a warning to Americans against the dangers of factionalism and disunion that destroyed the Roman Republic and later snuffed out the Italian republics, making Machiavelli a touchstone for balancing civic order with republican freedom in the tumultuous antebellum decades.[20] On their visits to the cathedral of Santa Croce in Florence, Americans, including Melville, made sure they visited the monuments to Galileo, Dante, Alfieri, Michaelangelo, and Machiavelli (15:122), a grouping that linked science, religion, art, and politics in a shrine to cultural nationalism; and Melville's Murray reminded readers that the Florentine republic began in the Piazza di Santa Croce when the citizens "made themselves *people,* according to the expressive term of the Chronicles."[21] While Ahab may, as Elizabeth D. Samet suggests in passing, display traits of "Machiavellian cynicism," *Pierre* builds on Macaulay's more complex revisionist views and integrates them into its primary themes.[22]

Internal evidence suggests that Melville knew both the *The History of Florence* and *The Prince* (which was available in the Bohn edition) because significant sections of *Pierre* follow the latter's most controversial maxims. Plinlimmon's recognition that people never turn the other cheek finds support in Machiavelli's insistence that princes should exercise power ruthlessly, and Plinlimmon's doctrine of a "virtuous expediency" (7:214) follows from Machiavelli's principle that princes must sometimes practice deception in order to maintain the state. Glendinning Stanly, Pierre's autocratic cousin, closely models such "Princely" behavior. For some time Glen has offered a honeymoon apartment in New York to Pierre and Lucy, but when Pierre explains that it will be for him and Isabel, not Lucy, Glen pretends not to know him and peremptorily dismisses him from his

---

20. *Florentine Histories,* 1: viii–ix.

21. *Handbook for Travellers in Northern Italy.,* 7th ed., 2 vols., vol. 2 (London: John Murray, 1858).

22. In *Willing Obedience: Citizens, Soldiers, and the Progress of Consent in America, 1776–1898* (Stanford, CA: Stanford University Press, 2004), Samet finds that Ahab overcomes Starbuck's scruples "with a combination of Machiavellian know-how and what Michael Rogin has called 'magnetic ascendancy'" (72), and she attributes to Ahab "a sincere belief in his own authority coupled with a Machiavellian cynicism about what it will take to suborn his crew" (74). Since Melville was recalling the "Florentine history" from his brother, he had probably read some Machiavelli before he finished writing *Moby-Dick,* although the novel never alludes explicitly to the diplomat.

house (7:239). By refusing to recognize Pierre, Glen can renege on his promise to provide his cousin and Isabel with an apartment and avoid the appearance of endorsing their relationship, something that would factionalize the family and lend credence to Pierre's anarchic behavior. At the end of the novel Glen attacks Pierre with a cowhide and Pierre kills him with two pistol shots. However rude and violent Glen may be, his death is clearly unjustified, a drastic consequence of Pierre's guilt and passion. Like Machiavelli's Prince, Glen desires order before sentiment and is willing to use dissimulation (pretending not to know Pierre) and force (the cowhide) in order to achieve his ends of preserving familial stability. Rogin perceptively sees that Pierre kills the part of himself that lives within the bounds of history and family: "Glen is Jacob to Pierre's savage Esau," Rogin observes, acknowledging the worldliness and cunning Glen represents.[23] In *Israel Potter* Melville calls Jacob "A tanned Machiavelli in tents" (8:46); Glen's manipulation of Pierre fully anticipates the comparison.

While it is easy to dismiss Glen Stanly as an aristocratic hypocrite, he is actually as complex as Machiavelli himself, a worldly sophisticate who recognizes that virtue without practical action is useless. Like Machiavelli Glen has traveled in France and Italy. Less profound than the Tuscan, Glen acquired from his travels a "fastidious superciliousness, which like the alledged [sic] bigoted Federalism of old times would not—according to a political legend—grind its daily coffee in any mill save of European manufacture" (7:218). Melville's "alledged" hedges his bets, allowing space for Federalist cosmopolitanism which, whatever its drawbacks, might have prevented Pierre's provincial overreaction to Isabel's exoticism. For the most part, "the less earnest and now Europeanized Glen" practices toward Pierre a "cool Tuscan policy," a canny strategy that holds "It is false that in point of policy a man should never make enemies. As well-wishers some men may not only be nugatory but positive obstacles in your peculiar plans; but as foes you may subordinately cement them into your general design" (7:219, 222). Glen's "policy" derives from *The Prince,* chapter 20, where Machiavelli argues "that it is advantageous for a prince to have enemies, which by preventing him from indulging in a dangerous repose, will enable him to win the esteem and admiration not only of his faithful, but of his rebellious subjects" (*History of Florence,* 471–72). The inferno world of *Pierre* is Dantean, to be sure; but in stopping short of Purgatory, let alone Paradise, it shares the moral realism of *The Prince* and exposes the perils of factionalism and familial discord in republics that Machiavelli

---

23. Rogin, *Subversive Genealogy,* 175.

146 / Chapter 4

Figure 13. Agasias of Ephesus, *The Borghese Gladiator,* .Musée du Louvre, Paris, France. First century BCE. Marble. Formerly known as the "Fighting Gladiator," this statue was found in the ruins of Nero's villa in 1611 and purchased by the Louvre in 1807.

found so distressing. Melville elaborates on Glen's cosmopolitan aestheticism with a flurry of Italian artistic allusions. After feigning ignorance of Pierre's identity, Glen turns to a friend to discuss the statue of the *Fighting Gladiator* in the Louvre (fig. 13).[24]

24. Melville may have seen this statue when he visited the Louvre on November 30, 1849 (15:31). Sculpted in Greece by Agasias of Ephesus (fl. 100 BCE) and taken from the Borghese Museum by Napoleon I in 1807, this statue was variously known as the *Fighter of Agasias* and the *Borghese Warrior*, as well as the *Fighting Gladiator*. The Louvre now calls it the *Borghese Gladiator*.

Infuriated by his cousin's indifference, Pierre leaps at him "like Spartacus" (7:239), absurdly identifying himself with the Louvre statue in a futile replay of the famous Roman slave revolt that led to death and defeat. As Wyn Kelley observes, Pierre here reveals his provincialism in a parody of conventional reactions to the city's moral complexity.[25] John P. McWilliams correctly sees Pierre as a failed Christian democrat who exposes the solipsism of Young American political principles;[26] yet by the end of the novel Pierre has gone even further, becoming like Spartacus a hopelessly overmatched pagan rebel whose impetuosity transforms him from subject to object, from agency to doomed revolt. In the context of post-1848 Italy, Pierre's emotional outburst darkly images the defeat of the Roman Republic, an erstwhile Christian democracy whose Mazzinian idealism outran Machiavellian reality. While Glen may represent the "evils of enlarged foreign travel" (7:218), Pierre represents the evils of provincial ignorance, an ignorance that, when threatened, responds murderously and futilely. Melville and Machiavelli share the fundamental Christian premise about humanity: people are born in sin. They are capable of redemption, as Dante argues, but most of them require strong enlightened leaders—a Virgil or Cosmo de Medici, whom Machiavelli praises for bringing order, wealth, and learning to Florence (*History of Florence,* 314–15). Successful rulers may need to break their promises and harm the few in order to help the many, perhaps Machiavelli's most infamous policy yet one which is grounded firmly on the premise of human evil, as is clear in this extended passage from chapter 18 of *The Prince,* "Whether princes ought to be faithful to their engagements":

> Now, as a prince must learn how to act the part of a beast sometimes, he should make the fox and the lion his patterns. The first can but feebly defend himself against the wolf, and the latter readily falls into such snares as are laid for him. From the fox, therefore, a prince will learn dexterity in avoiding snares; and from the lion, how to employ his strength to keep the wolves in awe. But they who entirely rely upon the lion's strength, will not always meet with success: in other words, a prudent prince cannot and ought not to keep his word, except when he can do it without injury to himself, or when the circumstances under which he contracted the engagement still exist.
>
> I should be cautious in inculcating such a precept if all men were good; but as the generality of mankind are wicked, and ever ready to

---

25. Kelley, *Melville's City,* 154.
26. *Hawthorne, Melville, and the American Character,* 166–74.

break their words, a prince should not pique himself in keeping his more scrupulously, especially as is it [sic] always easy to justify a breach of faith on his part. I could give numerous proofs of this, and show numberless engagements and treaties which have been violated by the treachery of princes, and that those who enacted the part of the fox, have always succeeded best in their affairs. It is necessary, however, to disguise the appearance of craft, and thoroughly to understand the art of feigning and dissembling; for men are generally so simple and so weak, that he who wishes to deceive easily finds dupes. (*History of Florence,* 459–60)

This passage looks forward to *The Confidence-Man* and its elaborate "feigning and dissembling" characters, especially the cosmopolitan Frank Goodman. Glen, a less duplicitous practitioner of Machiavellian policy, breaks faith with his cousin only after Pierre has broken his troth to Lucy, meaning that, as Machiavelli reasons, the "circumstances under which [Glen] contracted the engagement" no longer exist. Though he will not admit it to himself, Pierre's fantasies of Isabel betray his ignorance of that Dantean-Calvinistic-Machiavellian awareness "of Innate Depravity and Original Sin" that Melville praised in Hawthorne, Shakespeare, "and other masters of the great Art of Telling the Truth," among whom he surely counted Dante and Machiavelli (9:243, 244).

Pierre's destructive and self-serving idealism reaches its height when he allows Lucy to join him and Isabel in New York. Despite Pierre's conscious cruelty toward her, Lucy argues in a letter that "still we are one, Pierre; thou art sacrificing thyself, and I hasten to re-tie myself to thee, that so I may catch thy fire, and all the ardent multitudinous arms of our common flames may embrace" (7:309). Lucy's Dantean imagery of doomed lovers entwined in a shared inferno derives from Flaxman, as Schless noticed, yet it also iconically figures the doomed politics of Italian republicanism. Lucy's fatal infatuation with Pierre's revolutionary idealism resembles Margaret Fuller's sanctification of Mazzini, precisely the kind of hero-worship that Medusan gender politics destroys. The enthusiastic Charlie Millthorpe may be right when he says that society needs a new Curtius, a self-sacrificing Roman hero willing to plunge into the abyss to "save the whole empire of men" (7:281), but Pierre's "loftier heroism" hardly qualifies, for it sacrifices others along with himself in mutual immolation: "So Pierre turned round and tied Lucy to the same stake which must hold himself, for he too plainly saw, that it could not be, but that both their hearts must burn" (7:178). The metaphor prefigures the nihilistic conclusion that leaves Pierre, Lucy, and Isabel in a Shakespearean-Dantean Hell: "Well, be it hell," says Pierre in the novel's penultimate section; "I will mold a trumpet of the flames, and, with my breath of flame, breathe back my defiance!"—an Ahabian utterance that merits his doom (7:360). Glen, in contrast, blends European tradition with American individualism by fighting for family and honor even though he uses selfish means. He is, in short, both a fox and a lion, a figure that adumbrates Melville's move toward a ductile Machiavellian philosophy that draws on history and art to create a politics of compromise, accommodation, and pragmatism, one that develops in the 1850s and inspires him to experiment with fictional form and eventually turn away from linear narrative altogether.

MACHIAVELLIAN SATIRE IN "COCK-A-DOODLE-DOO!"

Machiavelli's narrative style and ironic tone offered stylistic resources for Melville as his satiric tone darkened even further in reaction to the growing crisis over slavery at home and the demise of republican movements in Europe. Macaulay's essay stressed Machiavelli's literary value by reminding readers that he wrote several dramatic comedies and a satiric novel along with his histories, political treatises, and correspondence, and in all genres showed "that his understanding was strong, his taste pure, and his sense of the ridiculous exquisitely keen"; he was a writer, Macaulay added in his own sally into sarcasm, "whose only fault was, that, having adopted some of the maxims then generally received, he arranged them more luminously, and expressed them more forcibly, than any other writer."[27] In an important essay on the rhetoric of *The Prince* Victoria Kahn declares that "the world of Machiavellian politics is intrinsically ironic, and the most effective mode of behavior in such a world is theatrical and hyperbolic," meaning that leaders may employ gesture and performance rather than principle to achieve their ends.[28] This is, of course, precisely the style of leadership that Ahab adopts and that Melville critiques in "The Specksynder," which claims that behind Ahab's "irresistible dictatorship" lie "arts and entrenchments" necessary in any powerful leader (6:147–48). Kahn makes a similar analysis of Machiavelli, who uses a "strategic style" that implicates readers in making ethical judgments by duplicating "on the poetic level the practical problem of judgment that the prince will have

27. Macaulay, "Machiavelli," *Edinburgh Review* 45: 262, 276.
28. "Virtù and the Example of Agathocles in Machiavelli's *Prince*," in Albert Russell Ascoli and Victoria Ann Kahn, *Machiavelli and the Discourse of Literature* (Ithaca, NY: Cornell University Press, 1993), 201.

to face—that of applying the rule of virtù to the particular situation at hand," or, as she quotes Roland Barthes on Machiavelli's work, "the structure of the discourse attempts to reproduce the structure of the dilemmas actually faced by the protagonists."[29] Such rhetorical indeterminacy is familiar to readers of "Bartleby, the Scrivener," "Benito Cereno," and *The Confidence-Man,* but rather than analyzing this style through poststructuralist theory we might find its origins in Machiavelli and its function within the historical conditions of the American 1850s. Machiavelli sees life as a constant battle between *virtù,* or individual valor in the Italian sense of the word,[30] and fortuna, or the uncontrollable events of history. All judgments, both those of princes and those of readers, are made within the limiting circumstances of particular situations, making all appeals to transcendent ideals or generalized rules irrelevant. Sometimes cruelty, violence, and deceit may effect a greater good than adherence to traditional ethical norms, as critics argue in defense of Babo's struggle for freedom in "Benito Cereno." Yet tension arises when a counterforce, in this case Amasa Delano, succeeds by the favor of fortuna, always a risk in politics and war. Delano is almost murdered on several occasions, and when he does take decisive action his men barely subdue a foe that is already exhausted by weeks of exposure and privation. "Benito Cereno" employs what Kahn calls a humanist "rhetoric of problematizing examples," a device Machiavelli uses to illustrate the limits of idealism in particular historical circumstances and force his readers, like Melville's, to examine their own ethical and moral values.[31]

Melville's second published story, "Cock-A-Doodle-Doo! Or, The Crowing of the Noble Cock Beneventano" (*Harper's,* December 1853), clearly marks his turn toward satire as a chief mode for confronting the challenges to republican idealism in both Italy and America of the 1850s. The narrator opens the tale with the jaunty remark that "In all parts of the world many high-spirited revolts from rascally despotisms had of late been knocked on the head.... All round me were tokens of a divided

---

29. Kahn, "Virtù," 207–8.

30. As the *OED* explains, virtù (or vertu) with its Italian sense of "valor" has never been current in English; rather, English adopted the French sense that means "the love of fine arts," as in Thomas Carlyle's famous denunciation of Italy as a "noble Nation sunk from virtue to virtù" (*Frederick the Great,* Book III). See *The Works of Thomas Carlyle,* vol. 1 (New York: Peter Fenelon Collier, 1897), 218.

31. Kahn, "Virtù," 212. Because "Benito Cereno" draws relatively little on Italian culture, I do not offer an extensive analysis of it here. Clearly, however, Risorgimento nationalism provides a political backdrop for the story and its plot cycle of oppression, liberation, and renewed oppression, as well as its theatricality and use of deception to gain freedom, owes much to Machiavellian thought.

empire" (9:268), an indifferent response to tyrannical regimes like Bomba's that verges on black humor. The title's allusion to Ferdinando Beneventano, whom Melville heard sing at the Astor Place Opera House in 1847 (9:694), suggests that the cock's fruitless crowing—by the end of the story its impoverished owner Merrymusk and his family are all dead, followed swiftly by the cock himself—parallels the futility of Italian art in Pierre's "City of Dis." Just before the story appeared Beneventano had performed in *Masaniello,* which *Putnam's Monthly* termed "one of the liberal operas" about "the progress and success of a popular insurrection."[32] Yet the *Putnam's* article offers no political analysis and focuses entirely on criticizing the scenery and singing, a disjunction of aesthetics and politics like that in "Cock-A-Doodle-Doo!" The narrator prizes the cock for its beauty and voice, and compares it to a "Field-Marshal" (Radetzky?), "Lord Nelson," and "the Emperor Charlemagne" (9:282), antirevolutionary figures all. No wonder his sympathy for the "unlucky risings of the poor oppressed *peoples* abroad" (9:274) is so shallow. Along with *Putnam's,* an ostensibly liberal publication, the narrator shares an elitist frame of reference that divides art from politics and sees poverty through rose-colored lenses: the cock, he says, "looked like some noble foreigner. He looked like some Oriental king in some magnificent Italian Opera" (9:282). When he unthinkingly calls the cock "Signor Beneventano" in the presence of Merrymusk, he immediately feels embarrassed, for the woodcutter lives in a different social world and misses the allusion. The narrator's culture of art, pleasure, indolence, and operatic performance veils political and social reality with imposing costumery and exaggerated gestures. Like a narrator from a Poe story, he cannot remember details of his visit to the opera the year before, neither the opera's title nor the precise role Beneventano played—"some royal character," is all he says, as he substitutes art for reality: "the proud pace of the cock seemed the very stage-pace of the Signor Beneventano" (9:283). Although opera played an important role in Risorgimento politics, even Americans as sympathetic as Walt Whitman seemed deaf to its political message.[33] Arias, whether natural or com-

---

32. "Music," *Putnam's Monthly* 2 (December 1853): 689. This is the same issue in which "Bartleby, the Scrivener" appeared.

33. For a measured view of opera's political impact, see Mary Ann Smart, "Liberty On (and Off) the Barricades," *Making and Remaking Italy,* 103–18. Robert D. Faner, *Walt Whitman & Opera* (Carbondale: Southern Illinois Press, 1951), notes that Whitman often recalled seeing *Masaniello* (10, 14, 49) and particularly admired the singing of Beneventano (41), but Faner says nothing about the political or social effect of these or other operas on Whitman. Rather, he stresses their formal influence on the diction, structure, rhythms, and sound of Whitman's poetry. Whitman's personal recollections of opera reveal similar apolitical views; see "The Old Bowery" in *Complete Poetry and Collected Prose,* ed. Justin Kaplan (New York: Library of America, 1982), 1185–92.

posed, the cock's or Beneventano's, mask injustice much as Italy's beautiful landscape masks its social, political, and economic conflicts. The story takes place in Massachusetts, itself a state torn between Know-Nothing reaction and Senator Daniel Webster's commercially motivated support for foreign revolutionaries.[34] Divided empires exist at home as well as in Europe, and the divisions are deepening, yet the Imperial Self that dominated Melville's early work is now an artifact of youthful innocence shunted aside by marginalized and obtuse narrators content to observe surfaces and avoid personal feeling or commitment. While the failure of Italy's "high-spirited revolts" justified Headley's low opinion of Italian fitness for self-rule, Melville saw in it more universal evidence of social fragmentation and the failure of community, even in the United States. In this jaundiced mood his ironic and satirical impulses come to the fore and make him more aware than ever that America needs its own Risorgimento.

REVOLUTIONARY FOLLIES
Kossuth, Mazzini, and Young America

After his move to Pittsfield in 1850, Melville drew further away from New York Italophiles and the second generation of Young Americans, what Edward L. Widmer calls "Young America II."[35] The Risorgimento came to his very doorstep in the surrogate for Mazzini, Louis Kossuth, the famous but failed Hungarian revolutionary who began his carnivalesque grand tour of the United States in December 1851 to plead for American support for European republicans, sparking a "Kossuth Fever," in Larry Reynolds's words, that swept the United States from 1851–52.[36] Just before leaving England, Kossuth had met with Mazzini and formed an alliance to promote national self-determination throughout Europe. When Mazzini appeared with Kossuth on a train platform in Birmingham, England, Melville's local paper, the *Pittsfield Sun*, reported that Mazzini "became almost as popular and the object of curiosity, as the Hungarian

---

34. Gemme, *Domesticating Foreign Struggles*, 71–72.
35. *Young America*, 185–86. In his "Prologue" Widmer says that "More than any writer, Herman Melville registered an acute disappointment with the failure of Young America, a psychic wound that coincided with his thrust at greatness" (17). Oddly, Widmer barely mentions *Pierre*'s withering satire of Young America's literary pretensions and thus understates, in my view, how early Melville diverged from the movement.
36. *European Revolutions*, 153–61.

himself."³⁷ In the United States Kossuth mentioned Mazzini frequently and favorably, publicity that kept the Risorgimento in the news despite its repression in Italy: "We [Hungary and Italy] have a common enemy," Kossuth declared to the New York press, "so we are brothers in arms for freedom and independence."³⁸ He also quoted Garibaldi's Churchillian injunction to his troops before the siege of Rome, an address Kossuth called "the most glorious speech I ever heard in my life" as the *Literary World* reported, thereby basking in the luster of the Risorgimento's best-known military hero as well as Mazzini's fame as its leading politician.³⁹

The Mazzini-Kossuth alliance stimulated the imagination of Kentuckian George N. Sanders who, as the new owner and editor of the *Democratic Review,* assumed de facto leadership of Young America. Sanders published a January 1852 article praising Kossuth and Mazzini as the current leaders of "Young Europe" and urging Americans to support them in their battle against the "Machiavellian" Austrians, an epithet that revealed his ignorance of Machiavelli's republican ideology.⁴⁰ The *Literary World* showed more enthusiasm for Kossuth than for *Moby-Dick,* which it reviewed unfavorably on November 15 and 22, 1851, by devoting a dozen columns in its four December issues to Kossuth's reception in New York and joining the chorus praising his eloquence, intellect, prudence, courage, and idealism. The usual crowd of Italophiles—Headley, Bellows, Bryant, Dana, George Bancroft, Sumner, Cornelius Mathews, Parke Godwin, and even President Charles King of Columbia College—paid homage to the Hungarian throughout the month. Duyckinck reprinted Walter Savage Landor's poem "To Kossuth on His Departure for America" that concluded with six lines designed to stoke Young American vanity and open American wallets:

Hungary! No more
Thy saddest loss deplore;
Look to the star-crowned Genius of the West,
Sole guardian of the opprest.

37. November 27, 1851, 2.
38. Quoted in Rossi, *Image of America,* 84.
39. December 27, 1851, 507. During the Battle of Britain, Churchill told the House of Commons, "I have nothing to offer but blood, toil, tears and sweat" (May 13, 1940); similarly, Garibaldi told his troops "what I have to offer you is fatigue, danger, struggle, and death."
40. "Mazzini—Young Europe," *Democratic Review* 30 (January 1852): 50. The article is presumably by Sanders. For Kossuth and Mazzini's relationship during this time, see Rossi's excellent chapter on Kossuth's American tour (*Image of America,* 75–90), and for Sanders and Mazzini, see both Rossi's chapter on "Mazzini and Young America," 90–104, and Gemme, *Domesticating Foreign Struggles,* 72–78.

Oh! That one only nation dared to save
Kossuth the true and brave.[41]

As a master of English idiom, a Protestant, an aristocrat, a constitutionalist, a moderate republican, and most importantly an avowed anti-Socialist, Kossuth charmed Americans with his charisma and rhetoric and gave a familiar, reassuring face to European radicalism. In comparison to the intellectual Mazzini, Kossuth seemed to Parke Godwin more deliberate, "comprehensive and solid."[42] Only the most skeptical Americans—among them Melville and Hawthorne—could resist him.[43]

Even in Pittsfield there was pressure on Melville to join Kossuth's crusade. His mother adored Kossuth and wondered why her son was not as religious as the Magyar patriot, while Sarah Morewood twitted Melville for his reclusiveness to which he replied, as Morewood wrote George Duyckinck, "if he left home to look after Hungary the cause in hunger would suffer."[44] Melville had surely seen the articles in the December *Literary World* and followed Kossuth's progress in the *New York Herald,* both of which he still received in Pittsfield, and the *Pittsfield Sun* set the local tone by reporting Kossuth's every move, reprinting his speeches and public prayers and publishing Henry P. Tappan's eight-stanza "Ode to Kossuth" on page 1.[45] In something no biographer has noticed, Kossuth actually made a whistle-stop visit to Pittsfield on May 18, 1852, on his way from Boston to Albany and delivered a short speech, declaring that he fought "by the authority of the Continental Congress and Almighty God,"[46] a calculated appeal to American patriotism that fired up the crowd and earned Kossuth a donation of twenty muskets. Melville's disgust with such theatrics surfaces in *The Confidence-Man* when Frank

41. *Literary World,* December 6, 452. The *Literary World* reported on artists' support for Kossuth on November 29 (431), on his earlier difficulties with the Austrian emperor on December 6 (445–46), on New York's enthusiasm on December 13 (469), and on his oratory and meetings on December 20 (481–82, 486).

42. Quoted from the *Phrenological Journal* in the *Literary World,* July 3, 1852, 11. Godwin had visited Mazzini on a recent visit to London.

43. In a letter to George N. Sanders of June 14, 1854, Hawthorne criticizes Kossuth's hedging on the slavery question in comparison to Mazzini's forthright desire for universal emancipation. See *The Centenary Edition of the Works of Nathaniel Hawthorne,* ed. Thomas Woodson et al. (Columbus: The Ohio State University Press, 1987), 17:230–31.

44. Parker, *Herman Melville,* 2:51, 49.

45. For Melville's disinterest in Kossuth see Parker, *Herman Melville,* 2:49, and for his mother's "excessive adulation" of Kossuth see 2:40, 51. I counted thirteen articles on Kossuth between January and June 1852 in the *Pittsfield Sun.* Tappan's "Ode to Kossuth," which compares Kossuth to Washington and identifies Kossuth's cause with America's, appeared in the *Sun* on January 15, 1852, 1.

46. *Pittsfield Sun,* May 20, 1852, 2.

Goodman quotes "gloomy souls" who believe that expecting "truth and the right" from American journalists "is little more sensible than for Kossuth and Mazzini to indulge hopes from the other" (10:165), a comment that reveals Melville's mature disdain for newspapers, popular politics, and revolutionary dreamers. He would have agreed with Hawthorne's satiric comment on American support for Kossuth when Miles Coverdale, the effete narrator of *The Blithedale Romance* (1852), claims that he could join the Hungarian for "one brave rush upon the levelled bayonets" if, and only if, the battle were held "within an easy ride of my abode" on a "mild, sunny morning, after breakfast."[47] Both Kossuth and Mazzini, like Melville's "fool of virtue" Pierre Glendinning, live outside history and ignore the anarchy and violence their policies arouse. They refuse to accept their failures and adjust their policies, and delude both themselves and their followers with fine rhetoric but little action.

"I and My Chimney," one of Melville's most genial antirevolutionary stories, makes a slighting reference to Kossuth that mocks both the Hungarian and his followers and contrasts their widespread yet superficial enthusiasm with the chimney's stable and solid traditionalism. The narrator calls the chimney a "grand seignior," an "autocrat," "the king of the house," and compares it to "the pyramids," to an altar "right worthy for the celebration of high mass before the Pope of Rome," and to Madame de Maintenon's residence at Versailles: "any man can buy a square foot of land and plant a liberty-pole on it, but it takes a king to set apart whole acres for a grand Trianon" (9:353, 358, 358, 365, 359, 354). Allan Emery sees in these and other political references a nationalist allegory of slavery and Union in which Melville takes a middle ground between the narrator's desire to preserve the chimney, a symbol of Unionism associated with Daniel Webster and the Compromise of 1850, and the wife's abolitionism, represented by her eagerness to diminish the chimney's unifying role.[48] Yet nearly all the political references are international: Caesar, Cardinal Wolsey, Henry VIII, Cromwell, Peter the Great, the partition of Poland, and of course the sarcastic allusion to Kossuth. As he surveys his abundant acreage the narrator confesses that it grows more weeds than grass: "Weeds, too, it is amazing how they spread. No such thing as arresting them—some of our pastures being a sort of Alsatia for the weeds. As for the grass, every spring it is like Kossuth's rising of what he calls the peoples" (9:355); that is, grass flourishes no better than Kossuth's

---

47. *Centenary Edition,* ed. Fredson Bowers and William Charvat, 3: 246–47.
48. Allan Moore Emery, "The Political Significance of Melville's Chimney," *New England Quarterly* 55, no. 2 (1982): 221–28.

revolution.[49] The main problem is not the "peoples," however; Jack Chase, after all, swore to cleave to them as he did to his shipmates (5:192). The problem is with "the public," which succumbs to charismatic leaders like Kossuth and Mazzini. Like the narrator of "Cock-A-Doodle-Doo," the aristocrat Kossuth and the expatriate theorist Mazzini understand little of the "peoples" they purport to serve and underestimate the need for strong central governments. The narrator's Unionist politics are closer to Melville's than Emery thinks. Underestimating the effect of failed democratic revolutions on Melville's thought, Emery like many critics uses White-Jacket's Jacksonian effusions as the baseline for judging Melville's political sympathies. By 1853, however, Melville recognized that nations, like chimneys, required deep foundations rooted in the history and customs of the people they represent. The chimney is not a one-dimensional symbol of monarchy but a complex icon merging liberty and authority, a formerly tall edifice "razeed," or shortened, by a former owner—a "regicidal act," the narrator calls it—and that now, "as a free citizen of this free land, stands upon an independent basis of its own" (9:356).[50] The chimney blends monarchy and republic by combining great age and a dominating appearance with picturesque individuality. By refusing to yield to the "pocketesque" (9:357), the utilitarian urge for efficiency, conformity, and rationality, the chimney retains its connection to the past while offering the narrator personal comfort in the present.

Melville extended his satire of revolution in "Charles' Isle and the Dog-King," like all of "The Encantadas" composed by the pseudonymous "Salvator R. Tarnmoor" who would, presumably, understand the extremes of Risorgimento nationalism. The sketch recounts a political experiment undertaken by the new republic of Peru when it grants the island to a soldier who fought bravely in the country's 1821 revolt against Spain. Ironically, he establishes a monarchy instead of a republic and subjects his citizens to a tyranny as vicious as any ancien régime: he proclaims martial law and "actually hunted and shot with his own hand several of his rebellious subjects" (9:147, 148). He protects himself from his "citizen-mob" with a bodyguard of "renegado strangers" (9:148), relying on

---

49. "Alsatia" is British slang for a refuge where officials could not arrest criminals (*OED*), a usage Melville could have picked up in conversation or from Francis Jeffrey's review of Scott in *The Modern British Essayists*. To avoid arrest, a character flees to the London district of Whitefriars, "then known by the cant name of *Alsatia*, and understood to possess the privileges of a sanctuary against ordinary arrests," Jeffrey explains (546). See *Modern British Essayists* 6 (Philadelphia: Carey and Hart, 1846), 543–48.

50. For a view corroborating mine, see Larry J. Reynolds, *European Revolutions*, 159–60, which argues that "much of the defiant conservatism in the work reflects that of the author" (160).

foreign troops in defiance of Machiavellian principles, and as Machiavelli predicted, the strangers, like "the foreign-born Pretorians, unwisely introduced into the Roman state" (9: 149) mutiny and banish the Dog-King to Peru.[51] Veering from one political extreme to another, they proclaim a republic which quickly degenerates into "a democracy neither Grecian, Roman, nor American. Nay, it was no democracy at all, but a permanent *Riotocracy,* which gloried in having no law but lawlessness" (9:149). These lawless republicans fancy themselves political heroes but are only one more noxious patch of weeds: "Each runaway tar was hailed as a martyr in the cause of freedom, and became immediately installed a ragged citizen of this universal nation. . . . It became Anathema—a sea Alsatia—the unassailed lurking-place of all sorts of desperadoes, who in the name of liberty did just what they pleased" (9:149–50). Devoid of order and masking anarchy with the rubrics of European republicanism—the American press conventionally called Kossuth a "martyr to freedom" and quoted Mazzini's call for a "universal Republic"[52]—Charles' Isle reprises the mob rule that plagued Florence and drove Machiavelli to warn reformers, "Let no one, when raising popular commotions, imagine he can afterwards control them at his pleasure, or restrain them from proceeding to the commission of violence" (*History of Florence,* 123).

In a letter to Duyckinck of February 2, 1850, Melville repeated the popular notion that "(as the divines say) political republics should be the asylum for the persecuted of all nations" (14:154), a noble sentiment identifying America as the typological "redeemer nation." By 1855 his short stories had dismantled this view with a transnational vision that condemns both monarchies and republics for their inability to construct a humane and democratic social order. Neither form of government provides by itself the combination of order and freedom necessary to successful nations, not even the "redeemer nation" of America, whose revolutionary promise now seemed as unlikely and insubstantial as the illusory republics of Kossuth and Mazzini.

---

51. In chapter 13 of *The Prince,* "Of Auxiliary, Mixed, and Native Troops," Machiavelli faults Pope Julius II and other rulers for relying on foreign troops and praises Cesare Borgia for replacing his French soldiers with native Italians.

52. For example, Henry P. Tappan calls Kossuth "the Hero and the Martyr" and "Freedom's youngest son" ("Ode to Kossuth," *Pittsfield Sun,* January 15, 1852, 1). The quotation from Mazzini is in "Mazzini—Young Europe," *Democratic Review* 30 (January 1852): 51.

REVOLUTIONARY HEROES
Machiavellian Politics in *Israel Potter*

After 1852, as Edward L. Widmer has shown, George Sanders's enthusiasm for Manifest Destiny, slavery, and the annexation of Cuba split Young America in half, leaving Melville and his circle in the antislavery camp.[53] Foreign policy also played a role, however, for as Joseph Rossi has shown, Sanders embraced Europe's "Red Republicans" far too warmly for many Americans and by 1855 his reputation had plummeted along with Mazzini's.[54] English supporters became frustrated with Mazzini's repeated attempts to foment insurrection and assassinate monarchs, and after the disastrous Milan uprising in February 1853 Mazzini lost moderate support in Italy as well as abroad.[55] His popular image was changing from savior of Italy to feckless conspirator and some Americans began to question whether they shared the ideals of the Risorgimento after all. Both *Harper's New Monthly Magazine* and *Putnam's Monthly Magazine,* which published all of Melville's writing after 1852, including his only serialized novel, *Israel Potter,* register this change in American opinion.

Harper's, for example, published favorable articles on both Kossuth and Mazzini in 1851 and 1852, but by 1855 an editorial portrayed Mazzini as an irresponsible creature out of a tale by Poe:

> Mazzini, with his wild, extravagant visions haunting him—lurking secretly among the mountain fastnesses—still finds means to speak his thought upon every measure of the hour, and to alienate some of the most ardent friends of Italian liberty by the eccentricity and exaggeration of his views. And were every yoke of foreign states withdrawn from Italy to-morrow, it is ten to one but the altercations of Italian patriots would involve that

---

53. *Young America,* 185–209. Sanders eventually wound up supporting the Confederacy during the Civil War.

54. Rossi, *Image of America,* 104. The *Democratic Review* advocated direct intervention in the Italian struggle for freedom and tried to galvanize American support with two long articles revisiting the events of 1848 and 1849: "Monarchy and the Republic in Italy. Campaigns of Charles Albert and of the Republicans," 31 (September 1852): 193–208, and "Campaigns of Charles Albert and of the Republicans. Second Campaign of Charles Albert," 31 (October 1852): 305–25. Relying heavily on Hugh Forbes's lectures, Sanders argued that Mazzini should be the leader of the new Italy and Rome should be its capital. He was appointed temporary consul to London in the early days of the Pierce administration and issued American passports to Mazzini and his friends; entertained Mazzini, Kossuth, Garibaldi, and other leading republicans at a famous Washington's Birthday dinner in 1854; and promised to supply the revolutionaries with weapons (95–97). Needless to say, he was soon recalled from diplomatic duty.

55. Mack Smith, *Mazzini,* 98–102; Rudman, *Italian Nationalism,* 104–19.

unfortunate country in a wilder and more bloody confusion than befalls her now.⁵⁶

Harper's editorials also registered an emerging discontent with facile identifications between European (particularly French) and American republicanism: "the memory of our revolution ... is greatly lowered by being compared continually with every miserable Cuban expedition and Canadian invasion, or every European émeute," and we should look to the nation's founders, not today's "gambling managers of modern political caucuses," to find the true "Young America."⁵⁷ In one of many indications that the *Literary World* had lost its enthusiasm for Young American ideology, Duyckinck favorably quoted this opinion and, as his weekly faded into obscurity, confined its articles on international politics to scattered attacks on Napoleon III and the pope.⁵⁸ As papal Rome and Bomba's Naples remained hostile to reform, old charges of Italian effeminacy, immorality, corruption, ignorance, violence, and unfitness for liberty resurfaced in a vitriolic anti-Catholic tirade in *Harper's* in 1855 by James Jackson Jarves, who targeted Mazzini for special obloquy: "All who have read the appeals of Mazzini to his countrymen will not fail to perceive that he relies chiefly on treachery and assassination—a wholesale repetition of the Sicilian vespers—to bring about a revolution."⁵⁹ In 1857 another *Harper's* editorial distinguished "Red Republicanism" from "American Republicanism" and concluded that "Humanity in Europe does not so much ask of us soldiers for Kossuth and Mazzini, as citizens trained in the school of Washington and Franklin,"⁶⁰ a position akin to Hawthorne's in *The*

---

56. "Our Foreign Gossip," section of "Editor's Easy Chair," *Harper's New Monthly Magazine* 11, no. 62 (July 1855): 275. The untitled piece on Kossuth appeared in 4:19 (December 1851): 40–47, and assured readers that "Kossuth comes to us as the exiled representative of those fundamental principles upon which our political institutions are based" (46). For Mazzini, see "Mazzini the Italian Liberal," 4:21 (February 1852): 404–8, a retrospective of his career that praises his work with Young Italy but recognizes his tendency to enthusiasm.

57. "Editor's Table," *Harper's New Monthly Magazine* 5 (July 1852): 265, 264. *Harper's* also published a series of cartoons satirizing Young America as childish, ineffective, and lazy; see issues 7:40 (September 1853): 574, and 9:49 (June 1854): 141–42.

58. *Literary World,* 3 July 1852, 10. For articles condemning Napoleon III see the issues of January 8, April 2, and May 21, 1853. Duyckinck joined in the attack on Pius IX for outlawing *Uncle Tom's Cabin* in the Papal States by reprinting a British poem that concludes "You can't be Pio! no—no no!" (June 25, 1853, 517), and he claimed precedence for the pun in *Yankee Doodle* as if trying to earn credit for his earlier liberalism (see chapter 2, note 8). The *Literary World* ceased publication at the end of 1853.

59. "Italian Life and Morals—Effects of Romanism on Society," *Harper's* 10 (February 1855): 331. Jarves included this article in his travel book, *Italian Sights & Papal Principles Seen through American Spectacles* (New York: Harper & Brothers, 1856).

60. "Editor's Table," 14 (February 1857): 413–14.

Blithedale Romance and Melville's in "I and My Chimney."

Putnam's, despite its more liberal and internationalist politics, also distanced itself from Mazzini and interventionism.[61] Publisher George Palmer Putnam, editor George William Curtis, and frequent contributor Parke Godwin counted themselves "friends of Italy" and showed early sympathy for Kossuth, yet gradually separated Italy's politics from its culture in such poems as the anonymous "Ode to Southern Italy" that buried vague hopes for Italian independence in a mass of picturesque clichés, or in its humorous account of travel in northern Italy that confined its politics to a few sarcastic comments about Austrians, or in the apolitical aestheticism of a poem on Dante that immediately preceded Melville's "The Apple-Tree Table."[62] In a notice of Englishman Richard Heber Wrightson's *History of Modern Italy* (1855) the writer, presumably Curtis, demurs from Margaret Fuller's high opinion of Italy's revolutionary leaders and sympathizes with Wrightson's "distrust and dislike of the Mazzini republicans": "we are disposed to agree with him in his conviction, that the 'conspirators' and theoretic democrats of Italy have played into the hands of the despots, foreign and domestic, who oppress that magnificent country."[63] A lighthearted 1857 article offered comic portraits of five exiles yet concluded with a serious call to avoid the "fanaticism of a Mazzini" and follow instead the model of Felice Foresti, who by now was a constitutional monarchist and American consul to Piedmont-Sardinia.[64] *Putnam's* was too cosmopolitan to indulge in the overt anti-Catholicism of *Harper's*, yet still held to an ideology linking republicanism and Protestantism. In "Should We Fear the Pope?" the writer argued that because American Catholics are participating more in democratic politics and experiencing the freedom it offers, "Rome is far more likely to become American, under the influences at work here, than America Roman."[65]

61. For a fine comparison of the politics of *Harper's* and *Putnam's*, see Post-Lauria, *Correspondent Colorings*, 165–209. For *Putnam's* literary politics, see Perry Miller, *Raven and the Whale*, 315–21. Unlike Miller, Post-Lauria does not specifically identify *Putnam's* as Young American progeny, but its literary nationalism and liberal politics clearly link it with the socially progressive, antislavery wing of the disparate movement. Also, the phrase "Young America" occurs repeatedly and favorably throughout the journal in contrast to *Harper's*, which scorned the term.

62. Richard Burleigh Kimball, "Cuba," *Putnam's Monthly Magazine* 1, no. 1 (January 1853): 3–16. This was *Putnam's* most conventionally Young American piece, sympathizing with Kossuth, criticizing Napoleon III, and advocating the annexation of Cuba and any other republic that wanted to join the Union. "Ode to Southern Italy, *Putnam's Monthly Magazine* 2 (July 1853): 23–24; [anonymous], "From Venice to Vienna," 1 (February 1853): 164–70; "A Few Days in Venice," 2 (July 1853): 60–66; and "On a Picture of Beatrice in Paradise," 7 (May 1856): 464.

63. "Editorial Notes," *Putnam's Monthly Magazine* 6 (September 1855): 328. Curtis became editor in March 1855.

64. "Italians in America," 9 (January 1857): 8.

65. *Putnam's Monthly Magazine* 5 (June 1855): 658.

Seemingly a progressive view, this argument in fact rests on the conservative premise that Roman Catholicism is inimical to republicanism and that an independent Italy will magically turn Protestant, views espoused earlier by Margaret Fuller.

In such fissures we find a growing unease with radical transnational republicanism across the political spectrum and an emerging recognition that Americans could support revolutionary nationalism only if it provided law, order, and religious and economic freedom. Melville's most nationalistic novel, *Israel Potter* (*Putnam's*, 1854–55), applies these criteria to the American Revolution and finds that, like all revolutions, it contains anarchic elements that require cunning diplomacy to control. By valorizing rebellion, revolutions sow the seeds of their own destruction and foster the moral and political chaos that subjects nations to the inexorable cycles of decline, fall, and resurrection predicted by Media's scroll. Machiavelli understood this and argued for counterbalancing liberty with authority:

> Republican governments, more especially those imperfectly organized, frequently change their rulers and the form of their institutions; not by the influence of liberty or subjection, as many suppose, but by that of slavery and licence; for with the nobility or the people, the ministers respectively of slavery or licentiousness, only the name of liberty is in any estimation, neither of them choosing to be subject either to magistrates or laws. When, however, a good, wise, and powerful citizen appears (which is but seldom), who establishes ordinances capable of appeasing or restraining these contending dispositions, so as to prevent them from doing mischief, then the government may be called free, and its institutions firm and secure; for having good laws for its basis, and good regulations for carrying them into effect, it needs not, like others, the virtue of one man for its maintenance. With such excellent laws and institutions, many of those ancient republics, which were of long duration, were endowed. (*History of Florence*, 157)

Either political extreme, the people or the nobles, cloaks its rule in "liberty" to justify anarchy or tyranny, licentiousness or slavery. Pierre illustrates this when he suddenly jumps from pampered aristocrat to impoverished plebeian, alternating like the fickle Florentines between fealty to tradition and hasty self-indulgence and becoming, in Melville's oxymoronic phrase, "the fool of Virtue" (7:358). Charles's Isle, the antebellum United States, and virtually all the republican governments during the European revolutions of 1848 exhibited the same violent political oscillations. In contrast, "powerful citizens" like Machiavelli's ideal leader Cosimo de' Medici, although wary of "the Medusa of republicanism," use their power judiciously to construct and enforce wise laws and bring the state an extended period of peace, wealth, freedom, and artistic creativity—the Italian Renaissance, which began in Cosimo's fifteenth-century Florence and still remains the high point of post-Roman Italian history.[66]

Israel Potter follows the advice of *Harper's* and looks to America's founders for models of revolutionary heroes. Loosing himself from the constraints of his source Melville chooses two types of Americans to portray different strategies for achieving nationhood through revolution, the wily diplomat Benjamin Franklin and the bold naval captain John Paul Jones. Melville compares Franklin to the biblical Jacob, who deceived his father, Isaac, in order to gain the paternal blessing that by rights belonged to his older brother Esau (Genesis 27):

> Viewed from a certain point, there was a touch of primeval orientalness in Benjamin Franklin. Neither is there wanting something like his scriptural parallel. The history of the patriarch Jacob is interesting not less from the unselfish devotion which we are bound to ascribe to him, than from the deep worldly wisdom and polished Italian tact, gleaming under an air of Arcadian unaffectedness. The diplomatist and the shepherd are blended; a union not without warrant; the apostolic serpent and dove. A tanned Machiavelli in tents. (8:46)

Melville's elliptical allusions convey the circumstantial necessity of diplomatic duplicity in order to maintain the state (or in Franklin's case create one), precisely the argument Machiavelli makes in chapter 18 of *The Prince*. Expertly playing the fox, which Machiavelli advises in this chapter, Franklin wears plain clothes and resides in the Latin Quarter to present an image of Yankee simplicity that masks his acuity (8:47). Some of his deceptions seem harmless, even comic, as when he mistranslates the label "Otard" on a bottle of wine as "poison" in order to filch it from the naïve Potter (8:51). More seriously, Franklin exploits Potter's patriotism by sending him on risky errands that end up depriving him of a share in the freedom he fights for. Israel—and his name resonates with Old Testament myth—gains his country's independence but loses his own. In times of

---

66. In "Jimmy Rose," a story about a prosperous New York merchant who loses his fortune and thereafter endures a life of genteel poverty, Melville compares Jimmy at his peak of success to "the great Florentine trader, Cosmo the Magnificent" (9:338). Although it is tempting to see in Jimmy's decline an allegory of Italy, the story has too few Italian references to bear such weight.

national crisis, Machiavelli realized, "self-preservation will often compel [the Prince] to violate the laws of charity, religion, and humanity"; therefore, any judgments of his motives "must attend only to results" (461). This last phrase, sometimes translated as "the end justifies the means,"[67] is in Italian "si guarda al fine," literally "one looks to the ends," a pragmatic criterion clearly suitable to war and the defense of nationhood. Franklin understands this well, and has no compunction sending Potter into the cannon's mouth—the "serpent and dove" indeed.

If Franklin is a fox, Jones is a lion, or perhaps more precisely the tool for Franklin's cunning diplomacy. J. G. A. Pocock suggests that Machiavelli's leaders inhabit a spectrum of virtù with new princes like the ruthless Cesare Borgia at one extreme and mythic lawmakers such as Moses or Romulus at the other: the first creates new states, the other builds them to last, roles taken respectively by Jones and Franklin.[68] Both men fight for American independence and unity, Franklin through diplomacy, Jones through war. Just as Franklin manipulates Potter he also manipulates Jones, who lives and breathes the "volcanic spirit" (8:57) of unbridled revolt that makes him, like Borgia, a relentless and unscrupulous enemy, a "prowling lion" (8:95) who is both "the gentleman and the wolf," or in his own words "a democratic sort of sea-king" like the equally charismatic and morally ambiguous Steelkilt (8:95, 96, 105, 90). Franklin makes the most of Jones's impetuosity and outright savagery, traits the narrator associates with the French revolution (8:63), and without approving any particular tactic he encourages Jones's predatory attacks on the English. Presentist ethical judgments of Jones ignore his crucial role in creating the conditions necessary for American success, particularly during those crises when, as Machiavelli advised, it is "safer to be feared than be loved" (457).[69] Cesare Borgia, Machiavelli's model prince, acted on this principle when he personally decided to assassinate four allies at Sinagaglia, an act that Machiavelli later condoned because it saved the country from a larger war, consolidated power in a time of anarchy, and rid the country of four unreliable and jealous princes, all greater evils than Borgia himself.[70] Similarly, Franklin never specifically approves Jones's tactics, which

---

67. See, for example, the long-standard translation of *The Prince* by Luigi Ricci and revised by E. R. P. Vincent for the Oxford World's Classics series and reprinted by the New American Library (1952), 94.

68. *The Machiavellian Moment*, 174–76.

69. For a different view of Jones as "Satanic," see Adler, *War in Melville's Imagination*, 82–83.

70. A long footnote in the introduction to the Bohn edition exonerates Machiavelli from any complicity in this "master-piece of treachery" and defends his diplomacy in a time of great crisis (*History of Florence*, xii). The Bohn edition recounts this event in the introduction, the

include flogging to death a sailor named Mungo Maxwell and burning the sailor's hometown when it refuses to exonerate Jones from the charge of murder (8:91). Jones is an American Borgia, a man who rages at Franklin, "My God, why was I not born a Czar!" (8:57), and who takes pride in his reputation as a "bloody cannibal . . . the captain who flogged Mungo Maxwell to death" (91). Nevertheless, he is crucial to American nationhood.

Melville's long description of the bloody fight between the *Bonhomme Richard* and the *Serapis* may seem like adventurous excess in an episodic novel, but reading it as the narrator suggests, as "a type, a parallel, and a prophecy" (8:120), reveals its figurative identity with the republican revolutions of Renaissance and Risorgimento Italy. The setting is the east coast of Britain which "wears a savage, melancholy, and Calabrian aspect" (8:121) like something out of a Salvator Rosa painting, and the *Richard*'s poop is a "tower of Pisa" where Potter stands with a spyglass like "Galileo on Fiesole" (8:115), a reference from *Paradise Lost* that combines John Milton's republicanism with memories of papal repression of science.[71] Mentioned five times in thirteen pages, the "tower of Pisa" allows Potter and Jones to tie a rope around the jibboom of the *Serapis* and bring it alongside the *Richard,* leaving between a watery lane "like that narrow canal in Venice which . . . is secretly crossed by the Bridge of Sighs" (8:125). The battle antitypes Italian history, as the narrator terms it more an "intestine feud, than a fight between strangers" (8:125), a conflict between "one family (the Guelphs)," or the British, and "another family (the Ghibelines [sic])," or the Americans (8:126). Jones is a wild-eyed revolutionary like George Sanders, an overenthusiastic Young American who supports "the rising of the peoples," however violent that rising may be. The *New York Citizen* predicted that the novel "will be greedily devoured by Young America" and the *Albion* of New York considered Melville "American enough to be a Know-Nothing," a political conflation that ironically rests the book's nationalistic claims on the very ideologies it questions, namely the nationalistic extremism of Young America

---

footnote, and again in an appendix that reprints Machiavelli's six-page dispatch on the matter. Machiavelli refers to it twice in *The Prince,* in chapters 7 and 8 (427, 433).

71. Describing Satan's enormous shield Milton writes, "the broad circumference / Hung on his shoulders like the Moon, whose Orb / Through Optic Glass the *Tuscan* Artist views / At Ev'ning from the top of *Fesole*" (I:287–89). Merritt Y. Hughes identifies the Tuscan artist as Galileo, whom Milton seems to have visited at Fiesole (*John Milton: Complete Poems and Major Prose* [New York: Odyssey Press, 1957], 218n). Melville acquired the *Poetical Works of John Milton* in 1849 and annotated it extensively on multiple occasions. See Robin Grey, *Melville and Milton: An Edition and Analysis of Melville's Annotations on Milton* (Pittsburgh: Duquesne University Press, 2004).

and the Know-Nothings.[72] Despite their lack of appreciation for Melville's irony, at least these reviewers understood that the novel addresses contemporary America: as the narrator says, "intrepid, unprincipled, reckless, predatory, with boundless ambition, civilized in externals but a savage at heart, America is, or may yet be, the Paul Jones of nations" (8:120). At the end of this harrowing chapter the narrator raises the same fundamental question that haunted *Typee*: "What separates the enlightened man from the savage? Is civilization a thing distinct, or is it an advanced stage of barbarism?" (8:130).

Rather than becoming a "second Rome," the United States may be on its way to becoming Bomba's Naples, as shown by Potter's miserable fate in Dantean London, the capital of the British Empire that has devolved into a "City of Dis" (166). When he finally returns to "the Fortunate Isles of the Free" after forty-five years of exile, he is almost run over by a "patriotic triumphal car" in Boston flying a banner that says "BUNKER-HILL. 1775. GLORY TO THE HEROES THAT FOUGHT!" (167). Narratively the date is July 4, 1826, but politically it is May 3, 1852, when Louis Kossuth stood before the Bunker Hill Monument and invoked the American dead in an extraordinarily flamboyant and patronizing speech even for him.[73] From the novel's dedication to the "Bunker-Hill Monument" to this closing scene Melville constructs a Machiavellian counternarrative to Kossuth's patriotic rhetoric in order to show how fluent oratory masks wartime horrors and obscures the dark truths that Machiavelli unflinchingly reveals in *The History of Florence* and *The Prince*. Abject, broken, impoverished, Potter has been driven by fortune, not virtù, an outcome that supports Lawrence Buell's characterization of the narrative as "an ironic meditation on the pseudo-polarity between republican freedom and the imperial yoke."[74] Deprived of strong leaders and wise laws, Potter has no real freedom at all, and his fate makes a mockery of Young Americans and others who refuse to restrain democratic extremes. Potter and Jones are both effectively exiled from the country they helped create[75] while foxes like Franklin, Melville's American Machiavelli, reap the rewards of the new republic.

---

72. Higgins and Parker, *Herman Melville: The Contemporary Reviews*, 460, 457.
73. The speech appeared in the *Pittsfield Sun*, May 13, 1852, 2
74. "Melville and American Decolonization," 224.
75. An article on Jones published in *Harper's* shortly after the final installment of *Israel Potter* concluded, "Neither the government of the United States nor that of Russia ever claimed his remains for burial or monumental honor, and the place of his sepulchre is unknown to the present generation!" "John Paul Jones," 11 (July 1855): 169. The last installment of *Israel Potter* appeared in *Putnam's* in March 1855.

THE "FIERY ALDEBARAN" OF ITALIAN REPUBLICANISM
"The Bell-Tower"

Melville's only tale set in Italy, "The Bell-Tower" was included as a pendant to *The Piazza Tales* and, unlike any other Melville tale, anthologized twice in the nineteenth century, a fact revealing later American interest in fiction with Italian locales (think Henry James and Constance Fenimore Woolson).[76] The story strives desperately for significance, beginning with its three epigraphs and ending with the hackneyed moral "pride went before the fall" (9:187), a disappointing conclusion to an ambiguous and unsatisfying tale. Critics have justifiably read it as an allegory of artistic vanity, slavery, religion, and technology.[77] Yet whatever else it is about, it is about Italy, specifically the politically tumultuous Renaissance that Melville knew from *The History of Florence* when republics rose and fell like Bannadonna's tower, a structure as fatally flawed as its historical analogue, the Leaning Tower of Pisa. The third epigraph, "*Seeking to conquer a larger liberty, man but extends the empire of necessity*" (9:174), is Melville's invention and summarizes the fate of republican movements since 1848 as well as the dilemmas faced by Babo, the Dog-King, John Paul Jones, and Israel Potter. Melville takes his memorable final three words from Thomas Carlyle's *Chartism* (1840), which characterizes human progress as a war "against the great black empire of Necessity and Night," and couples them with Machiavelli's critical view of popular government to create one of his most cynical comments on democracy.

Like *Israel Potter*, "The Bell-Tower" (1855) is historical fiction with contemporary significance. The story opens in the present and describes an Italian city mired in decay, "a once-frescoed capital, now with dank mould cankering its bloom"; nearby lies a fallen tower like "one steadfast spear of lichened ruin" (9:174). This unnamed city stands somewhere on the great Venetian plain where the tower originally offered a view of "the white summits of blue inland Alps, and whiter crests of bluer Alps off-shore," that part of Italy presently under Austrian rule. The narrative then returns to the Renaissance, when the state had been a wealthy republic that "voted to have the noblest Bell-Tower in Italy" (174): "Like Babel's, its base was laid in a high hour of renovated earth, following

---

76. According to Lea Bertani Vozar Newman, *A Reader's Guide to the Short Stories of Herman Melville* (Boston: G. K. Hall & Co., 1986), 80, "The Bell-Tower" was reprinted in *Little Classics: Tragedy,* ed. Rossiter Johnson (1874) and *A Library of American Literature from the Earliest Settlement to the Present Time,* ed. Edmund Clarence Stedman and Ellen Mackay Hutchinson (1889). "The Lightning-Rod Man," Newman notes, was reprinted once.

77. See the discussion in Newman, *Reader's Guide,* 87–92.

the second deluge, when the waters of the Dark Ages had dried up, and once more the green appeared" (9:174). The simile shadows Renaissance humanism with divine judgment and grounds the historical cycles of rise and fall in Old Testament myth, reminding readers of the follies of progressive history and its supposed goal, human equality. The democratic principle that merit outweighs birth applies when "the unblest foundling, Bannadonna" is chosen chief architect and repeatedly honored for his skill in constructing the three-hundred-foot tower (which some readers might have known was a hundred feet taller than Pisa's). But as Machiavelli predicted and as Melville confirmed in "Charles' Isle and the Dog-King," unchecked equality and democracy lead to corruption as surely as does despotism. When Bannadonna intemperately strikes and kills a workman, judge and priest excuse the act on grounds of "esthetic passion," a decision that privileges art over morality (9:176). The republic's chief magistrates are both "elderly men" and the image of their ancestors marks its custom seals, implying the city's superficial commitment to equal justice and excessive regard for its "illustrious founders" (9:179). Liberty for some is not liberty for all, as class divisions and oligarchy creep into republican institutions and, like America's noxious court decisions over slavery or the successes of the Know-Nothings at the ballot box, constrict the egalitarian impulse and further rend the national fabric.

Bannadonna is the Machiavellian usurper, an artist-prince who manipulates the aging magistrates with disingenuous deference and calculated theatrics that reveal their ignorance. He calls them "Eccellenza" and "illustrious magnificoes" while referring to himself as a "poor mechanic" or vassal, and when they hear a noise after leaving the bell tower he tells them some mortar fell but "knew its place" and didn't fall until the magistrates had left (9:178, 179). Such "ostentatious deference," a phrase that could have come from "The Specksynder," troubles the junior magistrate and prompts him to suspect "a certain sardonical disdain, lurking beneath the foundling's humble mien" (9:178–79). Bannadonna reveals his contempt by cloaking his bell-ringing automaton in a "domino" to exaggerate its mystery and play upon the magistrates' ignorance and fear. Viewing it behind this hooded cloak so disturbs them that they avoid further comment on it, "unwilling, perhaps, to let the foundling see how easily it lay within his plebeian art to stir the placid dignity of nobles" (9:178). Like the priests whom James Jackson Jarves derided for religious mummery, Bannadonna employs Roman Catholic accouterments—dominoes are worn by cathedral canons—to mystify and control state authorities and embody for American audiences a popular cultural fear, what Jenny

Franchot calls "the interlocking menaces of the 1850s: Romanism and slavery."[78]

The magistrates' ineffectiveness in the face of Bannadonna's populist and manipulative art reinforces American belief in the incompatibility of Catholicism and Republicanism and reveals the foundling as an Ahabian tyrant who exploits both the nobles and the masses to quench his Faustian pride. The whole city gathers eagerly to hear the first hour struck and waits at the tower's base in "expectation of some Shiloh," some redeemer, as Bannadonna stage-manages his mechanician's tricks into an unwittingly self-destructive apocalypse. When the hour strikes and the people hear only "a dull, mangled sound" they "become tumultuous" and turn into a "surging mob" (9:181, 182), yet another anarchic "citizen-mob." Bannadonna, of course, has died at the hand of his "iron slave" (9:184), a fate that links this tale with "Benito Cereno" and extends "the empire of necessity" to Bannadonna's own life. The superstitious magistrates shoot the automaton and bury it at sea, the bell cracks like the Liberty Bell the first time it is rung, and an earthquake, pure Machiavellian fortuna, destroys the bell tower and leaves it a "lichened ruin" to metonymize the entire Italian peninsula in the American imagination.

For all its success in transmuting Machiavellian policies into fictional form, "The Bell-Tower" exposes gaps in Melville's knowledge of Italy that prevented him from writing a *Marble Faun* or *Bravo,* let alone a Jamesian international novel. His grasp of Italian painting is weak so he invents a Florentine painter with the Spanish name Del Fonca and credits him with a vaguely described painting of Jael and Sisera and another (or perhaps the same one) that includes Deborah the Prophetess. His account of Bannadonna's flawed casting may come from Benvenuto Cellini's autobiography, as Robert Morseberger suggests, but so little else in the story corroborates this source that I doubt the attribution.[79] And it took the Northwestern-Newberry editors to correct Melville's flawed Italian, changing "Excellenza" to "Eccellenza" and "Signor" to "Signore" (9:621). In some sense Melville, like Bannadonna, overreached in this story and allowed his imagination to outrun his knowledge, as Fuller had done when she imagined a Protestant Italy. Still, Bannadonna's prostrate populist campanile tropes Mazzini's failing dreams of a republican Italy and offers a disturbing reminder that fortuna often trumps virtù. After considering the title "Benito Cereno and Other Sketches," Melville, or perhaps his

78. *Roads to Rome,* 174.
79. "Melville's 'The Bell-Tower' and Benvenuto Cellini," *American Literature* 44 (1972): 459–62.

editors, titled his collection of *Putnam's* fiction *The Piazza Tales* (1856), employing the Italian word for a plaza in the uniquely American sense of a front porch (*OED*). The collection begins with "The Piazza" and its narrator's politicized reminder that the story occurs "not long after 1848; and, somehow, about that time, all round the world, these kings, they had the casting vote, and voted for themselves" (9: 3); it concludes with "The Bell-Tower," a cynical parable where a corrupt state produces an equally corrupt art. To achieve true success, the serious artist must move from nationalist promotion to nationalist critique as Melville does in his final published work of fiction.

THE AMERICAN MACHIAVELLI
The Confidence-Man

The Confidence-Man (1857), a devastating satire of American values, substantiates Melville's earlier parallels between the stalled Risorgimento and 1850s America by employing Machiavellian irony to trace the fine line between virtue and corruption.[80] The previously mentioned "crazy beggar" with "his look of picturesque Italian ruin and dethronement" (10:195) corroborates the renewed disparaging view of Italy, as do references to the "moral poison" of Tacitus, the pessimistic chronicler of Imperial Rome (10:26), and to Joseph Marzetti, an Italian immigrant famous for pantomiming apes on Broadway, a distinct devolution from the favorable portrait of Carlo in *Redburn* (10:132). The herb doctor cites a "dungeoned Italian," presumably Silvio Pellico, as an example of recantation instead of stoicism; monks and "Papist converts" prove unfaithful; Frank Goodman dismisses Romans as suicidal pagans; Charlie Noble derides Seneca as a usurer; and Goodman complains that Rochefoucault and Machiavelli must have derived their dark views of human nature from the Son of Sirach, a pessmistic book in the Apocrypha (10:111, 150, 157, 198, 243).[81] Spoken by confidence men or their dupes, these allusions func-

---

80. A good explication of Melville's satirical aims is Jonathan A. Cook, *Satirical Apocalypse: An Anatomy of Melville's the Confidence-Man*, Contributions to the Study of World Literature, Number 67 (Westport, CT: Greenwood Press, 1996). Additional identification of the targets of Melville's satire is in Helen P. Trimpi, *Melville's Confidence Men and American Politics in the 1850s* (Hamden, CT: Archon Books, 1987).

81. My identifications of these and other allusions in *The Confidence-Man* are indebted to the notes in Brian Higgins and Hershel Parker, *The Confidence-Man* (New York: W. W. Norton, 2006) and Kathleen Kier, *A Melville Encyclopedia*, supplemented by my own research. For the

tion as rhetorical ploys designed to inspire trust by bonding with fellow Americans over renascent negative Italian stereotypes.

Most of the Italian allusions occur in the second half of the novel and involve the book's main character Frank Goodman, the final and dominant incarnation of the confidence man. As befits his cognomen of "cosmopolitan" Goodman is a transnational figure who competes with Melville's Benjamin Franklin as an American Machiavelli, a man who relies more on cunning than power to succeed in a culture that prides itself on self-reliance, common sense, opportunity, ambition, and a rough-hewn (if largely unpracticed) social equality. Such values can be, in the Machiavellian world, either virtuous or corrupting, and they require careful management if they are to redound to the social good. In *Foxes and Lions: Machiavelli's Confidence Men,* Wayne A. Rebhorn approaches Machiavelli as a literary figure whose princes—Borgia, the Medicis, Francesco Sforza—initiated a tradition of Renaissance tricksters evident in Boccaccio's *Decameron* through Shakespeare's Iago and Jonson's Alchemist to Milton's Satan and Melville's confidence man: "Machiavelli's princes are thus seminal figures for a wide array of characters. As much as a minor swindler operating his scam on the streets of New York, they are the true source of Melville's confidence man and his descendants."[82] By preferring the anachronistic term "confidence man" to "trickster," Rebhorn constructs a genealogy that links Machiavelli and Melville as satirists who employ fundamentally amoral characters to attack the hypocrisies and foibles of society. As the most successful confidence man in the novel, Goodman is more fox than lion, a performer who democratically shape-shifts through all the economic classes of a bumptious commercial society just as Franklin grew from "Poor Richard" to wealthy businessman and international diplomat yet still posed as a simple colonial. A self-styled "ambassador from the human race" (10:138, perhaps a Franklin allusion), Goodman incorporates good and evil in an amoral character whom Melville uses for a moral aim much as Milton used Satan. According to Rebhorn,

> Morally ambiguous confidence men thus bear eloquent witness to their creators' recognition that societies need limits as well as free spirits that transcend them, orderly structures as well as the animating though chaos-threatening energies embodied in individuals. They also need, as Machiavelli and other Renaissance writers recognized fully, the profound creativity of the confidence man, which may lead him to violate social

---

identification of Silvio Pellico, see Lang, "Melville's 'Dungeoned Italian.'"

82. Wayne A. Rebhorn, *Foxes and Lions: Machiavelli's Confidence Men* (Ithaca, NY: Cornell University Press, 1988), 11.

norms but is essential if societies are ever to escape the stultification and decadence produced by moribund structures and habits.[83]

Rebhorn's concise and discerning formulation illuminates how the cosmopolitan functions in Melville's novel: his mixed nature represents all humanity and strips people of the ideological veils that mask their essential self-interest, a Machiavellian strategy that exposes the true virtù of people and rulers alike.

Melville prepares for Goodman's identification with Machiavelli through indirection in the chapter immediately preceding Goodman's entrance. The misanthropic Missourian Pitch has just been gulled out of three dollars and passage-money by the confidence man disguised as a representative of the "Philosophical Intelligence Office," a sort of metaphysical employment agency. Recognizing his error only after the P.I.O. man has absconded, Pitch tries to figure out how he was swindled by "that threadbare Talleyrand, that impoverished Machiavelli, that seedy Rosicrucian—for something of all these he vaguely deems him—[which] passes now in puzzled review. Fain, in his disfavor, would he make out a logical case" (10:130). According to Kathleen Kier both Talleyrand and Franklin were associated with Rosicrucianism, and while I have found no links between Machiavelli and this sect of Christian mystics (their leading text was not published until well after Machiavelli's death), a common element of conspiratorial secretiveness might associate them in the popular mind.[84] Pitch is fumbling for an excuse to rationalize his mistake, and blindly accepts conventional prejudices that lump an aristocratic French diplomat with a secular Italian republican and a mystical religious sect, none of which adequately explains the P.I.O. man. Pitch comes closer to an explanation when he considers how the P.I.O. man's "undulating flunkyisms dovetail into those of the flunky beast that windeth his way on his belly" (10:130), the "serpent and dove" that combines Satan and Christ in such morally ambiguous figures as Franklin and *Pierre*'s Reverend Falsgrave.

Goodman then accosts the Missourian with a voice "sweet as a seraph's" and a "pitch" adapted to the commercial values of 1850s America: "A penny for your thoughts, my fine fellow" (10:130), he says, slapping Pitch on the shoulder. His words and appearance confound Pitch's paranoid rationalizations, for in this final incarnation the confidence man assumes his *least* "impoverished" disguise in order to play his *most* Machia-

---

83. Rebhorn, *Foxes and Lions*, 23–24.
84. *A Melville Encyclopedia: The Novels*, 2:884.

vellian role, an "ambassador" who negotiates between Christ and Satan for the soul of humanity. His elaborate international garb of "a Highland plaid, Emir's robe, and French blouse," an "Indian belt," and a "Nuremburgh pipe in blast, its great porcelain bowl painted in miniature with linked crests and arms of interlinked nations—a florid show" (10:131–32) amply justifies his cognomen of "cosmopolitan." In a sense the Missourian is perceptive when he compares Goodman to Joseph Marzetti, for a man playing an ape in a humorous theatrical performance masks the dark evolutionary truth behind such roles, making humans laugh unthinkingly at their own submerged bestiality. But the cosmopolitan is after bigger game than a bear-hunting frontiersman as he seeks to allay misanthropy with philanthropy through the very medium he disavows: "something Satanic about irony. God defend me from Irony, and Satire, his bosom friend" (10:136), says Goodman. What follows are conversations and encounters so satiric and ironic that they destabilize interpretation as much as Machiavelli's *Prince* upset political morality.

Perhaps the most devastating satire comes in chapter 26, "The Metaphysics of Indian-Hating," where as Rebhorn notices, Melville owes a specific debt to Machiavelli's account of Borgia's assassination of his allies at Sinagaglia. The cosmopolitan's newest friend and victim, Charlie Noble, recounts Judge James Hall's story of the Indian-hater Colonel John Moredock in a horrifying, deeply ironic chapter that seems to justify Indian extermination in the name of vengeance and westward expansion. Judge Hall offers the Indian chief Mocmohoc as proof of Indian savagery and deception, for like all Indians he is "a treaty-breaker like an Austrian" (10:146), a popular view of Austrians based on Hapsburg hegemony in Italy and Hungary. After two families move into Kentucky's Bloody Ground Mocmohoc's "dwindled tribe" relentlessly persecutes them until they consent to "a kind of treaty" (10:147). The families remain suspicious, however, because Mocmohoc, "though hitherto deemed a savage almost perfidious as Cæsar Borgia, yet now put on a seeming the reverse of this, engaging to bury the hatchet, smoke the pipe, and be friends forever" (10:148). The frontiersmen vow never to enter Mocmohoc's lodge together so that if he does murder them some will remain to care for their families and seek revenge, but Mocmohoc, as did Borgia, exercises "such fine art and pleasing carriage" that he wins their confidence, brings them all into his lodge to enjoy "a feast of bear's meat, and there, by stratagem, ended them" (10:148). Years later, when a captive hunter reproaches the chief for his treachery, he blames the gullible frontiersmen: "Treachery? Pale face! 'Twas they who broke their covenant first, in coming all together; they that broke it first, in trusting Mocmohoc" (10:148).

To such reasoning the judge solemnly intones, "Circling wiles and bloody lusts. The acuteness and genius of the chief but make him the more atrocious" (10:148). "Acuteness" and "genius" are attributes Machiavelli admired in princes, especially when they preserve the nation and prevent wider bloodshed. Judge Hall blames the Indian, but in the context of a "Metaphysics of Indian-Hating," which justifies exterminating an entire race, Mocmohoc's deed becomes a matter of self-defense. The threat of tribal extinction calls for desperate measures, and Mocmohoc employs them to save his tribe, a more virtuous motive than either vengeance or Manifest Destiny. Purely an invention of Melville's, the story of Mocmohoc portrays a transnational hero worthy of respect, as Frank Goodman acknowledges when he interrupts Charlie's story in order to refill his calumet (10:151), a simple gesture that pays homage to Mocmohoc's statecraft and identifies the cosmopolitan with the chief who smokes his pipe with men he later kills. Melville knew, and said so repeatedly in *Typee*, that savagism permeated so-called civilization and can only be managed, not eliminated (see 1:123–30, 195, 202–3).

Italy still holds truths for disenchanted Americans that they can access through its art, from Roman statuary and medieval poetry through Renaissance painting and modern tragedies. Only the flexibility and imagination of art comprehends the paradoxes of human nature and offers a footing in "this world of lies" ("Hawthorne and his Mosses," 9:244), and the cosmopolitan, an artist manqué, prefigures this aesthetic. In one of the novel's three metatextual chapters Melville asks, "Who did ever dress or act like your cosmopolitan? And who, it might be returned, did ever dress or act like harlequin?" (10:182). Of course Italian performers in the commedia dell'arte dressed and acted like harlequin, the conventional trickster whose deceptions force audiences to examine conventional beliefs and strive toward a more complex understanding of truth.[85] The cosmopolitan also imitates the beauty of classical Italian sculpture as Mark Winsome, Melville's parody of Emerson, notices by "scholastically and artistically eyeing the picturesque speaker, as if he were a statue in the Pitti Palace" (10:190), the art museum that also served as the home of the Medicis and, in Melville's day, the Grand Duke of Tuscany. The cosmopolitan blends harlequin, the art of the street, with classic statuary, the art of the aristocracy, in a single figure who embodies the aesthetic and political theories of Machiavelli. At the end of the novel, when he extinguishes the lamp,

---

85. John Bryant, *Melville and Repose: The Rhetoric of Humor in the American Renaissance* (New York: Oxford University Press, 1993), points out that William Jones, one of the minor literati in the Duyckinck circle, cited commedia dell'arte to illustrate his doctrine that "tyranny induces satire; freedom humor" (48). Art, it seems, can thrive under wildly variant political systems.

he illustrates the moral of "The Piazza": "truth comes in with darkness" (9:12). Yet as with Machiavelli's dark truths, the cosmopolitan's ironic worldview dissolves illusions and conventional wisdom, opening doors to fresh thought and, as Melville would find in his turn to poetry, fresh modes of expression.

5

The Triumph of Nationalism

Early Poems and Battle-Pieces

> To harmonize North and South is harder than fighting
> Austria or struggling with Rome.
> —Cavour, 1860, quoted in Bolton King, *A History of Italian Unity*

> Were the Unionists and Secessionists but as Guelphs and Ghibellines?
> If not, then far be it from a great nation now to act in the spirit that
> animated a triumphant town-faction in the Middle Ages.
> —Melville, "Supplement," *Battle-Pieces and Aspects of the War* (1866)

SOON AFTER completing *The Confidence-Man* Melville set off alone for the eastern Mediterranean and his long-awaited trip to Italy. No one knows precisely when he decided to turn from fiction to poetry, but it is clear that this trip inspired "At the Hostelry," "Naples in the Time of Bomba," "Fruits of Travel Long Ago," *Timoleon,* and *Clarel,* poems set in his primary destinations of Italy, Turkey, Greece, Egypt, and Palestine. And in his great book of Civil War poetry, *Battle-Pieces,* Risorgimento nationalism infuses his politics with a wrenching meliorism evident in the controversial "Supplement" and a melancholy brooding on national decline and fall that evokes the "ruins of Rome" topos. Historicizing Melville's earliest poems, notably "At the Hostelry" and "Naples in the Time of Bomba," is difficult because their dates of composition are uncertain and he worked on them for many years, returning to old manuscripts and revising and rearranging them on different principles.[1] Very likely,

---

1. The fullest discussion of dating "At the Hostelry" and "Naples in the Time of Bomba" is in Robert Allen Sandberg, "Melville's Unfinished *Burgundy Club* Book: A Reading Edition Edited from the Manuscripts with Introduction and Notes" (PhD diss., Northwestern, 1989), 12–28. See especially the chart on 24 listing the differing compositional stages of the poems and their accompanying sketches. All quotations from these poems, what I call Melville's "Nea-

as scholars from Howard Vincent on have speculated, Melville included some of these poems in the manuscript volume of poetry he entrusted to Evert Duyckinck in May 1860, hoping it would be published by the time he returned from his voyage around the world with his brother Tom.[2] This probability argues for examining his Italy-inspired poems as products of the decade beginning in 1857 and to treating them as intertexts for *Battle-Pieces*. In his recent book, *Melville: The Making of the Poet,* Hershel Parker establishes a rich aesthetic context for Melville's long interest in poetry; what I add here is a social and political context centered on the rise of a united Italy that occurred from 1857–61, the years when Melville turned his full energies to poetry and developed an elaborate transnational conceit: a parallel between Italy before and after 1860 and the United States before and after the Civil War.[3] This device is most evident in the Neapolitan diptych and in *Battle-Pieces,* substantial works that register Melville's reaction to the historical contexts covered in this chapter: his Italian tour, Garibaldi's conquest of the Kingdom of Two Sicilies, the unification of Italy, and the American Civil War.

After a decade of political dormancy, the Risorgimento took on new life in 1859 when Victor Emmanuel, with the help of the French, drove the Austrians from Lombardy and annexed it into his kingdom. Napoleon III, who feared a wider war for Italian unity, forced Piedmont into a hasty truce at Villafranca in July, a treaty widely viewed with disdain by Italian patriots and their supporters. The situation remained fluid and over the next nine months Cavour's diplomacy peacefully brought Tuscany, Modena, Parma, and the Romagna (the northern section of the Papal States) into the new Kingdom of Italy while ceding Savoy and Nice to France (fig. 14).

In May 1860 Garibaldi, with the king's covert support, led his legendary one thousand soldiers (*Il Mille*) to Sicily and in a series of brilliant battles liberated the island from Bourbon rule, crossed the Straits

---

politan diptych," are taken from this edition and cited parenthetically in the text by page and line number. The poems were first published in the Constable edition of 1922–24, and other important editions are *Collected Poems of Herman Melville,* ed. Howard P. Vincent (Chicago: Packard and Company, Hendricks House, 1947); Aaron Kramer, *Melville's Poetry: Toward the Enlarged Heart. A Thematic Study of Three Ignored Major Poems* (Rutherford: Fairleigh Dickinson University Press, 1972); and Gordon Poole, ed., *"At the Hostelry" And "Naples in the Time of Bomba"* (Naples: Istituto Universitario Orientale, 1989).

2. Vincent, *Collected Poems,* 476, 483. See also Shurr, *Companion,* 355, and Parker, *Herman Melville,* 2:418–25. My own work annotating these poems for the forthcoming Northwestern-Newberry edition of the unpublished writings shows that some allusions refer to post-1860 events: Italy's annexation of Venice in 1866 and Rome in 1870, Garibaldi's plan to dredge the Tiber in 1875, and Garibaldi's death in 1882.

3. Evanston, IL: Northwestern University Press, 2008.

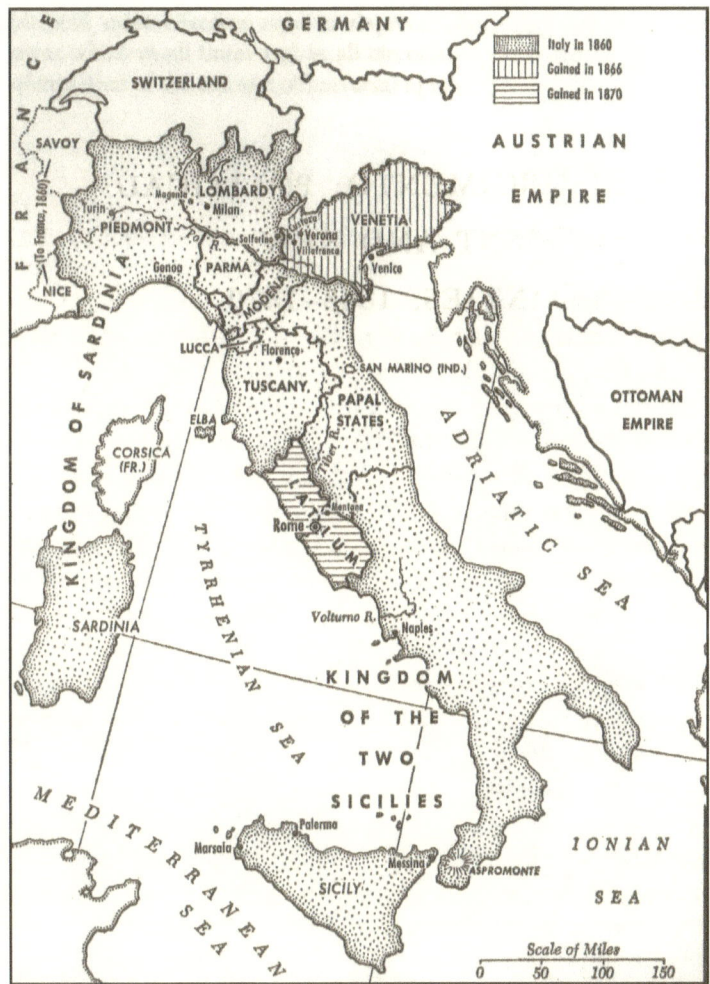

Figure 14. Map of Italy, 1859–70. Over a twelve-year period the Kingdom of Piedmont-Sardinia incorporated the entire peninsula into a new "Kingdom of Italy" under the House of Savoy. From Clough and Saladino, *A History of Modern Italy*, 62. Author photograph.

of Messina to Calabria, and in September entered Naples as its self-proclaimed "dictator." Piedmont saw its chance and drove southward, defeating Papal and Neapolitan troops and annexing most of the Papal States. On November 8, 1860, only two days after the election of Abraham Lincoln, Garibaldi handed over southern Italy to Victor Emmanuel, thereby uniting the peninsula except for Venice and Latium, the area around Rome. Garibaldi's Thousand had defeated an army of 100,000 men and unified north and south Italy for the first time in a millennium. "There is," write Beales and Biagini, "no comparable achievement in the settled history of modern Europe."[4] American interest in Italy reached a new peak as newspapers, magazines, and books celebrated Garibaldi's valor, Cavour's diplomacy, and Victor Emmanuel's leadership. The questionable radicalism of Mazzini and other "Red Republicans" now seemed totally irrelevant as Americans held numerous torchlight parades and civic meetings to celebrate the monarchy's military and diplomatic victories.[5]

Melville shared in and abetted popular enthusiasm for Italy, and Italian art and politics course through his life during his turn to poetry and infuse his poems with a cosmopolitan detachment from temporary enthusiasms and render them more philosophical than topical, more universal than partisan, more historic than contemporary. He began reading more systematically about Italy beginning in 1857 with Valery's *Travels in Italy* which he annotated in Florence, Giorgio Vasari's and Luigi Lanzi's histories of Italian painting which he borrowed from Evert Duyckinck in 1859, Hawthorne's *The Marble Faun* which he read aboard his brother Tom's ship in 1860, Elizabeth Browning's *Poems* (1860) which he acquired in 1864, and Robert Macpherson's *Vatican Sculptures* which he acquired in 1866. He may have owned Gibbon's *Decline and Fall of the Roman Empire* and would have run across significant references to Italy in his new volumes of Landor, Shelley, Ruskin, Leigh Hunt, and Moore's *Life of Byron*, all acquired between 1857 and 1865.[6] For his first season on the lecture circuit he chose the topic "Statues in Rome," anticipating the renewed popular interest in Italy. He received a letter inquiring about his poetry from Giovanni Spaggiari, an Italian exile living in New York, and was quoted favorably by a critic in the *Rivista di Firenze* of 1859, although he probably never knew about it.[7] In early 1861 he pursued the consul-

---

4. *Risorgimento*, 122.

5 Marraro, *American Opinion*, chronicles these outpourings of support extensively (225–304). Rossi, *Image of America*, says that Mazzini's influence had waned by 1858 (104). For an informed contemporary account of Mazzini's decline and Piedmont's ascent, see "Italy and the War," *New Englander* 17 (August 1859): 708–25.

6. For a thorough conspectus of Melville's reading and annotations from 1859–60, see Parker, *Herman Melville* 2:402–8, 433–41.

7. Melville received Spaggiari's letter in April 1859 informing him that a patriotic poem from *Mardi* had been published in Turin in Italian and would be republished in London, Rome, and New York in Spaggiari's forthcoming *Latin-English-Italian Anthology* (14:335, 669–71). The "patriotic poem" is an Italian version of an 1849 French translation of Yoomy's lyric in praise of Vivenza in chapter 154 of *Mardi* (3: 501–02; see Elizabeth Foster's discussion of its complicated textual history, 3: 669–70). The poem is quoted at length in the *Rivista di Firenze* 5 (1859), 187, toward the end of a long multipart essay on the state of journal publishing and literature in America, and is attributed to "il poeta Hermann Merville."

Figure 15. Alexander Jackson Davis, "Winyah," architectural drawing, 1853. Designed by Davis, a leading architect of the day, this "Tuscan villa" in New Rochelle, New York, was the country seat of Melville's family friend Richard Lathers, whom he frequently visited. From *Melville Society Extracts* 99 (December 1994): 18.

ship to Florence with the enthusiastic backing of his brother-in-law John Hoadley, who chaired the committee to celebrate Italian unification in Lawrence, Massachusetts, and although Melville had to terminate his consular quest when Lemuel Shaw suddenly died, it revealed his persistent interest in Italy and his continuing connection to American Italophiles, especially those in the newly empowered Republican Party.[8] As he had since 1853, he continued making trips to New Rochelle to admire the Italian art at Winyah, the Tuscan villa that Richard Lathers—the husband of Allan Melville's wife's sister—had built (fig. 15).[9] On July 6, 1859, he

8. Parker, *Herman Melville,* gives a thorough account of Melville's quest for a diplomatic appointment (2:460–66). Hoadley was a Republican, and Melville sought support from others in the new party such as Richard Henry Dana, Thurlow Weed, and Senator Charles Sumner, all of whom favored Italian nationalism. He also received numerous endorsements from Pittsfield Republicans. See also Harrison Hayford and Merrell Davis, "Herman Melville as Office-Seeker," *Modern Language Quarterly* 10 (1949): 168–73, 377–88.

9. Hennig Cohen, "Melville and the Art Collection of Richard Lathers," *Melville Society Extracts* 99 (December 1994): 1–25, lists 186 items from the collection of which approximately one-third are Italian in origin or theme. For Melville's visits to Winyah, see Parker, *Herman Melville,* 2:156–57, 476–77, 659–61. Eric Collum and Hershel Parker, "The Lost Lathers Collections: Suggestions for Further Research," *Melville Society Extracts* 99 (December 1994): 26–28, point out that most of Melville's visits to Winyah occurred before 1867 (26). Charles E. Brownell, "The Italianate Villa and the Search for an American Style, 1840–1860," in Jaffe, *Italian Presence in American Art,* identifies the mid-nineteenth century as the heyday of Italian-styled homes in the United States and cites Lathers's architect, Alexander Jackson Davis, as one of the earliest practitioners of the style (219). Both Parker, *Herman Melville* 2: figure 5 and Cohen (18) reproduce Davis's sketch of Winyah, and Brownell's illustrations of Italianate villas convincingly demonstrate Winyah's "Tuscan" characteristics.

wrote a letter that contains his first poem that we can date precisely, "Epistle to Daniel Shepherd," which questions Napoleon III's motives for supporting Piedmont in its war with Austria. And as American enthusiasm for Garibaldi's conquest of Naples reached its peak in the winter of 1860–61, he may have begun writing "At the Hostelry," which opens with a celebration of Garibaldi's victory.

When the Civil War struck in April 1861, the transnational ethos reversed pattern: Italy was uniting while America was dividing, making the new Kingdom of Italy a better example of successful nation-building than the United States. As Americans confronted the weaknesses of the federal system and the violent consequences of sectionalism and slavery, Garibaldi, the unifier of Italy, came to symbolize national union and the wisdom of subordinating republican ideals to an enlightened prince like Victor Emmanuel. In one of the great ironies for American exceptionalists, constitutional monarchies with strong central governments now appeared superior to federated republics. Melville's journals, lectures, and poems meditate on this irony and its significance for the Jacksonian democracy he once so ardently espoused. Garibaldi assumes mythic status in Melville's imagination, Rome resurfaces as a historical analogue to the United States, and the now-successful Risorgimento prompts Melville to question more deeply his own country's progressive view of history.

"THE GHOST OF ROME"
Italy as Tour and Lecture

Melville devoted more time and ink to Italy than any other country he visited on his Mediterranean trip of 1856–57. He spent two months there and devoted one-fourth of his journal to describing its art, architecture, landscapes, and social customs. Telegraphic rather than discursive, his journal mirrors his fast-paced travel through Scotland, England, the Levant, and Italy, a sharp contrast to Hawthorne's elaborate and polished accounts of his three leisurely years abroad. Unlike Hawthorne, Melville journeyed alone, struck up conversations with locals, and used vivid, charged images to record the discontent he sensed in the populace. When a merchant from Ancona complains bitterly about the pope's temporal wealth—"Estates of the Church–Estates of de Debel!" he grumbles—Melville notices an "Austrian man-of-war" hovering in the background (15:98), a deft collocation of dialogue and image that depicts a hypocritically materialistic papal regime supported by a foreign military power yet avoids explicit political comment, a technique Melville elaborates in his poetry. His first description of Sicily focuses on an image of political oppression: "The forts of Messina command the town, not the sea. Large tract of town demolished, so as to have rest at command from fort," a scene that recalls the vicious bombardment of Messina in 1848 that gave Ferdinand II the nickname "King Bomba" and that gave Melville the title for the second half of his Neapolitan diptych (15:100).[10] At Naples he notices the "clang of arms all over city. Burst of troops from archway. Cannon posted inwards," an image he inserts into "Naples in the Time of Bomba" (111–12; 11:11–45), and at the theater of San Carlo he remarks on the "Sentinel on stage &c," an emblem of government censorship (15:101, 102). He hears from an Englishman that Austrians had spied on Mike Walsh, the New York rabble rouser, and just riding in an Austrian coach from Florence to Venice gives him an eerie feeling: "Old fashioned vehicle. Mysterious window & face. Secret recesses. Hide. Old fashioned feeling" (15:97, 117). Clearly, Melville recognized a police state when he saw it.

Even in the face of oppression, however, Melville is no enthusiast for revolution, as his visit to Venice shows. He arrived on April 1, 1857, shortly after Emperor Franz Joseph of Austria appointed his brother Archduke Ferdinand Maximilian as governor of Venetia and Lombardy. On one hand Melville notices the "Austrain [sic] flags flying from three masts" in St. Mark's Square and the Foscari Palace "Occupied as barrack" by Austrian troops; on the other hand he recounts how his bantering guide, Antonio, "lost his money in 1848 Revolution & by travelling" and, in his hectoring for tips, would have made a "good character for Con. Man" (15:118, 119, 120). Symbols of foreign oppression alternate with a comic reminder of revolution as Melville strives to fathom the political subtext of a foreign locale. Does Antonio invoke the tragedy of 1848 to exploit presumed American sympathy for Italian nationalism and gain more tips? Or does Melville include this incident in his journal to remind himself that revolution still lurks under Austrian tyranny? As he floats down the Grand Canal with "Antonio the Merry" Melville thinks he spies Maximilian himself leaning over a parapet: "Anxious to settle it; & in my favor, for I consider that some of the feirce [sic] democracy would not look with disrespect upon the man who &c &c &c" (15:120). This cryptic entry requires some glossing. Maximilian was widely viewed as that rara avis, a Hapsburg liberal. He took office in February 1857 on the condition

---

10. Hershel Parker, following Jay Leyda (*Log*, 552), says that Melville saw Verdi conduct *Macbeth* in Messina on February 14, 1857 (*Herman Melville*, 2:321). While Melville did see Verdi's opera, the composer was not in Messina at this time; he was at his villa in northern Italy. See Mary Jane Phillips-Matz, *Verdi: A Biography* (New York: Oxford University Press, 1993), 354.

that he would command the local Austrian military, a move calculated to restrain the harsh conduct of Marshal Radetzky's successors.[11] Melville's "&c &c &c" likely refers to this step toward civilian rule as well as to Maximilian's comparatively high regard for the Italian people. Melville hopes that Italian democrats will "not look with disrespect" at Maximilian's overtures, take a gradualist approach toward reform, and avoid the bloody reversals of 1849. He is willing to compromise with enlightened authority, as advised in Media's scroll: "yet, in themselves, monarchies are not utterly evil. For many nations, they are better than republics; for many, they will ever so remain" (3:527). Evidently Melville didn't know that only a week earlier this "feirce democracy" did show "disrespect" by hoisting the Italian tricolor above the Austrian flag in St. Mark's Square, which might have moderated his optimistic meliorism.[12]

Behind Melville's scattered political musings lay the vast authority of the Roman Empire, a specter of unity and civic virtue that haunts his travels. At Salonica, Greece, he notices a Roman triumphal arch with the eagle still conspicuous, and he contrasts it with the surrounding misery of cheap wood structures and abject poverty (15:55). Passing under the aqueduct of Valens in Constantinople, he observes how "In these lofty arches, ivied & weatherbeaten, & still grand, the ghost of Rome seems to stride with disdain of the hovels of this part of Stamboul" (15:62), as if the city had reached its apex 1,500 years earlier and steadily declined ever since. On first entering Rome after four and a half tiring months of solitary travel he confesses that the city "fell flat on me"; soon, however, he experiences the power of "Gigantic Rome": the enormous equestrian statues of "Monte Cavallo" before the Quirinale Palace, the "colossal statuary" in the Basilica of St. John Lateran, a massive painting of Samson in the Rospigliosi Gallery, all merit the adjective "gigantic" (15:106, 107, 108, 110). Naples he enjoyed for its lively, Broadway-like crowds, Florence offered incredible museums, Venice was unique, but Rome preyed on him like a recurring dream. It was, he knew, "nothing independent of associa-

---

11. The *Times,* London, February 23, 1857, 10, and February 24, 10
12. The *Times,* London, April 1, 1857, 10. The flags were run up overnight on March 23, the anniversary of the Battle of Novara in 1849 when the Austrians defeated Piedmont, ending Charles Albert's hopes to unify northern Italy. Because the ropes needed to raise and lower the flags had been cut, they remained flying most of March 24. Eventually Maximilian advocated a series of reforms including home rule for Venetia and Lombardy and an Italian Federation under the pope, the latter an idea first broached by the neo-Guelph Vincenzo Gioberti (1801–52) and still supported by Catholic conservatives. However, none of these reforms appeased Venetian and Milanese republicans who remembered Radetzky's lash and Pio Nono's collaboration. For Maximilian's policies, see King, *Italian Unity,* 1:52–53; for Gioberti, see Beales and Biagini, *Risorgimento,* 61.

tions" (15:106)—but what associations! Keats, Shelley, Marius, Edward Gibbon, Tiberius, Beatrice Cenci, Cesare Borgia, Machiavelli arose before his mental eye as his own literary allusions materialized in places and portraits. Meaning expands as the statue he identified with John Ushant now reinforces his deepening sense of historical repetition: "Dying Gladiator. Shows that humanity existed amid the barberousness [sic] of the Roman time, as it now [sic] among Christian barberousness. Antinous, beautiful" (15:106). History, morality, and aesthetics interfuse in Rome's powerful iconography that alternately inspires and exhausts the weary Melville, making him unsure whether he was, in the formulation he conceived in *Clarel,* a tourist or a pilgrim, a philistine reading guidebooks or an acolyte of art (12:95).

Associations—the mental baggage we carry to every new scene—dominate Melville's perceptions and prove Emerson's maxim in "Self-Reliance" that we may seek Rome, and Naples, "the Vatican, and the palaces," but "My giant goes with me wherever I go."[13] Melville's giant is America itself. Ben Lomond, the Bosphorus, the Dead Sea, and Lake Como all remind him of Lake George (15:50, 65, 83, 121); the pyramids form an irregular line "like Notch of White Mountains" and their inner chambers are like "Mammoth Cave" (15:76, 75); the marble shards on the Acropolis look "like blocks of Wenham [Massachusetts] ice" and the Parthenon's ruins look like the "North River breaking up" (15:99). The Tiber reminds him of the Ohio, Venice reminds him of Boston and the New York Battery, the Grand Canal recalls the Susquehanna, Turin looks like Philadelphia, and, as mentioned earlier, Naples's Strada di Toledo resembles Broadway: "Dined & walked for an hour in Strada di Toledo. Great crowds. Could hardly tell it from Broadway. Thought I was there" (15:107, 117, 119, 122, 102). American travelers conventionally compared foreign and native scenes, as Headley's comparison of the Toledo and Broadway suggests (see chap. 1, 50); but Melville's similes occur more frequently than theirs and his lyricism constructs psychological and metaphoric links as, Whitman-like, he absorbs disparate scenes into highly personalized transnational images. He dedicated *Pierre* to "Greylock's Most Excellent Majesty," the whalelike mountain he could see from his study window; when he sees the Roman Colosseum he envisions the "Hopper of Greylock," a metaphor that fuses past and present, artifical and natural, local and foreign (7:vii; 15: 106). And of course the reverse would be true:

---

13. The classic work on associationalism in the United States is Terence Martin, *The Instructed Vision: Scottish Common Sense Philosophy and the Origins of American Fiction* (New York: Kraus Reprint Corp., 1969). For the Emerson quotations, see *Essays and Lectures* (New York: Library of America, 1983), 278.

once having noticed this similarity, Melville could never look out his study window again without seeing the Colosseum. America truly would be, in his mind, a second Rome.

Rome's reinvigorated centrality to Melville's imagination surfaces in his first literary effort after returning from Italy, his lecture "Statues in Rome" (1857). To Robert Milder, its most recent critic, the lecture is uncharacteristically idealistic, a temporary "aesthetic withdrawal" from contemporary realities that explains its failure to please audiences.[14] Yet at least one newspaper, as Hershel Parker recounts, found Melville's elision of politics and theology reassuring.[15] In fact, the lecture fuses politics and aesthetics with the muted comparisons Melville had practiced in his journal, for he knew that any work on "Rome" carried political connotations that his audiences would grasp, notably regard for law, order, and civic virtue. The lecture reinforces these connections by constructing what Parker calls "a rudimentary democratic theory of art appreciation" that opens the pleasures of "Art" (with a capital "A") to, as Melville says, the "rude and uncultivated" as well as the "polite and polished" (9:398).[16] Working without visual aids, he compares Roman statues to modern character types, for example a bust of Socrates to an "Irish comedian" and the head of Julius Caesar to a railroad president (9:400–1). He quickly complicates such philistine comparisons by adding that while these works reveal a commonplace humanity, they "are often deceptive, and a true knowledge of their character is lost unless they are closely scrutinized," as when the pleasing countenance of Tiberius masks "the monster portrayed by the historian" (9:402). An untutored identification with the past quickly develops into a meditation on the relative truths of word and image, history and art, and an implicit recognition that neither has ontological status in the quest for truth. Even religious differences melt away under the powerful appeal of popular iconography, as when Melville terms the Dying Gladiator a man "Christian in all but the name" (9:405). Protestantizing Rome as did Fuller, Melville argues that "though the ancients were ignorant of the principles of Christianity, there were in them the germs of its spirit" (9:404). The lecture's ideology seems invisible only because its symbols no longer signify, no longer carry the "pleasing and cherished associations" that Melville and his audience share

---

14. Robert Milder, "'The Connecting Link of Centuries': Melville, Rome, and the Mediterranean, 1856–1857," in *Roman Holidays: American Writers and Artists in Nineteenth-Century Italy*, ed. Robert K. Martin and Leland S. Person (Iowa City: University of Iowa Press, 2002), 222, 220.

15. *Herman Melville*, 2:369.

16. *Herman Melville*, 2:358.

(9:399). The lecture bespeaks a powerful conservative, antirevolutionary ideology that preserves the best of the past while denigrating science, progress, and political change, an ideology suited to the Risorgimento's embrace of monarchy.

Additional comparisons make this conservative turn increasingly pointed. Melville prefers the timeless art of the Vatican to the mechanical inventions of the Patent Office, the durable Colosseum to the fragile Crystal Palace, the satires of Juvenal to the novels of Dickens, and rhetorically asks, "shall the scheme of Fourier supplant the code of Justinian?" (9:408). By juxtaposing a French socialist with a Roman jurist Melville exploits American contempt for "Red Republicans" to exalt Rome's association with unity, peace, and the rule of law. He aims his strongest metaphor directly at his bickering countrymen: "As the Roman arch enters into and sustains our best architecture, does not the Roman spirit still animate and support whatever is soundest in societies and states?" (9:408). In the late 1850s, the ghost of Rome haunts a dividing America that sorely needs triumphal arches to validate its faltering republican experiment. If political idealists would express their dreams in art rather than in social reform, perhaps they would be more effective, the meaning I take from a passage near the conclusion: "The ancients of the ideal description, instead of trying to turn their impracticable chimeras, as does the modern dreamer, into social and political prodigies, deposited them in great works of art, which still live, while states and constitutions have perished, bequeathing to posterity not shameful defects but triumphant successes" (9:409). Art can be a more durable expression of social value than "states and constitutions," not antithetical to politics but another and more universal expression of it. "Statues in Rome" works through this difficult concept as Melville assesses the meaning of his Italian travels and ponders the function of art in an insecure nation. As he would discover in *Battle-Pieces,* and as Lincoln would realize when he asked Garibaldi to join the Union army, national unity could be well served by the symbols of ancient Rome.

THE CULT OF GARIBALDI

After Mazzini, Garibaldi was the best-known Italian to emerge from the revolutions of 1848. In what is probably the first portrait of him published in America, a daguerreotype taken in New York and printed as the frontispiece for Theodore Dwight's *Roman Republic of 1849* (1851),

Figure 16. Giuseppe Garibaldi, 1851. Frontispiece, Theodore Dwight, *The Roman Republic of 1849*. Daguerreotype. This is the first image of Garibaldi published in the United States and reveals the plebeian image he began cultivating during his stay in New York City.

he appears calm, thoughtful, and plainly dressed in nonmilitary clothing (fig. 16), a "drastic change" from the flamboyantly garbed figure depicted in earlier European illustrations, as Lucy Riall has observed.[17] The *Democratic Review* for September 1852 published an even more strikingly plebeian image of Garibaldi, sharply differentiating him from the splendidly aristocratic Louis Kossuth (figs. 17 and 18), a contrast that later served Garibaldi well. The next month the *Democratic Review* introduced Garibaldi to Young America by cloaking him in the mantle of Roman idealism, muting his revolutionary ideology, and enveloping him with the nostalgic aura of classical heroism in contrast to the cerebral and febrile Mazzini (fig. 19): "The type of his [Garibaldi's] character is antique, and belongs rather to one of Plutarch's heroes as Plutarch has painted them, than to any which our own times or the Middle

---

17. *Garibaldi: Invention of a Hero* (New Haven, CT: Yale University Press, 2007), 111–12. Riall brilliantly analyzes both the cultural and political functions of the "Garibaldi cult" and dissects the reasons for its success, particularly in establishing a prototype of Italian national identity that moderated revolutionary excess with republican principles.

The Triumph of Nationalism / 187

Figure 17. Giuseppe Garibaldi, 1852. Frontispiece, *United States Magazine and Democratic Review* 31 (September 1852). This is the first image of Garibaldi to appear in an American periodical. It continues the democratization of Garibaldi's public persona.

Figure 18. Lajos Kossuth, 1851. *Harper's New Monthly Magazine* 4 (December 1851): 40. In contrast to Garibaldi, Kossuth appears more aristocratic.

Figure 19. Giuseppe Mazzini, 1852. Frontispiece, *Democratic Review* 30 (January 1852). Mazzini's role as the intellectual leader of the Risorgimento comes through effectively in this engraving.

Ages offer."[18] Melville, whose own reading of Plutarch influenced his conception of Roman history, drew on such popular associations in "At the Hostelry" when he painted Garibaldi as one of "Plutarch's men" (Sandberg 80, 1:43). By the time Garibaldi reappeared on the American scene in 1858 he had openly disavowed Mazzini and subordinated his republicanism to the monarchy of King Victor Emmanuel II. In the 1859 war against Austria Garibaldi commanded the romantic *Cacciatori delle Alpi,* a daring cavalry of irregulars who swooped out of the mountains to harass the Austrians from the rear while traditional warfare continued on the plains. By placing patriotism before politics, Garibaldi conformed to American nationalist idealism and greatly increased his stature in the United States, as an article in Melville's local weekly, the *Berkshire County Eagle,* asserted:

> It is, by the way, a curious fact that this same Garibaldi, who fought so bravely against the French some ten years ago, would now be enlisted in the very cause to which they are so great a support; and it proves that

---

18. "Second Campaign of Charles Albert," *Democratic Review* 31 (October 1852): 313.

Garibaldi is no ranting Red Republican, but can lay aside all personal prejudices, and really and patriotically devote himself to the great cause of Italian amelioration and liberty—a cause in behalf of which Louis Napoleon and the French seem now to be powerful instruments.[19]

Pragmatic yet principled, selfless yet individualistic, a revolutionary in the service of a monarch, Garibaldi represented the ideological paradoxes at the core of an America striving for national unity yet riven with increasing sectionalism, an America on the eve of its own civil war.

American newspapers followed the Italian war closely, especially the new illustrated journal *Harper's Weekly* that thrived on publishing engravings of battle scenes, officers in full military regalia, and charts of military movements. One of Melville's favorite magazines, *Harper's Weekly* offered detailed analyses of the conflict every week and even printed three folio-sized maps of northern Italy so readers could better follow military maneuvers (May 28, July 9, and July 30, 1859). Melville's local newspapers, the *Pittsfield Sun* and the *Berkshire County Eagle,* unabashedly supported the king and Garibaldi. The *Sun* of May 12 reminded readers of "the evils under which Italy was suffering from foreign despotism, ecclesiastical thraldom, and the tyranny of domestic rulers," specifically Austria, the pope, and the king of Naples, and on June 3 the *Eagle* printed William Cullen Bryant's attack on Austrian perfidy.[20] Nor were Italy's French allies to be entirely trusted. Although Napoleon III argued that he aided Sardinia only "to restore to freedom one of the finest parts of Europe," Risorgimento enthusiast Senator Charles Sumner expressed highly qualified confidence in the emperor in the July 1 *Eagle.*[21] In this transnationally charged political atmosphere, on July 6 Melville wrote a letter in the form of a poem inviting his brother Allan's law partner friend Daniel Shepherd to Arrowhead:

Come, Daniel, come and visit me:
I'm lost in many a quandary:
I've dreamed, like Bab'lon's Majesty:
Prophet, come expound for me.
—I dreamed I saw a laurel grove,
Claimed for his by the bird of Jove,

19. "Who Is Garabaldi [sic]?," *Berkshire County Eagle,* June 24, 1859.
20. *Sun,* "Exciting War News," 1; *Eagle,* "Italy and Austria," 1.
21. *Sun,* "Three Days Later from Europe," June 30, 1859, 1; *Eagle,* "Senator Sumner on the Italian War," 1.

> Who, elate with such dominion,
> Oft cuffed the boughs with haughty pinion.
> Indignantly the trees complain,
> Accusing his afflictive reign.
> Their plaints the chivalry excite
> Of chanticleers, a plucky host:
> They battle with the bird of light.
> Beaten, he wings his Northward flight,
> No more his laurel realm to boast,
> Where now, to crow, the cocks alight,
> And—break down all the branches quite!
> Such a weight of friendship pure
> The grateful trees could not endure.
> This dream, it still disturbeth me:
> Seer, foreshows it Italy? (14:337–38)

Although scholars know little about Shepherd—all of the facts are summarized in the headnote to the letter—he presumably enjoyed discussing foreign politics over a glass of liquor, which the rest of the poem discusses in convivial detail.[22] What counts here is the precision of Melville's allusions to Italian politics and his desire to discuss them with a presumably knowledgeable and interested friend. Framed as a dream-allegory, the poem questions Napoleon III's motives and implies that French domination may follow Italian independence. The "bird of Jove" is Austria's double eagle, the "chanticleers" represent the French, and the laurel branches are the Italian states.[23] As much as Italy needs rescuing, Melville wonders whether its "laurel grove" can sustain the weight of French "friendship," a burdensome bond that contrasts sharply with the relationship the poet envisages with Shepherd. Melville shares Sumner's distrust of Napoleon III and asks if Italy may simply be trading one foreign ruler for another. Prophetically, Melville wrote the poem the same day Napoleon asked Franz Joseph of Austria for a truce, an act that betrayed the Italian cause and led to the notorious Treaty of Villafranca on July 9 which allowed Austria to remain in parts of northern Italy. Melville's prescience indicates a keen understanding of European politics and Louis Napoleon's strate-

---

22. Parker, for example, limits his discussion to the poem's indications about Melville's drinking habits (*Herman Melville*, 2:401).

23. These glosses were first inferred in Melville, *Representative Selections*, ed. Willard Thorp (New York: American Book Company, 1938), 425n. Thorp misread one line as "bird of love," yet still connected the image with Austria. My reading in the period suggests that Melville was using generally understood metaphors and national stereotypes.

gies. He knew that expressions of friendship from the lips of a Napoleon meant little, for, unlike the enlightened rulers he later praised in "The Age of the Antonines," modern emperors will sacrifice noble ideals—the "laurel" that wreathes Italy's separate states—to political expediency—here, Napoleon's fear of republics. Constitutional authority depends on the character of its executives, and Napoleon III, as Sumner suspected, was more concerned with self-preservation than principle.

The looming Italian war may have prodded Melville to compose not only "Daniel Shepherd" but some of the six Italian poems in "Fruit of Travel Long Ago" with their air of danger, unrest, unease, and possible death in a land whose tradition of "fatal beauty" is about to explode.[24] The first five stanzas of "Pausilippo (In the Time of Bomba)" exhibit "Daniel Shepherd's" tetrameters and, by recalling Silvio Pellico's "Clandestine arrest" for writing a "patriot ode / Construed as treason; trial none; / Prolonged captivity profound" (11:298; 31, 33–35), remind readers of Italy's wrongs at the hands of foreign oppressors. "In a Bye-Canal" evokes the mystery of Venice when the narrator spies the "loveliest eyes of scintillation" peering through a lattice as he floats by in a gondola (11:292; 13). While the eyes are presumably female, and their invitation sexual, they partake of the unwholesome spying Melville experienced in the Austrian-dominated city, and the poem's allusion to Jael, the Israelite woman who slew the Canaanite general Sisera, injects horror into an otherwise tranquil scene. "Venice" and "Milan Cathedral" offer celebratory verbal postcards of their subjects, but "Pisa's Leaning Tower" imagines the structure as "A would-be suicide" (11:294; 11), an ominous note reminiscent of "The Bell-Tower." "In a Church of Padua" compares a confessional to a "Dread diving-bell!" in which priests descend "into consciences / Where more is hid than found" (11:295; 14, 16–17), a metaphor that suggests both papal dungeons and the futility of Roman Catholic rites.

Garibaldi received even more acclaim after his successful invasion of Sicily and Naples confirmed his reputation as a man of integrity, one who refused the dishonorable treaty of Villafranca and stayed true to his vision of a united Italy. Even the splenetic Henry Adams rushed from Rome to Palermo to witness the triumph of the Thousand and meet the great

---

24. William H. Shurr, *The Mystery of Iniquity: Melville as Poet, 1857–1891* (Lexington: University Press of Kentucky, 1972), 47–75, calls these six poems the "Italian section" of *Timoleon*, where they were first published in 1891 (173). Taking a philosophical and formal approach to these works, Shurr believes that the poems "form a unified whole, comprising a small anatomy of Melville's moral and imaginative universe, with issues of pride and sexuality, the possibility of suicide, the crushing of the defiant man—a universe presided over by [Milan Cathedral,] still another of his massive white symbols for divinity" (173). These insights nicely complement my historical analysis.

"Dictator," who, he concluded in a letter to the *Boston Courier,* "was all he was ever said to be," a brave, honest, charismatic leader who "looked in his red shirt like the very essence and genius of revolution, as he is."[25] Later, in his autobiography, Adams wrote, "At that moment, in the summer of 1860, Garibaldi was certainly the most serious of the doubtful energies in the world; the most essential to gauge rightly."[26] By that fall Garibaldi was the most famous leader of the Risorgimento in the world. Newspapers reported his every move, periodicals embellished their pages with engravings of his colorful troops, scholars translated his memoirs, and journalists wrote fawning hagiographies. His image was everywhere, on tins of Virginia tobacco and bottles of perfume, a picture of a soldier with piercing blue eyes, a gentle smile, a thick beard, long hair, and square shoulders, dressed in a brilliant red shirt (fig. 20).

As the most romantic military hero of the day, Garibaldi's exploits inspired even more Risorgimento poetry, including poems by Elizabeth Barrett Browning and Walter Savage Landor as well as Whittier, Lowell, and Longfellow.[27] By early 1861 the *Christian Examiner* of New York asked, "Garibaldi—who has not heard of him? Who does not feel interested in his success? Who but wishes to know something more about him than what is reported in newspapers?"[28]

The American press eagerly shaped Garibaldi's legend to fit the contours of national ideology. Theodore Dwight rushed into print his translation of Garibaldi's memoirs (1859) and argued that the Italian cause was providentially designed to fulfill "some of the most glorious prophesies and promises recorded in the Bible, especially in overturning popery."[29] Such a typology effectively enlisted Garibaldi as a New World enemy of the anti-Christ and satisfied Protestant fears of unwittingly supporting a Catholic. The Beadle Publishing Company initiated its "Dime Biographical Library" with Orville J. Victor's *The Life of Joseph Garibaldi, The Liberator of Italy* (1860) and advertised the book as "Garibaldi, the Washington of Italy," a catchphrase repeated frequently in popular jour-

25. "Henry Adams and Garibaldi, 1860," *American Historical Review* 25 (January 1920): 245, 248. Adams met Garibaldi aborad the US Navy ship *Iroquois* and published seven letters about his visit in the *Boston Courier* in the summer of 1860.
26. *The Education of Henry Adams,* ed. Ernest Samuels (Boston: Houghton Mifflin Company, 1973), 95, 94.
27. Peterson, "Echoes of the Italian Risorgimento:" passim.
28. J. B. Torricelli, "Garibaldi," *Christian Examiner* 70 (1861): 110.
29. Giuseppe Garibaldi, *The Life of General Garibaldi. Written by Himself. With Sketches of His Companions in Arms,* trans. Theodore Dwight, 1st ed. (New York: A. S. Barnes and Burr, 1859). Dwight reprinted the frontispiece he had used for *The Roman Republic of 1849* to reinforce Garibaldi's democratic image (fig. 16).

Figure 20. Tin of Virginia tobacco with Garibaldi's image, c. 1868. Library of Congress. Commercial exploitation of the general's striking appearance, here in his famous red shirt, was rampant during the 1860s in both England and the United States.

nals.[30] Victor claimed that Garibaldi was of noble descent and compared him favorably to Roman generals, Napoleon Bonaparte, St. Paul, Martin Luther, Cromwell, and Washington. Like them, he was "the representative man" who carried out "the purposes of Divinity itself" in the service of a cause ordained by Providence.[31] *Harper's Weekly* devoted its June 9 and November 17, 1860 covers to full-length engravings of the general, first showing him astride a white horse leading men into battle (fig. 21), then portraying his head only, appearing calm and controlled as in the iconic *Democratic Review* frontispiece.

Periodicals extended the Americanization of Garibaldi by describing him in Protestant and Jacksonian tropes that merged him into the American vision of historical progress. Writing for the conservative *North American Review,* Henry Tuckerman characterized Garibaldi as "one of

30. Adams scornfully dismissed this comparison as mere cant: "Europeans are fond of calling him the Washington of Italy, principally because they know nothing about Washington. Catch Washington invading a foreign kingdom on his own hook, in a fireman's shirt!" ("Henry Adams and Garibaldi, 1860," 246). Adams did not realize that Americans had already appropriated the phrase themselves.

31. O[rville] J. Victor, *The Life of Joseph Garibaldi, the Liberator of Italy* (New York: Beadle and Company, 1860), 9–10n, 70, 81, 92, 97, 61. Some of the wrappers carried the title "Garibaldi, the Washington of Italy."

194 / Chapter 5

Figure 21. "General Giuseppe Garibaldi." *Harper's Weekly,* June 9, 1860, 1. News of Garibaldi's invasion of Sicily had recently reached the United States and *Harper's* expressed confidence in his success with this dramatic cover.

Nature's noblemen," a phrase formerly reserved for Andrew Jackson.[32] And J. B. Torricelli, reviewing five French and Italian books on Garibaldi for the *Christian Examiner,* affirmed the millennialist strain: Garibaldi is "*predestined* to be the deliverer of Italy, the messenger of the Almighty to

---

32. [Henry T. Tuckerman], "Rev. Of Italy in Transition; or Public Events and Private Scenes in the Spring of 1860, by William Arthur," *North American Review* 92 (1861): 35.

whom the commission was given to prepare his own countrymen for a new life."[33]

Of equal importance with his military success was Garibaldi's return to his farm on Caprera. Such a repudiation of power, like George Washington's, recalled the legendary Roman hero Cincinnatus who was called from his fields to lead the Roman army and, after defeating the foe, returned to the plow, preferring agrarian peace to military conquest. A central trope in the press, this comparison sanitized Garibaldi for American consumption. *Littell's Living Age* reprinted a British assessment that portrayed Garibaldi as "another Cincinnatus" whose "chief glory is, that, being a ringleader of rebels, he is the servant of order."[34] Orville Victor considered Garibaldi's renunciation of dictatorship even greater than Washington's refusal of a crown: "George Washington, retiring from his power as commander-in-chief of the American army, to his farm at Mount Vernon, glad to return to the quiet of home, was an act [sic] of great moral sublimity: but that of Garibaldi far transcends it."[35] "Cincinnatus," Garry Wills argues, "was an icon meant by the Enlightenment to *replace* churchly saints with a resolutely secular ideal," an aim that targets perfectly both Washington and Garibaldi.[36] For Americans who fancied their own republic a second Rome, Garibaldi provided one more link in a typological chain that extended back through Washington and the Pilgrims to ancient Rome and consecrated America's rebellious spirit with the halo of providential order.

Whatever the reality of his politics, the Garibaldi represented to the American public was neither a Mazzinian social democrat nor a slavish monarchist. Such balance gave him admirers from across the American political spectrum. Longfellow covertly compared him to a volcanic Titan in the poem "Enceladus" (1859), while the more radical Whittier apostrophized him as "God's prophet" in "Garibaldi" (1869).[37] This was precisely the kind of energy that made Garibaldi a popular choice for a command in the Union army, that drove immigrant volunteers to form the "Garibaldi Guard," and that made his autograph as valuable as Washington's, John Hancock's, or Kossuth's at an 1864 benefit for the Union cause.[38]

33. Torricelli, "Garibaldi," 137.
34. "The Sicilian Game," *Littell's Living Age* 27 (December 1860): 737, 736.
35. *Life of Joseph Garibaldi*, 101.
36. *Cincinnatus: George Washington and the Enlightenment* (Garden City: Doubleday, 1984), 23.
37. Peterson, "Echoes of the *Italian* Risorgimento," 239, 235. My own reading of "Enceladus" sees the Titan as more generally representative of Italy itself, not any particular person.
38. For Lincoln's offer of a Union command and the Garibaldi Guard, see Introduction, p. 2n. For Garibaldi's autograph, see Stanton Garner, *The Civil War World of Herman Melville* (Law-

"AT THE HOSTELRY"
Deconstructing Garibaldi

Melville first read of Garibaldi's feats in a San Francisco newspaper in October 1860; conceivably, he could have begun his verses on Garibaldi then.[39] Or he might have begun them the following July 1 when he and Evert Duyckinck visited the steam sloop *Iroquois* at the Brooklyn Navy Yard (*Log*, 641), walking the same deck that Garibaldi had trod while the ship was protecting American interests in Palermo.[40] At some point he may have discussed the general with his cousin Henry Gansevoort who had been in Italy with his family from late 1859 until August 1860, or seen the photographs of Garibaldi and his son Menotti in cousin Kate Gansevoort Lansing's photograph album of famous Europeans.[41] Whatever the sources, Herman and his extended family were well aware of Garibaldi-mania, a cause Melville advanced in his Neapolitan diptych, "At the Hostelry" and "Naples in the Time of Bomba."

Although seldom studied, in one form or another these poems have been included in the Melville canon since the Constable edition of 1922–24 and textual scholars have thoroughly, if inconclusively, debated its structure, intent, and dates of composition. Of their 1,428 lines, approximately 200 allude to Garibaldi, Cavour, and the Risorgimento. Garibaldi allusions occur in three places: the beginning and end of the first poem and the end of the second poem. They thus frame the entire diptych and provide a link between the two parts. A different persona narrates each diptych, and the topics shift uneasily between history, politics, and

---

rence: University Press of Kansas, 1993), 297.

39. Parker, *Herman Melville*, 2:449–50.

40. The *Iroquois* left New York for Palermo on January 19, 1860 to protect American lives and property. Garibaldi came aboard on June 20, 1860, shortly after he had taken the city. The ship operated in the Mediterranean into 1861 and was recalled to serve in the Civil War. See *Dictionary of American Fighting Ships,* Vol. III ([Washington, DC: Navy Department, Office of the Chief of Naval Operations, Naval History Division, 1968], 460). Melville and Duyckinck were visiting Richard Lathers at Winyah and, as Duyckinck recorded in his diary, went to the Navy Yard to visit the "Iroquois, fresh from the Mediterranean and Garibaldi" (*Log,* 641).

41. For Henry Gansevoort, see Garner, *Civil War World,* 16, 56; Kate Gansevoort Lansing's album is in the Gansevoort-Lansing Collection, New York Public Library, and the photos are on 37. Garibaldi wears a dark bowler and heavy coat while holding a cigar. Menotti wears full military regalia and stands with a sword. Henry Gansevoort fought in the Civil War and Melville followed him closely (Garner, passim); "Cousin Kate" (1838–1918) figures largely in Parker's biography. She collected photographs of European statesmen and artists from 1859–71 and they run the gamut from Joan of Arc and Napoleon Bonaparte through a large group of contemporary Italians including Victor Emmanuel I, Francis II of Naples, Mazzini, Cavour, Pius IX, and Cardinal Antonelli. One group includes likenesses of Michelangelo, Titian, Salvator Rosa, Dante, Murillo, and other artists Melville mentions.

art as other voices intrude to complicate the issue of authorial presence with what Robert Sandberg calls an "adjustment of screens."[42] Allusions to Garibaldi connect every voice, however, and offer differing perspectives on this complex hero. "At the Hostelry," narrated by the Marquis de Grandvin, begins with 100 lines recounting Garibaldi's victories in Sicily and the annexations leading up to Rome's incorporation into Italy in 1870; it concludes with a biographical reminiscence of Garibaldi's year of exile in New York, particularly his residence on Staten Island at the home of Antonio Meucci, an inventor and candlemaker. Thickly sandwiched in between is a long debate on the merits of the "picturesque" dramatized in the voices of thirty "Old Masters" such as Jan Steen, Adrian Brouwer, William Van de Velde, Tintoretto, Rubens, and Paolo Veronese. "Naples in the Time of Bomba," narrated by Major Jack Gentian, recounts the major's entry into Naples during the last years of Ferdinand II's reign and draws heavily on Melville's own experiences during his 1857 visit to Naples. The poem interfuses these scenes with disturbing recollections of Neapolitan history, including some of its darkest moments. Then, in a surprising turn, it concludes with an elegy for Garibaldi. As in his paired short stories set in America and England—"The Paradise of Bachelors and The Tartarus of Maids," "The Two Temples," and "Rich Man's Pudding, Poor Man's Crumbs," first called "diptychs" by Jay Leyda[43]—the paired poems connect disparate times and places to create a contrapuntal, transnational whole with Garibaldi as historical figure and poetic symbol bridging two distinct moments in recent Italian history.

"At the Hostelry" opens with a rush of details that authoritatively demonstrates Melville's familiarity with popular representations of Garibaldi's finest moment—the conquest of Sicily and Naples in 1860. A John Tenniel cartoon from *Punch* that was reprinted in the July 7, 1860 *Harper's Weekly*, while Melville was at sea, anticipates the poem's opening metaphor by depicting Garibaldi as a "Modern Perseus" rescuing Sicily-Andromeda from "Bomba Junior," Francis II caricatured as a grotesque sea monster (fig. 22).

"At the Hostelry" applies this iconography to Garibaldi's liberation of Naples, a city

> long in chains
>   Exposed dishevelled by the sea—

---

42. "'The Adjustment of Screens': Putative Narrators, Authors, and Editors in Melville's Unfinished Burgundy Club Book," *Texas Studies in Literature and Language* 31 (1989): 426–50.

43. Jay Leyda, ed., *The Complete Stories of Herman Melville* (New York: Random House, 1949), xx–xxi.

Figure 22. John Tenniel, "Garibaldi the Liberator; or, The Modern Perseus." *Harper's Weekly,* July 7, 1860, 432. This richly allusive cartoon celebrating Garibaldi's conquest of Sicily first appeared in *Punch* and was immediately reprinted in *Harper's Weekly.*

> Ah, so much more her beauty drew,
> Till Savoy's red-shirt Perseus flew
> And cut that fair Andromeda free. (79; 1:10–14)

The cartoon uses the same iconography as chapter 55 of *Moby-Dick* where Ishmael refers to Guido Reni's and William Hogarth's depictions of Perseus rescuing Andromeda (6:261). Melville's poetic allusion suggests that he not only saw the *Harper's* cartoon but also noticed its alterations that

Figure 23. Guido Reni, *Perseus and Andromeda* (1635–36). Galleria Pallavicini Rospigliosi, Rome, Italy. Oil. Alinari / Art Resource, NY.

paint a more positive picture of Garibaldi's military exploits. In Guido's painting (fig. 23) Perseus descends astride Pegasus, brandishing a sword in a recognizable pose of military valor, like the *Harper's Weekly* cover (fig. 21); in contrast, Hogarth's Perseus (fig. 24), unquestionably supernatural and mythic, flies through the air unaided, holding the head of Medusa.

Tenniel's cartoon changes these representations in several important ways. It eliminates Pegasus and gives his wings to Garibaldi, angelizing

Figure 24. William Hogarth, *Perseus Rescuing Andromeda.* Detail of engraving from Lewis Theobald's *Perseus and Andromeda: A Verse Drama* (1730). Courtesy of the New Bedford Whaling Museum.

him and reinforcing his moral distance from the sea monster, now transformed into Francis II, the misshapen prince of Hell.[44] It gives Garibaldi a spear, linking him with St. George as well as Perseus, a common archetypal

---

44. "The Entry into Naples," a poem published on the front page of *Harper's Weekly* a few months later, clothed Garibaldi's triumph in the rhetoric of millennialism, explicitly comparing him to "an angel from the skies" and "Heaven's own chosen king" (October 13, 1860). Such metaphors almost transform Garibaldi into an evangelical Protestant.

comparison that Melville used in *Moby-Dick* and one that further sanctifies Garibaldi's efforts (6:363). Importantly, Andromeda wears clothes, lessening her sexuality;[45] Medusa disappears, eliminating the chief emblem of Perseus's violence; and Garibaldi wears a Roman uniform, placing him in the service of the imperial state. These alterations conform the story of Perseus and Andromeda to Victorian and American ideology by validating accepted gender roles and obsessions with empire while eliding the dangerous "Medusa of Republicanism."[46] They are iconographic euphemisms, calculated changes designed to obscure the brutality behind the Perseus myth that Ishmael invoked when he compared Ahab to Cellini's statue. Although Garibaldi rebels against authority, his noble aims justify his deeds in a Machiavellian economy of war that repays violence with national independence.

Immediately after the allusion to Perseus and Andromeda, the poem turns toward the more mundane facts of Garibaldi's life, which moderate his mythic stature. Recalling popular descriptions of Garibaldi, the poem terms him "The banished Bullock from the Pampas" (79; 11:23) and a "red Taurus plunging on" (79; 11:29), metaphors that combine New World and Old, Garibaldi's participation in republican revolutions in Brazil and Uruguay with astrology. Behind "Taurus" lies Garibaldi's oft-noted rashness and impetuosity, as well as Torino ("little bull") or Turin, the seat of Victor Emmanuel who quietly supported Garibaldi's invasion. More mundane historical facts follow as Garibaldi arrives in Naples by rail, not on a white horse, just after his foe "King Fanny" has ignominiously packed his bags and fled to the papal fortress of Gaeta. Garibaldi's mechanized entrance links him with the industrial order that would soon dominate Europe and America and threaten the classic ideals that Garibaldi popularly represented. Melville's Garibaldi blends linear and cyclic patterns of history as an apostle of unpredictable change, a mixture of ancient myth and commonplace modern reality.[47]

Melville thus participates in Garibaldi-mania mainly to deconstruct it, anticipating Lucy Riall's method in *Garibaldi: Invention of Hero* and

---

45. For a good analysis of Andromeda's figurative role in nineteenth-century British culture, see Adrienne Auslander Munich, *Andromeda's Chains: Gender and Interpretation in Victorian Literature and Art* (New York: Columbia University Press, 1989).

46. For the Victorian reaction to the Risorgimento, see O'Connor, *The Romance of Italy*.

47. William Bysshe Stein, *The Poetry of Melville's Late Years: Time, History, Myth, and Religion* (Albany: State University of New York Press, 1970), interprets Garibaldi as a figure of cyclic history, a Dionysian reformer of the failed linear history of Christianity (229). Such a reading, while valuable, disregards the historical fact that Garibaldi liberated Naples from one king only to give it to another. Like many Melville critics who prefer to view Melville as disruptive and iconoclastic, Stein overemphasizes liberty and ignores authority.

her conclusion that "the creation of the myth of Garibaldi reflects both the political possibilities of modern communication techniques and the scavenging tendencies of nationalist rhetoric, which seeks to construct a popular and persuasive political ideology by appropriating and manipulating pieces of existing discourse and practice."[48] For example, after liberating Naples Garibaldi's name shines in the "halls of history" (80; 1.36) as

> one who in no paladin age
> Was knightly—him who lends a page
> Now signal in time's recent story
> Where scarce in vogue are "Plutarch's men,"
> And jobbers deal in popular glory. (80; 11:40–44)

Even while these lines criticize newspapers' inflated rhetoric they share the rhetoric of Garibaldi's obituaries in the press, evidence that Melville tinkered with the poem until 1882. E. L. Godkin praised Garibaldi's "heroism of the antique type, the simple type which Plutarch has painted, but the reproduction of which in our time the newspapers are making less and less possible, because its largest element was its unconsciousness, and the modern hero finds it difficult to be unconscious."[49] A. V. Dicey saw knightly valor succumbing to utilitarian warfare, where mechanized armies, steel ships, and growing imperialism left no room for the "romance and generosity" of a Garibaldi.[50] The *New York Tribune* considered Garibaldi "the last heroic figure in Italian history," and *Harper's Weekly* prepared a special full-page engraving depicting the highlights of Garibaldi's career (fig. 25).[51]

A revolutionary hero cloaked in Roman virtue, Garibaldi is one of Melville's "kingly commons," perhaps the last of his kind, a hero whose unquestioned merit reveals the shallowness of contemporary "popular glory." Yet he is also, as Lucy Riall has shown, a product of the "jobbers," a simple man elevated into living legend for the entertainment of newspaper readers and commodified as "picturesque" by well-intentioned writers like Dwight, Tuckerman, and even the caustic Adams. Whether wearing the regalia of the gaucho or the Roman legion, Garibaldi is one of Godkin's self-conscious modern heroes, as much a construct of his time as a force shaping it. The "popular glory" that surrounds him parallels the process Melville described in a late letter complaining about the publish-

---

48. Riall, *Garibaldi*, 389.
49. E. L. Godkin, "Garibaldi," *Nation*, June 8, 1882, 477.
50. A. V. Dicey, "Garibaldi and the Movement of 1848," *Nation*, June 29, 1882, 541–42.
51. "Necrology," *New York Tribune Index* (1882), xv; *Harper's Weekly*, June 17, 1882, 381.

Figure 25. "Giuseppe Garibaldi: Died at Caprera, June 2." *Harper's Weekly*, June 17, 1882, 381. Thomas Nast drew the robed figure of Garibaldi and based it on his earlier sketch of the general in a cartoon commemorating the demise of papal power in Rome (*Harper's Weekly*, February 20, 1875, 161).

ing house of Harper: "This species of 'fame' a waggish acquaintance says can be manufactured to order, and sometimes is so manufactured thro the agency of a certain house that has a correspondent in every one of the almost innumerable journals that enlighten our millions from the Lakes to the Gulf & from the Atlantic to the Pacific" (14:492–93).

As an icon of modern heroism, Garibaldi runs the risk of being absorbed by a greedy and commercial age of increasing utilitarianism and capitalism. The Marquis de Grandvin, ever practical, realizes that some loss of heroic stature inevitably follows fame. Revolutionary idealism must give way to practical diplomacy in order to make Italy "A unit and a telling State / Participant in the world's debate" (80; 1.65–66). The greater good may now be better served by a canny politician like Cavour: "Few deeds of arms, in fruitful end / The statecraft of Cavour transcend" (80; 1.67–68). With the successive incorporation of Florence, Ancona, Venice, and finally Rome into a unified republic, Italy's leaders must turn their attention to practical matters:

> Swart Tiber, dredged, may rich repay—
> The Pontine Marsh, too, drained away.
> And, far along the Tuscan shore
> The weird Maremma reassume
> Her ancient tilth and wheaten plume. (81; 1.94–98)

William Bysshe Stein reads these lines as a criticism of Garibaldi, who actively supported these projects during the 1870s and thus betrayed his idealism with utilitarianism.[52] But in Garibaldi's time these projects were considered visionary attempts to recapture the glories of ancient Rome by making Italy a more industrialized and progressive nation. And because they are agricultural improvements, they link Garibaldi even more closely with Cincinnatus, a figure whose heroic stature rests on combining the military with the agricultural. It is not so much Garibaldi whom Melville criticizes as it is the inflated imagery and rhetoric of contemporary media.

Still, real questions about Garibaldi's fame exist. Can his reputation survive his popularity? Or will he be reduced to a mere advertising image, a picture on a tin of smoking tobacco, a product of the "jobbers" at Beadle's, the cartoonists at *Punch* and *Harper's Weekly*, or the columnists at the *Nation*? In the conclusion of "At the Hostelry" the marquis wonders whether Garibaldi's fame can survive the coming age of utilitarianism. Consider his costume:

> The Cid, his net-work shirt of mail,
> And Garibaldi's woolen one:
> In higher art would each avail
> So just expression nobly grace—
> Declare the hero in the face? (94; 8.11–15)

Is Garibaldi's noble physiognomy sufficient to overcome his unheroic garb? Can he retain the heroic associations of the Cid even though he is customarily portrayed wearing ordinary clothes instead of armor? These ques-

---

52. *Poetry of Melville's Late Years*, 228–29. For Garibaldi's interest in making the Tiber navigable, see Mack Smith, *Garibaldi*, 189–90.

tions, as Gordon Poole has noticed, are implicit in the long debate on the picturesque that takes up most of "At the Hostelry."[53] Although the debate is finally inconclusive, Jan Steen's pragmatic response suggests the dilemma Garibaldi faces as he becomes a more and more legendary figure:

> Utility reigns—Ah, well-a-way!—
> And bustles along in Bentham's shoes.
> For the Picturesque—suffice, suffice
> The picture that fetches a picturesque price! (82; 2.17–20)

Garibaldi becomes little more than an advertising gimmick, a cheap means of increasing magazine sales or selling tobacco. The Garibaldi of history fades before the Garibaldi created by the media, an artificial and picturesque figure that serves the interests of publishers, not the ideals of revolution. This more ambiguous vision of Garibaldi informs the end of "At the Hostelry":

> There's Garibaldi, off-hand hero,
> A very Cid Campeadór,
> Lion-Nemesis of Naples' Nero—
> But, tut, why tell that story o'er!
> A natural knight-errant, truly,
> Nor priding him in parrying fence,
> But charging at the helm-piece—hence
> By statesmen deemed a lord unruly. (95; Sequel 17–24)

These lines capture the debate between cool-headed politicians like Cavour and Victor Emmanuel over Garibaldi's long-term value. The king respected Garibaldi's military genius and encouraged him when it served his ends, but, when Garibaldi recklessly set off on a buccaneering expedition against Rome in 1862 the Piedmontese army confronted his irregulars at Aspromonte and wounded the general so seriously he almost lost a leg. When he assaulted Rome again in 1867 the army defeated him at Mentana and the king placed him under house arrest on Caprera where he remained a virtual prisoner until 1871.[54] With the revolution over, "the dragons penned or slain, / What for St. George would then remain!" (95–96; Sequel 39–40), asks the marquis. It is a question that Garibaldi, cast aside by the king he had so ardently supported, must have asked

---

53. "At the Hostelry," xxviii–xxxi.
54. Mack Smith, *Garibaldi*, 122–81.

himself.

The final lines of "At the Hostelry" confirm Garibaldi's paradoxical nature: he resists both the historical typologies that seem to explain him and the picturesque aura conferred by the popular press. "A don of rich erratic tone," evidently a conservative member of the Burgundy Club, reminds the audience of Garibaldi's days on Staten Island. Were he born today, the don asserts, the "Red Shirt Champion" would never

> quit his trading trips,
> Perchance, would fag in trade at desk,
> Or, slopped in slimy slippery sludge,
> Lifelong on Staten Island drudge,
> Melting his tallow, Sir, dipping his dips,
> Scarce savoring much of the Picturesque! (96; Sequel 56–61)[55]

The don's linear view of history as progressively more common and ignoble presages Henry Adams's pessimism, where primal "forces" such as Garibaldi suffer from increasing entropy. To this bleak outlook a "cultured wight / Lucid with transcendental light" (96; Sequel 62–63) responds with a cyclical view of history:

> Pardon, but tallow none nor trade
> When, thro' this Iron Age's reign
> The Golden one comes in again;
> That's on the card. (96; Sequel 64–67)

While it's always tempting to find caricatures of Emerson in Melville's writings, this "transcendental" view is decidedly non-Emersonian. "All history resolves itself very easily into the biography of a few stout and earnest persons," Emerson wrote in "Self-Reliance,"[56] privileging the individual above events. Both the cynical don and the "cultured wight" disagree with Emerson's view and see men as products of their historical situation, whether it extends into an infinite and unpredictable future

---

55. Both Stein (245) and William H. Shurr (*Mystery of Iniquity*, 216) read these lines autobiographically, taking them as references to Melville's own dreary career in the custom house, a suggestion Poole, in the best published edition of the poem, repeats (39n). Yet Melville worked on Manhattan, not Staten, island and seldom drudged at a desk, instead walking the docks in the open air as, in his own words, an "outdoor Custom House officer" (*Log*, 818). Of course, the lines allude directly to Garibaldi's 1850–51 exile on Staten Island, a fact well known at the time and mentioned in all standard biographical dictionaries today. Melville's poem is trying to enter history, not evade it, to engage experience, not retreat into autobiography.

56. *Essays and Lectures*, 267.

or returns to a familiar past. The puzzle of Garibaldi is that he seems to be all three, one of Adams's primal energies exhausting itself in supreme effort, a picturesque Roman hero returned to usher in a golden age of Italian prosperity and independence, and a "representative man" who incorporates the spirit of the age so completely that it seems to have flowed from his veins. Garibaldi illustrates the impossibility of deciding whether man makes history or history makes man. Instead of an Emersonian motto, Melville presents a multivoiced, inconclusive debate on fundamental issues. The eloquent Marquis de Grandvin, perhaps more gracious than Melville himself, ends this "rhyming race" with a moderate position on the relationship between history and the self:

> Angel O' the Age! Advance, God speed.
> Harvest us all good grain in seed;
> But sprinkle, do, some drops of grace
> Nor polish us into commonplace. (96; Sequel 74–77)

Drawing upon his famous reserve of geniality, the marquis appeals for a middle way that sustains the mystique of Garibaldi ("the drops of grace") even while acknowledging the inevitable leveling of the advancing age of utilitarianism.

"NAPLES IN THE TIME OF BOMBA"
An American Garibaldi

"Naples in the Time of Bomba" counterpoints "At the Hostelry" by suggesting the limits of individual agency as a moderating force on history. Whereas "At the Hostelry" focuses on Garibaldi's life and major accomplishments, "Naples" mentions him only once, at his death, in lines tacked on after 1882 and, in their last iteration, presumably spoken by the poem's narrator, Major Jack Gentian. Sandberg's analysis of the manuscript indicates that Melville added this narrator around 1875–77 and fleshed him out in sketches only loosely connected with the original poem, which focuses on Naples in 1857 and relies heavily on the travel journal.[57] What I find striking about Jack is his similarity to Garibaldi, a man who represents the contradictory values of authority and individualism, violence and

---

57. "Melville's Unfinished *Burgundy Club* Book," 24.

peace, aristocracy and democracy, republicanism and monarchism, all the paradoxes of modern nationalism that beset both the United States and Italy. The framing devices of the Burgundy Club sketches re-vision Melville's original poem as Jack's narrative to his fellow Burgundians sometime in the late 1870s or even early 1880s, after Garibaldi's death. Of Southern stock, Jack grew up in the North and fought for the Union, losing an arm to the blind force of historical necessity. Like Garibaldi he is brave, impulsive, straightforward, and rash, and startles genteel society by swearing like a "Roman consul exhorting his infantry." No one, however, mistakes his natural merit, his noble bearing that inspires respect even in a New York "cabby" (98). On the surface democratic, Jack is in fact a natural aristocrat, that rare American who maintains the dignity of tradition yet fights on the side of a leveling utilitarianism. Postwar Jack understands how war complicates notions of individual valor and turns yesterday's hero into today's geriatric amputee, even as Garibaldi has fallen in esteem since 1860. Jack and his auditors would know of Garibaldi's two quixotic forays on Rome and his house arrest on Caprera. They might even have read about his escape to France in 1870 where he commanded a republican regiment in the Franco-Prussian War, or about his utopian plans to redirect the Tiber in 1875. With the postbellum "Iron Age" of utilitarianism well under way, Garibaldi seemed more and more of a historical curiosity, an eccentric whose reputation required reassessment and deflation, a theme cautiously advanced in some of the obituaries and overtly presented in William Roscoe Thayer's revisionist 1888 *Atlantic Monthly* pieces.[58]

Jack bears further comparison with Garibaldi by virtue of his membership in the Society of the Cincinnati, an international republican knighthood memorializing American-French cooperation during the Revolutionary War. Composed of Revolutionary War officers, their direct descendants, and French allies, the Cincinnati was America's only hereditary association, and included Melville's maternal grandfather General Peter Gansevoort. From its beginning in 1783 the society was steeped in controversy stemming from its aristocratic tendencies and foreign connections. Although Washington agreed to serve as its first president, on the advice of the anti-Federalist Jefferson he accepted only on condition that the society refrain from politics and moderate its elitism. Wills notes that after 1786 Washington never wore the Cincinnati's distinctive badge

---

58. "The Makers of New Italy," *Atlantic Monthly* 61 (November 1888): 656–67; "The Close of Garibaldi's Career," *Atlantic Monthly* 62 (December 1888): 758–65. In *The Life and Times of Cavour,* 2 vols. (Boston: Houghton Mifflin Company, 1911), Thayer portrays Garibaldi as a romantic radical whose success would have been impossible without Cavour's diplomacy and Victor Emmanuel's support.

obverse

reverse

Figure 26. Medal, Society of the Cincinnati, c. 1790. Reproduced by permission of The Society of the Cincinnati, Washington, DC. The obverse (front) depicts Cincinnatus at the plow, with shipping and villages in the distance; the reverse depicts three senators presenting a sword to Cincinnatus with his wife, child, and house behind him. Many versions of this basic design exist, and this one, the "Andrews-Richard Anderson Eagle," represents the prevailing type when Melville's grandfather General Peter Gansevoort joined the society. See Minor Myers, Jr., *The Insignia of the Society of the Cincinnati,* especially page 52.

and concludes that "Washington retained his membership in the Society only to check it."[59] When the France of Lafayette metamorphosed into the France of Robespierre, the society came under suspicion from conservative Federalists, for it now seemed allied with anarchy and rampant republicanism. Caught in the ongoing debate between authority and individualism, the Society of the Cincinnati served as a lightning rod for American uncertainty about the nature of republican ideology.

Ideological controversies surrounding the Cincinnati and a lingering personal sense of aristocratic pride explain Melville's obsessive rewriting of Jack's biography and his sketches on the society. For his service in the American Revolution Jack's grandfather, a South Carolinian, earned "the eagle-wings in gold of the Cincinnati, a venerable order whereof he who still reigns 'first in the hearts of his countrymen' was the original head" (99). Since membership passed to the oldest son, Jack, like Melville's cousin Guert Gansevoort, inherits the badge, and he insists on wearing it rather than his Grand Old Army medallion.[60] The badge consists of a gold American eagle displaying Cincinnatus at his plow on one side and receiving his sword on the other (fig. 26). It hung from a blue ribbon bordered with white in honor of the French Bourbon flag.

Some of the major's friends believe the badge betrays an aristocratic tendency, even "a weakness for certain gewgaws that savor of the monarchical"; but the narrator responds, "an inherited badge of the Cincinnati, every American however ultra in his democracy, must allow to be something of which no other American need be ashamed" (99). "The Cincinnati," a superseded sketch by one of the most conservative Burgundians, defends "the guillotined victim" Louis XVI and recalls "the violent democratic crusade" that began shortly after his death and briefly discredited the society (140). In another version of Jack's biography, one "Colonel Josiah Bunkum," an unreflecting voice of Radical Republicanism, the cash nexus, and utilitarianism, attacks the Cincinnati as archaic, impractical, antidemocratic, and monarchical. Yet, "Justly proud art thou of thy decoration of the Cincinnati" (143), asserts a subsequent fragment, while another calls Jack "a democrat, though less of the stump than of the heart" (135). Embodying conservative, liberal, and radical ideas, Jack remains as politically capacious as Garibaldi. He personifies the political paradoxes of Revolutionary America allied with monarchical France, Union officers of Southern heritage, modern military heroes with ancient Roman virtues, and Jacksonian Americans claiming inherited nobility.

59. *Cincinnatus,* 142, 145.
60. For the complicated and somewhat indeterminate history of the Gansevoort Cincinnati badge, see Parker, *Herman Melville* 2:518, and Garner, *Civil War World,* 166.

Like Garibaldi, Jack extends the typology of Cincinnatus-Washington into the present, an ambiguous iconography of military valor combined with pastoral humility that justifies force by moderating ambition. The inability of Jack's friends to understand these contradictions reveals their shortcomings, not Jack's. Outdated though he may seem to a "Bunkum," Jack, with his missing arm, dignity, geniality, and magnanimity, is a picturesque reminder of genuine heroism and patriotism. Encompassing contradictory ideologies, he surpasses any single ideology save that of the "representative man," the Emersonian ethos popularly applied to Garibaldi. Yet as a man enmeshed in history he complicates even that transcendental lure, that sop to individualism that mitigates the forces of historical necessity so obviously formative in Jack's life. Parker, following Michael Rogin, suggests that Melville's customhouse badge—which he wore daily when he was writing these poems—reminded him of the Cincinnati badge and what Rogin terms his "moral right" to wear it.[61] One need not accept this psychological speculation to recognize that the Cincinnati motif symbolizes Melville's recognition that history alternately demands aristocratic authoritarianism and democratic individualism, paradoxical qualities embodied in Cincinnatus, Washington, Garibaldi, and Jack Gentian.

Historical paradox riddles Jack's meditation in "Naples in the Time of Bomba" and explains why Melville thought him an appropriate narrator for the original poem. In 1857 Bomba reigns, frivolity dominates, and the revolutions of 1848 have faded from memory. Although Jack enjoys the gaiety and thoughtlessness of the Neapolitan mob, he knows the "shocking stories bruited wide, / In England which I left but late, / Touching dire tyranny in Naples" (111; 2.4–6), an allusion to Gladstone's famous letters of 1851 and the increasing English recognition of Bomba's horrors. Seeing through the gay façade into the darkness of Bomba's tyranny, Jack notices cannons turned toward the populace instead of the sea, troops mustered in a daily show of force, political prisoners in the Castel dell'Ovo, spies masquerading as blind beggars, and sycophantic Jesuits ready to rationalize Bomba's "lawless power" (124; 8.69). Naples in 1857 combines the ethical ambiguities of *The Confidence-Man* with the political repression Melville observed firsthand on his Italian tour. Jack knows Neapolitan history and recalls such abuses of authority as Queen Joanna I's murder of her husband and Tiberius's exile of Agrippina, Germanicus's noble wife. As twinned perversions of patriotism and filial loyalty, these events paint tyranny as the Janus face of anarchy, a fundamental paradox in Neapolitan history that culminates in the present reign of "A brag-

---

61. *Subversive Genealogy*, 291; Parker, *Herman Melville* 2:830.

212 / *Chapter 5*

gadocio Bourbon-Draco!" (127; 9.87). Underneath a smiling face, Naples is bubbling with Vesuvian fire, as Jack sees emblems of revolution everywhere: Vesuvius itself, of course, "a Power even more nitrous and menacing than the Bomb-King himself" (116); "Mariners in red Phrygian caps" (124; 8.48), the cap of proletarian revolt; and allusions to "Parthenope" (125; 9.12; 147, 148), both the ancient name of Naples and the short-lived republic established by French Jacobins in 1799.

The most horrifying event in Neapolitan history that Jack recalls is Masaniello's abortive revolt of 1647, which conjoins politics and art in a welter of associations that, dreamlike, move across centuries to resonate with the French Revolution of 1789 and the Medusan iconography darkly shadowing Garibaldi's deeds. When Jack hears the lilting song of a fruit girl selling blood oranges, a fruit whose very name blends the mixed horror and beauty of Medusa, specters from the past crop up as he remembers Masaniello's revolt:

> Lo, there,
> A throng confused, in arms, they pass,
> Arms snatched from smithy, forge and shop:
> Craftsmen and sailors, peasants, boys,
> And swarthier faces dusked between—
> Brigands and outlaws; linked with these
> Salvator Rosa, and the fierce
> Falcone with his fiery school;
> Pell-mell with riff-raff, banded all
> In league as violent as the sway
> Of feudal claims and foreign lords
> Whose iron heel evoked the spark
> That fired the populace into flame.
> And, see, dark eyes and sunny locks
> Of Masaniello, bridegroom young,
> Tanned marigold-cheek and tasseled cap;
> The darling of the mob; nine days
> Their great Apollo; then, in pomp
> Of Pandemonium's red parade,
> His curled head Gorgoned on the pike,
> And jerked aloft for God to see.
> A portent. Yes, and typed the years,
> Red after-years, and whirl of error
> When Freedom linkt with Furies raved

> In Carmagnole and cannibal hymn,
> Mad song and dance before the ark
> From France imported with *The Terror!*" (122; 7.143–69)

Melville probably takes his details from the *Penny Cyclopedia* which explains that three days after a treaty granting tax relief and amnesty the Neapolitan mob turned on Masaniello and "his head was cut off, fixed on a pole, and carried to the viceroy,"[62] a startling homology to Babo's fate in "Benito Cereno." Although neither Rosa nor Falcone took part in the revolt, legend associated them with it and gave their famous paintings of robbers and brigands a spurious authenticity. In contrast with Joel T. Headley's identification of Masaniello with George Washington, Jack thinks Masaniello prefigures the anarchy that overtook France in 1789 where peasant mobs sang the "Carmagnole" as they danced before the guillotine, an anarchy not unlike the "riotocracy" that Melville satirized in "Charles' Isle and the Dog-King." Jack's reading of history is understandable given that he lost an arm suppressing revolt in his own country, and that even such a revolutionary document as Thomas Paine's *Common Sense* used the example of Masaniello to warn against anarchy.[63] Yet the overlay of painting and opera along with the "iron heel" of an oppressive foreign authority engender reader sympathy if not support for Masaniello's doomed revolt and place the Amalfi fisherman in a long line of Roman and Italian republicans from Brutus and Rienzi through Mazzini and Garibaldi.

As a historical figure exalted into legend until his name metonymized the romance of revolution, Masaniello adumbrates the literary glorification that engulfed Garibaldi. Although Jack questions whether Masaniello is any better than the "foreign lords" he opposes, as a figure from picturesque Neapolitan history the decapitated Masaniello, like the decapitated Medusa whose head can still petrify enemies, assumes a literary afterlife as an ambiguous symbol of combined victimization and oppression. Figuratively, Masaniello requires readers to take a more complex view of history than Jack and serves purposes similar to Babo, John Brown, and Billy Budd, all ambiguous figures of revolt and murderous violence

---

62. "Anniello, Tommaso," *Penny Cyclopedia*, 1:32.

63. Paine cites Masaniello to bolster his argument for immediately framing an American consititution: "If we omit it now, some Massanello [*sic*] may hereafter arise, who laying hold of popular disquietudes, may collect together the desperate and the discontented, and by assuming to themselves the powers of government, may sweep away the liberties of the continent like a deluge." See *Thomas Paine's Common Sense: The Call to Independence*, ed. Thomas Wendel (Woodbury, NY: Barron's Educational Series, 1975), 99.

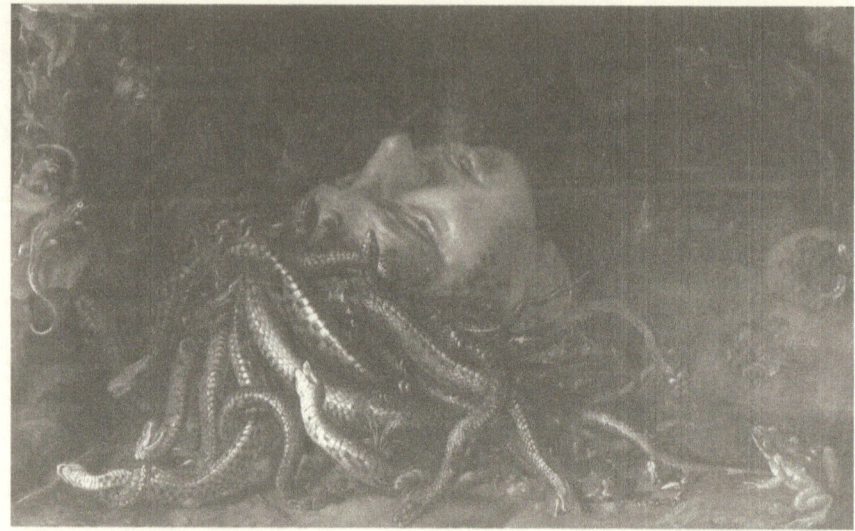

Figure 27. **Head of Medusa**, c. 1600. Once attributed to Leonardo da Vinci, it is now considered the work of a Flemish artist of the late sixteenth century. Uffizi, Florence, Italy. Alinari/Art Resource, NY.

who are at once apotheosized and punished. Like "weird John Brown" in "The Portent" in *Battle-Pieces* (11:5), Masaniello too portends revolution and civil strife; like Babo, his severed head enforces a moral, however mysterious; and like Billy, he is young, handsome, naïve, and violent. All four resist authority and die trying, and all four inspire songs and stories that outlive their abortive revolts. Theirs is an aesthetics of violence like the one that Herman Swanevelt, one of the ghostly painters in "At the Hostelry," discerns in Leonardo da Vinci's *Head of Medusa* (fig. 27):

> Like beauty strange with horror allied,—
> As shown in great Leonardo's head
> Of snaky Medusa,—so as well
> Grace and the Picturesque may dwell
> With Terror. Vain here to divide—
> The Picturesque has many a side. (83; 2.65–70)

By mediating the revolutionary excess of decapitation through the beauty of art, whether the (falsely attributed) painting of Leonardo's or Shelley's poem on the painting, Melville offers a covert intertextual recognition of art's political dimensions.[64] Revolution too has a "beauty strange with

64. The *Head of Medusa* was attributed to Leonardo in 1783, an error that remained un-

horror allied," a combination imaged in Garibaldi, revolution's current dominant icon. And this of course was the great distinction Americans drew between the French and the Italian revolutions: the Risorgimento, despite its history of political assassinations and terrorist attacks, avoided the anarchy of regicide and the sheer horror of the guillotine, the symbol of revolt gone mad, and thus comported with the meliorizing ideology of American politics. Garibaldi's elevated classicism sanitized revolutionary excess and allowed him to function as an American hero, a rebel with a cause. Like Jack, whose Cincinnati medal blends both revolution and monarchy and Roman imperialism and American democracy, Garibaldi retains a personal integrity that justifies his simultaneous exhortations to the mob and submission to the king. Unlike Robespierre or Napoleon, Garibaldi is magnanimous to his enemies, constrains the mob, and retires when his aims are fulfilled. Medusan iconography images the violence of rebellion and the sexual exclusiveness of revolutions fought mainly to liberate white men; but, as wielded by Perseus-Garibaldi and artistically rendered by Melville-Cellini-da Vinci-Shelley, the Medusa myth restrains revolutionary excess by giving the victims power even in death and justifying their murder with the overriding need for order. Unabated revolutionary activity kills Masaniello, Babo, and Robespierre—the beheaders beheaded. Garibaldi, a "knight-errant" with the common touch, both a "Perseus" and a "candle-dipper," offers a secure icon to represent violent historical change, one approved by Americans and, I believe, Melville as well.

When Garibaldi reenters the diptych at the end, he seems to bring order to chaos:

She [Naples as Andromeda] sobbed, she laughed, she rattled her chain;
Till the Red Shirt proved signal apt
Of danger ahead to Bomba's son,

---

corrected until 1907. The painting was the nineteenth century's standard referent for finding both beauty and horror in Medusa, a tradition that began with Goethe and ran through Shelley, Hawthorne, Pater, Swinburne, and William Morris. Although Melville could have seen this painting at the Uffizi in 1857, his lines probably come from Shelley's poem "On the Medusa of Leonardo Da Vinci in the Florentine Gallery": "Its horror and its beauty are divine," Shelley wrote, "Yet it is less the horror than the grace / Which turns the gazer's spirit into stone" as "the tempestuous loveliness of terror" mirrors "all the beauty and the terror there" (ll. 4, 9–10, 33, 38, *Poetical Works*, 250). This poem is included in the edition of Shelley's *Poetical Works* that Melville acquired in 1861 (Sealts, *Melville's Reading*, #469). For a conspectus of Romantic and Victorian appropriations of the Medusa myth see Jerome McGann, "The Beauty of the Medusa," and for a study of Shelley's poem see Grant Scott, "Shelley, Medusa, and the Perils of Ekphrasis" in *The Romantic Imagination: Literature and Art in England and Germany*, ed. Frederick Burwick and Jurgen Klein (Amsterdam: Rodopi, 1996), 315–32.

> And presently freedom's thunder clapt,
> And lo, he fell from toppling throne—
> Fell down, like Dagon on his face,
> And ah, the unfeeling populace!
> But Garibaldi:—Naples' host
> Uncovers to her deliverer's ghost,
> While down time's aisle, mid clarions clear
> "Pale glory walks by valor's bier." (130–31; 12.50–60)

The final image presents Garibaldi in all his contradictory power, as a live hero toppling monarchy yet initiating anarchic terror ("the unfeeling populace" that might revenge itself on its oppressors) and as a dead hero monumentalized in the language of the popular press. Now liberated, Naples must learn to use its freedom wisely and take its place in a unified Italian nation. Its turbulent history suggests difficulties, however, and for both the United States and Italy achieving unity after civil war will prove elusive.

"CHRISTIANITY AND MACHIAVELLI"
Risorgimento Ideology in *Battle-Pieces*

Unlike the stuttering composition of the Neapolitan diptych and Burgundy Club sketches, *Battle-Pieces* (1866) forms a unified book of poems chronologically arranged by the event each memorializes. The poems' themes and tropes are mostly drawn, as Stanton Garner demonstrates, from the immediate events Melville read about in the *Pittsfield Sun, Berkshire Eagle, Harper's Weekly, The Rebellion Record*, and witnessed firsthand when he visited the front in April 1864. Even after supplying this rich context Garner calls for further study of the poems' biblical, Greek, and Roman allusions, an invitation to read the book within the transnational context of the American Risorgimento that leads, I believe, to more closely aligning Melville's ideology with Federalism than Garner allows.[65] Risorgimento nationalism hovers over *Battle-Pieces* to insist that modern nation-states require both a strong central authority and respect for regional differences, a delicate balance Melville tries to achieve with-

---

65. *Civil War World*, 443. Southern apologetics mark Garner's analyses and lead him to read several poems ironically, such as "Gettysburg: The Check" (247) and "The House-Top" (255–57). In the latter poem Garner astonishingly places Melville on the side of rebellion, riot, and anarchy. Garner explains his ironic approach on 68–78.

out sanctioning racial oppression, sectional rivalries, or national disloyalty. Italy's experience after unification was instructive. Anxious to establish a uniform society, Piedmont imposed its civil code on all of its new dominions. Piedmontese law was widely accepted in the central states of Tuscany and Romagna, but in the South, notably Sicily and Calabria, it provoked the "Brigand Wars" of 1861–65 that pitted rural bandits, poor peasants, and recalcitrant Bourbonists against the northern-dominated government. Cavour's diplomatic skills might have smoothed differences between the regions but his untimely death in 1861 left the government under inept politicians unable to modify the stern policies of Victor Emmanue1.[66] Only 2 percent of the population held voting rights which, along with Pius IX's threat to excommunicate Catholics who participated in Italian politics, effectively created a parliamentary oligarchy.[67] These divisions of region, class, and religion prompted the famous proverb attributed to Massimo D'Azeglio, "having made Italy, it remains to make Italians."[68] War alone had failed to create a nation, a lesson *Battle-Pieces* preaches explicitly in its "Supplement" as it gestures simultaneously toward national unity and a cosmopolitan acceptance of regional difference.

Melville grounds his meliorism in Roman history, in 1866 still a respected text for North and South alike but one capable of being misread through the lens of sectional prejudice. The most explicit example comes in the author's note to "The Frenzy of the Wake," a poem voicing a Southerner's angry reaction to Sherman's march through Georgia in 1864. The note carefully distinguishes Sherman's scorched-earth policy from Pompey's decision to spare Roman cities in the civil war that ended the Roman Republic: "The war of Pompey and Caesar divided the Roman people promiscuously; that of the North and South ran a frontier line between what for the time were distinct communities or nations. In this circumstance, possibly, and some others, may be found both the cause and the justification of some of the sweeping measures adopted" (11:177). Sherman, obviously acting on orders from Lincoln, did what was "by military judges deemed to have been expedient" (11:176), a Machiavellian justification for tactics that preserved the Republic, unlike

66. Beales and Biagini, *Risorgimento,* 156–59, 152.
67. Lucy Riall, *The Italian Risorgimento: State, Society and National Unification* (New York: Routledge, 1994), 76–77. See also the hostile communications between Pius IX and Victor Emmanuel and the disillusioned reflections of Mazzini and Garibaldi in Clough and Saladino, *A History of Modern Italy,* 123–56.
68. Adrian Lyttleton, "Creating a National Past: History, Myth, and Image in the Risorgimento," in *Making and Remaking Italy,* provides the more accurate but less colorful translation: "the Italians have wanted to make a new Italy, but themselves to remain the old Italians" (70n48).

Pompey's more restrained and ineffective policies. In contrast to the note's cool analysis, the poem's anguished speaker voices the most extreme of Southern values: he hates Blacks and the American flag, he hopes Union soldiers will "wither" under the blazing Southern sun, and he yearns to avenge Sherman's depredations as Jael avenged Sisera's oppression of Israel by driving a nail through his head (11:97–98; 20, 9–12). Melville's note confesses that this allusion, though composed before Lincoln's assassination, implies Southern satisfaction with Lincoln's death, but somewhat disingenuously remarks that, "after consideration, it is allowed to remain" (11:176). The North may be an iron-charioted Sisera, as Stanton Garner argues, but Sisera was the instrument Jehovah chose to punish Israel for doing evil, and he trusted himself to Jael because her family was at peace with Sisera's king.[69] In other words, Sisera was an agent of God betrayed by an ally, and identifying Southerners with Jael places them in an equivocal ethical position. Melville allows the imputation of Southern vengeance to remain because not all Southerners are honorable any more than are all Northerners. The note reminds readers "that, by the less intelligent classes of the South, Abraham Lincoln, by nature the most kindly of men, was regarded as a monster wantonly warring upon liberty" (11:176), a convenient stereotype that rationalizes secession and slavery and substitutes vengeance for penitence. "The Frenzy" of the poem's speaker, clearly from the South's "less intelligent classes," allows neither forgiveness nor understanding of his Northern foe. By placing the poem immediately after the "March to the Sea," which spends six stanzas celebrating Sherman's march and two final stanzas questioning its necessity, Melville positions himself as an objective analyst who understands how military expedients can contribute to the greater good.

The next poem but one, "The Surrender at Appomattox," answers the question asked in the final stanza of "The March to the Sea": "Was the havoc, retribution?" (11:96; 91) and implicitly endorses Northern tactics because they conquered treason and preserved freedom:

> The warring eagles fold the wing,
>   But not in Cæsar's sway;
> Not Rome o'ercome by Roman arms we sing,
>   As on Pharsalia's day,
> But Treason thrown, though a giant grown,
>   And Freedom's larger play. (11:100; 9–14)

---

69. *Civil War World*, 377.

Both North and South share in the glory of the Roman eagle, yet symbols alone do not confer right any more than typological appeals to Roman history. Caesar defeated Pompey at Pharsalus, Greece, in 48 BCE and extinguished the last hope for a republican Rome, but the Union's republican (and Republican) victory over the South renews America's claim to be a "second Rome" that, with the demise of slavery, promises an even "larger play" of freedom than the first Rome. All men, regardless of color or region, can eventually share in the possibilities of democracy as the Union inherits and extends Roman *civitas* beyond anything dreamed of in either the past or Victor Emmanuel's warring, divided, class-ridden "New Italy."

The South has its share of Roman virtue too, but it emanates from individuals rather than policies or institutions, a romantic ideal ultimately inadequate to successful nation-building. The pair of poems titled "Stonewall Jackson" offers Northern and Southern views of the famous Confederate general, the first respectful but certain that Jackson "stoutly stood for Wrong" (11:59; 4), the second "(Ascribed to a Virginian)" presenting him as a "stoic" with a "Roman heart" who "followed his star" until it led to death (11:60; 9, 8, 23). The double perspective leaves Jackson's Roman qualities in question, for the Virginian admits that "much of doubt in after days / Shall cling, as now, to the war; / Of the right and the wrong they'll still debate, / Puzzled by Stonewall's star" (11:61; 47–50). The issue seems Machiavellian. Was Jackson's the "star" of virtù, or personal valor? Or was it a "star" more like John Brown's "meteor of war," a happenstance of blind fortuna? Similar ambiguity inheres in the Northerner's statement that Jackson is "True as John Brown or steel" (11:59; 12), another double-edged tribute especially given Melville's apparent disdain for Brown's tactics and the eerie portrait of him in "The Portent" (11:5).[70] Jackson remains worthy of remembrance, Melville writes in the "Supplement" (11:182), yet his ethical merits, like Brown's, remain uncertain.

"Lee in the Capitol," the penultimate poem in *Battle-Pieces*, dramatizes Robert E. Lee's appearance before a Senate committee in February 1866 and imagines him citing Roman precedent in a speech cautioning Northern senators against harsh reprisals. Roman imagery invests the poem with daunting grandeur as Lee views the Capitol with its dazzlingly white marble and "vaulted walks in lengthened line / Like porches erst upon the Palatine" (11:164; 49, and 168; 204–5). He asks the senators to avoid taking "Sylla's way" (11:168; 187), a reference to Sulla's proscrip-

---

70. See Garner, *Civil War World*, 43–48, for an overview of the Melville family's attitude toward Brown and the ambiguities of "The Portent," and see also 242–43 for an analysis of the two Jackson poems that differs in several respects from mine. Parker finds Melville indifferent to Brown's trial (*Herman Melville*, 2:411).

tions of his enemies in the latter days of the Republic, and he makes a transnational argument for tolerating Southern customs in his parable of a Moor's daughter who refuses to recant her faith for Christianity. The South has no hope, he tells the senators, "Unless you do what even kings have done / In leniency—unless you shun / To copy Europe in her worst estate—/ Avoid the tyranny you reprobate" (11:168; 197–200). Europe's "worst estate" likely refers to the harsh penalties Ferdinand II imposed on Naples after 1849 that Melville recorded in "Naples in the Time of Bomba," but it could more generally reference imperial revenge from any era. More puzzling is Lee's appeal to monarchical "leniency." Without an example it is difficult to know what Lee means, for even the comparatively lenient monarch Victor Emmanuel solved his *Questione Meridionale,* or Southern Question, by sending 100,000 troops to crush the Calabrian brigands. Lee remains a tragic figure, a man who went to war against the ideals of his own ancestors, including George Washington, "Founder of the Arch the Invader warred upon: / Who looks at Lee must think of Washington; / In pain must think, and hide the thought, / So deep with grievous meaning it is fraught" (11:165; 70–74). Washington constructed in America the "Roman arch" of national unity that supports "whatever is soundest in societies and states" (9:408), the metaphor from "Statues in Rome" that posits Rome as the keystone of American political ideals. Melville wants to ennoble Lee but realizes that his time is past, much like Garibaldi's after Aspromonte and Mentana. The General's pleas fall on deaf ears and the poem concludes with the North indulging in the shallow optimism of redemptive teleology: "Faith in America never dies; / Heaven shall the end ordained fulfill, / We march with Providence cheery still" (11:169; 211–13). Lee understands that national unity requires magnanimity and toleration, but his argument lacks force and leaves the South dependent on the questionable charity of the federal government.

If the South's claim to Roman virtue is weak, so is the North's, a key point of "The House-top. A Night Piece (July, 1863)." An imagined vision of the New York City draft riots, the poem paints the largely Irish Catholic rioters in colors usually applied to French revolutionaries: the narrator hears the "Atheist roar of riot" amid the baleful glare of "red Arson," compares the rioters to "ship-rats / And rats of the wharves," and digs at Catholic belief by characterizing the calls for order issued by New York's Archbishop John Hughes as "priestly spells" (11.64; 8, 10, 11–12, 13. Melville's note to Froissart's account of the atrocities committed by French seditionists reinforces the Gallic connection and contextualizes the immediate horror within his lifelong antipathy for mobs (11:175). Order is restored only when Federal troops arrive:

> Wise Draco comes, deep in the midnight roll
> Of black artillery; he comes, though late;
> In code corroborating Calvin's creed
> And cynic tyrannies of honest kings;
> He comes, nor parlies; and the Town, redeemed,
> Gives thanks devout; nor, being thankful, heeds
> The grimy slur on the Republic's faith implied,
> Which holds that Man is naturally good,
> And—more—is Nature's Roman, never to be scourged. (11:64; 19–27)

The poem's endorsement of military justice drives Garner to an ironic reading that condemns the narrator more than the mob, but given Melville's consistent criticism of mobs and revolutions most other critics take the poem literally, even if they find its moral disturbing.[71] Draco's laws may have been harsh—they punished nearly every crime with death—but the Athenians were overjoyed at finally having written laws in place of the capriciously enforced rules of an oral code.[72] Similarly, New Yorkers were glad when Federal troops ended the arson, lynchings, beatings, racial terror, and destruction of property that four days of rioting inflicted on their city, taking over one hundred lives in the worst riot the city had experienced. If such violence does not corroborate Calvin's belief in human depravity, the dark principle Melville associated with all deeply thinking minds in "Hawthorne and His Mosses," what does? Americans must learn to accept what many Risorgimento nationalists realized by 1859: the cynic tyranny of an honest king may be preferable to anarchy and civil strife. The irony in the poem is actually directed at "the Town,"

---

71. Garner, *Civil War World*, 255–57, 276–79. For literal readings, see Shurr, *Mystery of Iniquity*, 39–40, and Karcher, "The Moderate and the Radical," 220–21. Garner believes the narrator is a member of the radical Republican Union League Club, a pro-war organization dedicated to supporting Lincoln and the Union. Even if that were true—and there is no evidence to support it—Melville might well have endorsed the club's desire for order since he knew several of its members, including George W. Curtis and Henry T. Tuckerman. Garner seriously understates the brutality of the mob's attacks on blacks, women, and police officers, which were characterized by beatings, hangings, drownings, and mutilation, and elides the rapid erosion of support for the protest among German workers. Order was restored without martial law, and the draft resumed peacefully the following month. See Iver Bernstein, *The New York City Draft Riots: Their Significance for American Society and Politics in the Age of the Civil War* (New York: Oxford University Press, 1990), esp. 3–72. David Devries and Hugh Egan attempt to resolve the debate in "'Entangled Rhyme': A Dialogic Reading of Melville's *Battle-Pieces*," *Leviathan: A Journal of Melville Studies* 9 (October 2007) by arguing that Melville has "created a lyric that resists an authoritative reading" (27). Although their analysis of multiple "voices" in the poem is insightful, by insisting on its "indeterminacy" they devalue Melville's larger political aims and ethical values.

72. "Draco," *Encyclopedia Britannica*, 11th ed.

those naïve citizens who ignore the Calvinistic implications of the riot and continue to believe in "the Republic's faith" that human beings—or at least Northerners—are essentially good. The final lines counter White-Jacket's argument that Americans deserve the exemption from flogging granted Roman citizens (5:142) and contemptuously indict those who ignore the "grimy slur" of civil disorder. "The Town" indulges in the same shallow self-congratulation as the "cheery" Senate in "Lee in the Capitol," preferring to view history optimistically as linear rather than cyclic and ignoring the North's capacity for evil and discord.

Melville achieves his most nuanced appeal for accommodating Southern rights in his notorious "Supplement," an essay whose conservatism has troubled readers from the first.[73] Carolyn Karcher, who has praised Melville's progressive views on race, regretfully finds that the supplement, by contending that the franchise should be granted to former Confederates immediately but to former slaves only gradually, "betrays a greater sense of kinship with white Southerners than with blacks." Melville lapses, Karcher avers, "into a racial consciousness he had exposed as dangerously delusive in *Moby-Dick* and *The Confidence-Man*" and moves close "to the racial logic, if not to the anti-black prejudices, governing [President Andrew] Johnson's program of 'restoration.'"[74] Within the context of the American Risorgimento, however, Melville is merely applying Machiavellian thinking to a difficult national question, a solution he may have borrowed from John William Draper's *Thoughts on the Future Civil Policy of America* (1865), a book Garner believes Melville consulted as he wrote the supplement.[75] Draper's emphasis on strong central government and racial separation may have influenced Melville's thinking on these topics in the "Supplement." Draper was a professor of chemistry at the University of the City of New York who gave a series of lectures from December 1864 to March 1865 at the New-York Historical Society and used them as the basis for this book on postwar policy. He argues that nations undergo endless cycles of birth and death

---

73. The Republican *New York Times* wryly warned Radicals such as Thaddeus Steven and Charles Sumner of the supplement's "treasonable language," the Democratic *Herald* praised its "laudable spirit," and the *New York Independent* published a long critique that condemned the piece as "mischievous" (Higgins and Parker, *The Contemporary Reviews,* 509, 513, 526).

74. Karcher, "The Moderate and the Radical," 229.

75. Garner, *Civil War World,* 511n83. Sealts, *Melville's Reading,* #190, says Melville owned the fourth edition of 1865, but the first edition was published that year and the fourth edition in 1868. WorldCat does list a fourth edition in 1865 but I suspect there is a misprint of some kind to account for this anomalous entry. Draper's book was reprinted six times by 1875 and reissued in a memorial edition in 1886 that reprinted the 1865 text. I use a reprint of that edition: John William Draper and George Frederick Barker, *Thoughts on the Future Civil Policy of America. Memoir of John William Draper, 1811–1882* (New York: Garland Pub., 1974).

but inexorably evolve toward large, unified states with strong central authorities as did Rome: "Rome never would have permitted a divided empire in Italy: the Lion will tolerate no competitor in his desert, the Eagle will endure no companion in the air." In his chapter on the effects of emigration, certainly a concern in the North with former slaves now free to venture northward, he cites Machiavelli's division of society into three orders of men as the basis for his analysis: "a superior order, who understand things through their own unassisted mental powers; an intermediate order, who understand things when they are explained to them; a lower order, who do not understand at all." When Rome allowed these groups to intermingle, it corrupted the previously homogenous race and created the "festering mass" of today's Italians, a mixed race that clings to Roman Catholic superstition and papal authority, the two great obstacles faced by contemporary Italy: "With the noblest aspirations, what can Italy do in presence of the anachronism of Rome?"[76]

Draper's Machiavellian analysis of society surfaces in the "Supplement's" most controversial section, a long paragraph advising differential citizenship for white Southerners and former slaves. Melville taxonomizes those Southerners who were "politically misled by designing men" (11:184) as coeval with Northerners in inheriting not authoring slavery, and advises toward them a prudent combination of magnanimity and law: "Benevolence and policy—Christianity and Machiavelli—dissuade from penal severities toward the subdued" (11:185). Southern whites, "who stand nearer to us in nature," should be immediately reenfranchised, but "the blacks, in their infant pupilage to freedom," require a "paternal guardianship" (11:185). Superior Northerners, intermediate Southerners (except perhaps for the "less intelligent classes"), and uneducated former slaves correspond rather neatly to Machiavelli's three orders of society. Certainly this is racist and patronizing, but to a nation confronting a problem no other civilization had faced—the sudden emancipation of four million persons of another race under a government nominally committed to democracy and equality—it seemed like a rational, scientific, even ethical response, the enlightened tone that Draper projects in his treatise. Blacks will eventually earn citizenship, as Melville predicts in "Formerly a Slave" (11:115), but at present it is unwise to enfranchise a servile population and risk further enmity from a white South that remains as dangerous as the people of southern Italy who started the Brigand Wars, a comparison evident in a key passage in the "Supplement":

76. Draper, *Thoughts*, 240, 111–12, 76.

And there are fears. Why is not the cessation of war now at length attended with the settled calm of peace? Wherefore in a clear sky do we still turn our eyes toward the South, as the Neapolitan, months after the eruption, turns his toward Vesuvius? Do we dread lest the repose may be deceptive? In the recent convulsion has the crater but shifted? Let us revere that sacred uncertainty which forever impends over men and nations. (11:185)[77]

Melville excavates vintage Machiavelli in reverencing the "sacred uncertainty" of politics that disrupts both anarchy and tyranny in an endless historical cycle,[78] and concludes this section of the supplement with a warning against perverting "the national victory into oppression for the vanquished," a policy that would only divide Northern Unionists and prompt "any honest Catos" to oppose federal policy. Cato (the younger, 95–46 B.C.E.) was a fervent republican who supported his former opponent Pompey in order to prevent civil war and the ascendancy of Julius Caesar. According to Plutarch, when Pompey asked Cato to join his regime, Cato refused so he could remain free to criticize the government. Shortly thereafter he advised Pompey against enacting recriminatory laws against his former opponents, precisely the advice the supplement offers to the North.[79] "Plutarch's men," whether Garib-

77. Compare "The Apparition," which employs volcanic imagery in its description of a mountain rising up from a pastoral glen: "So, then, Solidity's a crust— / The core of fire below; / All may go well for many a year, / But who can think without a fear / Of horrors that happen so?" (11:116; 11–15). Like the awareness of human depravity Melville counsels throughout his works, even the most peaceful societies must acknowledge the lurking potential for rebellion in their midst.

78. See, for example, *The History of Florence:*
> provinces amid the vicissitudes to which they are subject, pass from order into confusion, and afterwards recur to a state of order again; for the nature of mundane affairs not allowing them to continue in an even course, when they have arrived at their greatest perfection, they soon begin to decline. In the same manner, having been reduced by disorder, and sunk to their utmost state of depression, unable to descend lower, they, of necessity, re-ascend; and thus from good they gradually decline to evil, and from evil again return to good. The reason is, that valour produces peace; peace, repose; repose, disorder; disorder, ruin; so from disorder order springs; from order virtue, and from this, glory and good fortune. (202-3)

79. "Pompeius being thus declared consul prayed Cato to come to him to the suburbs: and on his arrival Pompeius received him in a friendly manner with salutations and pressing of hands, and after acknowledging his obligations he entreated Cato to be his adviser and his assessor in the consulship. But Cato replied, that neither had he said what he first said out of evil disposition towards Pompeius, nor had he said what he last said in order to win his favour, but did everything for the interest of the state; accordingly he observed that he would give Pompeius his advice when he was privately invited, but that in public, even if he should not be invited, he would certainly say what he thought. And he did as he said. In the first place, when Pompeius

aldi or Cato, think for themselves, as does Melville in this controversial afterpiece.

Schooled by Roman history, Machiavelli's politics, and Garibaldi's military triumphs and failures, Melville creates in the supplement a blueprint for an American Risorgimento that will outstrip Italy's: "Were the Unionists and Secessionists but as Guelphs and Ghibellines? If not, then far be it from a great nation now to act in the spirit that animated a triumphant town-faction in the Middle Ages" (11:187). Italy, still torn by traditional feuds and fearful of the Medusa of republicanism, was by 1866 a tarnished model for the United States. America too has confronted Medusa, the "Gorgon in her hidden place" that haunts the maternal icon in "America," and has emerged like Andromeda freed by Perseus a wiser and more powerful nation with "Law on her brow and empire in her eyes" (11:121; 30, 45).[80] Under the "iron dome" that Michael Rogin identifies as the triumphal symbol of law in *Battle-Pieces,* a dome with Italian frescoes lining its interior and a statue wearing a liberty cap on its peak, the United States combines the Risorgimento's original republican idealism with the order and stability of a strong central government, effectively dissolving the ancient opposition of republic and monarchy. The supplement is essentially optimistic, for it presumes that Northern lenity will encourage Southern loyalty and eventually lead to black enfranchisement, reinstating Redburn's vision of a continental nation of nations (4:169) and fulfilling America's providential role as the Redeemer Nation. The essay concludes with these hopeful words: "Let us pray that the terrible historic tragedy of our time may not have been enacted without instructing our whole beloved country through terror and pity; and may fulfillment verify in the end those expectations which kindle the bards of Progress and Humanity" (11:188).

---

was proposing laws with new penalties and severe proceedings against those who had already bribed the people, Cato advised him not to care about the past, but to attend to the future, for he said, it was not easy to determine at what point the inquiry into past offences should stop, and if penalties be imposed after the offences, those would be hardly dealt with who were punished by a law which they were not breaking at the time of their wrong-doing. In the next place, when many men of rank were under trial, some of whom were friends and relations of Pompeius, Cato observing that Pompeius was giving way to the greater part of them and yielding, rebuked him firmly and roused him up" (*Plutarch's Lives,* trans. Aubrey Stewart and George Long, 3 [London: George Bell & Sons, 1892]: 550). After Caesar's victory Cato committed suicide rather than live under tyranny, an event Ishmael alludes to in the opening chapter of *Moby-Dick* (6:3).

80. Deak Nabers, "'Victory of LAW': Melville and Reconstruction," *American Literature* 75 (March 2003), examines the legal justifications for Reconstruction and finds in them a profound tension between the "aims of law and empire" (19). The Roman analogy was one way of reconciling these aims, and complements Nabers's insightful analogies between Melville's violations of poetic "law" in *Battle-Pieces* and the Union's violations of positive law (such as *habeas corpus*) during the war.

Melville's optimism echoes Draper who predicted that as a result of the war "there shall exist on this continent one Republic, great and indivisible, whose grandeur shall eclipse the grandeur of Rome in its brightest days—sovereign among the Powers of the earth;... There is indeed a manifest destiny before us" if only Americans will realize that "Liberty, therefore, is always, if such a paradox may be excused, liberty under restraint."[81] For Draper this meant subordinating the individual to the nation, a lesson Melville partly accepted, as in his gradualist approach to black citizenship, yet modified with his belief that religious sentiment—"Christianity and Machiavelli"—could leaven civic duty with compassion. The final poem in *Battle-Pieces*, "A Meditation," expresses an almost transcendental faith in "the god within the breast" of individual soldiers who even on the battlefield treat their enemies as brothers and fellow men (11:170; 13). The poem's title and much of the troubled questioning in *Battle-Pieces* shares the pensive mood of "Casa Guidi Windows," particularly those in a footnote Browning wrote to accompany her lines describing the day Leopold II granted his subjects some basic civil rights: "Since when the constitutional concessions have been complete in Tuscany, as all the world knows. The event breaks in upon the meditation, and is too fast for prophecy in these strange times.—E.B.B."[82] This is the only passage in the entire volume that Melville triple-checked. Clearly, he meditated deeply and long on Italy in all its historic and contemporary manifestations, from the authoritarian arguments of Media's scroll to the exaltation of Roman virtue in "Statues in Rome" and the celebration of Garibaldi's victories in "At the Hostelry." While the Civil War chastened his outlook, he remained hopeful that an American Risorgimento might avoid the mistakes of Italy's and still prove the exceptional nature of his country.

---

81. Draper, *Thoughts*, 239–40.
82. Cowen, *Melville's Marginalia*, 1:366. The footnote is in Melville's copy of *Poems*, 2 (New York: C. S. Francis, 1860), 386, and occurs in Part I, line 583 of "Casa Guidi Windows."

6

"The Italian Turn of Thought"

Clarel *and Late Writings*

> There is no steady unretracing progress in this life; we do not advance through fixed gradations, and at the last one pause:—through infancy's unconscious spell, boyhood's thoughtless faith, adolescence's doubt (the common doom), then scepticism, then disbelief, resting at last in manhood's pondering repose of If. But once gone through, we trace the round again; and are infants, boys, and men, and Ifs eternally.
>
> —Ahab, *Moby-Dick* (1850)

> It was a very different Italy which I spent my life dreaming of, not the impoverished and humiliated country which we now see ruled by the dregs of the nation.
>
> —Giuseppe Garibaldi, 1880

AHAB'S VIEW of personal development as an endless cycle between faith and doubt bears literary fruit in Melville's last two decades, when the heady days of Risorgimento nationalism and the American Civil War ended and led both Italy and the United States away from republican idealism into the Iron Age of industrialism. Materialism, greed, and the cult of progress dominated both countries and drove former democratic idealists like Melville even further into "manhood's pondering repose of If" (6:492). Although many critics find his later works disengaged from reality, viewed within the transnational and transhistorical context of Risorgimento nationalism, Melville's late poetry, like *Battle-Pieces,* breathes and lives in the world of experienced event, seeking not universals but confronting particulars and measuring them against the professed and inevitably tarnished ideals of political, religious, and philosophical orthodoxies. The constant questioning, backtracking, indecisiveness, and contradiction in *Clarel*

(1876) mirror the shifting political landscape of the 1860s and 1870s, a time when definitions of national identity were being questioned in both the Old World and the New. The nobility of the "Roman Spirit" that Melville praised in "Statues in Rome" infuses *Timoleon* (1891), and his interest in Garibaldi continues when he memorializes the hero's death in 1882 in the final lines of his Neapolitan diptych. *Billy Budd* echoes *Battle-Pieces* in its insistence on law, and the differing claims that Billy and Captain Vere make on the moral imagination reflect the ambiguity of Garibaldi's heroism and the *realpolitik* of Machiavelli.

After 1860, as Leonardo Buonomo observes, Italy was no longer Arcadia: "The country that to many Americans had once seemed the perfect opposite of an increasingly industrialized and preeminently urban United States was now seen as being in danger of becoming too much like the land across the Atlantic."[1] One contemporary Italian put it quite simply: "the *dolce far niente* of the time of yore exists no longer."[2] In *Clarel*, Rolfe, the character most critics consider closest to Melville's sentiments, agrees: "Eden nor Athens shall come back:— / And what's become of Arcady?" (12:158; 2.8.36–37).[3] As the Kingdom of Italy became just one more European power with colonial ambitions, economic schemes, and internal dissensions, Americans felt nostalgia for the Old Italy with its "dear little old-fashioned Italian grand-dukes," as Mrs. Light puts it in James's *Roderick Hudson* (1875), and William Wetmore Story had to struggle to preserve the picturesque Roman past in his popular novel *Roba di Roma* (1862).[4] Story's plight prefigured the realistic portrayals of Italian life by James and William Dean Howells and paved the way for the melodramatic historical romances of Francis Marion Crawford that inundated America's late-nineteenth-century reading public, creating a "politics of the picturesque" that opposed the charm of the picturesque to the deadening reality of modern industrialism, a phenomenon Melville had foreseen when he coined the word "povertiresque" in *Pierre* (7:276–77).[5] In the postbellum environment for both Italy and America, Melville saw that both countries were falling short of their revolutionary ideals as they followed the siren

1. *Backward Glances*, 92.
2. Count A. Maffei, *Brigand Life in Italy. A History of Bourbonist Reaction* (1865), as quoted in Beales and Biagini, *Risorgimento*, 285.
3. All parenthetical references give volume, page, book, canto and line numbers to *Clarel*, vol. 12 of *The Writings of Herman Melville*.
4. James, *Novels 1871–1880* (New York: The Library of America), 330. Vance, *America's Rome*, describes Story's struggle and his new preface and footnotes to the 1887 edition that explained "when Liberty came in, song went out" (2:138).
5. Vance, *America's Rome* 2:145–46, 229–54. Crawford published over a dozen Roman novels between 1887 and 1909.

song of "progress" and its blindly linear view of history.

For a time Italy nonetheless retained a special place in American cultural politics precisely because its national triumphalism justified the progressive view of history subscribed to by political liberals like Horace Greeley and religious liberals like Henry Whitney Bellows, whose Unitarian church Melville joined.[6] By the time the Risorgimento achieved its ultimate goal of making Rome the capital of a united Italy in 1870, about the time Melville began writing *Clarel*, Melville was living in New York among strong partisans of pope and king—modern Guelphs and Ghibellines. Roman Catholics, primarily Irish Democrats, organized dozens of meetings to condemn the papal ouster and heard countless sermons through the fall of 1870 in opposition to Victor Emmanuel.[7] Some partisans even hoped that the pope would relocate to America, ironically justifying the early fears of nativists and Know-Nothings. In reaction, Protestants organized a huge countercelebration of "Italian Unity" on January 12, 1871, at the Academy of Music on Fourteenth Street. Hundreds of New York's leading citizens attended, including several men once associated with Melville: William Cullen Bryant, George William Curtis, and George P. Putnam. Many who could not attend sent letters of support, among them Melville's old friends Senator Charles Sumner, Richard Henry Dana Jr., Bayard Taylor, Henry T. Tuckerman, and Rev. Orville Dewey. From his home in Concord, Ralph Waldo Emerson sent a letter of regret praising Italy's "emancipation"—a word implicitly linking its people with America's newly freed slaves.[8] One of the main speakers was Greeley, who recalled the failure of the Roman Republic of 1849 and believed that Italian unity fulfilled the republican dream. Another was Melville's pastor Bellows, who defended the separation of church and state and advised the Roman Catholic Church to expect no special treatment in a free country:

> If she can persuade the people to adopt her creed and policy, she has a perfect right to do it. She has a right freely to express her opinion of Protestantism and to exhibit its weakness and peril and sinfulness, to call it unchristian and immoral if she will, and to prove her words if she can. Protestantism may do the same by her.[9]

   6. For Melville's attendance at Bellows's church, see Walter Donald Kring, *Henry Whitney Bellows* (Boston: Skinner House, 1979), 479–81, and Kring's "Introduction" to Donald Yannella and Hershel Parker, eds., *The Endless, Winding Way in Melville: New Charts by Kring and Carey* (Glassboro, NJ: Melville Society, 1981), 1–9.
   7. Marraro, "American Opinion on the Occupation of Rome in 1870," *South Atlantic Quarterly* 54 (1955): 221–42.
   8. *New York Times*, January 14, 1871, 2.
   9. *New York Times*, January 13, 1871, 2.

Bellows's ominous final sentence justified Protestant criticism of Catholicism, a resonant theme that Melville continued to mine in one of his most ambitious works, the 18,000-line epic poem *Clarel*.

THE POLITICS OF *CLAREL*

Because of its compelling philosophical and religious debates, *Clarel* has provoked a wealth of theological commentary. Critics have seen it variously as optimistic, pessimistic, tragic, Roman Catholic, Hebraic, agnostic, and existential.[10] The poem's many voices, digressions, dreams, and reveries encourage these diverse spiritual readings, while its inhuman settings among the ancient buildings of Jerusalem and the barren landscapes of Palestine paint an inhospitable material world that drives readers toward inward meditations on mind and spirit. Frustrating any sense of personal discovery, however, the narrative's circular structure—it begins and ends in the same place, Jerusalem—implies endless questing in a wearisome cycle of seeking, finding, and losing. In the major plot line, the poem's eponymous hero, Clarel, finds love in the Holy Land, leaves his beloved so she can properly mourn her father's death, and returns to find her dead. Love and death, sin and redemption, isolation and community all revolve in endless cycles of discovery and loss that stunt human spiritual growth. John Milton's *Paradise Lost* (1667), to which *Clarel* is often compared, offers a coherent linear narrative that links divine and human history in a rational and hopeful spiritual plan, famously justifying God's ways toward man.[11] In *Clarel*, while some individuals maintain their faith—Derwent the Anglican clergyman, a few Roman Catholic priests and monks, perhaps Rolfe the humanistic sailor and Ungar the dispossessed Confederate veteran and lapsed Catholic—there is no general plan of salvation. The hopeful spiritual hierarchy of the *Divine Comedy* gives way to a religious pessimism repeatedly imaged in Italian metaphors of existential isolation, such as Jerusalem compared to "the city Dis aloof," a monastery

---

10. For a fine introduction to these and other themes as well as a thorough bibliography through 1982, see Vincent Kenny, "Clarel," in *A Companion to Melville Studies*, 374–406. The two most recent books on *Clarel*, Goldman's *Melville's Protest Theism* and Potter's *Melville's* Clarel *and the Intersympathy of Creeds*, continue the emphasis on the poem's religious and philosophical themes.

11. For a good analysis of Melville's debt to Milton as well as a more optimistic reading of *Clarel* than I offer here, see John T. Shawcross, "'Too Intellectual a Poet Ever to Be Popular': Herman Melville and the Miltonic Dimension of Clarel," *Leviathan: A Journal of Melville Studies* 4 (March and October 2002): 71–90.

"Pale as Pompeii disinterred," or the "dead Medusa stare" of the desert (12:114, 1.36.29; 105, 1.33.15; 266, 3.1.135). Italy's artistic heritage, so richly displayed in "At the Hostelry," fades away like the the frescoes of Fra Angelico "whose tender pigments melt from view" and resurfaces in the gloomy dungeons of Piranesi that mirror St. Paul's dreadful "mystery of iniquity" (12:65; 1.18. 30; 12:248–49; 2.35.24).[12] Such landscapes and paintings provide no redemptive patterns and make salvation a personal matter, an individual soul's insistence on its divinity in the face of silence. Theological readings of the poem, then, even those as sound as Stan Goldman's *Melville's Protest Theism,* remain frustrated by Melvillean uncertainty and ambiguity, and ultimately offer no satisfying theological system.[13]

For all the obsession in the poem with matters "beyond human ken," as Hawthorne said of Melville in 1856,[14] *Clarel* exists in a particular time and place in its genesis, composition, and setting. Hershel Parker believes that Melville wrote the poem between 1870 and 1875 as a conscious advance on *Battle-Pieces,* while Walter Bezanson thinks that Melville started it in 1867 and Kenny suggests 1866.[15] Everyone agrees that the poem draws heavily upon Melville's 1856–57 trip to the Holy Land, which implies a long incubation period, but less studied is the fact that he wrote it during his years as a customs inspector in New York, a city that exerted immense influence on his writing and was undergoing rapid political and cultural changes in the decades following the Civil War.[16] While the poem itself contains no precise indication of its narrative present, references to the Paris Commune (12:197, 2.25.107; 12:456,

---

12. See Shurr, *Mystery of Iniquity,* 47–75, for the wasteland images and symbols in *Clarel,* some of which may derive from Robert Browning's "Childe Roland to the Dark Tower Came" (71–73). The Piranesi allusion is explored at length by Samuel Otter, "How *Clarel* Works," in *A Companion to Herman Melville,* ed. Wyn Kelley (Malden, MA: Blackwell Publishing, 2006), 476–80. Cohen, "Melville and the Lathers Collection," 23, thinks the allusion refers to an unnamed print at Winyah, and we know that Melville owned at least one Piranesi print himself, the *Arch of the Emperor Marcus Aurelius,* which is reproduced in Robert K. Wallace, "Melville's Prints: David Metcalf's Prints and Tile," *Harvard Library Bulletin,* n.s., 8, no. 2 (Winter 1997): 5.

13. As the half-title to Goldman's book testifies, *The Hidden and Silent God in* Clarel, whatever theology (or theodicy) that emerges is equivocal at best. Goldman concludes, "Protest theism is not to be mistaken for theological certainty, for a formulation of creed or maxim" (169).

14. Nathaniel Hawthorne, *The English Notebooks 1856–1860,* ed. Thomas Woodson and Bill Ellis, *Centenary Edition,* 22:163.

15. Parker, *Herman Melville,* 2:687; Bezanson, "Historical and Critical Note" to *Clarel* (12:531); Kenny, "Clarel" in *Companion to Melville Studies,* 378.

16. See Kelley, *Melville's City,* as well as a more focused study, Hans Bergmann, *God in the Street: New York Writing from the Penny Press to Melville* (Philadelphia: Temple University Press, 1995), which traces the city's journalistic discourse in *The Confidence-Man* (1857).

4.20.125–33) place its action no earlier than March 1871, and its publication date of 1876 draws inevitable comparisons to the American Centennial. Lawrence Buell suggests that "one of its dimensions is a postbellum meditation on the national destiny in light of the fate of democratic revolutions in the nineteenth century generally," and the richest contextual study of *Clarel* to date, Hilton Obenzinger's *American Palestine*, situates the poem in the religio-historical subgenre of Holy Land narratives, a context that links it with Mark Twain's *Innocents Abroad* (1869) and other contemporaneous books about Palestine.[17] As these varied studies show, *Clarel* is not just about the author's experiences, American politics, or Palestine; rather, it is a cosmopolitan epic whose manifold ideologies demand a transnational perspective.

The moderate politics of the Risorgimento and the philosophical pragmatism of Italian thinkers like Machiavelli echo throughout the poem. When Walter Bezanson concludes that "No one, including the narrator, offers a defense of revolutionaries" (12:758n), he means *French* revolutionaries, for factoring the Risorgimento into *Clarel*'s political mix creates a more nuanced commentary on the complexities of revolution, nationalism, history, and progress than any single voice in the poem can sustain, even the narrator's. Three characters who never meet but nonetheless engage dialogically across the poem's length express these multiple concerns. Two are the only Italians in the poem: Celio, the hunchback orphan and Christian rebel who was born in Rome and now lives with the Franciscans in Jerusalem's Terra Santa monastery, and Brother Salvaterra, a young Franciscan monk from Tuscany who blindly accepts traditional Roman Catholic superstitions and legends. The third is the French Dominican priest, a more sophisticated defender of Catholicism who served in Napoleon III's legislature and argues (like a good Bonapartist) for Rome's special place in world history. Neither they nor any of the poem's other characters are isolated questers after religious knowledge but historically contingent individuals obsessed with issues crystallized in the Risorgimento. Rather than marking a break with Melville's earlier work, then, *Clarel* addresses the continuing problems of the American Risorgimento, especially the long aftermath in Italy and the United States that consolidated power among northern elites, replaced religious salvation with material achievement, and diminished the promise of democracy. As modern "second Romes," both America and Italy replicate the historical cycle of decline and fall and drive Melville to interrogate more deeply

---

17. Buell, "Melville the Poet," *The Cambridge Companion to Herman Melville*, ed. Robert S. Levine (Cambridge: Cambridge University Press, 1998), 148; Obenzinger, *American Palestine: Melville, Twain, and the Holy Land Mania* (Princeton, NJ: Princeton University Press, 1999).

the claims of democracy, republicanism, and individualism he had once so ardently championed.

CELIO AND RISORGIMENTO SECULARISM

Melville critics usually classify Celio with Mortmain, Ungar, and Agath as one of *Clarel*'s four "monomaniacs" or "misanthropes."[18] Such useful taxonomies can mask important distinctions, however. Ungar is the only character to use the word "monomania," and other characters besides these four—notably Brother Salvaterra and the Dominican priest—exhibit equally single-minded convictions. Celio deserves special attention both within this group and the poem's larger cast because he is among the few who interrogate ideology with experience yet who remains true to his high-minded quest for personal belief, providing a spiritual example that indelibly affects the poem's central character, Clarel himself.

A secular idealist, Celio would necessarily applaud the Risorgimento's crowning achievement, the pope's loss of temporal power; yet he is unable to profit from that change, for he now lives in Jerusalem, a city suffocating with religious tradition. "By birth a Roman" (12:36; 1.12.11), the orphaned Celio left Italy when a cardinal commended him to the Franciscans in Jerusalem. The monks find him humble and unassuming, yet they distrust his lack of religious zeal: "he showed no zest / Of faith within, faith personal" (12:37; 1.12. 30–31). He prefers to wander around the holy sites assessing their significance for himself. Celio stages a Risorgimento of the soul by refusing to accept the "civic honorable place" that the Franciscans seek for him (12:37; 1.12.52). Instead, he goes his own way,

> Unpledged, unhampered. So that still
> Leading a studious life at will,
> And prompted by an earnest mind,
> Scarce might he shun the fevered sway
> Of focused question in our day.
> Overmuch he shared, but in that kind
> Which marks the Italian turn of thought,
> When, counting Rome's tradition naught,
> The mind is coy to own the rule

---

18. See Bezanson's influential "A Critical Index of the Characters" (12:613–35). Vincent Kenny, *Herman Melville's Clarel*, usefully discusses how these "misanthropes" represent a seductive but ultimately insufficient alternative belief system (186–98).

> Of sect replacing, sect or school.
> At sea, in brig which swings no boat,
> To founder is to sink. (12:37–38; 1.12. 58–69)

These last two lines are often quoted as evidence of the need to believe, to find somewhere a "lifeboat of faith," as Goldman puts it.[19] Yet in the context of Risorgimento thought, epitomized in Cavour's motto "A Free Church in a Free State," religious and political freedom are worth the risk of sinking. In post-1870 Italy, with "Rome's tradition naught," Celio can indulge that "Italian turn of thought" that owes more to Roman stoicism and Italian Renaissance humanism than it does to Christianity. He is "coy"—that is shy, reluctant, even unwilling—to replace his abandoned Catholic faith with some other "sect or school," yet his "earnest mind" prevents him from avoiding contemporary philosophical issues. He chooses the intellectual rigors of the "unpledged, unhampered" life of the mind, a skeptic of all creeds and a disciple of none.

A revolutionary of the spirit, Celio is, as Kenny suggests (quoting a notation that Melville made in his copy of *Don Quixote*), "a god-like mind without a God"; similarly, Goldman considers Celio one of the poem's "heroic doubters," a person whom doubt energizes into further searching; more specifically, Shirley M. Dettlaff terms him a "Hebraic doubter."[20] Rather than rush into the comfort of a new sect, Celio considers his own circumstances, and measures the value of external faith by his personal experiences and feelings. One such experience is disappointed love, which gnaws at him and proves the insufficiency of the Dantean ideal: "Never the hunchback may be loved," he laments, "Never! for Beatrice—Bice—O, / Diminutive once sweet, made now / All otherwise!" (12:38; 1.12.79–82). Celio understands that Dante could idealize Beatrice only because she never grew into "riper womanhood" (1.12.85), an insight that predicts Clarel's loss of his beloved, Ruth. Rather than seizing his moment with her, Clarel bows to Jewish protocols that prevent him, a Gentile, from participating in mourning for her dead father; he leaves her to seek his own spiritual goals and consequently misses her emotional maturation and untimely death. Clarel's devastating experience confirms Celio's view of the New World as "joyless and ironic too!" (12:39; 1.12.104), and validates Celio's turn to the pagan past of his Roman heritage.

19. *Melville's Protest Theism*, 135.
20. Kenny, "Clarel," *Companion*, 376; Goldman, *Melville's Protest Theism*, 85; Dettlaff, "'Counter Natures in Mankind': Hebraism and Hellenism in Clarel," in *Melville's Evermoving Dawn: Centennial Essays*, ed. John Bryant and Robert Milder (Kent, OH: Kent State University Press, 1997), 201.

History thus enters the poem through Celio, one of the few characters to acknowledge the power of culture to shape identity: "The Past, the Past is half of time, / The proven half," he argues (12:39; 1.12.111–12), and cites the Pantheon, Santa Croce, Trajan's hall, and Titus's Arch for their power to connect the individual to both Roman and Jewish history:

> Tho' all be whim of mine,
> Yet by these monuments I'm schooled,
> Arrested, strangely overruled;
> Methinks I catch a beckoning sign,
> A summons as from Palestine. (12:39; 1.12.133–37)

Celio knows that the Church of Santa Croce lies on soil relocated from Palestine, that Jewish laborers erected the Forum Trajanum, and that the Arch of Titus bears the image of the seven-branched candlestick and other Jewish artifacts.[21] Such material evidence demonstrates that Celio's identification with Palestine is in fact no "whim" but rather an informed recognition of cross-cultural indebtedness, a form of higher criticism that grants special status to no single religion or nation. "Even Papal Rome," Celio muses, may be a mere "appanage" or "colony" of the Holy Land (12:39–40; 1.12.140–42), making the Holy See derivative of a larger historical process and, therefore, justifying its decline within a new, unified, and more classically Roman Italian nation.

Celio's historical vision contrasts sharply with Hilda's in *The Marble Faun,* in which Hilda also ruminates on the legendary seven-branched Jewish candlestick. Said to be lost in the Tiber, the candlestick may be recovered, Hilda thinks, and could inspire seven American poets to collaborate on a seven-part allegorical poem that would emit "the intense white light of Truth!"[22] Whereas Hilda wants to Americanize Jewish tradition and absorb it into Protestant Christianity, Celio seeks to understand it, even if it creates intellectual chaos. Far from revealing greater "truth," Palestine evokes the "upstart element" of "novel doubt" (12:40, 1.12.150; 1.13.6), what Melville in his European journal calls "the great curse of modern travel—skepticism" (15:97). At the Arch of Ecce Homo Celio finds no viable linkages between Judaism, Rome, and Christianity, and begins to see history as a series of disruptions and betrayals rather than a covenant between God and man. Historically (rather than theologically), Christ brought only false promises and impossible dreams, jarring discon-

---

21. See Melville, *Clarel,* 12:39, 1.12.120–32, and Bezanson, "Discussions," 12:729.
22. Hawthorne, *The Marble Faun: or, the Romance of Monte Beni,* ed. William Charvat, Roy Harvey Pearce, and Claude M. Simpson, *Centenary Edition,* 4:371.

nects from experience as irrelevant as Hilda's wish for an Americanized candlestick. As Celio says of Christ, "Nearing thee / All footing fails us; history / Shows there a gulf where bridge is none" (12:42; 1.13.80–82). Christ replaces the "Medusa shield" and like it "In beauty and in terror too / Shalt paralyze the nobler race," that is, Romans (1.13.95–97). In his quest for individual rather than institutional salvation, Celio pushes so far into history's depths that he identifies with the "bad Jew" Cartophilus, the man who taunted Christ and became the legendary Wandering Jew (12:43; 1.13.110–18). Philosophy seeks Hilda-esque unity and coherence, but history teaches disruption and disjuncture.

Celio, as the narrator tells us, is a modern version of Savonarola and Leopardi, Italian martyrs to free thought (12:43–44; 1.14.1–9).[23] Girolamo Savonarola (1452–1498), a charismatic Dominican, exposed papal corruption and helped establish a short-lived Christian republic in Florence. Along with two of his followers he was hanged on a cross and burned for defying Pope Alexander VI, Cesare Borgia's father and one of the most corrupt men ever to hold the papacy.[24] Despite his un-Melvillean asceticism and mysticism, as a critic of unjust authority and advocate of republican polity Savonarola stands, like Billy Budd, as one of those ambiguously appealing revolutionary figures who holds fast to ideals even at the price of chaos and death. Celio's skepticism and philosophical independence align him with Savonarolan idealism and republicanism and make him a worthy inheritor of Italian resistance to corruption in church and state. Similarly, Giaocomo Leopardi (1798–1837), the Italian romantic poet, gained fame for his early poems extolling Italian nationalism. He could have become a priest and gained employment in the Papal States, but instead he accepted a wandering life of poverty in order to pursue his craft in freedom. Does not such a man, Melville's narrator later asks (12:263–64; 3.1.12–24), deserve immortality as much as St. Teresa?

Celio takes his place in this line of Italian martyrs to papal authority when he questions the efficacy of Roman Catholic mourning rites, which he observes from afar in Part 1, Canto 14. In darkness, lit only by torches, a line of laymen and Franciscan monks from the Terra Santa monastery winds out of the city along a path said to be the route of the

---

23. Because there are no special sources for Melville's knowledge of Savonarola, Leopardi, and Alexander VI, the facts in this paragraph are based on the biographical articles in the *Encyclopedia Britannica*, 11th edition (1911), a representative summary of late-nineteenth-century Anglo-American thought on Roman Catholicism and Italian history.

24. Melville presumably alludes to Alexander VI, Rodrigo Borgia, in his epigraph to "At the Hostelry": "Be Borgia Pope, be Bomba King, / The roses blow, the song-birds sing" (Sandberg, "Melville's Unfinished *Burgundy Club* Book," 78). One other Borgia, Callixtus III, also served as pope, but his nephew Rodrigo was the better known.

Virgin Mary's funeral train. When they stop at Mary's "tomb alleged" (12:45; 1.14.71), Celio reacts with both heart and head, illustrating the balance of emotion and intellect characteristic of the "Italian turn of thought": "Out sobbed the mourners, and the tear / From Celio trickled; but he mused— / Weak am I, by a myth abused" (12:46; 1.14.81–83). When the monks' journey ends at the supposed tomb of Lazarus, they chant the famous verse from 1 Corinthians 15:55, "*O death, where is thy sting? O grave, / Where is thy victory?*" (12:46; 1.14.107–8), foreshadowing (and undermining, in my view) the poem's final line, "death but routs life into victory" (12:499; 4.35.34). Celio seeks religion without superstition, a faith that combines emotion and intellect in a historically defensible system of belief. To him, Lazarus's "vacant tomb" is nothing but "A void cell," no different than Christ's empty tomb, a similarity that proves "Raiser and raised divide one doom; / Both vanished now" (1.14.112–16). Through Celio the overwhelming presence of death in *Clarel* projects back into history, death without redemption save through the existential nobility of the free inquirer. Savonarolan idealism leads to Leopardian pessimism and eventuates in Celian fatalism, a line of Italian thinking that privileges individual freedom and defiance of authority even at the cost of personal annihilation.

What most distinguishes Celio from the poem's other seekers is his indelible impact on Clarel. The two men first lock glances at Lower Gihon, a reservoir outside Jerusalem where Nehemiah, the American millennialist, has guided Clarel. Clarel feels "A novel sympathy" (12:35; 1.11.58) for Celio, but says nothing, and the two part with only a flicker of spiritual recognition passing between them. The next morning, under a brilliant Palestinian sun that bathes the landscape with its "indifferent . . . beam" and makes the story of Christ seem but a "dream" (12:47; 1.15. 9, 13), and as a muezzin's cry reminds readers that here in Jerusalem "now the Crescent rides the Cross" (12:48; 1.15.37), Celio's night-doubts seem plausible, validated by the multiplication of belief systems represented in the pagan "orb supreme" (12:47; 1.15.6) and the Islamic call to prayer. In this context of expanding religious alternatives, the narrator asks whether friendship, perhaps even a homoerotic relationship, between the two young men is possible:

> But what's evoked in Clarel's mien—
> What look, responsive look is seen
> In Celio, as together there
> They pause? Can these a climax share?
> Mutual in approach may glide

> Minds which from poles adverse have come,
> Belief and unbelief? (12:48–49;1.15.50–56)

For a moment, meaningful human contact seems possible, as with this probing stare "Celio knew his mate" and hovers with "an overture that scorned debate" (12:49; 1.15.68, 71). Perhaps because of the latent eroticism of the "responsive look," Clarel, "shy, unsure" (1.15.72), hesitates just enough to make Celio turn away in a "recoil of heart" (1.15.76) that forecloses friendship.[25]

This scene echoes similar ones so common in Hawthorne's fiction, where two people reach out to each other only to find one unable to reciprocate: Hester and Dimmesdale in *The Scarlet Letter* (1850), Miriam and Kenyon in *The Marble Faun,* and, more homoerotically, Hollingsworth and Coverdale in *The Blithedale Romance.* Inevitably, an emotionally cold male—the second character in each pair—makes some gesture, says some word, that prevents communion and cuts short a budding relationship. The Clarel/Celio divide carries political as well as personal implications, for each represents a country in need of the other. America needs Italy's cosmopolitan aesthetics and history, and Italy needs America's energy and will. Melville's narrator clearly indicts Clarel in this failed exchange, saying "Ah, student, ill thy sort have sped: / The instant proffer—it is fled!" (12:49; 1.15.79–80), and he goes on to describe Clarel's "repentant" (1.15.82) visit to the Franciscan convent a few days later, after he has learned Celio's name. By then, of course, it is too late: Celio has moved to another part of Jerusalem and, overtaken by illness, has died alone with his face turned to the wall (12:67; 1.19.8–16), one of those Melvillean blanknesses that confront skeptics as different as Ahab and Bartleby. But as another nautical metaphor makes clear, Celio's brig, unlike the *Pequod,* has neither foundered nor sunk. Clarel's last glimpse of Celio imagines him as a distant boat sailing away under a rising sun, a powerful metaphor of futurity:

> What speck is that so far away
> That wanes and wanes in waxing day?
> Is it the sail ye fain had spoken
> Last night when surges parted ye?
> But on, it is a boundless sea. (12:49; 1.15.87–91)

---

25. In late 1851 Melville wrote to Hawthorne: "When the big hearts strike together, the concussion is a little stunning" (14:213). The metaphor, however muted in the Clarel-Celio relationship, certainly carried special significance for Melville.

Unable to share Celio's "Italian turn of thought," the ability to consider alternative sectarian beliefs or human relationships without necessarily accepting any one as final, Clarel is the one at risk of foundering. After his talk with Nathan the apostate, Clarel is more sexually confused than ever, and finds that

> every thought
> Of Ruth was strangely underrun
> By Celio's image. Celio—sought
> Vainly in body—now appeared
> As in the spiritual part,
> Haunting the air, and in the heart. (12:65–66; 1.18.51–56)

Obsessed, Clarel locates Celio's journal (whose contents the poem never reveals) and finds "a second self therein" (12:68; 1.19.26)—not so much a mirror image, as William H. Shurr contends,[26] but more an idealized figure of what Clarel wishes he himself could be, a person able "to brave / All questions on that primal ground / Laid bare by faith's receding wave" (12:68; 1.19. 27–29). The Arnoldian metaphor of a barren beach of faith competes with the Melvillean metaphor of the "boundless sea" upon which Celio endlessly sails, an opposition that suggests one more set of alternatives that frustrate and confuse Clarel.[27] Entitled "The Fulfilment," Part I, Canto 19 implies a material immortality as Celio lives on through both Clarel and the eponymous poem. He has forced the young American, and Young America, to confront those "second selves" (death, homoeroticism, passion, doubt) that they typically avoid. When Clarel finally visits Celio's grave, placed in consecrated ground by Franciscans earnest to claim a convert, he sees through the monks' "mistimed zeal" (12:121; 1.40.13) and accepts Celio for what he really is, "one / Not saved through faith, nor Papal Rome's true son" (12:121; 1.40. 15–16). In a heartfelt meditation, Clarel accepts Celio's final appeal: "Remember me! For all life's din / Let not my memory be drowned" (12:122; 1.40. 25–26). By taking possession of Celio's journal, thoughts, and feelings, Clarel replicates psychologically the larger American pattern of self-discovery through contact with "Rome" that William Vance has noticed.[28]

26. *Mystery of Iniquity*, 83.

27. The most thorough study of Arnold's influence on Melville remains Walter Bezanson, "Melville's Reading of Arnold's Poetry," *PMLA* 69 (June 1954): 365–91. Although Melville did not mark "Dover Beach" in his copy of Arnold's *New Poems* (acquired 1871), Bezanson believes that "its central image of the withdrawing sea of faith is germane to the 'wasteland' metaphors of *Clarel*" (390).

28. *America's Rome*, 1:xxiv.

240 / Chapter 6

Celio's crucial role is reaffirmed toward the end of *Clarel* when the pilgrims visit their last holy site, the birthplace of Jesus at the Church of the Star in Bethlehem. Like an opposite bookend, Brother Salvaterra, the only other Italian in the poem, guides the pilgrims on a sacramental tour that ironically promotes Celian skepticism. A native of Tuscany, Salvaterra has recently joined the Franciscan order and ardently believes all of Catholicism's legends and superstitions. His commentary provokes varying reactions among the pilgrims, from Derwent's indulgent skepticism and Rolfe's functionalist pragmatism (superstition helps maintain faith) to Clarel's urgent wish to believe as unquestioningly as the monk. But the poem's overvoice mocks Salvaterra's exaggerated devotion, asceticism, ignorance, and provincialism: "Ah, fervor bought too dear: / The fingers clutching rope and cross; / Life too intense; the cheek austere / Deepening in hollow, waste and loss" (12:428; 4.14.159–62).

One of *Clarel*'s key confrontations between belief and skepticism, Brother Salvaterra's sly attempt to proselytize Ungar is often considered by critics to be a moment of spiritual, even specifically Catholic, triumph. Noticing Ungar's apparent Catholic sympathies at the Manger, Salvaterra takes advantage of this "lapse within the soldier's thought" and gently tells him, "True sign you bear: your sword's a cross" (12:431, 4.14.15; 4.14.21), startling Ungar into uncertain assent that Vine characterizes as a moment of transfiguration (12:434; 4.15.12). In reality, this canny "Ascetic insight" (12:431; 4.14.14) merely exploits Ungar's "lapse" and provides spiritual sanction to his violent vocation of soldier of fortune.[29] Where St. Francis easily converted the knight Angelo Tancredi (12:432; 4.14.41–54), Salvaterra's stratagem fails to convert the mercenary Ungar, a failure that suggests the impotence of contemporary Franciscanism. As their names imply, Salvaterra is the philosophical opposite of Celio, as earth is opposed to heaven (*cielo*).[30] Salvaterra's name and order recall the Terra Santa monks, and his credulity, like theirs at Mary's tomb, betrays a faith requiring the reified proofs of artifacts and sites. Celio's name connotes more than "heaven"; as the first person indicative of *celiare*, "to jest," it suggests "jesting at heaven," even as Derwent jests about Salvaterra's literalist faith. When Derwent terms the Tuscan "unmanly" (12:433; 4.14.94), an observation that, according to Rolfe, Machiavelli made of Jesus,[31] it points more

29. Obenzinger, *American Palestine*, while noting Derwent's sarcasm, believes Salvaterra's observation "gives Ungar a stolid, heroic stature unique among the characters the pilgrim-party encounters," a heroism Melville also accepts (156). Read against Risorgimento anticlericalism and nationalism, however, both Salvaterra and Ungar appear as reactionaries willing to ignore history (the pope's loss of temporal power, the Civil War) to maintain philosophical unity.

30. Bezanson suggests the anagram cielo as a source for Celio's name (12:618).

31. I have been unable to locate this particular attribution in Machiavelli; his objection to

to Salvaterra's innocence and ineffectuality than his physical appearance. Salvaterra recalls the deluded Syrian monk whom Rolfe and Clarel meet in Part 2, Canto 2.18, a devout young eremite who, as a consequence of his Christ-like fast in the wilderness, imagines that he has spoken with Satan. Rolfe, one of the poem's most balanced observers, questions the pathetic monk's story as mere "ecstasy of fast?" (12:191; 2.18. 157), only a more obvious and less dangerous delusion than Salvaterra's literalism. Certainly, in comparison to Celio's brave confrontation with his darkest self, Salvaterra's unquestioning acceptance of Catholic superstition, especially so late in the poem, appears embarrassing and misplaced. It is not surprising that an older monk interrupts Salvaterra at the height of his proselytizing (12:432; 4.14.49–53), and that Salvaterra's tour ends with a donkey lapping holy water from the sacred shell: "Well," says Derwent, "things have come to pretty pass— / The mysteries slobbered by an ass!" (12:437; 4.16.43–44).

Celio's struggle to believe frames the poem and forms a cautionary tale, not only for Clarel, but for New Italy as well. The secular nation may oust papal authority, but it cannot ignore either the deeper history that undergirds Rome or the persistence of Catholic superstition. Roman stoicism and paganism keep Celio, and by extension all young Italians, from acceding too readily to new sects. Italy will be wise to avoid the religious extremism that affects Nathan the Zionist or Nehemiah the millennialist or the self-flagellating Syrian monk or even Brother Salvaterra, the credulous Franciscan. Had Clarel accepted Celio's friendship, he would never have begun his pilgrimage and might have found love with Ruth. His final fantasy of the poem's dead includes Celio "As in a dampened mirror glassed" (12:493; 4.32.89), a befogged image of lost intimacy. Both nations and individuals must accept their place in larger historical processes in order to achieve secular salvation, an existentially "Free Church" beyond anything that Cavour imagined.

THE DOMINICAN'S DEFENSE OF ROME:
Melville's Religious Satire

In Part 2 of *Clarel* the pilgrims encounter a more cosmopolitan defender of the church in the French Dominican priest, an informed proponent of politicized Catholicism. A strong, athletic, powerful, frank, intelligent, and

---

Christianity's ethic of humility is well known.

persuasive man (12:214; 2.25.19–27), in sharp contrast to the effeminate and ineffectual Salvaterra and Syrian, the Dominican is a worldly and confident advocate of Roman Catholic hegemony who powerfully represents the Church Militant. Because he claims to have served in the French legislature, he styles himself a "staunch Catholic Democrat" (12:215; 2.25.81), a pragmatic moderate loyal to authorities in both church and state. His claim does not bear historical scrutiny. There is no record of a priest serving in the French legislature under Napoleon III (1852–1870), the likely period when the Dominican would have been elected; in fact, high-ranking ecclesiastics were expressly forbidden from serving.[32] If Melville knew this, he could intend the Dominican for another incarnation of the confidence-man, a man who easily insinuates himself into others' company. When the Dominican hears Rolfe, Vine, and Derwent singing a Latin hymn, he leaves his own group of French pilgrims in order to engage these three Protestants in conversation. Even though they may "slight the rule / Of Rome," he tells them, their joyful song reveals the satisfaction that Catholic rites offer souls in need (12:213; 2.25.12–15): "Ah Rome, your tie! may child clean part? / Nay, tugs the mother at the heart!" (2:25.1–2). Unlike Celio's blend of pagan, republican, imperial, and Hebraic Rome, the Dominican's Rome is aggressively Roman Catholic and strictly papal. As he explains, Rome has absorbed the Reformation and now opposes further reform with its "riot of reason quite set free," "sects bisected," and "Relapse barbaric":

> Rome is the Protestant to-day:
> The Red Republic slinging flame
> In Europe—she's your Scarlet Dame.
> Rome stands; but who may tell the end?
> Relapse barbaric may impend,
> Dismission into ages blind—
> Moral dispersion of mankind. (12:216; 2.25.103–12)

At this point, in a dramatic gesture that Brother Salvaterra would appreciate, the Dominican drops upon one knee and prays for the trio's salvation.

The Dominican's attack on the Paris Commune—"The Red Republic slinging flame"—would have resonated sympathetically with many New Yorkers of the early 1870s. Fears of communistic revolutions among

---

32. See Eric Anceau, *Les Députés du Second Empire: Prosographie d une Élite du XIXe Siècle* (Paris: Honoré Champion Éditeur, 2000), 33 and passim.

the city's lower classes were commonplace, and many commentators worried that New York could turn into another Paris. Yet the Commune lasted only two months, from March 18 to May 24, 1871, and local events undermined Catholic claims to democratic ideals. On July 12, 1871, the simmering conflict between New York's Protestants and Catholics exploded in violence when the city militia killed sixty Irish and their sympathizers in a riot stemming from an Orange parade down Eighth Avenue.[33] Specters of Astor Place and the Draft Riots, both of which Melville opposed, were resurfacing as he began *Clarel*. Catholic political ideology suffered another blow when, in October 1871, William Marcy Tweed, the Protestant "Boss" of Tammany Hall, suffered the first of many indictments for misuse of public funds. Herman's brother Gansevoort had once aspired to leadership in the Tammany organization, but that was twenty years ago, and the Democratic machine had grown corrupt and venal. Heavily dependent on Irish Catholic voters, consistently vigorous opponents of the Risorgimento, Tammany Hall seemed hypocritically aligned with forces of order abroad—the pope—and forces of disorder at home—the Irish mob. The Dominican shares Tammany Hall's position but masks it with his charm, argumentative vigor, and dubious claims of legislative service and democratic beliefs.

Characteristically, Derwent tries to end the Dominican's unwelcome conversation amicably (12:216; 2:25.120–24), but like the proselytizing Salvaterra the French priest persists. Rome, he argues, remains "fixed in form" (2.25.130) while adjusting to "new times": "But deep / Below rigidities of form / The invisible nerves and tissues change / Adaptively" (12:217; 2.25.132–35). Neither science nor nature touches on such hidden mysteries, he says, since they deal with mere matter. In lines often quoted to show Melville's respect for Roman Catholicism, the Dominican explains: "'Tis Abba Father that we seek, / Not the Artificer" (2.25.158–59).[34] Many of *Clarel*'s best critics see in these arguments Melville's Catholic sympathies, and they find, as does Bezanson, the Dominican symbolizing "THE PERMANENCE AND THE ADAPTABILITY OF THE CHURCH" ("Historical and Critical Note," 12:622).[35] The Dominican's

33. Burrows and Wallace, *Gotham*, 1002–8. Over 25,000 Parisians died when the royalists defeated the communards in May 1871 (1003).

34. Goldman believes the Dominican is "right" (123).

35. In one of the more balanced assessments of *Clarel*'s Roman Catholic sympathies, Joseph G. Knapp cites "endurance" as the church's chief attraction for Melville (*Tortured Synthesis: The Meaning of Melville's* Clarel [New York: Philosophical Library, 1971], 100). Kenny, *Herman Melville's* Clarel, believes Melville valued the church because of its "endurance as a natural institution" (135) and its ability to overcome its own corruption (136). Ronald C. Mason, *The*

"ability to wrestle with contraries," Goldman asserts, distinguishes him from Brother Salvaterra and gains him the respect of both the narrator and the pilgrims.[36] Almost alone among *Clarel*'s commentators, Zephyra Porat condemns the Dominican as "anti-intellectual," an unthinking religious ideologue as seduced by the "folly of the cross" (12:348; 3.22.331) as Brother Salvaterra or Christodulus (the blind abbot of Mar Saba).[37] In the context of the American Risorgimento, the Dominican's arguments reveal, as he himself says, that "Crafty is Rome" (12:214; 2.25.36). Celio knew from experience, and Melville's pastor Henry Bellows intimated in his 1871 remarks demanding that the church prove its attacks on Protestantism, that priestly arguments can inveigle unwary listeners into her grasp and must be forthrightly challenged.

The Dominican lays before the surprised pilgrims a grand reactionary scheme of Catholic essentialism that inverts conventional tropes and resists the tide of current events. Rome, not Protestantism, represents reform; republicanism, not Rome, is the Scarlet Whore of Babylon; the Dark Ages lie ahead, not behind. Where Ishmael saw humanity united under a "just Spirit of Equality" overseen by the "great democratic God" (6:117), the Dominican appeals to the common bonds of centralized Catholic authority:

> If Rome could fall
> 'Twould not be Rome alone, but all
> Religion. All with Rome have tie,
> Even the railers which deny,
> All but the downright Anarchist,
> Christ-hater, Red, and Vitriolist. (12:218; 2.25.173–78)

Such essentializing propositions deny individual spiritual and intellectual freedom and the very architecture of *Clarel* itself, which traces the multiple religious quests of nearly a dozen characters in constant debate.[38] More important, such premises deny history. Rome already *has* fallen to the Kingdom of Italy, as the Dominican well knows, and in New York some of the greatest threats to order come from lower-class Irish

---

Spirit Above the Dust: A Study of Herman Melville (London: Lehmann, 1951), contends that "Rome emerges from Melville's prolonged dialectical disputation with nearly all the honours" (241).

36. Goldman, *Melville's Protest Theism*, 89.

37. See Porat, "Towards the Promethean Ledge: Varieties of Sceptic Experience in Melville's Clarel," *Journal of Literature & Theology: An Interdisciplinary Journal of Theory and Criticism* 8 (March 1994): 33.

38. See Potter, *Melville's* Clarel, for the multiple religious traditions in the poem, esp. 150–210.

Catholics loyal to the pope. But the Dominican refuses to accept defeat: "In rout / Sword-hilts rap at the Vatican, / And, lo, an old, old man comes out: / 'What would ye?' 'Change!' 'I never change'" (12:215; 2.25. 59–62). This story recalls Melville's parody of Pius IX in *Mardi,* Hivohitee MDCCCXLVIII, "an old, old man; with steel-gray eyes, hair and beard, and a horrible necklace of jaw-bones" (3:360–61). Pius IX, who served until his death in 1878, had become even more reactionary over the years. His *Syllabus of Errors* (1864) "rejected liberalism, democracy and toleration" and his Doctrine of Papal Infallibility (1869) made disagreements with his policies impossible.[39] He refused to negotiate Vatican rights with the Kingdom of Italy and spent his last days isolated from the new country rapidly developing around him, much like the suspicious "priest-king of Vatikanna" in *Mardi* (3:467). The Dominican's statement about "invisible nerves and tissues" adapting to change, like his claim to have served in the French legislature, is mere debate strategy designed to muddle his opposition. *Clarel,* far from supporting Catholicism, actually satirizes a church out of touch with the postbellum world in both the United States and Italy. Melville's brother-in-law, the Radical Republican John C. Hoadley whom Hershel Parker calls "the best nineteenth-century critic of *Clarel,*" had no trouble identifying the poem's critique of Catholicism: in his own copy, next to a line recording Derwent's lament for the perversion of Christianity, Hoadley wrote "Rome!—even if the author didn't mean it!"[40]

The French priest is the flip side of Mortmain, the Swedish radical who fought for republicanism during the revolutions of 1848. A secular Christian idealist reminiscent of Mazzini, Mortmain has spent twenty-five years nursing his bitterness over the failures of 1848. Whereas Mortmain lost his revolutionary struggle to renewed totalitarianism, the Dominican has lost his conservative struggle to maintain papal power. With the defeat of Napoleon III, in fact, the Dominican must have lost his supposed seat in the French legislature, which may be why he is now a tour guide in Palestine. As defeated representatives of revolution and authority, Mortmain and the Dominican rationalize their failures with universal claims that appeal to unsupportable ideals rather than historical experience. Mortmain has turned to a fatalistic neo-Calvinism and now believes that "Man's vicious: snaffle him with kings" (12:145; 2.3.180), while the Dominican rationalizes the pope's defeat by arguing that only his spiritual power really matters:

---

39. Beales and Biagini, *Risorgimento,* 153.
40. Quoted in Parker, *Herman Melville,* 2:811, 810.

> Weigh well the Pope. Though he should be
> Despoiled of Charlemagne's great fee—
> Cast forth, and made a begging friar,
> That would not quell him. (12:218; 2.25.181–84)

Of course, if that were true, why did the pope cling to temporal power in the first place, or refuse to accept the separation of church and state crucial to Risorgimento nationalism? The Dominican shifts ground in order to account for all contingencies, even while presuming to argue from unchanging principles. Both the ultramontane priest and the Mazzinian revolutionist Mortmain, the Guelph and Ghibelline Melville denounced in the "Supplement" to *Battle-Pieces,* ignore the compromises of the Risorgimento—a secular constitutional monarchy with limited democracy—and turn to totalizing opinions about human nature that ignore the variable needs and histories of both individuals and nations.

The priest's crafty argument provokes a two-canto discussion between Derwent and Rolfe, with Derwent good-naturedly dissenting from the Dominican's extreme position and Rolfe talking himself into it. Derwent argues from current events, the republicanism sweeping over Europe that is destroying authority and rendering the pope's future uncertain:

> since all
> The bias of the days that be
> Away leans from authority,
> And most when hierarchical;
> So that the future of the Pope
> Is cast in no fair horoscope;
> In brief, since Rome must still decay;
> Less care I to disown or hide
> Aught that she has of merit rare. (12:221.2.26.77–85)

The more the church loses its temporal power, the more humanity can appreciate its spiritual value, an argument long made by Mazzini and other Italian nationalists. Derwent specifically alludes to the Risorgimento's triumph, "that tidal fall / Of Rome in Southern Europe" (2.26.103–4), and confidently offers a prediction: "Rome's guns are spiked; and they'll stay so. / The world is now too civilized / For Rome" (12:222; 2.26.117–19). Derwent's optimism may seem shallow, but he has good historical evidence for his position. Rolfe, in contrast, argues from personal belief, insisting that only Rome still understands that "man's heart is what it used to be" (12:223; 2.26.159)—a distant echo of Melville's own early Calvinism.⁴¹ Rolfe, lacking Celio's "Italian turn of thought," feels threatened by "this vile liberty" imbibed from American culture, an Emersonian individualism that taught him "to reverence naught, not even herself" (2.26. 151–53). Critics conventionally consider Rolfe's view to be the closest to Melville's own thinking: Robert Penn Warren calls Rolfe "an idealized version of Melville himself," and Walter Bezanson calls him "a partial self-portrait."⁴² But Rolfe is actually quite far from the Melville of 1876 (or even 1850), for he sees the world in strict binaries, black-and-white antitheses that ignore both Celio's skepticism and Derwent's meliorism. In Europe's revolutions, Rolfe argues, only "Rome and the Atheist have gained: / These two shall fight it out—these two" (12:222; 2.26.140–41), a position that he outlined earlier when he defended Volney, Chateaubriand, and Lamartine against the "Red Caps" of 1848 (12:183; 2.16.41–51). If Rolfe represents any part of Melville's thinking, then it is the historically naïve and idealistic position—reminiscent of Emerson—that principles alone govern human behavior.

Strong evidence undermining the Dominican's views comes from Clarel, who is "perplexed" both by them and Rolfe's seeming assent (12:224; 2.27.7–10). As Celio's "second self," Clarel knows that Rome is more than any one religion, certainly more than any one man (here the now-infallible Pope Pius IX), and that its power and authority compound Christianity, paganism, imperialism, republicanism, and a wealth of other creeds and ideologies. Rome's strength lies in its diversity and flexibility, its ability to change (witness the New Italy) while maintaining a material reality that connects people to the past. The Dominican, like the Franciscan Brother Salvaterra, seeks comfort in the moral clarity of extremes, and he directly challenges the "Italian turn of thought" that seeks knowledge without hastily committing to one particular belief. As John Milton knew, neither Dominicans nor Franciscans have a monopoly on salvation. Melville marked a passage in his copy of *Paradise Lost* that places both orders in a "Paradise of Fools," a limbo reserved for those who hope to gain Heaven through their own effort (III, 479–480, 496).⁴³ John

---

41. Shurr, *Mystery of Iniquity,* 115–20, links the Calvinism articulated by Rolfe and Ungar with Melville's earlier Calvinistic utterances, most famously in "Hawthorne and His Mosses"; Herbert, *Moby-Dick and Calvinism,* finds Melville moving away from and even parodying Calvinism by the time of *Moby-Dick.* I agree with Herbert that "problems of doctrine were for [Melville] continuous with problems of experience" (15), meaning that one can find support for believing in evil without subscribing to a specific dogma such as Calvinism.

42. See Warren, "Introduction," in *Selected Poems of Herman Melville* (1970; New York: Barnes & Noble, 1998), 40, and Bezanson, "Historical and Critical Note" (12:587). See also Kenny, *Herman Melville's Clarel,* 206 and 249n.

43. Robin Grey and Douglas Robillard, "Melville's Milton: A Transcription of Melville's

Shawcross convincingly argues that Melville remembered this passage in a Mar Saba canto, "Before the Gate" (12:295; 3.10.1–42).[44] I think that Milton's passage also informs Clarel's puzzled reaction to the Dominican and implicitly problematizes the authority of all priestly arguments. Ultimately, the Dominican's worldview is only one more sectarian appeal to unquestioned orthodoxy that denies current history and masks self-interest with lofty principles.

Later debates about Roman Catholic hegemony similarly undermine the Dominican's position. Ungar is an Anglo-Catholic Confederate veteran who has turned soldier of fortune, and in his criticisms of democracy, Reconstruction, progress, and contemporary religion he seems to Bezanson "very close to Melville's own sensibility" (12:634). As a participant in the American Risorgimento, however, he is one more papistic Guelph in Melville's nexus of political extremists. He rebelled against a just authority during the Civil War and fought in the name of reactionary ideals: secession, states' rights, and slavery. Although he believed "holding slaves was aye a grief— / The system an iniquity" (12:403; 4.5.148–49), he hypocritically fought in its behalf, supporting one of the few undeniable evils in Melvillean ideology.[45] He is as much a political as a racial hybrid, of "Anglo brain, but Indian heart" (12:403; 4.5.140), a "countryman" of Rolfe, Vine, and Clarel yet, unlike these American Protestants, "sprung from Romish race" (12:419; 4.10.180) and consequently comfortable with Roman Catholic hegemony. He idealizes the Middle Ages, praises Charlemagne's submission to the church, condemns democracy, denies progress, and inveighs against the "new uprising of the Red" in the Paris Commune (12:456; 4.20.126) as presage of "the Dark Ages of Democracy" (12:460; 4.21.139)—an inverted figure startlingly like those the Dominican used. Instead of learning from the lessons of current history, Ungar illogically exalts both Marcus Aurelius (12:454; 4.20.44–52) and Christ (12:458; 4.21.37–44), man and God, stoic and savior, to justify his extreme pessimism and personal opposition to reform.

Certainly, there are elements in Ungar's relentless diatribes that Melville voices elsewhere, notably "credence to Calvin" (12:462; 4.22.38) in

---

Marginalia in His Copy of *The Poetical Works of John Milton*," *Leviathan: A Journal of Melville Studies* 4 (March and October 2002): 131.

44. See Shawcross, "Too Intellectual a Poet," 88–89, which points out the relevant section in *Paradise Lost* (Book III, 451–97) where Milton indicts priests, as well as many others, who try to enter Heaven's gate on the strength of their own vain exploits. Shawcross includes Celio among these false martyrs, a reading I dispute.

45. See Karcher, *Shadow Over the Promised Land*, for Melville's lifelong antipathy to slavery, and her essay "The Moderate and the Radical" for his later, more moderate views on racial equality.

"The House-top," antipathy for French radicalism, and praise for Marcus Aurelius in "The Age of the Antonines." That poem, however, valorizes Aurelius as a "pagan gentleman" who achieved peace through "law made will" (11:286; 6, and 287, 25), behavior opposite to Ungar's rebellious nature and continuing violence as a soldier of fortune. Ungar, like Ahab, ignores all viae mediae, a position that finally shocks Rolfe out of his unease with his American "vile liberty" into a new appreciation for the contingencies of human experience. To Ungar's extreme pessimism, darker by far than anything Celio envisions, Rolfe replies: "Yes, God is God, and men are men, / Forever and for aye. What then? / There's Circumstance—there's Time; and these / Are charged with store of latencies / Still working in to modify" (12:459; 4.21.74–78). The three Americans admit that there is some justification for Ungar's bleak outlook, particularly given the horror of the Civil War (12:460; 4.21.140–59), which the narrator earlier calls a "True Bridge of Sighs" (12:401; 4.4.77) that divided American history into two eras. Yet Ungar's defense of the Confederacy picks at the wounds Melville tried to heal in his "Supplement" to *Battle-Pieces*. Ungar is no Cincinnatus, Washington, or Garibaldi who returns to his farm when the fighting concludes. Rather, he seeks renewed violence as a hired gun for the Ottoman Empire, pursuing a "business," Derwent reminds Rolfe, that drives "men through fires / To Hades, at the bidding blind / Of Heaven knows whom" (12:464; 4.23. 42–44) and belies Ungar's concern for children "Ground up by Mammon in the mill" (12:464; 4.23. 42–44, 50). Ungar's sword is *not* a cross; Christianity cannot justify war. And no matter how incisive and germane Ungar's criticisms of contemporary society may be, his self-confessed "monomania" (12:459; 4.21.101–2) and hypocritical behavior invalidates his confused and extremist philosophy.[46]

In *Clarel* Melville insists on the necessity of Celian skepticism, the "Italian turn of thought" epitomized in the Risorgimento's pragmatic blend of revolutionary idealism and monarchical authority in order to achieve national unity, however tenuous. While I have aligned Melville with the Protestant republican view of the New Italy, he knew that there were other sides to the question as well. The largest view of the poem must take into account the Dominican's alluring quest for order, Mort-

---

46. Outside of a few poems in *Battle-Pieces,* such as "Lee in the Capitol," Melville has little positive to say about the Confederate military. In "Bridegroom Dick" (1876) Melville's speaker excoriates the "Rebs" for refitting the captured Union ship *Cumberland* as a battering ram whose blows "strike below the belt" and so "replace / The openness of valor while dismantling the grace" (11:213; 416–18). There is nothing chivalrous about any modern war, North or South, making Garibaldi all the more an exception.

main's disillusion with revolutions, and Ungar's persistent rebelliousness. All three speakers address major events in nineteenth-century political history, such as the excesses of French communism, the failures of 1848, and the collapse of Reconstruction, as well as the overarching threat of materialism, codified as "Mammon" throughout the poem.[47] Yet insofar as these men resist change, they prove less influential on Clarel than the gentle skeptic Celio does. In *Clarel,* Melville supports Celio's skeptical perspective, a perspective enforced by reading the poem within its contemporary historical context when doubt pervaded thought on nearly all matters, from religion to politics to science.

COSMIC WRECKAGE:
The Remains of Pax Romana

Hilton Obenzinger argues persuasively that *Clarel* demonstrates the futility of teleology, whether figured as Jewish Zionism, Puritan typology, or American millennialism.[48] Rome too, state and church, provides Melville an apt metaphor for such historical indeterminacy. As the pilgrims wind over an upland plateau, they notice "crumbled aqueducts" and "shattered pottery," scattered ruins that remind the narrator of "the shards of tile-like brick" found around Richborough castle in Kent, a former Roman fort (12:195; 2.20.29, 31, 33). He further observes: "What breadth of doom / As of the worlds in strata penned— / So cosmic seems the wreck of Rome" (2.20. 37–39). Gone also is Rome's mythic power as Margoth, the atheist geologist, persistently hammers away at its symbolism: "As the Phlegræan fields no more / Befool men as the spookish shore / Where Jove felled giants, but are known— / The Solfatara and each cone / Volcanic—to be but on a par / With all things natural" (12:196; 2.20.52–57). The Roman landscapes and artifacts that empowered Melville's fiction have been stripped of larger meaning and reduced to objects of scientific scrutiny by books like Barthold Niebuhr's *Roman History* (1827–28), a trend Melville complained about in his journal (15:97) and Rolfe laments to Clarel: "Zion, like Rome, is Niebuhrized" (12:108; 1.34.19). Memorials of the decline of Imperial Rome are everywhere: England, France, Italy, Palestine, as well as in several prints Melville probably owned by

---

47. See Trachtenberg, *The Incorporation of America,* for the social and economic context for the attacks on "Mammonism" in *Clarel.*

48. *American Palestine,* especially the discussion of Nathan the American Zionist, 95–113.

this time.[49] They surface in the eight-line poem "The Ravaged Villa," which describes a ruined Roman dwelling where "The weed exiles the flower; / And, flung to kiln, Apollo's bust / Makes lime for" (11:266; 6–8). "Mammon," Melville's code word for Gilded Age materialism, dominates modern life and constructs hubristic towers that, like Bannadonna's, rest on corrupt foundations and will eventually join the cycle of historical decline and fall.[50] Memorials to the temporal and spiritual fall of Papal Rome are also in the making (*Clarel* itself is one such memorial). And someday, memorials to the fall of the United States, the New Italy, and other modern nations will also arise. Human beings need order, yet time and history and the growing human desire for progress militate against any *single* order, whether in politics or art, and thus lead Melville to his deepest questioning of Western civilization.

At the conclusion of *Battle-Pieces* Melville hoped that the United States might undertake its own Risorgimento and emerge as the true heir of Rome, fusing republic and empire under the iron dome of democracy merged with law. Without explicitly vitiating that vision, *Clarel* reminds readers that all empires decay in the endless cycles of history. Of this too modern Italy is an emblem, as Garibaldi ruefully observed in 1880: "It was a very different Italy which I spent my life dreaming of, not the impoverished and humiliated country which we now see ruled by the dregs of the nation."[51] Melville voices similar opinions through the grim Mortmain and the jocular Don Hannibal, two former revolutionaries who rue their radicalism but in very different tones. Mortmain sounds as disillusioned as Garibaldi in his fatalistic acceptance of revolutionary failure:

> And what is stable? Find one boon
> That is not lackey to the moon
> Of fate. The flood ebbs out—the ebb
> Floods back; the incessant shuttle shifts
> And flies, and weaves and tears the web.
> Turn, turn thee to the proof that sifts:
> What if the kings in Forty-eight
> Fled like the gods? Even as the gods

---

49. See, for example, the well-known print *Byron Contemplating the Coliseum* reproduced in Wallace, "Melville's Prints" (1997), 10. Lathers owned several paintings of Roman ruins as well (Cohen, "Melville and the Lathers Collection," esp. prints numbered 27, 37, 174, and 176).

50. Perhaps, as Hennig Cohen suggests, "The Ravaged Villa" is based on Melville's memory of the villa of Maecenas near Naples (*Selected Poems of Herman Melville* [New York: Fordham University Press, 1964], 230–31).

51. Quoted in *Great Lives Observed: Garibaldi,* ed. Denis Mack Smith (Englewood Cliffs, NJ: Prentice-Hall, 1969), 174.

> Shall do, return they made; and sate
> And fortified their strong abodes;
> And, to confirm them there in state,
> Contrived new slogans, apt to please—
> Pan and the tribal unities.
> Behind all this still works some power
> Unknowable, thou'lt yet adore.
> *That* steers the world, not man. (12.4. 92–108)

Once a social idealist whose "Precocities of heart outran / The immaturities of brain," Mortmain now bitterly denounces reform and wears a skull cap in place of a liberty cap to underscore his pessimism (12:147, 2.4.52–53;12: 140; 2.2.1–22). More hopefully, the weaving imagery in this passage recalls Ishmael's reconciliation of human desire with circumstance in "The Mat-Maker" and "A Bower in the Arsacides" and points toward the Roman stoicism that accepts life's "fine hammered steel of woe" (6:424). In one of the most nuanced discussions of Melville's view of history, William H. Shurr finds that this and other examples in *Clarel* confirm Melville's belief in a cyclic theory of history,[52] a belief evident since *Mardi* and fortified by the Roman typologies of the American and Italian Risorgimentos.

One of Shurr's examples could have been Señor Don Hannibal Rohon Del Aquaviva, Derwent's old friend who lost an arm and a leg in his fight for "Mexic liberty" (12:450; 4.19.63). Like Mortmain, Don Hannibal is a victim of revolution, but he responds to his fate with good humor and a desperado philosophy like Ishmael's. Don Hannibal's linguistically eclectic name indicates his cosmopolitanism, combining as it does the greatest enemy of the Roman Republic, French and Italo-Spanish surnames, and Spanish titles in a comic and transnationally resonant name.[53] Because Mexico first gained independence in 1821, which would put Don Hannibal in his late seventies in the poem, it seems likely that he fought for Mexican independence in 1866 under Benito Juárez and against Maximilian I, the Hapsburg puppet of Napoleon III whom Melville saw in Venice. By virtue of his wounds he blends revolutionary Ahab with conservative Jack Gentian, or as he calls himself "A *reformado* reformed" (12:450; 4.19.72), a revolutionary now willing to accept the traditional authority of "poor Old Spain" (12:450; 4.19.67) in exchange for national stability and peace. He has learned the lesson of Garibaldi the monarchist and

---

52. *Mystery of Iniquity*, 81–94.

53. Bezanson notes some of the name's puns (aqua vitae) and its linguistic eclecticism (12:623, 832n).

rejected the lesson of Mortmain the republican and so avoided Mortmain's bitterness. Don Hannibal (who uses the fractured Italian "excellenza" [4.19.151]) is a more hopeful Celio, "still in quest" (4.19.48) for a place to escape the rising tide of proletarianism of England and the "Eternal hacking"—wars and revolutions—of contemporary democracies (12:452; 4.19.118). Mortmain and Don Hannibal show that victory and defeat are two sides of the same coin that flips endlessly in the hand of circumstance. History dominates agency in an endless ebb and flow of political action and reaction, and both individuals and nations must proceed with humility and caution before giving in to either excessive despair or unwarranted hope. Although a minor, late entry in Melville's political ruminations, Don Hannibal, in his devil-may-care cosmopolitanism and fondness for "Wine and the weed" (12: 452; 4.19.115), parallels the Marquis de Grandvin and may come closer to Melville's attitude than any other late character.

One of Melville's most nostalgic poems, "The Age of the Antonines," sharply contrasts modern civilization with the Roman Empire and the monarchs who took it to its glorious pinnacle in the second century. Melville enclosed a copy of the poem in a letter to Hoadley (14:452–54), telling him that he based it on a passage in Gibbon, presumably the section contending that the Roman Empire reached its peak under Nerva, Trajan, Hadrian, and the "two Antonines," Antoninus Pius and Marcus Aurelius, all emperors from 96–180.[54] Melville owned an engraving of a bust of Antoninus Pius and a handsome illustration in *Vatican Sculptures* (fig. 28) which presents a calm and forceful image of this ideal emperor who reigned over a period considerably more

> peaceful than Europe's tumultuous present:
> While faith forecasts millennial years
> Spite Europe's embattled lines,
> Back to the Past one glance be cast—
>   The Age of the Antonines!
> O summit of fate, O zenith of time
> When a pagan gentleman reigned,
> And the olive was nailed to the inn of the world

---

54. Melville's edition of Gibbon has not been identified. In volume 1, chapter 2, Gibbon uses the phrase "the age of the Antonines" at least three times, and in chapter 3 he says of Antoninus Pius and Marcus Aurelius, whom he calls "the two Antonines," "their united reigns are possibly the only period of history in which the happiness of a great people was the sole object of government." See *The Decline and Fall of the Roman Empire*, ed. D. M. Low (New York: Pocket Books, 1962), 1:16, 28, 35, 56

Figure 28. Antonius Pius, from Robert MacPherson, *Vatican Sculptures* (1863), plate 105. This line drawing may have contributed to Melville's favorable description of the Roman emperor in "The Age of the Antonines." Author's photograph.

> Nor the peace of the just was feigned.
> A halcyon Age, afar it shines,
> Solstice of Man and the Antonines. (11:286, 1–10)

Nostalgia supplies what the present denies as Melville now finds the "zenith of time" 1,700 years in the past, reversing progressive theories of history. Roman paganism brought to Europe the "olive" of peace, unlike contemporary Christianity which perpetuates "embattled lines" between England, France, Germany, and Russia and drives Christian nations into uneasy alliances with former enemies, for example the infamous Triple Alliance of Italy, Austria, and Germany (1882). Neither the demagoguery of "the pulpit-drum" nor the illusory spiritual promises of a "Paradise pledged or sought" were necessary to achieve peace and stability under the Antoninines, stoic leaders who validate Celio's low opinion of Christianity. "We sham, we shuffle, while faith declines— / They were frank in the Age of the Antonines" (11:286; 19–20), the poem continues, as it celebrates reason and "the fluent thought" that led Celio to accept death rather than live with the hypocrisy of modern religions. The poem, which may have been written at the same time as *Clarel*,[55] glosses Celio's "Italian turn of thought" as a truly "Roman turn of thought" rooted firmly in Aurelian skepticism and stoicism. It constitutes a historically grounded reproach to the self-aggrandizing rationalizations of unrepentant rebels like Ungar and reinforces what Melville made clear in *Battle-Pieces*: peace is most likely, the poem continues, "Under law made will," where the "parvenu" of democracy accepts the rule of "the foremost of men the best" (11:285–86; 25, 22, 28).[56] The poem ends as it began, on a measured hope for a moral politics: "Ah, might we read in America's signs / The Age restored of the Antonines." "Signs," especially without knowing for sure when Melville composed the poem, is too cryptic a word to identify with any distinct historical event; yet the sentiment shows that America can still fulfill its Roman destiny, an idea that supports Gail Coffler's contention that "after the fragmentation of the Civil War years, Melville developed an enlarged respect for the unifying and preservative powers encompassed in the idea of 'Rome,' as exhibited in Roman law, in Roman architecture, in the military order that solidified the Roman Empire, and in the assimilative catholicity of the Roman Church."[57] Except for the last point, which I believe Melville questions in *Clarel*, what Melville proposed in "Statues in Rome" remained true for him in his final years: "the Roman spirit [does] still animate and support whatever is soundest in societies and states" (9:408).

The best image for the historical place of the Risorgimento in Melville's later thought comes from "The Conflict of Convictions," the third poem in *Battle-Pieces*: "I know a wind in purpose strong— / It spins

---

55. For dating the poem see Parker, *Herman Melville* 2:421, 816, and Garner, "Aging with the Antonines," in Sanford E. Marovitz and A. C. Christodoulou, eds., *Melville "Among the Nations"* (Kent, OH: Kent State University Press, 2001), 285.

56. In the printed version Melville substituted the word "parvenu" for "leveller" which appears in his letter to Hoadley (14:454). The change softens somewhat his criticism of the radical democratic politics associated with "leveling," perhaps the populism spreading over late-nineteenth-century America. Other significant changes include adding explicit references to Europe and America, neither of which occurs in the Hoadley letter.

57. "Classical Iconography," 275. The date Melville acquired his copy of Gibbon and the edition he used remain unknown, but as Bezanson's notes in *Clarel* show, Melville mined Gibbon repeatedly in his later years (12:720n).

against the way it drives" (11:10; 63–69). This naturalistic conjoining of opposites in violent, presumably purposive movement illustrates Melville's view of history as a force that moves in endlessly unpredictable directions, undermining and re-forming ideology in a constant vortex of uncertainty. America was no more whole after the Civil War than before, and like Italy it might never attain true nationhood—that is, a single people with a common cultural identity. And this goal might not even be desirable, for the choice, as *Clarel*'s many voices make clear, is not between paired opposites, compelling as these may be (I think of Shirley Dettlaff's insightful contrast of Hebraism and Hellenism);[58] rather, the choices are multiple, with "sects bisected" and interlaced across boundaries of ethnicity, religion, and nation. Catholic Democrats, Roman atheists, American Zionists, ex-Confederate Catholics of mixed Native American and European blood—all move through Melville's poem in a bewildering array of unstable identities. *Clarel*, so recalcitrant that even its best readers puzzle over basic issues of diction, voice, and syntax, illustrates rather than resolves the problem of giving lasting form to thought.[59] Yet this is no cause for hermeneutical despair; rather, like those Roman statues that both capture timeless ideals and depend upon circumstance, *Clarel* embodies the whirlwinds of its own time, the endless resurgences of faith and despair that cycle, like history, through every thoughtful person.

MACHIAVELLI AND THE MEDUSA OF REVOLUTION IN *BILLY BUDD*

Billy Budd, Sailor addresses the conflict between authority and liberty central to the American Risorgimento more subtly and completely than any other Melville work. As Barbara Johnson has argued, there are as many interpretations of *Billy Budd* available as there are readers.[60]

---

58. "'Counter Natures in Mankind.'"

59. Robert Milder, one of *Clarel*'s closest readers, finds that even in lines crucial to his argument "it is hard to determine what attitude—and whose attitude—is communicated" ("In Behalf of 'Dearth,'" *Leviathan: A Journal of Melville Studies* 1 [October 1999]: 66). Milder argues that the Northwestern-Newberry reading "death" in 1.28.29 should be revised to read "dearth."

60. Barbara Johnson, "Melville's Fist: The Execution of Billy Budd," in *The Critical Difference: Essays in the Contemporary Rhetoric of Reading* (Baltimore: Johns Hopkins University Press, 1980), 79–109. Good overviews of the story and its long, contentious critical history are available in Merton M. Sealts, Jr., "Innocence and Infamy: Billy Budd, Sailor," in *A Companion to Melville Studies*, 408–30, and *Critical Essays on Melville's* Billy Budd, Sailor, ed. Robert Milder (Boston: G. K. Hall, 1989), 3–18.

Rather than offer yet another reading here, I wish to historicize Johnson's deconstructionist approach by suggesting that the story's resistance to unified interpretations is not only part of its linguistic apparatus but also its historical situation. Both language and history resist objective interpretation, a key lesson of the American Risorgimento, and *Billy Budd* participates in both. The tale is very much a "political fiction" as Milton Stern has long argued,[61] but its politics are not confined to those of the Great Mutiny, the French Revolution, or the *Somers* affair. The story's slender web of Italianate allusions entangles its meanings in the bedeviling ambiguities and paradoxes of Risorgimento nationalism and the constellation of iconography, imagery, and allusions associated with it. Consequently, *Billy Budd* takes on the urgency and uncertainty of the central transnational experience in Melville's lifetime. John Wenke has it right when he says that "The ambiguity of *Billy Budd* is an essential, functional concomitant to Melville's fictionalized confluence of historical, political, and moral forces as they impinge upon an individual's—Vere's—consciousness and action,"[62] a confluence whose many eddies include the Risorgimento.

Set in the Mediterranean on a British warship in the summer of 1797, *Billy Budd* combines the historical specificity of *Israel Potter* and *Battle-Pieces* with the philosophic speculativeness of *Clarel*. The Machiavellianism of Benjamin Franklin, the mediatory politics of the "Supplement," and the skepticism of Celio interfuse in a historical moment that foreshadows the Risorgimento—Napoleon Bonaparte's creation of the Cisalpine Republic in Northern Italy in July 1797. Napoleon, still a general, led into Italy one of those "proselyting armies of the French Directory" that England fears will extend republicanism to its own shores (54). The mutinies at Spithead and the Nore confirmed these fears and prompted the Admiralty to send the *Bellipotent* "to join the Mediterranean fleet" and then on to isolated reconnaissance duty (54). Although the worst excesses of the French Revolution were over, no one could know that, and with her so-called liberation of Italy France seemed bent on universal conquest. Billy's sally about "the Rights of Man" necessarily bears political freight, for even if he refers only to his former ship, that ship has been deliberately christened with a name that evokes "the enemy's red meteor

---

61. "Introduction," *Billy Budd Sailor (An Inside Narrative)* (Indianapolis: Bobbs-Merrill Company, 1975), xix. See also his reading of the story as primarily concerned with nature and experience, not philosophy and ideals in *The Fine-Hammered Steel of Herman Melville* (Urbana: University of Illinois Press, 1957), 206–39.

62. "Melville's Indirection: Billy Budd, the Genetic Text, and 'the deadly space between,'" in *New Essays on Billy Budd*, 118.

of unbridled and unbounded revolt" (54). Moreover, Handsome Sailors are known to consort with shipmates who look like the motley crew that Anacharsis Cloots brought before the first French Assembly (43), a revolutionary throng of the world's oppressed. In this historical context John Claggart is right to harbor suspicions of Billy's political loyalties. As I pointed out in chapter 3, Billy's androgyny, singing ability, and Apollonian beauty link him with the Italian organ-grinder Carlo as a potential revolutionary who threatens established order, and Melville's dedication of the tale to Jack Chase distantly recalls Jack's proud identification with the Roman agitator Rienzi. Revolutionary potential, in fact, is integral to the Handsome Sailor archetype, whether in the allusion to him as a "nautical Murat" (as I mentioned in chapter 1) or in the metaphor he shares with Garibaldi (the "red Taurus plunging on" in "At the Hostelry") when Billy's shipmates fancy him as their "grand sculptured Bull" who appears in the foretop "tossed up as by the horns of Taurus" (44). The narrator specifically compares Billy to Apollo (48) and Hercules (51), putting him in the category of just murderers whose noble aims outweigh normally prohibited means.[63] When Billy strikes and kills Claggart he seems even to Captain Vere a just, godly murderer: "It is the divine judgment on Ananias! Look!" he says, pointing to Claggart's dead body, and then exclaims, "Struck dead by an angel of God! Yet the angel must hang!" (100–101). Vere understands instantly that he confronts a Machiavellian moment when unjust means bring about just ends, as in Peter's condemnation of Ananias in Acts 5. But because Claggart's death upsets the order of the state, Vere just as quickly moves to a further Machiavellian premise, that the state must be preserved. Vere seems to understand that Billy's is more an act of fortuna than virtù, more fate than will, and thus carries with it no imputation of heroism, which distinguishes it from Garibald's angelized rescue of Sicily-Andromeda. While Vere could be viewed as a Machiavellian tyrant who ought to be deposed and Billy as the agent of a healthy rebellion needed to rebalance liberty and authority, nothing in the story suggests this possibility, and Vere's larger aim of defeating the French justifies in pragmatic terms the execution of one young seaman. Vere is no decisive and self-assured Cesare Borgia, no Prince; rather, if he fits anywhere in the Machivellian universe it is as the detached and ration-

---

63. For a full analysis of the irony and moral ambiguity implicit in the allusions to Hercules and Apollo, plus a discerning comment on Melville's comparison of Billy to the unreliable Roman historian Fabius, see Gail Coffler, "Religion, Myth, and Meaning in the Art of *Billy Budd, Sailor*" in *New Essays on* Billy Budd, 54–57. Hercules, Coffler points out, "used his strength to commit both good and evil deeds," and Apollo was known as "the archer of death." Melville quotes Martial's sarcastic lines on Fabius, Coffler adds (see *Billy Budd,* 53), to satirize readers who dismiss the truths of myth and fiction in favor of the supposed objectivity of history.

alizing diplomat himself, which Melville suggests in Claggart's gazing at Vere as one might have gazed at the biblical patriarch Jacob, the "tanned Machiavelli in tents" of *Israel Potter* (8:46).⁶⁴

In the pantheon of justifiable rebels Billy is closest to Masaniello, the Amalfi fisherman whose youth, beauty, innocence, and "Tanned marigold-cheek" (122; 7.153) prefigure Billy and his "rose-tan" cheek (119). As Apollonian Billy is idolized by the crew so was Masaniello "The Darling of the mob; nine days / Their great Apollo"; but then the mob (as Melville knew mobs do) reversed itself and beheaded him, "a portent"(122; 7.159–60, 164). Both Masaniello and Billy are ironic martyrs to the "Rights of Man," like "weird John Brown" portents of larger rebellions to come. And both are Medusa-figures, Masaniello by virtue of decapitation and Billy because he mutely turns his antagonist Claggart to the petrification of instant death (Auber's Masaniello play was entitled *La Muette [mute] de Portici*). Both assume legendary status in song and story as spokesmen for their respective proletarian "nations," Masaniello for Neapolitans oppressed by Spain and Billy for impressed seamen under the control of officers like Claggart, who may very well be of foreign birth (64–65).⁶⁵ Both violate gender norms by combining feminine attractiveness with masculine strength, Masaniello with his "curled head" and "dark eyes and sunny locks," and Billy even more strongly with his "feminine" facial complexion and narrative comparisons to a "mother" and to Georgiana in Hawthorne's "The Birthmark" (Sandberg, 122; *Budd,* 50, 51, 53). Simultaneously appealing and appalling, unpredictable, volatile, and violent, as Billy's sudden death-blow at Claggart and Masaniello's diseased ravings demonstrate, these two young men incite mutiny, rebellion, and anarchy even as they seek justice for wrongs committed against them and their fellows. Innocence is their blinder, for they are ordinary people whose instincts and heart drive them to actions society finds intolerable and even their compatriots cannot support, yet history and literature confer on them the status of mythic heroes. Both Masaniello and Billy become, in spite of themselves, transmuted into beautiful and terrible Medusas of revolution.

---

64. While Vere ponders Claggart's accusations that Billy is plotting mutiny, Claggart gives his captain "a look such as might have been that of the spokesman of the envious children of Jacob deceptively imposing upon the troubled patriarch the blood-dyed coat of young Joseph" (96). In one of the rare discussions of Machiavelli in the story, Anthony Hutchinson, *Writing the Republic: Liberalism and Morality in American Political Fiction* (New York: Columbia University Press, 2007), finds Hannah Arendt's association of Vere with Machiavellian virtue narrowly restrictive, and counters her views with those of John Patrick Diggins and Lionel Trilling (84–92).

65. Claggart could even be French and therefore associated with more dangerous revolutionary tendencies than Billy himself. See Larry J. Reynolds, "Billy Budd and American Labor Unrest: The Case for Striking Back" in *New Essays on* Billy Budd, 42–43.

Billy has not truly subsumed his will to his monarch's. Although he pledges fealty to his king and knows "it was his duty as a loyal bluejacket to report in the proper quarter" the mutinous overtures of the afterguardsman (85), in failing to do so he betrays his country and its laws. A compound of revolutionary ideologies, Billy allows French anarchism and suspicion of authority to trump the Risorgimento's constitutional monarchism, making him a "Red Republican" despite his assertions of loyalty to the crown.[66] Vere knows that the average sailor, particularly after the mutinies at Spithead and the Nore, is incapable of distinguishing among gradations of rebellion. With the example of Garibaldi unavailable in 1797, Vere can only look to a figure like Timoleon, who murdered his brother in order to save Corinth from Tyranny, an event that inspired one of Melville's last poems: "The time was Plato's. Wandering lights / Confirmed the atheist's standing star; / As now, no sanction Virtue knew / For deeds that on prescriptive morals jar" (11:257; 121–24). Forms, laws, codes, circumstances, and consequences—the death of an officer at the hands of a sailor—are all we can consider in an imperfect, Machiavellian world. The report of Billy's execution by a British naval chronicle confirms Vere's reasoning by reducing the complex and upsetting circumstances of Claggart's death to the cultural stereotypes of the day: Claggart uncovered a plot, apprehended the ringleader, and the culprit drew a knife and stabbed him in the heart. Prompt and salutary punishment followed (130–31). Given the self-congratulatory virtue of the "public," which Melville satirized in *The Confidence-Man* and in his Burgundy Club manuscript the "House of the Tragic Poet,"[67] what else could be expected from a newspaper? The naval chronicle displays, as the Cosmopolitan sarcastically observed of freedom of the press in *The Confidence-Man*, the "*freedom of Colt's revolver*" (10:165).

Vere is a tragic figure for he should represent a law-abiding nationalism as did Garibaldi and Nelson yet he lacks their supreme self-confidence. He maintains the *Bellipotent* in sufficient fighting trim to defeat the *Athée*, but his juridical decisions leave behind (as *Billy Budd* criticism

---

66. One of the strongest indictments of Billy as a mutineer is Lyon Evans, Jr., "'Too Good to be True': Subverting Christian Hope in Billy Budd," *New England Quarterly* 55 (September 1982): 331–44.

67. A "literary editor" offers the following analysis of his audience: "The People, God bless them, always and everywhere have a certain animal good sense and honesty. Feeling themselves to be ignorant as to most matters lying outside of their practical interests, they lay no claim to universal culture. But the Public, on the contrary, thinks itself highly cultivated, yes, and as to everything, nor has it any inkling of suspicions that possibly it may be a bit mistaken here" (69). This is, of course, quite similar to Jack Chase's distinction between the public and the people in *White-Jacket* (5:192).

demonstrates) a legacy of legal and ethical confusion that might have been avoided had he read less Montaigne and more Machiavelli. Nelson faced a circumstance similar to Vere's when he abruptly tried and hanged Prince Francesco Caraccioli, the seventy-year-old Republican naval commander of the Parthenopean Republic. Robert Southey, a Nelson sympathizer whose *Life of Nelson* Melville read and annotated while he wrote *Billy Budd*, considered Caraccioli's summary execution "the only blot upon [Nelson's] public character."[68] Melville elides this moment in *Billy Budd*'s references to Nelson (57–58) and didn't even mark it in his copy of Southey's *Life,* but he knew about it and had to recognize its similarity to Vere's case. Melville wanted the Nelson of *Billy Budd* to remain an English John Paul Jones whose just murders and nationalist ideals excuse his savage excess. Defending Nelson from Southey's charges would have detracted both from Melville's compact narrative and his contrast between Nelson and Vere, the man of action versus the man of thought. Nelson's "cool Tuscan policy" of shameless, summary execution in the name of order triumphs over Vere's superstitious religiosity, evident when Vere deifies Billy as "an angel of God" and again when Vere dies uttering Billy's name as if it were some incantation against damnation. Perhaps in 1797 such beliefs were credible; in 1891 they were not. Garibaldi was the last knight-errant, the last chivalrous hero, and even he lived to be brought down by "King common-place." Melville never mentions Garibaldi's vainglorious attempts to conquer Rome on his own in 1862 and 1867 in defiance of King Victor Emmanuel's orders, both futile attempts that ended in ignominious defeat.[69] Such omissions suggest that Melville participates with the "jobbers" in shoring up the glory of the age's last candidates for heroism, Nelson and Garibaldi, while refusing to grant such unmitigated status to Vere. Even though Vere and Billy are, like Garibaldi,

68. Robert Southey, *The Life of Nelson,* ed. E. R. H. Harvey (London: Macdonald, 1953), 166. Southey devotes seven pages to Caraccioli's death and issues "a severe and unqualified condemnation of Nelson's conduct" (171). Caraccioli's correct name was Caracciolo, and he was forty-six not seventy, just two facts that illustrate the distortions, half-truths, and inaccuracies that Southey perpetrates and Melville presumably believed. Harvey's edition is well annotated and includes a long appendix on "The Naples Controversy" (301–39). "Nelson's action has been supported on the ground that the trial and punishment of this leading rebel was calculated to restore order in Naples," Harvey notes (171n), an argument curiously similar to those of Melville critics who defend Vere. For Melville's use of Southey, see the notes in Hayford and Sealts, *Billy Budd,* 144–52. For Melville's markings and annotations, see Cowen, *Melville's Marginalia* (1987), 2:516–35.

69. In 1862 the Italian army stopped Garibaldi at Aspromonte in the toe of Italy, where he was seriously wounded in the foot; in 1867 the French army stopped him at Mentana, inside the Papal State (Beales and Biagini, *Risorgimento,* 150). These events were fully reported in the American press, and *Harper's Weekly* ran a cover illustration of a frustrated Garibaldi nursing his wounded foot (October 25, 1862).

members of "great Nature's nobler order" (115), Melville's "inside narrative" exposes their weaknesses, real or imagined, and refuses to grant either of them the heroic status of Garibaldi or Nelson, mythic though it may be. As Elizabeth Samet acutely observes, "the heart of *Billy Budd* is not Melville's admiration for naval heroes but the way in which he imagines the dynamics of two very different kinds of authority," basically the charismatic and the legalistic, a distinction roughly analogous to mine between Garibaldi-Nelson and Vere.[70]

By 1891, when Melville wrote his last draft of *Billy Budd,* the age of heroes was over. Melville's deliberately ragged-edged narrative answers negatively the questions posed by the Marquis de Grandvin about Garibaldi ("our Cid") near the conclusion of "At the Hostelry":

Well now, in days the gods decree,
Toward which the levellers scything move
(The Sibyl's page consult, and see)
Could this our Cid a hero prove?
What meet emprise? What plumed career? (95)

These lines counterpoint the idealization of the past in "The Age of the Antonines" and confirm the narrator's statement that *Billy Budd* "is no romance" (53): there are no dragons to slay, no knights-errant to ride to the rescue, no neatly rounded plots with happy endings to satisfy readers that all's right with the world. The phrase "under the circumstances" occurs multiple times in *Billy Budd* and implies that contingency, necessity, fate, chance, and subjectivity—Machiavelli's *fortuna*—drive decisions that will always remain questionable, for they are, as Benito Cereno realized at the end of his life, made by humans, not nature (9:116). Melville's particular insight is that art not life creates heroes, whether it is the art of the journalists and "jobbers" who promoted Garibaldi, the art of an incomplete masterpiece like *Billy Budd,* or the enduring statuary of ancient Rome that offers access to the reign of the Antonines.

One last statue shadows Melville's thoughts on the American Risorgimento. In 1888 the Sons of Italy and other groups dedicated the Garibaldi statue (fig. 29) in Washington Square, an event Melville surely knew about and perhaps might have attended. As reported in the *New York Times,* Mayor Hewitt viewed the statue "as a warning against domestic strife

---

70. Samet, *Willing Obedience,* 193 and 221. While I cannot go so far as Samet in finding Vere "democratic," her entire chapter on *Billy Budd,* "A Singular Absence of Heroic Poses" (178–221), offers an excellent "Burkean" reading of the story that respects both Billy's moral innocence and Vere and Claggart's allegiance to duty.

Figure 29. Garibaldi statue, Washington Square, New York City. The statue was dedicated in 1888.

and as a perpetual monitor of that love of union for which Italy and the United States have each in the crises of their destiny made such heroic sacrifices," reviving the theme of national unity as the common goal of both countries.

Professor Vincenzo Botta, Henry Tuckerman's old friend and the husband of the now-deceased Anne Lynch, gave the major address and praised Garibaldi in language that might have sprung from Melville's Neapolitan diptych: "England has her Arthur and his Knights, Spain her Cid, and France her Jeanne d'Arc. But it has been the privilege of Italy to possess in this age, which cannot be called heroic, an actual hero, whose devoted patriotism and deeds of arms bear comparison with those of the Paladins of old, and whose historic reality needs no aureola of myth or legend to give it splendor." Botta almost makes Garibaldi a "Handsome Sailor," for he notes that he "was a sailor and a son of a sailor" and "possessed the characteristic virtues of that class in an eminent degree. He was honest, frank, and loyal," energetic, indomitable, modest, "simple in his manners," and endowed with "an irresistible magnetic power." Even more than that he was a "Brutus," a "Curtius," and a "Cincinnatus," a latter-day Roman hero well worthy of the honor New York has bestowed upon him.[71] Significantly, Botta includes Cavour and Victor Emmanuel in his remarks but (at least in the newspaper report) fails to mention Mazzini, an indication of how far the Christian idealist and committed republican had fallen in American esteem. Heroic authority triumphs over personal liberty, military prowess over theoretical politics, action over ideals, and centralized government over federalism, presaging a new world order well suited to the United States of the twentieth century.

---

71. "To Garibaldi's Memory," *New York Times*, June 5, 1888, 8.

Works Cited

Adams, Henry. *The Education of Henry Adams*. Ed. Ernest Samuels. Boston: Houghton Mifflin Company, 1973.
Adler, Joyce Sparer. *War in Melville's Imagination*. New York: New York University Press, 1981.
Alighieri, Dante. *The Vision; or Hell, Purgatory, and Paradise of Dante Alighieri*. Ed. Henry Cary. New York: D. Appleton and Company, 1858.
"Americans in Italy." *New-England Magazine* 1 (July 1831): 50–54.
Amfitheatrof, Erik. *The Enchanted Ground: Americans in Italy, 1760–1980*. Boston: Little, Brown and Company, 1980.
Anceau, Eric. *Les Députés du Second Empire: Prosographie d'une Élite du XIXe Siècle*. Paris: Honoré Champion Éditeur, 2000.
Anderson, Benedict. *Imagined Communities: Reflections on the Origin and Spread of Nationalism*. Rev. ed. New York: Verso, 1991.
Anthon, Charles. *A Classical Dictionary....* New York: Harper and Brothers, 1841.
Ascoli, Albert Russell, and Krystyna von Henneberg, eds. *Making and Remaking Italy: The Cultivation of National Identity Around the Risorgimento*. New York: Berg, 2001.
Bailey, Brigitte. "Gender, Nation, and the Tourist Gaze in the European 'Year of Revolutions': Kirkland's *Holidays Abroad*." *American Literary History* 14 (March 2002): 60–82.
Baker, Paul. *The Fortunate Pilgrims: Americans in Italy, 1800–1860*. Cambridge, MA: Harvard University Press, 1964.
Ball, Robert. "On the Dying Gladiator." *Royal Irish Academy, Proceedings* 6 (1853/1857): 152–54.
Barnum, Jill, Wyn Kelley, and Christopher Sten, eds. *"Whole Oceans Away": Melville and the Pacific*. Kent, OH: Kent State University Press, 2007.
Beales, Derek, and Eugenio F. Biagini. *The Risorgimento and the Unification of Italy*. London: Pearson Education Limited, 2002.
Bean, Judith Mattson, and Joel Myerson, eds. *Margaret Fuller, Critic: Writings from the New-York Tribune, 1844–1846*. New York: Columbia University Press, 2000.

Bercaw, Mary K. *Melville's Sources.* Evanston, IL: Northwestern University Press, 1987.

Bergmann, Hans. *God in the Street: New York Writing from the Penny Press to Melville* Philadelphia: Temple University Press, 1995.

Berkshire County Eagle, 1855–63.

Bernstein, Iver. *The New York City Draft Riots: Their Significance for American Society and Politics in the Age of the Civil War.* New York: Oxford University Press, 1990.

Berthold, Dennis. "Class Acts: The Astor Place Riots and Melville's 'The Two Temples.'" *American Literature* 71 (September 1999): 429–61.

———. "Melville, Garibaldi, and the Medusa of Revolution." *American Literary History* 9 (Fall 1997): 425–59.

Bezanson, Walter. "Melville's Reading of Arnold's Poetry." *PMLA* 69 (June 1954): 365–91.

Bhabha, Homi K. "DissemiNation: Time, Narrative, and the Margins of the Modern Nation." In *Nation and Narration,* ed. Homi K. Bhabha, 291–322. New York: Routledge, 1990.

Billington, Ray Allen. *The Protestant Crusade 1800–1860: A Study of the Origins of American Nativism.* New York: Rinehart & Company, 1938.

Bourne, Randolph. "Trans-national America." *Atlantic Monthly* 118 (July 1916): 86–97.

Branch, Watson. "The Etiology of Melville's *Mardi.*" *Philological Quarterly* 64 (Summer 1985): 317–36.

———. "The Quest for *Mardi.*" In *A Companion to Melville Studies,* ed. John Bryant, 123–43. New York: Greenwood Press, 1986.

Brooks, Van Wyck. *The Dream of Arcadia: American Writers and Artists in Italy, 1760–1915.* New York: Dutton, 1958.

Brown, Charles H. *William Cullen Bryant.* New York: Charles Scribner's Sons, 1971.

Brownell, Charles E. "The Italianate Villa and the Search for an American Style, 1840–1860." In *The Italian Presence in American Art 1760–1860,* ed. Irma B. Jaffe, 208–30. New York: Fordham University Press, 1989.

Browning, Elizabeth Barrett. *The Complete Poetical Works of Elizabeth Barrett Browning.* Ed. Harriet Waters Preston. Boston: Houghton Mifflin Company, 1900.

Bryant, John. *Melville and Repose: The Rhetoric of Humor in the American Renaissance.* New York: Oxford University Press, 1993.

———. *Melville Unfolding: Sexuality, Politics, and the Versions of* Typee. Ann Arbor: University of Michigan Press, 2008.

Bryant, William Cullen. *Letters of a Traveller; or, Notes of Things Seen in Europe and America.* New York: George P. Putnam, 1850.

Buell, Lawrence. "American Literary Emergence as a Postcolonial Phenomenon." *American Literary History* 4 (Autumn 1992): 411–42.

———. "Melville and the Question of American Decolonization." *American Literature* 64 (June 1992): 215–37.

———. "Melville the Poet." In *The Cambridge Companion to Herman Melville,* ed. Robert S. Levine, 135–56. Cambridge: Cambridge University Press, 1998.

Bulwer, Edward Lytton. *Rienzi.* Ed. E. H. Blakeney. New York: E. P. Dutton & Co., 1911.

Buonomo, Leonardo. *Backward Glances: Exploring Italy, Reinterpreting America (1831–1866).* Madison, NJ: Fairleigh Dickinson University Press, 1996.

Burrows, Edwin G., and Mike Wallace. *Gotham: A History of New York City to 1898.* New York: Oxford University Press, 1999.

Byron, George Gordon, Lord. *The Selected Poetry of Lord Byron.* Ed. Leslie A. Marchand. New York: Modern Library, 1951.

"Campaigns of Charles Albert and of the Republicans. Second Campaign of Charles Albert." *United States Magazine and Democratic Review* 31 (October 1852): 305–25.

Carlyle, Thomas. *Frederick the Great.* Vol. 1 in *The Works of Thomas Carlyle.* New York: Peter Fenelon Collier, 1897.

———. *On Heroes Hero-Worship and the Heroic in History.* 1841; London: Oxford University Press, 1974.

Casali, Giovanni Francesco Secchi de. "Italy in 1846." *American Whig Review* 5 (April 1847): 357–70.

———. "Times and Life of Machiavelli." *United States Magazine and Democratic Review* 20 (May 1847): 401–7.

Chai, Leon. *The Romantic Foundations of the American Renaissance.* Ithaca, NY: Cornell University Press, 1987.

Characteristics of Men of Genius: A Series of Biographical, Historical, and Critical Essays. Ed. John Chapman. The Catholic Series. London: J. Chapman, 1846.

Ciccarelli, Andrea. "Dante and the Culture of the Risorgimento: Literary, Political or Ideological Icon?" In *Making and Remaking Italy: The Cultivation of National Identity Around the Risorgimento,* ed. Albert Russell Ascoli and Krystyna von Henneberg, 77–102. New York: Berg, 2001.

Clough, Shepard B., and Salvatore Saladino. *A History of Modern Italy: Documents, Readings, and Commentary.* New York: Columbia University Press, 1968.

Coffler, Gail. "Classical Iconography in the Aesthetics of *Billy Budd, Sailor.*" In *Savage Eye: Melville and the Visual Arts,* ed. Christopher Sten, 257–96. Kent, OH: Kent State University Press, 1991.

———. *Melville's Classical Allusions: A Comprehensive Index and Glossary.* Westport, CT: Greenwood Press, 1985.

———. "Religion, Myth, and Meaning in the Art of *Billy Budd, Sailor.*" In *New Essays on Billy Budd,* ed. Donald Yannella, 49–82. Cambridge: Cambridge University Press, 2002.

Cohen, Hennig. "Melville and the Art Collection of Richard Lathers." *Melville Society Extracts* 99 (December 1994): 1–25.

———, ed. *Selected Poems of Herman Melville.* New York: Fordham University Press, 1964.

Collum, Eric, and Hershel Parker. "The Lost Lathers Collections: Suggestions for Further Research." *Melville Society Extracts* 99 (December 1994): 26–28.

Connelly, Owen, and Jesse Scott. "Joel Tyler Headley." In *Dictionary of Literary Biography,* vol. 30, 107–11. Chicago: Gale Group, 1984.

Cook, Jonathan A. *Satirical Apocalypse: An Anatomy of Melville's* The Confidence-Man. Westport, CT: Greenwood Press, 1996.

"The Corinne, Or Italy, of Madame De Stael." *Southern Literary Messenger* 15 (July 1849): 377–84.

Cowen, [Wilson] Walker. *Melville's Marginalia.* 2 vols. Harvard Dissertations in American and English Literature. Ed. Stephen Orgel. New York: Garland Publishing, 1987.

Cranch, Christopher P. "Lines on the Late Carnival at Rome." *Literary World* 13 (April 1850): 376.
Curti, Merle. "Young America." *American Historical Review* 32 (October 1926): 34–55.
Dekker, George. *The American Historical Romance.* New York: Cambridge University Press, 1987.
Dettlaff, Shirley M. "'Counter Natures in Mankind': Hebraism and Hellenism in *Clarel.*" In *Melville's Evermoving Dawn: Centennial Essays,* ed. John Bryant and Robert Milder, 192–221. Kent, OH: Kent State University Press, 1997.
Devries, David, and Hugh Egan. "'Entangled Rhyme': A Dialogic Reading of Melville's *Battle-Pieces.*" *Leviathan: A Journal of Melville Studies* 9 (October 2007): 17–33.
Dewey, Rev. Orville. *The Old World and the New; or, a Journal of Reflections and Observations Made on a Tour in Europe.* 2 vols. New York: Harper & Brothers, 1836.
Dicey, A. V. "Garibaldi and the Movement of 1848." *Nation,* 29 June 1882, 540–42.
Dickens, Charles. *Pictures From Italy.* Ed. David Paroissien. New York: Coward, McCann & Geoghegan, 1974.
Dictionary of American Fighting Ships. Vol. 3. Washington, DC: Navy Department, Office of the Chief of Naval Operations, Naval History Division, 1968.
Dictionary of Modern Italian History. Ed. Frank J. Coppa. Westport, CT: Greenwood Press, 1985.
Dimock, Wai Chee, and Lawrence Buell, eds. "American Literary Globalism," a special issue of *ESQ: A Journal of the American Renaissance* 50 (2004).
———. *Empire for Liberty: Melville and the Poetics of Individualism.* Princeton, NJ: Prince-ton University Press, 1989.
———. *Through Other Continents: American Literature Across Deep Time.* Princeton, NJ: Princeton University Press. 2006.
———, and Lawrence Buell, eds. *Shades of the Planet.* Princeton, NJ: Princeton University Press, 2007.
Doyle, Don H. *Nations Divided: America, Italy, and the Southern Question.* Athens: University of Georgia Press, 2002.
Draper, John William, and George Frederick Barker. *Thoughts on the Future Civil Policy of America. Memoir of John William Draper, 1811–1882.* Rpt. 1865 ed. of *Thoughts on the Future Civil Policy of America.* New York: Garland Pub., 1974.
Duban, James. *Melville's Major Fiction: Politics, Theology, and Imagination.* Dekalb: Northern Illinois University Press, 1983.
Dwight, Theodore. *The Roman Republic of 1849; With Accounts of the Inquisition, and the Siege of Rome, and Biographical Sketches.* New York: R. Van Dien, 1851.
"Editorial Notes." *Putnam's Monthly Magazine* 6 (September 1855): 328.
"Editor's Table." *Harper's New Monthly Magazine* 5 (July 1852): 264–65.
"Editor's Table." *Harper's New Monthly Magazine* 14 (February 1857): 413–14.
Emerson, Ralph Waldo. *Essays & Lectures.* Ed. Joel Porte. New York: Library of America, 1983.
Emery, Allan Moore. "The Political Significance of Melville's Chimney." *New England Quarterly* 55, no. 2 (1982): 221–28.
Encyclopedia Britannica. 11th ed. New York: Encyclopedia Britannica Company, 1910–11.
"The Entry into Naples." *Harper's Weekly,* October 13, 1860, 1.
"European Politics." *North American Review* 21 (July 1825): 141–53.

Evans, Jr., Lyon. "'Too Good to be True': Subverting Christian Hope in *Billy Budd.*" *New England Quarterly* 55 (September 1982): 323–53.
Faner, Robert D. *Walt Whitman & Opera.* Carbondale: Southern Illinois Press, 1951.
Ferguson, Robert A. *Reading the Early Republic.* Cambridge, MA: Harvard University Press, 2004.
"A Few Days in Venice." *Putnam's Monthly Magazine* 2 (July 1853): 60–66.
Fisher, Marvin. *Going Under: Melville's Short Fiction and the American 1850s.* Baton Rouge: Louisiana State University Press, 1977.
Flexner, James Thomas. *The Light of Distant Skies, 1760–1835.* New York: Harcourt, Brace, 1954.
Forsyth, Joseph. *Remarks on Antiquities, Arts, and Letters, During an Excursion in Italy, in the Years 1802 and 1803.* Ed. Keith Crook. Newark: University of Delaware Press, 2001.
Franchot, Jenny. *Roads to Rome: The Antebellum Protestant Encounter with Catholicism.* Berkeley: University of California Press, 1994.
Freccero, John. "Medusa and the Madonna of Forlì: Political Sexuality in Machiavelli." In *Machiavelli and the Discourse of Literature,* ed. Albert Russell Ascoli and Victoria Kahn, 161–78. Ithaca, NY: Cornell University Press, 1993.
Fredricks, Nancy. *Melville's Art of Democracy.* Athens: University of Georgia Press, 1995.
"From Venice to Vienna." *Putnam's Monthly Magazine* 1 (February 1853): 164–70.
Fuller, Margaret. "American Artists in Italy, &c." *Literary World* 26 (May 1849): 458.
———. *These Sad but Glorious Days: Dispatches from Europe, 1846–1850.* Ed. Larry J. Reynolds and Susan Belasco Smith. New Haven, CT: Yale University Press, 1991.
Garibaldi, Giuseppe. *The Life of General Garibaldi. Written by Himself. With Sketches of His Companions in Arms.* Trans. Theodore Dwight. New York: A. S. Barnes and Burr, 1859.
Garner, Stanton. "Aging with the Antonines." In *Melville "Among the Nations,"* ed. Sanford E. Marovitz and A. C. Christodoulou, 277–86. Kent, OH: Kent State University Press, 2001.
———. *The Civil War World of Herman Melville.* Lawrence: University Press of Kansas, 1993.
Gay, H. Nelson. "Garibaldi's American Contacts and His Claims to American Citizenship." *American Historical Review* 38 (October 1932): 1–19.
Gellner, Ernest. *Nations and Nationalism.* Ithaca, NY: Cornell University Press, 1983.
Gemme, Paola. *Domesticating Foreign Struggles: The Italian Risorgimento and Antebellum American Identity.* Athens: University of Georgia Press, 2005.
———. "Joel Tyler Headley." *Dictionary of Literary Biography.* Vol. 183, 162–67. Chicago: Gale Group, 1997.
Giamatti, A. Bartlett, ed. *Dante in America: The First Two Centuries.* Binghamton: State University of New York Press, 1983.
Gibbon, Edward. *The Decline and Fall of the Roman Empire.* Ed. D. M. Low. New York: Pocket Books, 1962.
Gilman, William H. *Melville's Early Life and Redburn.* New York: New York University Press, 1951.
Giovannini, G. "Melville's *Pierre* and Dante's *Inferno.*" *PMLA* 64 (March 1949): 70–78.

Godkin, E. L. "Garibaldi." *Nation,* 8 June 1882, 477.
Goethe, Johann Wolfgang. *Italian Journeys.* Trans. W. H. Auden. New York: Pantheon, 1962.
Goldberger, Avriel H. "Introduction." *Corinne, or Italy,* xv–liv. New Brunswick, NJ: Rutgers University Press, 1987.
Goldman, Stan. *Melville's Protest Theism: The Hidden and Silent God in* Clarel. DeKalb: Northern Illinois University Press, 1993.
Gollin, Rita. "*Pierre's* Metamorphosis of Dante's *Inferno.*" *American Literature* 39 (January 1968): 542–45.
Greeley, Horace. *Hints Towards Reforms, in Lectures, Addresses, and Other Writings.* New York: Harper & Brothers, 1850.
Grey, Robin. *Melville and Milton: An Edition and Analysis of Melville's Annotations on Milton.* Pittsburgh, PA: Duquesne University Press, 2004.
———, and Douglas Robillard, eds. "Melville's Milton: A Transcription of Melville's Marginalia in His Copy of *The Poetical Works of John Milton.*" *Leviathan: A Journal of Melville Studies* 4 (March and October 2002): 117–204.
Griffin, Susan M. *Anti-Catholicism and Nineteenth-Century Fiction.* Cambridge: Cambridge University Press, 2004.
Grossman, James. *James Fenimore Cooper.* 2nd ed. The American Men of Letters Series. NP: William Sloane Associates, 1949.
Guggisberg, Hans R. "American Exceptionalism as National History?" In *Bridging the Atlantic: The Question of American Exceptionalism in Perspective,* ed. Elisabeth Glaser and Hermann Wellenreuther, 265–76. Cambridge: Cambridge University Press, 2002.
Handbook for Travellers in Northern Italy. 7th ed. 2 vols. London: John Murray, 1858.
Handbook of Rome and Its Environs, A. 5th ed. London: John Murray, 1858.
Harper's New Monthly Magazine, 1850–1860.
Harper's Weekly, 1859–82.
Haskell, Francis and Nicholas Penny, eds. *Taste and the Antique: The Lure of Classical Sculpture 1500–1900.* New Haven, CT: Yale University Press, 1981.
Havely, Nick. "Introduction." In *Dante's Modern Afterlife: Reception and Response from Blake to Heaney,* 1–14. New York: St. Martin's, 1998.
Hawthorne, Nathaniel. *The Blithedale Romance.* Ed. Fredson Bowers and William Charvat. Vol. 3 of *The Centenary Edition of the Works of Nathaniel Hawthorne.* Columbus: The Ohio State University Press, 1965.
———. *The English Notebooks 1856–1860.* Ed. Thomas Woodson and Bill Ellis. Vol. 22 of *The Centenary Edition of the Works of Nathaniel Hawthorne.* Columbus: The Ohio State University Press, 1997.
———. *The Letters, 1853–1856.* Ed. Thomas Woodson et al. Vol. 17 of *The Centenary Edition of the Works of Nathaniel Hawthorne.* Columbus: The Ohio State University Press, 1987.
———. *The Marble Faun: or, the Romance of Monte Beni.* Ed. William Charvat, Roy Harvey Pearce, and Claude M. Simpson. Vol. 4 of *The Centenary Edition of the Works of Nathaniel Hawthorne.* Columbus: The Ohio State University Press, 1968.
Hayford, Harrison, and Merrell Davis. "Herman Melville as Office-Seeker." *Modern Language Quarterly* 10 (1949): 168–83, 377–78.
Headley, J[oel] T[yler]. *Italy and the Italians, in a Series of Letters.* Ed. Evert A. Duyckinck. No. 1. The Home Library. Prose Series. New York: I. S. Platt, 1844.

———. *Letters from Italy.* Wiley and Putnam's Library of American Books. New York: Wiley and Putnam, 1845.

———. *Letters from Italy.* New and Revised edition. New York: Baker & Scribner, 1848. [This is identical to the 1845 edition except for eight pages added to the preface.]

Heimert, Alan. "*Moby-Dick* and American Political Symbolism." *American Quarterly* 15 (1963): 498–534.

"Henry Adams and Garibaldi, 1860." *American Historical Review* 25 (January 1920): 241–55.

Herbert, T. Walter, Jr. *Moby-Dick and Calvinism: A World Dismantled.* New Brunswick, NJ: Rutgers University Press, 1977.

Hertz, Neil. "Medusa's Head: Male Hysteria under Political Pressure." 1983; rpt. with a postscript in *The End of the Line: Essays on Psychoanalysis and the* Sublime, 160–93. New York: Columbia University Press, 1985.

Higgins, Brian, and Hershel Parker, eds. *Herman Melville: The Contemporary Reviews.* New York: Cambridge University Press, 1995.

Hillard, George Stillman. *Six Months in Italy.* Boston: Houghton, Mifflin and Company, 1853.

Hobsbawm, E. J. *Nations and Nationalism Since 1780: Programme, Myth, and Reality.* 2nd ed. Cambridge: Cambridge University Press, 1990.

Hoogenboom, Ari. "American Exceptionalism: Republicanism as Ideology." In *Bridging the Atlantic: The Question of American Exceptionalism in Perspective,* ed. Elisabeth Glaser and Hermann Wellenreuther, 43–65. Cambridge: Cambridge University Press, 2002.

Howard, Leon. *Herman Melville: A Biography.* Berkeley: University of California Press, 1951.

Hutchinson, Anthony. *Writing the Republic: Liberalism and Morality in American Political Fiction.* New York: Columbia University Press, 2007.

"Italian Exile, The." *New-England Magazine* 1 (1831): 10.

"Italian Peninsula, The." *Littell's Living Age,* August 9, 1856, 383.

"Italian Revolutions in 1848, The." Rev. of Fanny Kemble, *A Year of Consolation. New Englander* 7 (February 1849): 72–94.

"Italy." Rev. of Theodore Lyman, *The Political State of Italy. North American Review* 12 (January 1821): 198–229.

"Italy." Rev. of [William Beckford,] *Italy: With Sketches of Spain and Portugal. North American Review* 40 (April 1835): 417–47.

"Italy and the War." *New Englander* 17 (August 1859): 708–25.

Jaffe, Irma B., ed. *The Italian Presence in American Art 1760–1860.* New York: Fordham University Press, 1989.

James, Henry. *Novels 1871–1880.* New York: The Library of America, 1983.

Jarves, James Jackson. "Italian Life and Morals—Effects of Romanism on Society." *Harper's New Monthly Magazine* 10 (February 1855): 320–34.

———. *Italian Sights & Papal Principles Seen through American Spectacles.* New York: Harper & Brothers, 1856.

Jefferey, Francis. Rev. Sir Walter Scott, *The Fortunes of Nigel* (1822). In *Modern British Essayists,* 6:543–48. Philadelphia: Carey and Hart, 1846.

Johnson, Barbara. "Melville's Fist: The Execution of Billy Budd." In *The Critical Difference: Essays in the Contemporary Rhetoric of Reading.* Baltimore: Johns Hopkins

University Press, 1980.

Kadir, Djelal, ed. "America, the Idea, the Literature." *PMLA* 118 (Spring 2003).

Kahn, Victoria. "Virtù and the Example of Agathocles in Machiavelli's *Prince.*" In *Machiavelli and the Discourse of Literature,* ed. Albert Russell Ascoli and Victoria Ann Kahn, 195–217. Ithaca, NY: Cornell University Press, 1993.

Kaplan, Amy, and Donald Pease, eds. *Cultures of United States Imperialism.* Durham, NC: Duke University Press, 1993.

Karcher, Carolyn L. "The Moderate and the Radical: Melville and Child on the Civil War and Reconstruction." *ESQ: A Journal of the American Renaissance* 45 (1999): 187–257.

———. *Shadow Over the Promised Land: Slavery, Race, and Violence in Melville's America.* Baton Rouge: Louisiana State University Press, 1980.

Kelley, Wyn. *Melville's City: Literary and Urban Form in Nineteenth-Century New York.* Cambridge: Cambridge University Press, 1996.

Kemp, Mark A. R. "*The Marble Faun* and American Postcolonial Ambivalence." *Modern Fiction Studies* 43, no. 1 (1997): 209–36.

Kennon, Donald R., and Thomas P. Somma. *American Pantheon: Sculptural and Artistic Decoration of the United States Capitol, Perspectives on the Art and Architectural History of the United States Capitol.* Athens: Ohio University Press, 2004.

Kenny, Vincent. "Clarel." In *A Companion to Melville Studies,* ed. John Bryant, 374–406. New York: Greenwood Press, 1986.

———. *Herman Melville's* Clarel: *A Spiritual Autobiography.* New York: Archon Books, 1973.

Kier, Kathleen. *A Melville Encyclopedia: The Novels.* 2 vols. New York: Whitston Publishing, 1990.

Kimball, Richard Burleigh. "Cuba." *Putnam's Monthly Magazine* 1, no. 1 (January 1853): 3–16.

King, Bolton. *A History of Italian Unity: Being a Political History of Italy from 1814 to 1871.* 2 vols. London: James Nisbet, 1899.

Kirkland, Caroline. *Holidays Abroad; or Europe from the West.* 2 vols. New York: Baker and Scribner, 1849.

Knapp, Joseph G. *Tortured Synthesis: The Meaning of Melville's* Clarel. New York: Philosophical Library, 1971.

Kramer, Aaron. *Melville's Poetry: Toward the Enlarged Heart. A Thematic Study of Three Ignored Major Poems.* Rutherford: Fairleigh Dickinson University Press, 1972.

Kramer, Michael P. *Imagining Language in America: From the Revolution to the Civil War.* Princeton, NJ: Princeton University Press, 1992.

Kring, Walter Donald. *Henry Whitney Bellows.* Boston: Skinner House, 1979.

Lang, Hans-Joachim. "Silvio Pellico, Melville's 'Dungeoned Italian.'" *Melville Society Extracts* 58 (May 1984): 4–5.

Levander, Caroline S., and Robert S. Levine, eds. "Hemispheric American Literary History." Special issue of *American Literary History* 18 (Summer 2006).

Levine, Robert S. "'Antebellum Rome' in *The Marble Faun. American Literary History* 2 (Spring 1990): 18–38.

———. *Conspiracy and Romance: Studies in Brockden Brown, Cooper, Hawthorne, and Melville.* Cambridge: Cambridge University Press, 1989.

Leyda, Jay, ed. *The Complete Stories of Herman Melville.* New York: Random House, 1949.

———. *The Melville Log: A Documentary Life of Herman Melville, 1819–1891.* 2 vols. New York: Gordian Press, 1969.
Literary World, The. Ed. Evert Duyckinck. New York, 1847–53.
Longfellow, Henry Wadsworth. *The Divine Comedy of Dante Alighieri.* Vol. 9 of *The Writings of Henry Wadsworth Longfellow.* Cambridge: Houghton Mifflin & Co., 1886.
Lowell, James Russell. "Dante." *Among My Books,* Second Series. Boston: Houghton Mifflin Company, 1876.
Lueck, Beth L. *American Writers and the Picturesque Tour: The Search for National Identity, 1790–1860.* New York: Garland Publishing, 1997.
Lyman, Theodore. "The Statue Called the Dying Gladiator." *Old and New,* December 2, 1870, 718–28.
Lynch, Anne C. *Memoirs of Anne C. L. Botta.* New York: J. S. Tait & Sons, 1894.
———. "Nightfall in Hungary." *Literary World* 12 (January 1850): 37.
Lyttleton, Adrian. "Creating a National Past: History, Myth, and Image in the Risorgimento." In *Making and Remaking Italy: The Cultivation of National Identity Around the Risorgimento,* ed. Albert Russell Ascoli and Krystyna von Henneberg, 27–74. New York: Berg, 2001.
Macaulay, Thomas Babington. "Machiavelli." Rev. *Oeuvres Complètes de Machiavel,* traduites par J. V. Perier. *Edinburgh Review* 45 (March 1827): 259–95. Rpt. in *Essays, Critical and Miscellaneous. The Modern British Essayists.* Vol. 1. Philadelphia: Carey and Hart, 1847–49.
"Machiavelli." *North American Review* 41 (July 1835): 70–94.
Machiavelli, Niccolò. *The Florentine Histories.* Trans. C. Edwards Lester. 2 vols. New York: Paine and Burgess, 1845.
———. *The History of Florence, and of the Affairs of Italy, from the Earliest Times to the Death of Lorenzo the Magnificent; together with The Prince. And Various Historical Tracts.* London: Henry G. Bohn, 1847.
———. *The Prince.* Trans. Luigi Ricci and revised by E. R. P. Vincent. New York: New American Library, 1952.
Mack Smith, Denis. *Garibaldi: A Great Life in Brief.* New York: Alfred A. Knopf, 1956.
———, ed. *Great Lives Observed: Garibaldi.* Englewood Cliffs, NJ: Prentice-Hall, 1969.
———, ed. *The Making of Italy 1796–1870.* London: Macmillan, 1988.
———. *Mazzini.* New Haven, CT: Yale University Press, 1994.
Malachuk, Daniel S. "The Republican Philosophy of Emerson's Early Lectures." *New England Quarterly* 71, no. 3 (1998): 404–28.
Manning, Susan, and Andrew Taylor, eds. *Transatlantic Literary Studies: A Reader.* Baltimore: Johns Hopkins University Press, 2007.
Marchand, Leslie A. *Byron: A Biography.* Vol. 2. New York: Knopf, 1957.
Marraro, Howard. "American Opinion on the Occupation of Rome in 1870." *South Atlantic Quarterly* 54 (1955): 221–42.
———. *American Opinion on the Unification of Italy.* New York: Columbia University Press, 1932.
———. "Lincoln's Offer of a Command to Garibaldi: Further Light on a Disputed Point of History." *Journal of the Illinois State Historical Society* 36 (1943): 237–70.
Martin, Terence. *The Instructed Vision: Scottish Common Sense Philosophy and the Origins*

of American Fiction. New York: Kraus Reprint Corp., 1969.

Mason, Ronald C. *The Spirit Above the Dust: A Study of Herman Melville.* London: Lehmann, 1951.

Mathews, Cornelius. "Long Life to His Holiness." *Yankee Doodle,* October 2, 1847, 248.

"Mazzini the Italian Liberal." *Harper's New Monthly Magazine* 4 (February 1852): 404–8.

"Mazzini—Young Europe." *United States Magazine and Democratic Review* 30 (January 1852): 50.

McGann, Jerome J. "The Beauty of the Medusa: A Study in Romantic Literary Iconology." *Studies in Romanticism* 11 (1972): 3–25.

McWilliams, John P. *Hawthorne, Melville, and the American Character: A Looking-Glass Business.* Cambridge: Cambridge University Press, 1984.

Melville, Herman. *Billy Budd, Sailor (An Inside Narrative).* Ed. Harrison Hayford and Merton M. Sealts, Jr. Chicago: University of Chicago Press, 1962.

———. *Collected Poems of Herman Melville.* Ed. Howard P. Vincent. Chicago: Packard and Company, Hendricks House, 1947.

———. *The Confidence-Man.* Ed. Brian Higgins and Hershel Parker. New York: W. W. Norton, 2006.

———. *Israel Potter: His Fifty Years of Exile.* Ed. Hennig Cohen. New York: Fordham University Press, 1991.

———. *The Writings of Herman Melville.* Ed. Harrison Hayford, Hershel Parker, G. Thomas Tanselle, et al. 14 vols. Chicago: Northwestern University Press and the Newberry Library, 1968–.

Milder, Robert. "'The Connecting Link of Centuries': Melville, Rome, and the Mediterranean, 1856–1857." In *Roman Holidays: American Writers and Artists in Nineteenth-Century Italy,* ed. Robert K. Martin and Leland S. Person, 206–25. Iowa City: University of Iowa Press, 2002.

———. "In Behalf of 'Dearth.'" *Leviathan: A Journal of Melville Studies* 1 (October 1999): 63–69.

———. "Introduction." *Critical Essays on Melville's Billy Budd, Sailor,* 3–18. Boston: G. K. Hall, 1989.

Miller, Edwin H. *Salem Is My Dwelling-Place: A Life of Nathaniel Hawthorne.* Iowa City: University of Iowa Press, 1991.

Miller, Perry. *The Raven and the Whale: The War of Words and Wits in the Era of Poe and Melville.* New York: Harcourt, Brace and Company, 1956.

Milton, John. *John Milton: Complete Poems and Major Prose.* Ed. Merrit Y. Hughes. New York: Odyssey Press, 1957.

Mitgang, Herbert. "Garibaldi and Lincoln." *American Heritage* 26 (October 1975): 34–39, 98–101.

Moers, Ellen. "Performing Heroinism: The Myth of Corinne." In *Literary Women,* 173–210. New York: Oxford University Press, 1976.

"Monarchy and the Republic in Italy. Campaigns of Charles Albert and of the Republicans." *United States Magazine and Democratic Review* 31 (September 1852): 193–208

Moore, Maxine. *That Lonely Game: Melville, Mardi, and the Almanac.* Columbia: University of Missouri Press, 1975.

Moore, Thomas. *The Works of Lord Byron: With His Letters and Journals, and His Life.* 17 vols. London: John Murray, 1833.

Morseberger, Robert. "Melville's 'The Bell-Tower' and Benvenuto Cellini." *American Literature* 44 (1972): 459–62.
"Mrs. Browning's Italian Poem." *Literary World* 5 (July 1851): 7.
Munich, Adrienne Auslander. *Andromeda's Chains: Gender and Interpretation in Victorian Literature and Art*. New York: Columbia University Press, 1989.
"Music." *Putnam's Monthly* 2 (December 1853): 689.
Myers, Jr., Minor. *The Insignia of the Society of the Cincinnati*. Washington, D.C.: The Society of the Cincinnati, 1998.
Nabers, Deak. "'Victory of LAW': Melville and Reconstruction." *American Literature* 75 (March 2003): 1–30.
Neil, J. Meredith. *Toward a National Taste: America's Quest for Aesthetic Independence*. Honolulu: University Press of Hawaii, 1975.
Newman, Lea Bertani Vozar. "Hawthorne's Summer in Florence: Reliving a Honeymoon, the Dante Connection, and the Nascent *Marble Faun*." In *The Poetics of Place: Florence Imagined*, ed. Irene Marchegiani Jones and Thomas Haeussler, 53–70. [Florence, Italy]: Leo S. Olschki Editore, 2001.
———. "Melville's Copy of Dante: Evidence of New Connections Between the *Commedia* and *Mardi*." *Studies in the American Renaissance* (1993): 305–38.
———. *A Reader's Guide to the Short Stories of Herman Melville*. Boston: G. K. Hall & Co., 1986.
New York Times, 1851–1888.
New York Tribune, 1844–1882.
Noble, David W. *Death of a Nation: American Culture and the End of Exceptionalism*. Minneapolis: University of Minnesota Press, 2002.
"Notices of New Books." Rev. *The Florentine Histories*. *United States Magazine and Democratic Review* 17 (September 1845): 237–38.
Obenzinger, Hilton. *American Palestine: Melville, Twain, and the Holy Land Mania*. Princeton, NJ: Princeton University Press, 1999.
O'Connor, Maura. *The Romance of Italy and the English Political Imagination*. New York: St. Martin's Press, 1998.
"Ode to Southern Italy." *Putnam's Monthly Magazine* 2 (July 1853): 23–24.
Odell, George Clinton Densmore. *Annals of the New York Stage*. 15 vols. 1927; rpt. AMS Press, 1970.
"On a Picture of Beatrice in Paradise." *Putnam's Monthly Magazine* 7 (May 1856): 464.
[O' Sullivan, John L.?] "The Revolutionary Secret Societies of Italy." *United States Magazine and Democratic Review* 9 (September 1841): 260–76.
Otter, Samuel. "How *Clarel* Works." In *A Companion to Herman Melville*, ed. Wyn Kelley, 476–80. Malden, MA: Blackwell Publishing, 2006.
"Our Foreign Gossip." *Harper's New Monthly Magazine* 11, no. 62 (July 1855): 275.
Paine, Thomas. *Thomas Paine's Common Sense: The Call to Independence*, ed. Thomas Wendel. Woodbury, NY: Barron's Educational Series, 1975.
Parker, Hershel. *Herman Melville: A Biography*. 2 vols. Baltimore: Johns Hopkins University Press, 1996, 2002.
———. *Melville: The Making of the Poet*. Evanston, IL: Northwestern University Press, 2008.
Pellico, Silvio. *Memoirs of Silvio Pellico; or My Prisons*. Trans. Hubert P. Lebfevre and M. J. Smead. New York: J. H. G. Langley, 1844.

———. *My Prisons, Memoirs of Silvio Pellico.* Trans. Mrs. Andrews Norton. Cambridge [MA]: C. Folsom, 1836.

Penny Cyclopedia of the Society for the Diffusion of Useful Knowledge, The. 14 vols. London: Charles Knight, 1833–43.

Peterson, Roy Merel. "Echoes of the Italian Risorgimento in Contemporaneous American Writers." *PMLA* 47 (1932): 220–40.

Phillips-Matz, Mary Jane. *Verdi: A Biography.* New York: Oxford University Press, 1993.

Pittsfield Sun, 1850–64.

Plutarch's Lives. Trans. Aubrey Stewart and George Long, 3 [London: George Bell & Sons, 1892]: 550.

Pocock, J. G. A. *The Machiavellian Moment: Florentine Political Thought and the Atlantic Republican Tradition; with a New Afterword by the Author.* 2nd ed. Princeton, NJ: Princeton University Press, 2003.

Poe, Edgar Allan. *Essays and Reviews.* Ed. G. R. Thompson. New York: Library of America, 1984.

———. *Poetry and Tales.* Ed. Patrick Quinn. New York: Library of America, 1984.

Poole, Gordon, ed. *"At the Hostelry" and "Naples in the Time of Bomba."* Naples: Istituto Universitario Orientale, 1989.

Porat, Zephyra. "Towards the Promethean Ledge: Varieties of Sceptic Experience in Melville's *Clarel.*" *Journal of Literature & Theology: An Interdisciplinary Journal of Theory and Criticism* 8 (March 1994): 30–46.

Porte, Joel. *In Respect to Egotism: Studies in American Romantic Writing.* Cambridge: Cambridge University Press, 1991.

Post-Lauria, Sheila. *Correspondent Colorings: Melville in the Marketplace.* Amherst: University of Massachusetts Press, 1996.

Potter, William. *Melville's* Clarel *and the Intersympathy of Creeds.* Kent, OH: Kent State University Press, 2004.

Ramazani, Jahan. "A Transnational Poetics." *American Literary History* 18 (Summer 2006): 332–59.

Rebellion Record: A Diary of American Events with Documents, Narratives, Illustrative Incidents, Poetry, Etc., The. Ed. Frank Moore. 11 vols. New York: G. P. Putnam and Van Nostrand, 1861–68.

Rebhorn, Wayne A. *Foxes and Lions: Machiavelli's Confidence Men.* Ithaca, NY: Cornell University Press, 1988.

Reinhold, Meyer. *Classica Americana: The Greek and Roman Heritage in the United States.* Detroit: Wayne State University Press, 1984.

"Retrospective View of the State of European Politics, Especially of Germany, since the Last Congress of Vienna." *United States Magazine and Democratic Review* 1 (October 1837): 123–42.

Review of Madame de Stael, *Corinne; or, Italy. Southern Literary Messenger* 15 (July 1849): 377–84.

"Review of *History of the Italian Republics,* by J. C. L. Simonde De Sismondi; in Lardner's Cabinet Cyclopaedia." *Southern Quarterly Review* 1, no. 1 (1842): 157–93.

Review of *Italy, Past and Present,* by L. Mariotti, and *The Genius of Italy,* by Robert Turnbull. *The Literary World* 2 (June 1849): 473–74.

"Review of *Six Months in Italy.*" *North American Review* 77 (October 1853): 522–28.

"Revolutionary Secret Societies of Italy, The." *United States Magazine and Democratic*

Review 9 (September 1841): 260–76.

Reynolds, David S. *Beneath the American Renaissance: The Subversive Imagination in the Age of Emerson and Melville*. Cambridge, MA: Harvard University Press, 1989.

Reynolds, Larry J. "*Billy Budd* and American Labor Unrest: The Case for Striking Back." In *New Essays on Billy Budd,* ed. Donald Yannella, 21–48. Cambridge: Cambridge University Press, 2002.

———. *European Revolutions and the American Literary Renaissance*. New Haven, CT: Yale University Press, 1988.

Riall, Lucy. *Garibaldi: Invention of a Hero*. New Haven, CT: Yale University Press, 2007.

———. *The Italian Risorgimento: State, Society and National Unification*. New York: Routledge, 1994.

Robbins, Bruce. "Introduction Part I: Actually Existing Cosmopolitanism." In *Cosmopolitics: Thinking and Feeling Beyond the Nation,* ed. Pheng Cheah and Bruce Robbins, 1–19. Minneapolis: University of Minnesota Press, 1998.

Robillard, Douglass. *Melville and the Visual Arts: Ionian Form, Venetian Tint*. Kent, OH: Kent State University Press, 1997.

Rogers, Samuel. *The Poems of Samuel Rogers*. New York: Hurst & Co., Publishers [1853].

Rogin, Michael Paul. *Subversive Genealogy: The Politics and Art of Herman Melville*. Berkeley: University of California Press, 1985.

Rossi, Joseph. *The Image of America in Mazzini's Writings*. Madison: University of Wisconsin Press, 1954.

Rowe, John Carlos. *At Emerson's Tomb: The Politics of Classic American Literature*. New York: Columbia University Press, 1997.

Rudman, Harry W. *Italian Nationalism and English Letters: Figures of the Risorgimento and Victorian Men of Letters*. London: George Allen & Unwin Ltd., 1940.

Ruland, Richard, ed. *The Native Muse: Theories of American Literature*. Vol. 1. New York: E. P. Dutton & Co., 1976.

Samet, Elizabeth D. *Willing Obedience: Citizens, Soldiers, and the Progress of Consent in America, 1776–1898*. Stanford, CA: Stanford University Press, 2004.

Sandberg, Robert Allen. "'The Adjustment of Screens': Putative Narrators, Authors, and Editors in Melville's Unfinished Burgundy Club Book." *Texas Studies in Literature and Language* 31 (1989): 426–50.

———. "Melville's Unfinished *Burgundy Club* Book: A Reading Edition Edited from the Manuscripts with Introduction and Notes." PhD diss., Northwestern University, 1989.

Schless, Howard H. "Flaxman, Dante, and Melville's *Pierre*." *Bulletin of the New York Public Library* 64 (February 1960): 65–82.

Scott, Grant. "Shelley, Medusa, and the Perils of Ekphrasis." In *The Romantic Imagination: Literature and Art in England and Germany,* ed. Frederick Burwick and Jurgen Klein, 315–32. Amsterdam: Rodopi, 1996.

Sealts, Merton M., Jr. "Innocence and Infamy: *Billy Budd,* Sailor." In *A Companion to Melville Studies,* ed. John Bryant, 407–30. Westport, CT: Greenwood Press, 1986.

———. *Melville's Reading: Revised and Enlarged Edition*. Columbia: University of South Carolina Press, 1988.

"Second Campaign of Charles Albert." *United States Magazine and Democratic Review* 31 (October 1852): 305–25.

Sells, Lytton. *The Paradise of Travellers: The Italian Influence on Englishmen in the Seventeenth Century.* Bloomington: Indiana University Press, 1964.

Shawcross, John T. "'Too Intellectual a Poet Ever to be Popular': Herman Melville and the Miltonic Dimension of Clarel." *Leviathan: A Journal of Melville Studies* 4 (March and October, 2002): 71–90.

Shelley, Percy Bysshe. *The Complete Poetical Works of Percy Bysshe Shelley.* Ed. William Michael Rossetti. London: John Slark, 1885.

Shields, John C. *The American Aeneas: Classical Origins of the American Self.* Knoxville: University of Tennessee Press, 2001.

"Should We Fear the Pope?" *Putnam's Monthly Magazine* 5 (June 1855): 650–59.

Shurr, William H. "Melville's Poems: The Late Agenda." In *A Companion to Melville Studies,* ed. John Bryant, 351–74. New York: Greenwood Press, 1986.

———. *The Mystery of Iniquity: Melville as Poet, 1857–1891.* Lexington: University Press of Kentucky, 1972.

"Sicilian Game, The." *Littell's Living Age* 27 (December 1860): 734–48.

Six Months in Italy. Rev. *North American Review* 77 (October 1853): 522–28.

Smart, Mary Ann. "Liberty On (and Off) the Barricades: Verdi's Risorgimento Fantasies." In *Making and Remaking Italy: The Cultivation of National Identity Around the Risorgimento,* ed. Albert Russell Ascoli and Krystyna von Henneberg, 103–18. New York: Berg, 2001.

Southey, Robert. *The Life of Nelson.* Ed. E. R. H. Harvey. London: Macdonald, 1953.

Spencer, Benjamin Townley. *The Quest for Nationality: An American Literary Campaign.* Syracuse, NY: Syracuse University Press, 1957.

Spengemann, William C. *A Mirror for Americanists: Reflections on the Idea of American Literature.* Hanover, NH: University Press of New England, 1989.

Stafford, John. *The Literary Criticism of "Young America": A Study in the Relationship of Politics and Literature, 1837–1850.* Berkeley: University of California Press, 1952.

Staud, John. "'What's in a Name?' The *Pequod* and Melville's Heretical Politics." *ESQ: A Journal of the American Renaissance* 38 (4th quarter 1992): 339–59.

Stebbins, Theodore E., Jr. *The Life and Work of Martin Johnson Heade: A Critical Analysis and Catalogue Raisonné.* New Haven, CT: Yale University Press, 2000.

———. *The Lure of Italy: American Artists and the Italian Experience, 1760–1914.* Boston: Museum of Fine Arts, 1992.

Stein, William Bysshe. *The Poetry of Melville's Late Years: Time, History, Myth, and Religion.* Albany: State University of New York Press, 1970.

Sten, Christopher, ed. *Savage Eye: Melville and Visual Arts.* Kent, OH: Kent State University Press, 1991.

Stern, Milton. *The Fine-Hammered Steel of Herman Melville.* Urbana: University of Illinois Press, 1957.

———. "Introduction." *Billy Budd Sailor (An Inside Narrative),* vii–xliv. Indianapolis, IN: Bobbs-Merrill Company, 1975.

Stone, Geoffrey. *Melville.* New York: Sheed & Ward, 1949.

Taylor, Bayard. *Views A-foot: or Europe Seen with Knapsack and Staff.* 2 vols. in one. 9th ed. New York: George P. Putnam, 1850.

Thayer, William Roscoe. "The Close of Garibaldi's Career." *Atlantic Monthly* 62 (December 1888): 758–65.

———. *The Life and Times of Cavour.* 2 vols. Boston: Houghton Mifflin Company, 1911.

———. "The Makers of New Italy." *Atlantic Monthly* 62 (November 1888): 656–68.
Thomas, M. Wynn. "Walt Whitman and Risorgimento Nationalism." *Literature of Region and Nation*. Ed. Winnifred M. Bogaards. Saint John, New Brunswick, Canada: Social Sciences and Humanities Research Council of Canada and University of New Brunswick in Saint John, 1998.
Thompson, John Reuben. "A Retrospect of 1849." *Literary World* 5 (January 1850): 14.
Thoreau, Henry David. *Walden and Civil Disobedience*. Ed. Owen Thomas. New York: W. W. Norton & Company, 1966.
Times, The. London. 1857.
Torricelli, J. B. "Garibaldi." *Christian Examiner* 70 (1861): 108–37.
Trachtenberg, Alan. *The Incorporation of America: Culture and Society in the Gilded Age*. New York: Hill & Wang, 1982.
Trimpi, Helen P. *Melville's Confidence Men and American Politics in the 1850s*. Hamden, CT: Archon Books, 1987.
[Tuckerman, Henry T.] "E. Felice Foresti." *Atlantic Monthly* 4 (November 1859): 525–40.
———. *Essays, Biographical and Critical: or, Studies of Character*. Boston: Phillips, Sampson and Company, 1857.
———. *Isabel; or, Sicily: A Pilgrimage*. Philadelphia: Lea and Blanchard, 1839.
———. *The Italian Sketchbook. By an American*. Philadelphia: Key & Biddle, 1835.
———. Review of Gabriele Rossetti, *Rome in the Nineteenth Century* (1846). *Literary World*, 20 October 1847, 301.
———. Review of William Arthur, *Italy in Transition; or Public Events and Private Scenes in the Spring of 1860*. *North American Review* 92 (1861): 15–56.
———. "To Pius IX: in 1848" and "To the Same: in 1849." *Literary World*, September 1, 1849, 201.
———. "A Word for Italy." Review of Joel Tyler Headley's *Letters from Italy* (1845). *United States Magazine and Democratic Review* 17 (September 1845): 202–12.
Tuttleton, James C. *The Sweetest Impression of Life: The James Family and Italy*. New York: New York University Press, 1990.
Tuveson, Ernest Lee. *Redeemer Nation; the Idea of America's Millennial Role*. Chicago: University of Chicago Press, 1968.
Vance, William L. *America's Rome*. 2 vols. New Haven, CT: Yale University Press, 1989.
Verduin, Kathleen. "Dante in America: The First Hundred Years." In *Reading Books: Essays on the Material Text and Literature in America*, ed. Michele Moylan and Lane Stiles, 16–51. Amherst: University of Massachusetts Press, 1996.
Victor, O[rville] J. *The Life of Joseph Garibaldi, the Liberator of Italy*. New York: Beadle and Company, 1860.
Vincent, Howard P. *The Trying-Out of Moby-Dick*. 1949; rpt. Kent, OH: Kent State University Press, 1980.
Viotti, Andrea. *Garibaldi: The Revolutionary and His Men*. Poole, UK: Blandford Press Ltd., 1979.
Wallace, Robert K. *Melville & Turner: Spheres of Love and Fright*. Athens: University of Georgia Press, 1992.
———. "Melville's Prints: David Metcalf's Prints and Tile." *Harvard Library Bulletin*, n.s., 8, no. 2 (Winter 1997): 3–36.

———. "Melville's Prints and Engravings at the Berkshire Athenaeum." *Essays in Arts and Sciences* 15 (1986): 59–90.

Warren, Robert Penn, ed.. *Selected Poems of Herman Melville*. 1970; rpt. New York: Barnes & Noble, 1998.

Weisbuch, Robert. *Atlantic Double-Cross: American Literature and British Influence in the Age of Emerson*. Chicago: University of Chicago Press, 1986.

Wenke, John. "Melville's Indirection: *Billy Budd,* the Genetic Text, and 'the deadly space between.'" In *New Essays on Billy Budd,* ed. Donald Yannella, 114–44. Cambridge: Cambridge University Press, 2002.

White, Hayden. *Metahistory: The Historical Imagination in Nineteenth-Century Europe*. Baltimore: Johns Hopkins University Press, 1973.

Whitman, Walt. *Complete Poetry and Collected Prose*. Ed. Justin Kaplan. New York: Library of America, 1982.

———. *Leaves of Grass: Comprehensive Reader's Edition,* ed. Harold W. Blodgett and Sculley Bradley. New York: W. W. Norton & Company, 1965.

Whittier, John Greenleaf. *The Complete Poetical Works of Whittier*. Ed. Horace E. Scudder. Boston: Houghton Mifflin Company, 1894.

Widmer, Edward L. *Young America: The Flowering of Democracy in New York City*. New York: Oxford University Press, 1998.

Wilentz, Sean. *Chants Democratic: New York City and the Rise of the American Working Class, 1788–1850*. New York: Oxford University Press, 1984.

Wills, Garry. *Cincinnatus: George Washington and the Enlightenment*. Garden City, NY: Doubleday, 1984.

Wolanin, Barbara A. "Constantino Brumidi's Frescoes in the United States Capitol." In *The Italian Presence in American Art 1760*–1860, 150–64. New York: Fordham University Press, 1989.

Woodress, James. *Howells & Italy*. Durham, NC: Duke University Press, 1952.

Woolf, Stuart. *A History of Italy 1700–1860: The Social Constraints of Political Change*. London: Methuen & Co. Ltd., 1979.

Wright, Nathalia. *American Novelists in Italy: The Discoverers: Allston to James*. Philadelphia: University of Pennsylvania Press, 1965.

———. "Herman Melville and the Muse of Italy." *Italian Americana* 1 (1975): 169–84.

———. "*Pierre:* Herman Melville's *Inferno.*" *American Literature* 32 (May 1960): 167–81.

Yang, Jincai. *Herman Melville and Imperialism: A Cultural Critique of Melville's Polynesian Trilogy*. Nanjing: Nanjing University Press, 2001.

Yannella, Donald, and Hershel Parker, eds. *The Endless, Winding Way in Melville: New Charts by Kring and Carey*. Glassboro, NJ: Melville Society, 1981.

Index

Adams, Henry, 191–92, 202, 206–7
"The Age of the Antonines" (Melville), 249, 253–55, 262
Alfieri, Vittorio, 14
Alighieri, Dante: Cary's translation of and *Mardi,* 65–71; as catchword in American culture, 117; influence in *Clarel,* 234; influence in *Moby Dick,* 127–29; influence in *Pierre,* 68–70, 135–42, 145–48; influence on political satire in *Mardi,* 80–85; literary influence in *Mardi,* 22–23, 72–75, 92–94; Mazzini and, 44, 61, 65–66; Pius IX and, 86–92; political influence in *Mardi,* 75–80; transnationalism and, 75
Allen, William, 81
American exceptionalism, 5–16, 132
American Novelists in Italy (Wright), 10, 16
American Palestine (Obenzinger), 232
American Party. *See* Know-Nothings
American Revolution, 32, 39, 45, 161, 210
America's Rome (Vance), 5
Amfitheatrof, Erik, 32
Anderson, Benedict, 11, 58, 65
Anniello, Tommaso. *See* Masaniello
Anthony Burns riots, 134
anti-Catholicism, 11, 78, 134, 143; in America, 53–57, 99, 121, 159–60; in *Mardi,* 86, 91–93; Young America and, 56. *See also* Catholicism
antipapalism, 23, 86–92, 93, 97–98, 134
"The Apple-Tree Table" (Melville), 160
Astor Place Riots, 113, 117, 122, 243
"At the Hostelry" (Melville), 3, 175, 180, 196–207, 226, 262. *See also* Neapolitan diptych

Auber, Daniel, 50, 259
Aurora (Guido), 55
Avezzana, Giuseppe, 98
D'Azeglio, Massimo, 217

Backward Glances: Exploring Italy, Reinterpreting America (1831–1866) (Buonomo), 10
Baker, Paul R., 9, 32, 57
Balzac, Honoré de, 16
"Bartleby, the Scrivener" (Melville), 49, 133, 150
Battle-Pieces (Melville): Catholicism in, 217, 220; democracy in, 215, 219, 223, 248, 251, 253, 255, 259; disillusionment with Italy, 227; echoes in *Billy Budd,* 228; Karcher on, 26; Machiavelli's influence in, 216–26; Masaniello in, 213–14; nationalism and, 175–76, 185; overview, 23; Risorgimento and, 216–26, 251, 255; transnationalism in, 216, 220. *See also* "Supplement," *Battle-Pieces*
Bellini, Vincenzo, 45–46
Bellows, Henry Whitney, 20, 229–30
"The Bell-Tower" (Melville), 20, 132, 166–69, 191
Beneventano, Ferdinando, 150–52
"Benito Cereno" (Melville), 21, 87, 132, 150, 168, 213
Bentley, Richard, 93
Bezanson, Walter, 21, 231–32
Bhabha, Homi, 9
Billington, Ray Allen, 53
Billy Budd, Sailor (Melville): ambiguous

281

282 / Index

politics in, 79; classical allusions in, 17; dedication to Jack Chase, 107, 258; echoing *Battle-Pieces*, 228; French Revolution of 1789 in, 257–60; Machiavelli's influence in, 256–64; Risorgimento and, 256–57, 260–62; sexual politics in, 135; tension between revolt and authority in, 21, 38; transnationalism in, 21, 257
"The Birthmark" (Hawthorne), 259
Blake, William, 68, 69*fig.*
The Blithedale Romance (Hawthorne), 155, 159–60, 238
Boccaccio, Giovanni, 170
Bomba. *See* Ferdinand II
Bonaparte, Louis-Napoleon (Napoleon III), 34, 36–37, 98; in *Clarel*, 232, 242, 245; Duyckinck on, 159; in "Epistle to Daniel Shepherd," 180, 189–91; Italian unification and, 176; in *Mardi*, 84; in *Moby-Dick*, 122; Rogin on, 21
Bonaparte, Napoleon, 84, 123, 194, 257
Borgia, Cesare, 163–64, 170, 172, 183, 258
Botta, Anne C. Lynch. *See* Lynch, Anne C.
Botta, Vincenzo, 20, 263–64
Botticelli, Sandro, 68
Bourne, Randolph, 8
Boyd, Henry, 66–67
The Bravo (Cooper), 9, 31, 45, 168
Briggs, Charles S., 51, 101
Brooks, Van Wyck, 9, 31–32
Brown, John, 134, 213, 219, 259
Browne, J. Ross, 129
Browne, Thomas, 68
Browning, Elizabeth Barrett, 115, 178, 192, 226
Browning, Robert, 43
Brumidi, Constantino, 18
Bryant, William Cullen, 19, 20, 34–35, 60, 114, 189, 229
Buell, Lawrence, 6, 7, 17, 165, 232
Bulwer-Lytton, Edward, 11, 43, 106
Buntline, Ned, 90
Buonomo, Leonardo, 10, 30, 32, 96, 228
Burgundy Club (Melville), 26, 206–8, 216, 260
Byron, George Gordon, 16, 26, 49; *Cacciatore Americani* and, 38–39; as political poet, 32–33, 108–12, 120

Cacciatore Americani, 38–39
Cacciatore delle Alpi, 188
Calhoun, John C., 81, 120
Calvinism, 83, 135
Caraccioli, Francesco, 261
Carbonarism, 36–43
Carlyle, Jane, 43
Carlyle, John Aitken, 68
Carlyle, Thomas, 43, 68, 77, 166
"The Carnival in Europe," 63–64
Cary, Henry, 22, 65–80, 94, 136–37, 140–41
"Casa Guidi Windows" (E. Browning), 115, 226
"The Cask of Amontillado" (Poe), 39
Catholicism: in America, 11–12, 97, 117, 124, 160–61; in *Battle-Pieces,* 217, 220, 223; in "Charles' Isle and the Dog-King," 168; in *Clarel,* 23, 92, 230–41, 241–48, 256; Emerson on, 229–30; in England, 112; Fuller on, 56, 90, 96; in "In a Church of Padua," 191–92; in *Mardi,* 86–92; in *Moby-Dick,* 120–21, 129; Rome and, 51–57. *See also* anti-Catholicism; antipapalism
Cato (the younger), 224
Cavour, Camillo Benso di: "At the Hostelry" and, 203–5; Botta on, 20, 264; *Clarel* and, 234, 241; Crimean War and, 133–34; Italian unification and, 13, 29, 116, 134, 176–78, 217; Neapolitan diptych and, 3, 196
Cellini, Benvenuto, 125, 168, 201
Cenci, Beatrice, 183
Chai, Leon, 6
Charles Albert, King of Piedmont, 49, 63–64, 85
"Charles' Isle and the Dog-King" (Melville), 156–57, 166–67, 168, 213
Chartism (Carlyle), 166
Childe Harold's Pilgrimage (Byron), 10, 26, 32–33, 49, 108–10
Christianity: in "The Age of the Antonines," 254–55; in *Battle-Pieces,* 216–26; Catholicism and, 55–56; in *Clarel,* 234–35, 245, 247, 249; and Machiavelli, 216–26; in *Mardi,* 78–80, 90–91; in "Statues in Rome," 185; in *White-Jacket,* 105
Ciccarelli, Andrea, 66
Cincinnatus, 195, 204
Cisalpine Republic, 36
"Civil Disobedience" (Thoreau), 40, 110

Civil War, U.S.: *Battle-Pieces* and, 26, 175, 177, 180, 216–26; *Clarel and*, 249; *Mardi* and, 134; *Moby-Dick* and, 130; overview, 2–6, 14–15, 19

Clarel (Melville): Bonaparte, Louis-Napoleon (Napoleon III) in, 232, 242, 245; Catholicism in, 23, 92, 230–41, 241–48, 256; Cavour and, 234; Christianity in, 234–35, 245, 247, 249; Dante's influence in, 68, 234; democracy in, 232–33; disillusionment with Italy, 227–28; *Divine Comedy* and, 230; French Revolution of 1789 in, 212–15, 232; Italy as setting, 20; as memorial to Imperial Rome, 250–56; multicultural influences in, 16; overview, 23; Pellico and, 40–41; politics of, 230–33; as religious satire, 241–50; Risorgimento and, 232, 233–41, 244–49; secularism in, 233–41; sexual politics in, 135; tension between revolt and authority in, 21; transnationalism in, 227, 232; U.S. Civil War, U.S., and, 249

"Cock-A-Doodle-Doo" (Melville), 149–52

Coffler, Gail, 17, 255

Cole, Thomas, 31, 54, 59

Coleridge, Samuel Taylor, 4, 66

Commedia (Dante). See *Divine Comedy*

Common Sense (Paine), 213

Communion of St. Jerome (Domenichino), 55

A Companion to Melville Studies (Shurr), 16

Compromise of 1850, 116, 130, 155

The Confidence-Man (Melville): cosmopolitanism in, 170–74; ethical ambiguities of, 211; historical context of, 58, 133, 175; irony in, 169, 172; Karcher on, 222; Kossuth and, 154; Machiavelli's influence in, 148, 150; as political satire, 169–74, 260

"The Conflict of Convictions" (Melville), 255

Congress of Vienna, 3, 38

A Connecticut Yankee in King Arthur's Court (Twain), 87

Conspiracy and Romance (Levine), 12

Cooper, James Fenimore, 9, 10, 31, 45

Coppola, Francis Ford, 4

Corinne; or Italy (Staël), 10, 35, 118

cosmopolitanism: in *The Confidence-Man*, 170–74; in *Pierre*, 145–48; theories of, 17–21, 50, 77; Young America and, 55–56

Course of Empire (Cole), 54, 59

Cranch, Christopher P., 115

Crawford, Francis Marion, 228

Crimean War, 133

Cultures of United States Imperialism (Kaplan and Pease), 5–6

Curtis, George William, 160, 229

cyclical theory of history, 23, 58–59, 82, 117, 134, 201, 206

Dana, Richard Henry, Jr., 229

"Daniel Shepherd" (Melville), 189–91

Dante. See Alighieri, Dante

Dante revival, 14, 66, 72, 76, 117, 138

Da Ponte, Lorenzo, 67

Death of a Nation (Noble), 7

Decameron (Boccaccio), 170

The Decline and Fall of the Roman Empire (Gibbon), 11, 106, 178

Dekker, George, 11

democracy: in "Battle-Pieces," 215, 219, 223, 248, 251, 253, 255; in "Charles' Isle and the Dog-King," 157, 166–67; in *Clarel*, 232–33; in *Mardi*, 81, 84; Mazzini and, 44–46; Melville and, 21, 24–25, 79–80, 180–82; in "Naples in the Time of Bomba," 207, 210; in *Pierre*, 132, 134, 147; Pius IX and, 245

Democratic Review. See *United States Magazine and Democratic Review*

Dettlaff, Shirley, 234, 256

Dewey, Orville, 19, 54–56, 87, 110

Dicey, A. V., 203

Dickens, Charles, 43

Dimock, Wai Chee, 7, 13, 25–26, 78, 92

"DissemiNation: Time, Narrative, and the Margins of the Modern Nation" (Bhabha), 9

Divine Comedy (Dante): *Clarel* and, 230; Emerson and, 8; influence on Melville, 61, 65–78; *Mardi* and, 22, 80–83, 92–94; *Moby-Dick* and, 128–29; *Pierre* and, 136, 140, 142

Domenichino, Zampieri, 244

Doré, Gustav, 67, 68

Doyle, Don H., 14

Draper, John William, 222–23, 225

Dream of Arcadia (Cole), 31, 32*fig*.

The Dream of Arcadia: American Writers and

Artists in Italy (Brooks), 31–32
Dred Scott decision, 134
Duban, James, 26, 100–101
Duyckinck, Evert: Cary and, 70; Fuller and, 98; Macready petition and, 113; Melville and, 19, 157, 176, 178, 196; as publisher, 51, 60, 116, 153, 177; Young America and, 44, 79, 114, 159
Dwight, Theodore, 42, 186, 194, 203
Dying Gaul. See Dying Gladiator
Dying Gladiator, 108–11, 113, 131, 183–84
"Dying Gladiator" (Byron), 49

Emerson, Ralph Waldo, 8, 11, 173, 183, 229; *Clarel*, opposition to, 206–7, 247; interest in Dante, 67–68
Emery, Allan, 155–56
"Enceladus" (Longfellow), 195
"Epistle to Daniel Shepherd" (Melville), 180, 189–91
Etchings of a Whale Cruise (Browne), 129
European Revolutions and the American Literary Renaissance (Reynolds), 6
European Revolutions of 1848, 20–21, 95
exceptionalism, American, 5–16, 132

"Fate" (Emerson), 8
Faulkner, William, 4
Ferdinand I, 37
Ferdinand II, 30, 101, 114, 181
Ferguson, Robert, 82
Field, David Dudley, 60
Fighting Gladiator, 146
Filicaja, Vincenzo da, 35, 73
Fisher, Marvin, 46
Fitzgerald, F. Scott, 4
Flaxman, John, 67–68, 135–38, 148
flogging, 105–13
Florentine Histories (Machiavelli), 142
Foresti, Eleutario Felice: as Carbonarist exile in New York, 19, 39, 41–43, 60–61; as consul to Genoa, 133, 160; Rogers and, 45; Whittier on, 116–17
"Formerly a Slave" (Melville), 223
Forrest, Edwin, 111
Forsyth, Joseph, 33–34, 59, 87–88, 96
Forsyth's Travels (Forsyth), 33–34, 87–88
Foscolo, Ugo, 39
Foster, Elizabeth, 80
Foxes and Lions: Machiavelli's Confidence Men (Rebhorn), 170

Franchot, Jenny, 11, 55, 87, 90, 167–68
Francis II, 2, 198, 200
Franklin, Benjamin, 162–63, 165, 170, 171, 257
Freccero, John, 127
Fredricks, Nancy, 24
French Revolution of 1789, 21, 79, 94, 97, 163; in *Billy Budd*, 257–60; in *Clarel*, 212–15, 232
French Revolution of 1848, 11, 101
"The Frenzy of the Wake" (Melville), 217
Friends of Italy, 130
"Fruits of Travel Long Ago" (Melville), 175
Fugitive Slave Law of 1850, 134
Fuller, Margaret: death of compared to Anna Garibaldi's, 115–16; imagery of eagles and vultures, 82; as Italophile in New York, 19; on America compared to Rome, 52; on Catholicism, 56, 90, 96; on Mazzini, 97–98, 148; on Pius IX, 62–64; Protestant Italy and, 97, 161, 168; Roman Republic and, 95–99, 101, 107

Gansevoort, General Peter, 208
Gansevoort, Guert, 210
Gansevoort, Henry, 196
"Garibaldi" (Whittier), 195
Garibaldi, Anna, 115–16
Garibaldi, Giuseppe: American reputation of, 192–96; "At the Hostelry" and, 3, 180, 196–207; cult of, 186–96; as guerilla warrior, 85; Kossuth on, 153; liberation of Sicily and Naples, 177–78, 192–94; Lincoln and, 2, 14, 18; "Naples in the Time of Bomba" and, 207–16; Nast cartoon, 254*fig.*; in New York, 19–20, 206; on failure of revolution, 251; Risorgimento and, 192–93, 215; Roman Republic and, 98, 133; statue in New York, 262–64; transnationalism and, 3. *See also* Risorgimento
Garibaldi: Invention of Hero (Riall), 201
"Garibaldi the Liberator; or, The Modern Perseus" (Tenniel), 197*fig.*, 198–201
Garner, Stanton, 216–17, 221
Gellner, Ernest, 30
Gemme, Paola, 12, 36, 44–45, 50
Ghibellines, 58, 78–79, 84, 94, 141, 144, 164, 229

Gibbon, Edward, 11, 16, 106, 178, 183, 253
Gilchrist, Alexander, 68
Giovannini, G., 135
Giovine Italia. *See* Young Italy
Gladstone, William H., 114
Godkin, E. L., 203
Godwin, Parke, 154, 160
Godwin, William, 4
Goethe, Johann Wolfgang von, 118, 126
Goldman, Stan, 234, 244
Gray, John Chipman, 66
Greeley, Horace, 20, 60, 95, 118–20, 128, 229
Greenough, Horatio, 18
Gregory XVI, 61–62, 86
Griffin, Susan M., 53
Guelphs, 58, 78–79, 84, 94, 141, 144, 164, 229
Guggisberg, Hans R., 7

Hawthorne, Nathaniel, 9–11, 16, 31, 59, 67–68, 80, 231; "The Birthmark," 259; *The Blithedale Romance,* 155, 159–60; *The House of Seven Gables,* 104; *The Marble Faun,* 9, 31, 59, 70, 168, 178, 235, 238; Melville on, 148; Melville's letters to, 101; on Fuller, 97–98; similarities of his fiction to *Clarel,* 238; travel journals contrasted with Melville's, 180
"Hawthorne and His Mosses" (Melville): America as "Redeemer Nation" in, 101; Americanizing Dante in, 117; Calvinism in, 83, 221; Christianity in, 79–80; literary nationalism in, 17, 45
Heade, Martin Johnson, 105
Headley, Joel Tyler: antipapalism and, 87; *Childe Harold's Pilgrimage* and, 110; Know-Nothings and, 54; *Letters from Italy,* 47, 50, 53, 63; Masaniello and, 213; on American travelers, 183; on Charles Albert, King of Piedmont, 49, 63–64; on Italian politics, 152; on Pius IX, 64; on Rome, 52, 89; Tuckerman-Headley debate, 22, 45–51
Head of Medusa, 214*fig.*
Heimert, Alan, 120
Hemingway, Ernest, 4
Herbert, T. Walter, 135
Hertz, Neil, 125
Hillard, George Stillman, 31, 110, 133

Hints Towards Reforms (Greeley), 118–20, 128
The History of Florence (Machiavelli), 134, 142, 144, 166
History of Modern Italy (Wrightson), 160
History of the Italian Republics in the Middle Ages (Sismondi), 11, 58
Hoadley, John, 79, 245, 253
Hobsbawm, Eric, 15
Hogarth, William, 198–99, 200*fig.*
Holidays Abroad (Kirkland), 31, 118
Homer, 70
The House of Seven Gables (Hawthorne), 104
"The House of the Tragic Poet" (Melville), 260
"The House-top. A Night Piece" (Melville), 220, 249
Howe, Julia Ward, 10
Howells, William Dean, 10, 53, 228
Hughes, Bishop John, 54, 97–98, 220
Hunt, Leigh, 114, 178

"I and My Chimney" (Melville), 155–56, 160
"In a Bye-Canal" (Melville), 191
"In a Church of Padua" (Melville), 191–92
Index Librorum Prohibitorum, 143
Innocents Abroad (Twain), 232
interculturalism, 14, 18, 24, 59
Iron Crown of Lombardy, 122–24
irony, 23, 74, 180; in *The Confidence-Man,* 169, 172; in "Hawthorne and His Mosses," 221; in *Israel Potter,* 165; in *Pierre,* 135–42
Irving, Washington, 9, 13
Isabel; or, Sicily. A Pilgrimage (Tuckerman), 45–47, 139
Israel Potter (Melville), 21, 23, 70, 145, 158–65, 257, 259; irony in, 165; transnationalism in, 161, 171, 173, 177
Italian-American analogy, 1–5
"The Italian Banditti" (Irving), 9
Italian People for National Independence and Constitutional Freedom, 60
Italian Sights and Papal Principles (Jarves), 87
Italian Sketchbook (Tuckerman), 45, 62–63
Italophiles in New York City, 19–20, 153
Italy: American views of, 30–35, 51–57, 57–59, 178; Carbonarism and, 36–43;

Catholicism as threat from, 51–57; cultural identity of, 30–35; Italian-American analogy, 1–5, 12; map (1815), 28*fig.*; map (1859–70), 176*fig.*; Melville's disillusionment with, 227–30; as mirror of American culture, 57–59; as model for U.S. transnationalism, 180, 184; political overview, 29–30; Tuckerman-Headley debate, 43–51; unification of, 13, 29, 116, 134, 176–78, 217
Italy, a Poem (Rogers), 33

Jackson, Thomas "Stonewall," 219
James, Henry, 9, 13, 47, 53, 168, 228
Jarves, James Jackson, 87, 159, 167
Jerrold, Douglas, 43, 114
Jews, in *Clarel,* 234–36
Johnson, Barbara, 256–57
Jones, James, 4
Jones, John Paul, 162–65
Jonson, Ben, 170

Kahn, Victoria, 149–50
Kansas-Nebraska Act of 1854, 134
Kaplan, Amy, 5–6
Karcher, Carolyn, 26, 222
Keats, John, 183
Kelley, Wyn, 19, 147
Kenny, Vincent, 231, 234
Kier, Kathleen, 171
Kingdom of Naples, 37. See also Naples
Kingdom of Two Sicilies, 2, 29–30, 176–77
Kirkland, Caroline, 19, 31, 118, 120
Knight, Charles, 87–88
Know-Nothings, 53–54, 134, 152, 164, 167
Kossuth, Louis (Lajos), 23, 152–57, 165, 186–87

Landor, Walter Savage, 43, 114, 153, 178, 193
Lansing, Kate Gansevoort, 196
Lanzi, Luigi, 178
Lathers, Richard, 179
Latini, Brunetto, 78
Leaves of Grass (Whitman), 76
Lee, Robert E., 219–20
"Lee in the Capitol" (Melville), 219

Leland, Henry P., 10
Le Mie Prigioni (Pellico), 39–41
Leopardi, Giacomo, 14, 235–36
Leopold II, Grand Duke of Tuscany, 30, 34, 88–89, 115, 173, 226
Lester, C. Edwards, 142–44
Letters from Italy (Goethe), 118, 126
Letters from Italy (Headley), 47, 50, 53, 63
Levine, Robert, 12
Leyda, Jay, 198
Life of Byron (Moore), 39, 178
The Life of Joseph Garibaldi, The Liberator of Italy (Victor), 194
Life of Nelson (Southey), 261
Life of William Blake, "Pictor Ignotus" (Gilchrist), 68
Lincoln, Abraham, 2, 13–14, 18, 185, 217–18
"Lines on the Late Carnival at Rome" (Cranch), 115
"Lines Written Among the Euganean Hills" (Shelley), 32–33
Literary World, 40, 60–63, 98, 114–17, 153–54, 159
Littell's Living Age, 133
Livy, 16
Lockwood, John, 105
Longfellow, Henry Wadsworth, 67, 68, 76, 88, 193, 195
Lowell, James Russell, 67, 77, 78–79, 193
Lynch, Anne C., 19–20, 45, 51, 115

Macaulay, Thomas Babington, 143–44, 149
Machiavelli, 132–74; anti-Catholicism and, 143; and Christianity, 216–26; influence in *Battle-Pieces,* 216–26; influence in *Billy Budd,* 256–64; influence in *Israel Potter,* 158–65; influence in Melville's poetry, 183; influence in *Pierre,* 135–36, 142–49; influence in "The Bell Tower," 166–69; Melville's discovery of, 134; Melville's indebtedness to, 23; *The Prince,* 134, 142, 144–50, 162, 172; three orders of society, 223–24; transnationalism and, 142
Mack Smith, Denis, 44, 133
Macpherson, Robert, 178
Macready, William Charles, 43, 114
Macready petition, 113
Mailer, Norman, 4
Making and Remaking of Italy: The Cultivation of National Identity Around the

Risorgimento, 12
Mandeville, John, 78
Mandeville's Travels (Mandeville), 78
Manifest Destiny, 44, 51, 52, 81, 132, 158, 173
Manzoni, Alessandro, 14, 39
Maramma (Maremma), 87–88, 91, 97
The Marble Faun (Hawthorne), 9, 31, 59, 70, 168, 178, 235, 238
"March to the Sea" (Melville), 218
Mardi (Melville), 38, 46, 101; anti-Catholicism in, 86, 91–93; Bonaparte, Louis-Napoleon (Napoleon III) in, 84; Cary's translation of Dante and, 65–71; Catholicism in, 86–92; Christianity in, 78–80, 90–91; Dante's literary influence in, 22–23, 72–75, 92–94; Dante's political influence in, 75–80; democracy in, 81, 84; *Divine Comedy* and, 22, 80–83, 92–94; early vision of Italy in, 4, 34; and Pius IX, 61–64, 86–92, 245; as political satire, 80; transnationalism in, 88, 92; U.S. Civil War, U.S., and, 134
Maroncelli, Piero, 39
Marzetti, Joseph, 169, 172
Masaniello (Auber), 50, 151, 259
Masaniello (Tommaso Anniello), 50, 101, 212–15, 259
Mathews, Cornelius, 44
Matthiessen, F. O., 25
Maximilian, Ferdinand, 181–82, 252
Mazzini, Giuseppe: antipapalism and, 97–98; church and, 246; Dante and, 44, 61, 65–66; democracy and, 44–46; Fuller on, 97–98, 148; Garibaldi's disavowal of, 188; Italian Republic and, 16, 20, 85, 96–98, 130, 133, 168; Kossuth and, 152–57; loss of support for, 158; Mack Smith on, 44–45, 133; radicalism of, 178; reputation in America, 158–60, 188, 264; Risorgimento and, 13, 43–44; Young Italy and, 4, 42–45, 117. *See also* Risorgimento
Mazzinism, 42, 44, 46, 97, 120
McWilliams, John P., 26, 79, 84, 147
Medici, Cosimo de, 127
"A Meditation" (Melville), 226
Medusa, 125–27
Medusa Rondanini, 126
Melville, Gansevoort, 243
Melville, Herman, 86–92; anti-Catholicism and, 56–57; antislavery and, 158; attacks on Pius IX in *Mardi,* 86–92; Byron and, 33; Cary's translation of Dante and, 65–71; Christianity and, 79–80; consulship to Florence, 178–79; cosmopolitanism and, 16–22; as customs inspector in New York, 231; democracy and, 21, 24–25, 79–80, 180–82; disillusionment with Italy, 227–30; *Divine Comedy's* influence on, 61, 65–78; Duyckinck and, 19, 157, 176, 178, 196; Forsyth and, 33–34; French Revolution and, 11; as Italophile in New York, 20–21; in Italy, 144, 175–80, 180–85; Kossuth and, 154; Machiavelli, discovery of, 134; Macready petition and, 113; mixed-genre narratives, 71–75; Murat and, 38; in Naples, 181–83; on Pius IX, 64; Pellico and, 40–41; Rogers and, 33; Roman Republic and, 99–100; in Rome, 182–84; Shelley and, 33; transnationalism and, 3, 21–22, 66; Young America and, 45–51. *See also* specific works by Melville
Melville: The Making of the Poet (Parker), 177
"Milan Cathedral" (Melville), 191
Milder, Robert, 184
Mill, John Stuart, 43
Milton, John, 68, 164, 170, 230, 247
A Mirror for Americanists (Spengemann), 5
Mitford, Mary, 106
mixed-genre narratives, 71–75
Moby-Dick (Melville): Bonaparte, Louis-Napoleon (Napoleon III) in, 122; Catholicism in, 120–21, 129, 223; Catholic symbolism in, 120–21; as critique of European Revolutions of 1848, 20–21; Dantean intertext in, 68, 117, 129–30; debts to lesser authors, 74; *Divine Comedy* and, 128–29; "Garibaldi the Liberator; or, The Modern Perseus" and, 198–200; Italian references in, 118–31; *Literary World* review of, 153; political symbolism in, 120–31; Risorgimento and, 113–17, 227–29; Roman Republic and, 99, 113–17; transnationalism in, 120
"*Moby-Dick* and American Political Symbolism" (Heimert), 120
The Modern British Essayists, 143

Monti, Vincenzo, 39
Moore, Thomas, 39, 178
Morseberger, Robert, 168
La Muette de Portici (Auber), 50, 151, 259
Murat, Joachim, 37–38
My Prisons (Pellico), 39–41

Naples: Bryant on, 35; compared to New York, 1, 4, 50; Forsyth on, 34; Gladstone on, 114; Headley on, 49; Lynch on, 115; Melville in, 181–83; Napoleon and, 36–37; as Parthenope, 36–37
"Naples in the Time of Bomba" (Melville): democracy in, 207, 210; Garibaldi and, 207–16; inspiration for, 103, 175, 181, 198; in "Naples in the Time of Bomba," 196; overview, 3. *See also* Neapolitan diptych
Napoleon III. *See* Bonaparte, Louis-Napoleon
Nast, Thomas, 254*fig.*
Nations and Nationalism (Gellner), 30
Neapolitan diptych (Melville): historical context of, 36, 40, 50, 103, 177, 181, 196, 228, 263; overview, 3, 20, 23; transnationalism in, 198. *See also* "At the Hostelry"; "Naples in the Time of Bomba"
Nelson, Horatio, 103, 261
Newman, Lea, 72, 75
Niebuhr, Barthold, 37, 250
"Nightfall in Hungary" (Lynch), 115
Noble, David W., 7

Obenzinger, Hilton, 232, 250
O'Brien, Tim, 4
"Ode to Kossuth" (Tappan), 154
"Ode to Southern Italy" (*Putnam's*), 160
The Old World and the New (Dewey), 54–55
Omoo (Melville), 57, 73, 76, 86, 93
"On the Medusa of Leonardo Da Vinci in the Florentine Gallery" (Shelley), 126
O'Sullivan, John L., 44

Paine, Thomas, 213
Paradise Lost (Milton), 70, 164, 230, 247
Parker, Hershel, 54–55, 81, 176, 184, 231, 245

Parthenopean Republic, 36
"Pausilippo (In the Time of Bomba)" (Melville), 40–41, 191, 198
Peabody, Sophia, 67
Pease, Donald, 5–6
Pellico, Silvio, 39–43, 49, 169, 191
The Penny Cyclopedia of the Society for the Diffusion of Useful Knowledge (Knight), 87–88, 213
Perseus and Andromeda (Reni), 199–200
Perseus Rescuing Andromeda (Hogarth), 198–200
Perseus with the Head of Medusa (Cellini), 125, 127, 201
The Piazza Tales (Melville), 166, 169–74
picturesque: in "At the Hostelry," 197, 203–6, 214; in *The Confidence-Man*, 133, 169; Garibaldi as, 85; in "I and My Chimney," 156; *in Italian Sketchbook,* 45; Italy as land of, 30–35, 59; in "Naples in the Time of Bomba," 211, 213; in Neapolitan diptych, 3; in "Ode to Southern Italy," 160; in *Redburn,* 101, 104; in *Roba de Roma,* 228; Tuckerman-Headley debate and, 49–50
Pierre (Melville): cosmopolitanism in, 145–48; Dante's influence in, 68–70, 135–42, 145–48; dedication of, 184; democracy in, 132, 134, 147; *Divine Comedy* and, 136, 140, 142; irony in, 135–42; Machiavelli's influence in, 23, 135–36, 142–49; moral ambiguity in, 171; as political satire, 135; povertiresque in, 228
"Pisa's Leaning Tower" (Melville), 191
Pius IX (Pio Nono): Hughes defends, 121; Kirkland on, 120; as liberal, 60–63; in *Mardi,* 86–91; as reactionary, 64, 113, 217, 245–47
Plutarch, 16, 188, 203, 224
Pocock, J. G. A., 163
Poe, Edgar Allan, 10–11, 39, 67, 106, 133
Poems (E. Browning), 178
political satire. *See* satire, political
Pompey, 217, 219, 224
Poole, Gordon, 204
"Poor Man's Pudding and Rich Man's Crumbs" (Melville), 49, 198
Porte, Joel, 24
"The Portent" (Melville), 213–14, 219
Post-Lauria, Sheila, 71
Prescott, William, 67

The Prince (Machiavelli), 134, 142, 144–50, 162, 172
The Princess Casamassima (James), 47
"Prisoners of Naples" (Whittier), 42–43
Protestantism, 47, 53–56, 160, 229, 244
Putnam, George Palmer, 160, 229

Ramazani, Jahan, 77
Raphael, 55
"The Ravaged Villa" (Melville), 251
Rebhorn, Wayne A., 170–72
Redburn (Melville), 20, 23, 99, 100–105, 169
Red Republicans: *Billy Budd* and, 260; Garibaldi and, 189; Mazzini and, 97, 101, 133, 178; *Moby-Dick* and, 130; Sanders and, 158; "Statues in Rome" and, 185
religious satire. *See* satire, religious
Remarks on Antiquities (Forsyth), 33
Reni, Guido, 55, 198–200
Representative Men (Emerson), 8
"Resurgemus" (Whitman), 14
Reynolds, David S., 24
Reynolds, Larry J., 6, 11, 20–21, 26, 79, 83–84, 98, 122
Riall, Lucy, 201, 203
Rienzi, Cola di, 106–7, 114, 213, 258
Rienzi, the Last of the Roman Tribunes (Bulwer-Lytton), 11, 106
Risorgimento: America and, 9, 12–21, 36–43, 51–54, 57–59, 60–61, 95–100, 132–33; *Battle-Pieces* and, 175–80, 216–26, 251, 255; *Billy Budd* and, 256–57, 260–62; *Clarel* and, 232, 233–41, 244–49; *The Confidence-Man* and, 169; Dante and, 66, 77–78; defined, 2–3; English and American sympathies for, 115; as framework for Italian nationhood, 12–13; Fuller on, 23; Garibaldi and, 192–93, 215; *Israel Potter* and, 158; Italian heroes of, 13; Machiavelli and, 142–43; *Mardi* and, 64, 83, 93–94; Mazzini and, 13, 43–44; Melville and, 4, 16, 20–25; *Moby-Dick* and, 113–17, 118, 120, 123, 227–29; *Pierre* and, 135–36, 140; poetry of, 35, 193, 196–97; *Redburn* and, 101; Renaissance vs., 14; Roman Republic and, 95–100; Rome and, 51–57; *White-Jacket* and, 105. *See also* Garibaldi, Giuseppe; Mazzini, Giuseppe
Risorgimento nationalism, 15, 21, 36–46, 54, 136, 156; *Battle-Pieces* and, 175, 216; *Billy Budd* and, 257; *Clarel* and, 246; *Moby-Dick* and, 227
Rivista di Firenze, 178
Roads to Rome (Franchot), 11
Roba di Roma (Story), 228
Robbins, Bruce, 77
Roderick Hudson (James), 9, 228
Rogers, Samuel, 33, 43, 45, 66, 114
Rogin, Michael Paul, 20–21, 26, 79, 135, 225
Roman Catholicism. *See* Catholicism
Roman History (Niebuhr), 250
Roman Newsboys (Heade), 105
Roman Republic, 58, 82, 95–131, 144, 217, 229, 252; *Moby-Dick* and, 113–17, 118–31; overview, 95–100; *Pierre* and, 147; *Redburn* and, 100–105; Risorgimento and, 95–100; *White-Jacket* and, 105–15. *See also* Rome
Roman Republic of 1849 (Dwight), 186
The Romantic Foundations of the American Renaissance (Chai), 6
Rome: American idealization of, 51–57, 160, 165, 219–23; *Clarel* and, 23, 241–50, 250–56; *Mardi* and, 85–90; Melville in, 182–84; *Moby Dick* and, 120, 128. *See also* Roman Republic
Rosicrucianism, 171
Rossetti, Gabriele, 43
Rossi, Joseph, 44
Rossi, Pellegrino, 63
Rowe, John Carlos, 24
Ruskin, John, 178

Samet, Elizabeth D., 144, 262
Sandberg, Robert, 197, 207
Sanders, George N., 153, 158, 164
satire, political, 23, 71–72, 185; in "Charles' Isle and the Dog-King," 156–57; in "Cock-A-Doodle-Doo," 149–52; in *The Confidence-Man*, 169–74; in *Mardi*, 80; in *Pierre*, 135
satire, religious, 241–50
The Scarlet Letter (Hawthorne), 238
Schless, Howard, 135
Scott, Sir Walter, 11, 139
Sedgwick, Catherine, 19
"Self-Reliance" (Emerson), 183, 206
Shades of the Planet (Dimock and Buell), 7

Shakespeare, 16, 68, 70, 148, 170
Shaw, Lemuel, 79, 179
Shawcross, John, 247
Shelley, Percy Bysshe, 32–33, 126, 178, 183
Shepherd, Daniel, 189–90
Sherman, William Tecumseh, 217–18
"Should We Fear the Pope" (*Putnam's*), 160
Shurr, William H., 15, 239, 252
de Sismondi, J. C. L. Simonde, 11, 58
Six Months in Italy (Hillard), 31, 133
Sketch-Book (Irving), 13
slavery: in America, 7, 14, 52; "The Bell-Tower" and, 166–68; E. Browning on, 116; in *Clarel*, 248; Dewey on, 55–56; *Dying Gladiator* and, 111; in "The Frenzy of the Wake," 218; Garibaldi and, 2, 18; in "I and My Chimney," 155; in *Mardi*, 81–84, 91; Melville and, 158; in *Redburn*, 103; in "Supplement," *Battle-Pieces*, 223; in "The Surrender at Appomattox," 218–19; Thoreau and, 134; Young America and, 44
"Slavery in Massachusetts" (Thoreau), 134
Society of Cincinnati, 208–10
Society of Friends of Italy, 114
"Song of Myself" (Whitman), 4
Southey, Robert, 261
Spaggiari, Giovanni, 178
Spartacus, 111
Spengemann, William C., 5
Staël, Germaine de, 10, 35, 118, 139
"Statues in Rome" (Melville), 178, 184–85, 228; *Battle-Pieces* and, 220; *Billy Budd* and, 17; Christianity in, 185; *Dying Gladiator* and, 110; *Moby-Dick* and, 128; *Timoleon* and, 226
Stebbins, Theodore E., Jr., 105
Steen, Jan, 198, 204
Stein, William Bysshe, 204
Stern, Milton, 257
"Stonewall Jackson" (Melville), 219
Story, William Wetmore, 228
Stowe, Harriet Beecher, 90
Sumner, Charles, 20, 189, 229
"Supplement," *Battle-Pieces* (Melville), 249; compromise and, 246; mediatory politics of, 79, 257; meliorism in, 175, 217; overview, 23; Southern rights and, 222–25; Stonewall Jackson in, 219. See also *Battle-Pieces*
"Surrender at Appomattox" (Melville), 218–19
Syllabus of Errors (Pius IX), 207

Tales of a Traveller (Irving), 9
Tammany Hall, 243
Tappan, Henry P., 154
"The Tartarus of Maids" (Melville), 117, 135, 198
Taylor, Bayard, 123, 229
Tenniel, John, 197*fig.,* 198–200
Thomas, M. Wynn, 15
Thompson, John Reuben, 114
Thoreau, Henry David, 8, 11, 40, 110, 134
Thoughts on the Future Civil Policy of America (Draper), 222
Through Other Continents (Dimock), 7
Ticknor, George, 67
Timoleon (Melville), 175, 228
"To Italy" (Filicaja), 35
"To Kossuth on His Departure for America" (Landor), 153
"To Pius IX" (Tuckerman), 62–63
Torricelli, J. B., 195
Tortesa, the Usurer (Willis), 139
"To the Apennines" (Bryant), 35
The Tragedy of Rienzi (Mitford), 106
Transfiguration (Raphael), 55
"Trans-national America" (Bourne), 8
transnationalism: *Battle-Pieces* and, 216, 220; *Billy Budd* and, 21, 257; *Clarel* and, 227, 232; Dante and, 75; Garibaldi and, 3; *Israel Potter* and, 161; Italy as model for U.S., 180, 184; Machiavelli and, 142; *Mardi* and, 88, 92; Melville and, 3, 21–22, 66; *Moby-Dick* and, 120; in Neapolitan diptych, 198; Pellico and, 41; short stories and, 132, 157; theories of, 6–9, 13, 15, 18–19, 22, 24–25, 50
"Traveling" (Melville), 115
Travels in Italy (Valery), 178
Triple Alliance, 254
Tuckerman, Henry Theodore: *Isabel; or, Sicily. A Pilgrimage,* 45–47, 139; *Italian Sketchbook,* 45, 62–63; Italian Unity celebration and, 229; as Italophile in New York, 10, 19–20; on "Casa Guidi Windows," 116; on Foresti, 42; on Garibaldi, 194, 203; on Italy's politi-

cal dilemma, 35; on Pellico, 40; on political maturity of Italy, 22; pro-Italy meetings in New York, 60; "To Pius IX," 62–63; Tuckerman-Headley debate, 45–51
Tuckerman-Headley debate, 45–51
Tuttleton, James, 9
Twain, Mark, 87, 232
Tweed, William Marcy, 243
"The Two Temples" (Melville), 87, 198
Typee (Melville): Christian missionaries in, 79; cultural imperialism in, 51; debts to lesser authors, 74; interculturalism and ethnocentrism in, 59; multicultural influences in, 16; savagism in, 173

Uncle Tom's Cabin (Stowe), 90
United States Magazine and Democratic Review, 32, 44, 47, 105, 186–88, 194
Valery, Antoine Claude, 178
Vance, William L., 5, 11, 86, 105, 239
Vasari, Giorgio, 178
Vatican Sculptures (Macpherson), 178, 253
"Venice" (Melville), 191
Verduin, Kathleen, 66
Victor, Orville J., 192–93, 195
Victor Emmanuel II: American Catholic opposition to, 229; annexation of Lombardy, 177–78; Botta on, 264; as constitutional monarch, 180, 188; Garibaldi and, 133–34, 261; as hero of Risorgimento, 13–15, 20; Kingdom of Italy and, 2, 217–20
Views A-Foot (Taylor), 123
Vincent, Howard, 176
da Vinci, Leonardo, 214

Walden (Thoreau), 8
Walsh, Mike, 181
Warren, Robert Penn, 247
Washington, George, 14, 195, 208, 220
Webster, Daniel, 81, 83, 152, 155
Webster, Noah, 76
Wenke, John, 257
White, Hayden, 11
White-Jacket (Melville): Christianity in, 105; democratic ritual in, 122; flogging in, 105–13; overview, 23; Roman Republic and, 99–100, 105–15
Whitman, Walt, 4, 11, 14, 15, 19, 76, 151
Whittier, John Greenleaf, 42–43, 114, 116–17, 193, 195
Wicksteed, Philip H., 73
Widmer, Edward L., 158
Willis, Nathaniel Parker, 19, 87, 139
Wills, Gary, 208
Winyah, 179
Woodress, James, 9
Wordsworth, William, 4
Wright, Nathalia, 9, 10, 16, 31, 135
Wrightson, Richard Heber, 160

Young America, 4, 79; anti-Catholicism and, 56; cosmopolitanism and, 55–56; Headley and Tuckerman and, 22; Kossuth and Mazzini and, 152–57; *Mardi* and, 61, 62, 84; *Moby-Dick* and, 116–17; *Pierre* and, 140–41; Roman Republic and, 97–101; Sanders's leadership and, 158–59, 164; Young Italy in, 42–51
Young Europe, 153
Young Italy, 4, 43–51, 62, 101, 104, 117

www.ingramcontent.com/pod-product-compliance
Lightning Source LLC
Chambersburg PA
CBHW030107010526
44116CB00005B/137